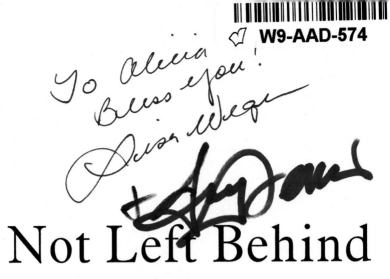

To Alicia
Bless you!
Lisa Weger

Not Left Behind

Going Back for the Offended

Advantage INSPIRATIONAL™

Jay Ferris & *Lisa Weger*

Not Left Behind - Going Back For The Offended
by James Jay Ferris and Lisa Weger

Copyright © 2005 by James Jay Ferris and Lisa Weger
All Rights Reserved
ISBN: 1-59755028-0

Published by: Advantage Books
                www.advbooks.com

Unless otherwise indicated, Bible quotations are taken from the HOLY
BIBLE, KING JAMES VERSION.

Scripture taken from the HOLY BIBLE, NEW INTERNATIONAL
VERSION Copyright ©1973, 1978, 1984 by International Bible Society.
Usage by permissionof Zondervan. All rights reserved."

Library of Congress Control Number: 2005924872

First Printing: April 2005

05 06 07 08 09 10 11   10 9 8 7 6 5 4 3 2 1

Printed in the United States of America

DEDICATION

To Carleen Ferris and Kurtis Weger:
"…and great grace was upon them all."
—Acts 4:33

ACKNOWLEDGEMENTS

Jay writes:

We leave it to the reader to test and prove whether these things be from God. As for Lisa and me, we are very grateful to the Lord for all that He has been able to do and say in the give and take of our correspondence with each other. In a sense, this book is a biography of relationship, and each of us has been blessed by the life revealed and shared.

I want to give thanks for all those about whom I have been able to say "my" and "mine" through the years. They have helped me in the living of a new life to understand the joy that must have belonged to the Apostle Paul when he addressed Timothy as "my dearly beloved son,"[1] saying "… as a son with a father, he hath served with me in the Gospel."[2] Together, Paul and Timothy wrote, "What is our hope, or joy, or crown of rejoicing? Are not even ye in the presence of our Lord Jesus Christ at his coming? For ye are our glory and joy."[3]

I want to thank some fathers in the Lord. Whatever they may have been to others, surely they have been as fathers to me: Frank Wren from Watford England; Lloyd Sweet, a true apostle to New England; Calvin Bacon, a pillar in the faith who took the best I could throw his way, and loved me anyway; and Herb Mirly who stands witness to the grace of God in the restoration of authentic apostolic ministry in the days of this correspondence.

I want to thank all those who were graced to love and embrace me in the days when I felt so strongly led to push the envelope of what was possible in Christ where relationship and intimacy are concerned—and to do so gender neutral. Thank you!

---

[1] 2 Timothy 1:2.   [2] Philippians 2:22.
[3] 1 Thessalonians 2:19–20.

I want to thank those who have read and given input and feedback concerning the correspondence of these pages.

Both Lisa and I owe a tremendous debt of gratitude to Pat Shepherd who has brought her gifts of encouragement to the life we have lived and to the formatting of these pages, in which that life is revealed. She saw and protected the chemistry of our conversation, letting us know—especially letting me know—when things written in other venues needed to go to "time out" as an appendix. She has helped us in our desire to keep this real and accurate, allowing the reader to come with us as we shared, so that nothing has been held back, and those things that were a part of the content—but not written in the chemistry of our exchange—are safely available in appendices, where they supply foundational truth without taking away from the flow of the chemistry.

In this, Pat has been of very great service, bringing her very considerable skills to the presentation of our sharing, and we are truly grateful.

Finally, we want to thank our spouses, who have given us the space to love one another in the Spirit and to do so in such a way that our marriages have been enriched rather than diminished. They have helped us to prove for ourselves that the oneness Jesus prayed and died for is within our reach even in this present age.[4] It is our hope that those who read our conversation will discover this reality for themselves—and do so in time for the "world to believe."

And Lisa adds:

I would like to thank all who have ever dared to love me, in whatever capacity you have been able to do so, investing in me with your love. It is my hope that, with this book, your investment will increase a thousand times over, and you will share in the satisfaction of knowing that your love has made a difference.

---

[4]John 17:21.

TABLE OF CONTENTS

JESUS AND THE WOMAN OF SAMARIA
by Gustave Doré (1832–1883)

How is it that thou, being a Jew, askest drink of me, which am a woman of
Samaria? for the Jews have no dealings with the Samaritans.... (John 4:9)

INTRODUCTION

First, a word about the cover:

We have chosen an engraving by Gustave Doré (1832–1883) of a well-known scene from the Bible, perhaps best known as "The Sarmaritan Woman at the Well." Our book is a correspondence that not only brought that picture and passage to mind, but also brought it to life.

In essence it is about those who are on the outside but with a heart to be inside. Perhaps the greatest cry of the human heart is for intimacy, and the greatest fear of the human mind is the fear of rejection.

The woman on the cover is a rejected woman.

We first read about her in the Gospel of John, Chapter 4, which is presented below. Here, we find not only that she is among those who have been rejected by reason of family, race, religion, nationality, and geography, but she has known personal rejection on a number of occasions as well. In sum, she is a beautiful personification of our human condition.

There is always the problem of trying to distinguish the accidental from the purpose driven, and so it is with this Biblical encounter. At first glance it appears to be an accidental or chance meeting between a woman who has questions and a Man who has answers. At first glance, the same could be said of the encounter that opens to you in these pages. As it was at the well in Samaria, the present conversation may seem shameless to some but may hold out a message of hope for others.

To the religious mindset of the Biblical time frame, the conversation appears to be illegal, and so it is today. But for those who were seeking a better life with better answers, then the encounter between the woman and the Man at the well was the beginning of something altogether new. It was new for her. It was new for her family, her race, religion, and nationality. The only thing that got left behind was her geography. The Man on the cover took her to a whole new place, where no one had ever gone before. In short, it was new for human history as well.

This book is that story, but it's not a story—it's true! If we had the whole script of what was said between the Man and the woman on that day so long ago, except for the language, it might not have been so different from what you will find here in the correspondence between a woman and a man who "bumped into each other" in cyberspace.

This book is the beginning of how it looked last year. And now, in summary, here is how it was understood almost two thousand years ago by a man named John:

Gospel of John, Chapter 4

1-3: When therefore the Lord knew how the Pharisees had heard that Jesus made and baptized more disciples than John, (Though Jesus himself baptized not, but his disciples,) He left Judaea, and departed again into Galilee.

It is interesting to note the reason Jesus departed for Galilee. Apparently, even back then there was a kind of "Market Watch," a religious market watch. The religious market watchers had noted that John's stock was going down and Jesus's stock was rising. Apparently they were not too happy about it: "Get out of town!"

4: And he must needs go through Samaria.

If you check the map in the back of your Bible, you can see that it was not too easy to get to Galilee without going through Samaria.

5: Then cometh he to a city of Samaria, which is called Sychar, near to the parcel of ground that Jacob gave to his son Joseph.

Looks like Jesus took the high road.

6: Now Jacob's well was there. Jesus therefore, being wearied with his journey, sat thus on the well: and it was about the sixth hour.

Even Jesus got genuinely pooped now and then. Anyway, He sits down at the well.

7: There cometh a woman of Samaria to draw water: Jesus saith unto her, Give me to drink.

Jesus starts a conversation. We are soon given to understand that it was an illicit conversation, perhaps for as many as three reasons; she's a woman, she's a Samaritan, and she may be of questionable reputation. Please note, none of these seem to phase Jesus. (Got to love it!)

If the Bible is careful to inform us about the disciples' absence, there must be a reason we need to know about it. When we explore the reason, it really gets to be quite comical—and quite revealing about some fundamentals, like eating, drinking, attitudes, sources, refreshments, etc. Please note that none of the disciples were around to take notes on the conversation that was about to take place. We are left to wonder who related this story to John. From all appearances, there were only two witnesses to the conversation, the woman and Jesus. If Jesus told John about it, that is interesting for us in one way. If the woman told John about it, that is interesting for us in other ways. In either case, the Holy Spirit considered it important enough to have John write it down for us. (I think it's important to consider this so that we don't miss the point.) I would like to be able to spend a little time here on the possible implications of which of them told John, and what that might reveal to us about them, and about the importance of their conversation, but perhaps another time. [:-)]

8: (For his disciples were gone away unto the city to buy meat.)

You have to admire her pluck! She gets right in Jesus's face. Perhaps she's playing with Him, just a little, but whatever, she meets Him eyeball to eyeball.

9: Then saith the woman of Samaria unto him, How is it that thou, being a Jew, askest drink of me, which am a woman of Samaria? for the Jews have no dealings with the Samaritans.

Jesus responds in kind. Right back in her face! He is very self-revealing in His response. If she is looking to play, it is very clear that Jesus is also a "player."

10: Jesus answered and said unto her, If thou knewest the gift of God, and who it is that saith to thee, Give me to drink; thou wouldest have asked of him, and he would have given thee living water.

The girl knows how to play tennis! Right back at Him.

11: The woman saith unto him, Sir, thou hast nothing to draw with, and the well is deep: from whence then hast thou that living water?

12: Art thou greater than our father Jacob, which gave us the well, and drank thereof himself, and his children, and his cattle?

13, 14: Jesus answered and said unto her, Whosoever drinketh of this water shall thirst again: But whosoever drinketh of the water that I shall give him shall never thirst; but the water that I shall give him shall be in him a well of water springing up into everlasting life.

You have to wonder what she might have expected from Jesus as a return shot after that one. [:-)]

WOW! Talk about taking her deep the first time out! Jesus is treating her not only as a full-fledged person, but as one with real substance and the ability to go places in the Spirit.

15: The woman saith unto him, Sir, give me this water, that I thirst not, neither come hither to draw.

Bingo! She bites! It is difficult to imagine a more honoring feminine response. This is wide open; fully vulnerable; and fully receptive! (This is the moment when she puts her waterpot down.)

16: Jesus saith unto her, Go, call thy husband, and come hither.

How about that for knowing how to play the game? Where did that response come from? Where was Jesus taking her now?? Looks to me like He was taking her to a depth and circumstance where there would be some serious need for "buddy breathing."

17: The woman answered and said, I have no husband.

Please note, she is right there with Him, no whiplash. It's like watching a final competition in professional ballroom dancing. The two are perfect together. She follows His lead with seamless perfection.

Jesus said unto her, Thou hast well said, I have no husband:

Jesus reassures her that she has made the right response. So, how did we get from water to husbands??? Hello??? (This is what I call reading the Scriptures with both eyes open.) Having been sent a wide-open signal from this woman, Jesus is having His way with her, in the best possible sense of the expression.

18: For thou hast had five husbands; and he whom thou now hast is not thy husband: in that saidst thou truly.

Dr. Jesus diagnoses her case.

19: The woman saith unto him, Sir, I perceive that thou art a prophet.

Today we would say, "You have just read my mail!!…"

"...so, as long as we seem to be on the same page, let's talk about worship." I hope your seat belt is fastened, here. It looks like hers was. I think she was sitting so close to Jesus at this point that they were using the same seat belt. (Boy, it's a good thing the disciples went to town.)

20: Our fathers worshipped in this mountain; and ye say, that in Jerusalem is the place where men ought to worship.

CRASH!!! This is a paradigm collision! Jesus lets her have the steering wheel, she takes a turn off the "husband road" subject, and now they're both side by side in the middle of the "worship road" subject. They are now headed for a place where no one has ever been before. Jesus had never taken his disciples there, and he didn't take the Jews there. He picks up a woman of questionable reputation and takes her to a place in the Spirit where no one has ever been before. Just a little honoring, I would say. All at once the place of worship is no longer a matter of earthly geography. It is in that moment revealed as a place of spiritual geography. He chose this conversation with this woman to reveal this eternal truth to mankind. It doesn't get too much better than that. Seems like Jesus had a way of revealing things to women first. Significant things like the resurrection, like what makes great lovers, like perfume as a preparation for a death that no one else is very clear about yet, like relationships that come from Him. Even Mel Gibson's "The Passion of the Christ" included that communication.

21-24: Jesus saith unto her, Woman, believe me, the hour cometh, when ye shall neither in this mountain, nor yet at Jerusalem, worship the Father. Ye worship ye know not what: we know what we worship: for salvation is of the Jews. But the hour cometh, and now is, when the true worshippers shall worship the Father in spirit and in truth: for the Father seeketh such to worship him. God is a Spirit: and they that worship him must worship him in spirit and in truth.

Still dancing with perfection. The woman is discussing theology with Jesus, and they are taking turns taking the lead. How good is that? [:-)]

25: The woman saith unto him, I know that Messias cometh, which is called Christ: when he is come, he will tell us all things.

WOW! Seems like most of the time He was keeping that a secret. He doesn't even wait for her to guess. He just comes right out and tells her. Be still my heart!!!

26: Jesus saith unto her, I that speak unto thee am he.

27: And upon this came his disciples, and marvelled that he talked with the woman:

Right about then the kids show up. Shucks! The conversation was apparently PG-13, so the TV gets shut off when they show up. It's bad enough in their minds that He's talking to a woman, never mind the content of the conversation, at least, for now.

... yet no man said, "What seekest thou?"

I've already shared some about this. This is a typical male response, "shutdown." No one wanted to risk a bruised ego by going there.

... or, "Why talkest thou with her?"

Nope, not going to risk it.

28,29: The woman then left her water-pot,

Perhaps it's enough to say that when a woman is really touched, she will leave her own water-pot behind.

... and went her way into the city, and saith to the men, Come, see a man, which told me all things that ever I did:

It certainly looks to me as though, if John knew the full extent of what passed between them, it did not seem necessary for him to tell us the whole conversation. A woman who has known six men, more or less as a woman knows a husband, has probably "done" a few more things than what John has related to us here. Perhaps he wasn't told all of the conversation or he wasn't prompted to tell us the whole thing, but this woman makes no bones about it to her "men" friends in the city.

"... is not this the Christ?

How about that, a Socratic Samaritan— and a woman in the bargain! [:-)]

30: Then they went out of the city, and came unto him.

For a woman of questionable reputation, she sure seems to have a lot of credibility with the townsfolk. (Can you say "Chemistry"?)

31: In the mean while his disciples prayed him, saying, Master, eat.

I think this is the solid food equivalent of a preoccupation with "water-pots."

32: But he said unto them, I have meat to eat that ye know not of.

This looks to me like the solid food version of the conversation that has just taken place with the woman.

33: Therefore said the disciples one to another, Hath any man brought him ought to eat?

Which being freely translated means, "You have nothing to draw with and the well is deep." Or "You have no fork, and there's no food in sight."

So now the "water" has become "meat," and the "meat" is apparently a job that needs to be done.

Looks like Jesus has "already" been doing the job at the well.

Do you think that Jesus might have had just a little "rejoicing" in His heart right about then??

"Show time!!" [:-)]

There it is again, including the "trailer." Please note, they believed in Him because of her.

Jesus honored the fruit of her testimony by remaining with them for a while. Isn't it nice for us that, now that He is no longer in the flesh, He can "abode" with us forever!?!?

Some believed because of Him directly.

Some people just won't settle for second-hand information, especially coming from a woman.

Please note the connection between His continued travel and His observation about honor. She of "another country" honored Him. His own did not. This passage is so rich in its implications that we could stay here for a year and not glean it all. Recently, one of the things that struck me is, it isn't a matter of information so much as it is a matter of love. The problem is that we are more comfortable with information, because love can get us killed. How can we know anything about love, let alone have the ability to explain it to others, if we are not willing to die? That's our problem, is it not?

34: Jesus saith unto them, My meat is to do the will of him that sent me, and to finish his work.

35: Say not ye, There are yet four months, and then cometh harvest? Behold, I say unto you, Lift up your eyes, and look on the fields; for they are white already to harvest.

36: And he that reapeth receiveth wages, and gathereth fruit unto life eternal: that both he that soweth and he that reapeth may rejoice together.

37, 38: And herein is that saying true, One soweth, and another reapeth. I sent you to reap that whereon ye bestowed no labour: other men laboured, and ye are entered into their labours.

39: And many of the Samaritans of that city believed on him for the saying of the woman, which testified, He told me all that ever I did.

40: So when the Samaritans were come unto him, they besought him that he would tarry with them: and he abode there two days.

41: And many more believed because of his own word;

42: And said unto the woman, Now we believe, not because of thy saying: for we have heard him ourselves, and know that this is indeed the Christ, the Saviour of the world.

43, 44: Now after two days he departed thence, and went into Galilee. For Jesus himself testified, that a prophet hath no honour in his own country.

7

Perhaps this is enough for openers.

As for the title of our correspondence, "Not Left Behind," being so close to another recent and very well-known series, we will have something to say about the understanding of the Scriptures reflected in that series, not in this volume but in a later book of our own, should there prove to be interest. For now, perhaps it's enough to quote the following:

"But of that day and hour knoweth no man, no, not the angels of heaven, but my Father only. But as the days of Noah were, so shall also the coming of the Son of man be. For as in the days that were before the flood they were eating and drinking, marrying and giving in marriage, until the day that Noah entered into the ark, And knew not until the flood came, and took them all away; so shall also the coming of the Son of man be. Then shall two be in the field; the one shall be taken, and the other left. Two women shall be grinding at the mill; the one shall be taken, and the other left. Watch therefore: for ye know not what hour your Lord doth come."[1]

Please note who is taken and who is left.

—Jay

It seems I've lived most of my life in a sea of denial—my own and others. Denial not of how bad things are, but rather of how good they can be. I'm talking human relationships here, about our experience of being human in relationship with others. There seems to have been a sub-response to others in my own life, and as I look around, the same is true in others' lives. After all, what I saw around me conditioned me to my own response. The possibility of full, unbridled, passionate loving relationships was not something I witnessed, let alone imagined. The pull of the world is to keep a level of mediocrity, a lukewarm response to one another. Enough closeness to count on one another as friends, but not enough to really go places deep inside one another, as lovers do. And so, the call of my heart is to be an exquisite lover of men, as Jesus was and told us to be, and the working of that love thru my flesh has, until now, only gone so far. My sense, and experience, is that is true for most of us.

Take heart, this is not a book about denial. This is a book about opening up to life, to love, to glorious passion expressed not only inwardly and privately to my Lord, but outwardly to those that He has

---

[1]Matthew 24:36–42.

put in my life in particular to love. It's a focus that goes beyond what feels good, sounds good, looks good, tastes good, smells good. It IS good, goodness only from Him, shared from an overflowing of Him thru Him to others. It's a book about two people discovering and affirming together the Love that He has for us individually in Him and for each other in Him. It's a book about Love and becoming Lovers in Him. It is a book made possible by coming out of denial and allowing for the possibility of belief, belief that what is happening is good, from Him, desired for us by Him, and only a taste of what is there for us in Him. It's just a taste of what Jesus meant when he was about to go to the cross and prayed to the Father, "I have given them the glory that you gave me, that they may be one as we are one; I in them and you in me." [2]

When I "met" Jay, over the Internet, I had been anticipating the unfolding of what I had already received as a message: that my life was about to change significantly and that it would involve a man much further along in his spiritual path. I was surprised that he was a "Christian" since at that time I was not inclined to follow what I perceived to be a "Christian" path. I saw more love outside the "church" than in it. And I didn't have a real understanding of the Bible, that it is, in essence, a love story. But I had an experience in my early 20s where I had felt the realness of Jesus and His Love, and while I had not pursued a "Christian" path of Bible study and Church going, I followed Jesus in my heart and beliefs. I believed He was the Son of God and I believed that He came here to tell us how much God loves us, and I believed that we were supposed to love one another as He loves us. I had a sense that what I saw in the Church—all of the ritual and the activities and the pressures to conform—wasn't "it." So I was cautiously open to Jay and his Christian message and became increasingly more open as I looked at the Bible and began to understand what it unfolds as seen thru Jay's eyes. At the same time, I was experiencing Jay as being so unlike what I feared: a closed, judgmental, rule-imposing "religious" man. In fact, early on—in his first email even—I sensed a depth of love and willingness and ability to share it in a Godly manner that struck a chord of recognition deep inside me, a chord so loud and strong that, like following Jesus, my only response could be a heartfelt "Yes!"

As I look back on it, all of my life has brought me to a place where I am ready to open and receive all that God wants for me, both in deeper understanding of Him as well as how He wants me to live in

---

[2]John 17:22–23.

His love with others. I suppose you could say that I've been observing, searching, trying on different methods and attitudes, driven by a desire deep within to break out of a cocoon, if you would, of "safety" and "acceptability." I've always sensed that there has to be more. Just before meeting Jay, a series of events, including what I believe now to be my Baptism in the Spirit and a consequent amazing experiential sense of the Spirit, prepared me even further along the path of receiving, rejoicing in, and wanting to fully immerse myself in the understanding and experience of Jesus and His Love. My hope is that there will be those among you whom the Lord has prepared in a similar way, and that you will be able to glean from my correspondence and growing relationship with Jay some idea of the Hope and Joy that was set before Jesus as He approached His cross.

—Lisa

CHAPTER 1

PASSING THROUGH SAMARIA

On Tuesday, December 16, 2003, Lisa Weger wrote to the David Deida discussion list at deida.com:

Well, I now know one thing to NOT do when you're a Deida newbie working on changing your relationship dynamics. You DO NOT talk about why your sex life has not worked in the past. That's like shooting yourself in the foot to see if it hurts. YIKES! The truth is, it's all BS anyway—all the "reasons" that kept us from intimacy. It's really about good old-fashioned fear, I believe. I'm becoming convinced that this DD [David Deida] work is on an energetic level and talking isn't. So for now I'm going to focus on a lot more non-verbal stuff—moaning, gazing, rubbing, pulling come to mind.

Lisa

On Thursday, December 18, 2003, Jay Ferris responded to Lisa's e-mail in a private communication.[1]

Lisa wrote:

Well, I now know one thing to NOT do when you're a Deida newbie working on changing your relationship dynamics....So for now I'm going to focus on a lot more non-verbal stuff—moaning, gazing, rubbing, pulling come to mind.

---

[1] Jay generally responds to Lisa's e-mails by taking a portion of what she writes, commenting on that, moving to the next portion of her e-mail, responding to that, and so on. This format will be followed here, with Lisa's remarks presented in italics. For the sake of space, in some cases not all of the text of Lisa's e-mails will be repeated.

11

Dear Lisa,

I don't know if or when I might ever send this response to what you have written here. Right now my common sense tells me that I should watch and learn for a while in order to get a better idea of where people are coming from on this list. But your paragraph above touched on, at least, three aspects relating to the possibility of or conditions for spiritual intimacy.

I would say therefore, that this is in some sense a journal entry, except that writing to a journal falls too far short of what is possible when writing to a person. Perhaps I can begin by confessing a few givens, the perceptions/realities out of which I write. At 65 years of age, I am convinced that the deepest longing of every human heart is for intimacy, and the greatest fear is the fear of rejection. In some sense the garbage of past experience lies beneath both the hope and the fear. I assume your talking about your sex life related to the one, and expressed fear hardly needs further comment. The "BS" is the garbage.

I know nothing about this "DD work" having only just arrived here from another source of exploration, so I have nothing to contribute from a "DD" perspective. Rather I have come to the exploration of intimacy from a Biblical perspective. The door of entry from a Biblical perspective is that, in the beginning God made them male and female in His image. (Genesis 1:27) In Ephesians 5:31–32, the door is opened further where the possibility of spiritual intimacy is concerned: "'For this reason a man will leave his father and mother and be united to his wife, and the two will become one flesh.' (This is a quotation from Genesis 2:24. Verse 25 immediately goes on to say: "And they were both naked, the man and his wife, and were not ashamed.") This is a profound mystery: but I am talking about Christ and the church."

In other words, sex is a parable. By that, I am not suggesting that sex cannot be fulfilling for its own sake, rather, I'm saying that sex at its best is only a picture of a greater intimacy, a spiritual intimacy. That the parable is a picture of Christ and the church does not mean that there is no longer any horizontal outworking of intimacy, because there most certainly is. The church spoken of in Ephesians is composed of many people who are intimate with each other because of intimacy with Him. At least, from a Biblical perspective, this is the way it is supposed to work, John 17:21 says, "that all of them may be one, Father, just as you are in me and I am in you. May they also be in us so that the world may believe that you have sent me." At this point I cannot proceed further without first asking your forgiveness for what may have been represented to you as "church."

The first time Jesus was introduced to humanity, it was said of Him, "Behold the lamb of God that takes away the sins of the world." John 1:29. To make this up-to-date in the terms we are using here, Jesus was announced as the garbage man, the one who takes away all the "BS." In other words, before anything else is possible where intimacy is concerned, the "BS" must first be removed. Actually, in its popular usage, "BS" is the very opposite of intimacy; it is false rather than true. For that reason, I would like to suggest "garbage" as a more helpful description of the problem or obstacle to intimacy.

Without trying to elaborate a complete theology of garbage removal, I would for the present share with you that all of us need to find a place to put our garbage. We are not very good at trash compacting, because when the pressure is on, the garbage sooner or later leaks out and ruins intimacy. Putting the garbage in the wrong place only messes up everything. They call it "littering," and it really should be against the law. Being in denial about our garbage is not very smart, because sooner or later everyone knows that we all have garbage.

There are places in all of us where we have never been, and the problem is that you can't get there alone, because if you went there alone it would not be the same place as it would be if you took someone else with you. Garbage is what keeps us from going there. We need a place to put the garbage. Jesus is the only one who can take away the garbage and leave everything clean. This to say, alone or with others, none of us can go to spiritually intimate places without taking Him with us.

There is no way around it/Him. If I am correct, that sex is a parable and that the point of the parable is Christ and the church, then not to get the point is to be left hung up on the plumbing. Where intimacy is concerned, the reality is spiritual, not plumbing. By this, I'm not saying that the plumbing cannot be part of the intimacy, only that the intimacy available to the plumbing is very limited.

An aspect of the sexual parable where both the Bible and the creation is concerned is the matter of circumcision. From the Bible we discover that the circumcision of the flesh is only a picture of the cutting off of a greater barrier to intimacy/sensitivity, the cutting off of our cluelessness, the cluelessness of our flesh, Colossians 2:11. Common sense and sexual awareness will tell you that circumcision should precede intimacy. As it is with the intimacy of the flesh, so must it be with spiritual intimacy. From a Biblical perspective, uncircumcised flesh is part of the garbage. Sooner or later it gets in the way of spiritual intimacy. When it does, the consequences are deadly, even worse than "shooting yourself in the foot."

Finally, your conclusion to abandon the verbal in favor of "moaning, gazing, rubbing, and pulling," raises another very important, if completely ignored, Biblical point. In the Greek, there are four loves that the Bible speaks about. More than likely you have heard of three of them; "agape," "phileo," and "eros." I'm also guessing that, [except] for the first, you know how they differ, so I won't go into that here, except to say that the Bible uses "agape" for love, both before and after the crucifixion. The meaning of agape, however, was changed by the crucifixion.

Agape: the purely spiritual love of one person for another. This love corresponds to the love of God or Christ for mankind.

Phileo: indicates one having love or strong affinity or preference for (from Greek word *philos* meaning beloved, dear, and loving).

Eros: physical love or sexual desire.

The greatest agape anyone knew about before the crucifixion was an agape that might possibly lay its life down for a friend. With the crucifixion a new agape was revealed, one that is willing to lay its life down for enemies: 1 John 3:16 and Romans 5:10. The fourth Greek word for love found in the Bible is "storge." You will find it in three places: Romans 1:31, Romans 12:10, and 2 Timothy 3:3.

Storge: the love one feels towards family members and animals.

This is a love that has to do with "moaning, gazing, rubbing, and pulling." Storge is the love of a mother for her infant. It is translated, "natural affection." It is natural to animals including birds, and it is natural to humans—or at least it used to be. It is communicated by look, and tone, and touch. It is the first awareness in new life that the new life might possibly be of value. When it is not there, the result is dysfunction. In fact, it is already evidence of dysfunction when it's missing. I should add that the other natural affections, phileo and eros, are also communicated by look and tone and touch. One result of the dysfunction due to a storge deficit is the attempt to compensate with misplaced eros.

While value or being valued can be communicated by look, and tone, and touch, so much more meaning can be communicated with words. In either case, the garbage must be removed or, at least, be properly disposed of as it is uncovered in the experience of intimacy.

· There is certainly much more that could be said on the subject from a Biblical perspective, but perhaps it is best for now to limit my response to the several points you touched on in your email.

As a fellow "newbie," I have just reread the rules, and saw that I can send this to you in private rather than via the whole list. I hope you will not be offended by my doing so. I sincerely mean all that I have said above and know by study and experience that it is true.

Sincerely,

Jay

On Friday, December 19, 2003, Lisa wrote:

Hello Jay,

I enjoyed reading what you had to say—I'm still digesting it—and wonder why you sent it to me and not as a general post? I haven't seen anything relating to Biblical terms in the Deida postings (I've only been reading them for a week or two) but would be interested in hearing others' take on this. I, personally, am not a Biblical scholar, but your thoughtfulness and translation into the here and now intrigued me. This whole issue of sexuality and spirituality is vast and certainly can be framed in several contexts. Thanks for sharing your frame of reference.

Lisa

On the same day, Jay responded:

Lisa wrote: *I enjoyed reading what you had to say—I'm still digesting it—* ...

Dear Lisa,

Thank you for your encouraging note.

...and wonder why you sent it to me and not as a general post? ...

Not having read the postings long enough to get a sense of where people were coming from, I was reluctant to stick my oar in. Your contribution, to which I responded, contained so much that I have been exploring for a number of years now, that I thought you might be a safe place to share some thoughts. I am encouraged that this seems to have been a correct impression.

15

...I haven't seen anything relating to Biblical terms in the Deida postings (I've only been reading them for a week or two), but would be interested in hearing others' take on this....

Perhaps, after reading the postings for a little longer, I might feel free to post it. I try to meet people where they are, and I'm still not sure of where they are on this list. Yesterday I received my first two books by David Deida, and I spent some time reading last night and this morning. I'm not yet ready to write a book review either, but I'm digesting, perhaps to that end.

...I, personally, am not a Biblical scholar, but your thoughtfulness and translation into the here and now intrigued me. This whole issue of sexuality and spirituality is vast and certainly can be framed in several contexts.

For the past 15 years I have been researching and working on a book, by the title I have already alluded to, **In Other Words, Sex Is a Parable.** In 1980 or so, I had a book published on the monetary implications of the Bible and am currently doing a rewrite on it for a Wall Street publishing firm. The monetary implications of the Bible turn out to be love. That's what I found in seven years of Biblical research on that subject.

If the current subject is of interest I would be glad to send you a little glimpse into my perspective on what I call, "relationships that come from God." In this connection, I should say that your posting today is exactly right. It has to do with "being," not "doing." "Doing" that is not grounded in "being" is always born out of our insecurities. Insecure people aren't much good to themselves or others. Spiritual being is a matter of revelation.

Sincerely,

Jay

On Monday, December 22, 2003, Lisa wrote:

Hello Jay-

Yes, I would be interested in a glimpse into your perspective. I will be out of pocket from Christmas Eve thru the weekend after New Year's but would look forward to a response by then. Thanks for the offer.

Take care,

Lisa

Dear Lisa

In February of 2000, I experienced a paradigm shift, and now, after four months of a broken heart, I don't think I ever want to be without one again.

In October of 1999, a friend, Nate Krupp, asked me to clean up three or four manuscripts that I had been working on for about 15 years. He said it was time, and he wanted to get them published as soon as possible. Nate's wife, Joanne, had finally published her book on women, which contains so much truth that she was unable to find anyone who would publish it for over eight years. Her book is called **Woman: God's Plan, Not Man's Tradition.**[2]

My three manuscripts dealt with the church as a new creation: **In Other Words, Sex Is a Parable; The Authority Crisis;** and **Circumcision: The Battle of Belonging.**

Nate had asked that I try to combine them. It hadn't been so easy, and then became impossible. I felt there was a real need to make the book more personal. So I began working on a chapter, tentatively titled "Getting Personal," which would be Chapter 17, a new last chapter.

In this chapter my intention was to be as transparent and vulnerable as possible. I was determined to let it all hang out. I say "determined" because the thought of being that vulnerable was very frightening. The fear was—and is—the fear of rejection.

As I was thinking about this my wife, Carleen, and I were on a walk together with some friends in our woods. We came to a new insight on the parable of the talents, Matthew 25: 14-30 [at the right].

Looking at the one talent slave, in context, we saw that the parable has little or nothing to do with financial investment, stock market investment, putting money in a bank, or even burying it in the ground. It is speaking about high-risk investment

The Parable of the Talents

[Jesus, speaking privately to his disciples on the Mount of Olives, said] "Again, it will be like a man going on a journey, who called his servants and entrusted his property to them. To one he gave five talents of money, to another two talents, and to another one talent, each according to his ability. Then he went on his journey. The man who had received the five talents went at once and put his money to work and gained five more. So also, the one with the two talents gained two more. But the man who had received the one talent went off, dug a hole in the ground and his master's money.

"After a long time the master of those servants returned and settled accounts with them. The man who had re-

---

[2]**Woman: God's Plan, Not Man's Tradition,** by Joanne Krupp, with a Foreword by Treena Kerr, published by Preparing the Way Press, in 1999.

ceived the five talents brought the other five. 'Master,' he said, 'you entrusted me with five talents. See, I have gained five more.'

"His master replied, 'Well done, good and fiathful servant! You have been faithful with a few things; I will put you in charge of many things. Come and share your master's happiness!'

"The man with the two talents also came. 'Master,' he said, 'you entrusted me with two talents; see, I have gained two more.'

"His master replied, 'Well done, good and faithful servant! You have been faithful with a few things; I will put you in charge of many things. Come and share your master's happiness!'

"Then the man who had received the one talent came. 'Master,' he said, "I knew that you are a hard man, harvesting where you have not sown and gathering where you have not scattered seed. So I was afraid and went out and hid your talent in the ground. See, here is what belongs to you.'

"His master replied, 'You wicked, lazy servant! So you knew that I harvest where I have not sown and gather where I have not scattered seed? Well then, you should have put my money on deposit with the bankers, so that when I returned I would have received it back with interest.

"'Take the talent from him and give it to the one who has ten talents. For everyone who has will be given more, and he will have an abundance. Whoever does not have, even what he has will be taken from him. And throw that worthless servant outside, into the darkness, where there will be weeping and gnashing of teeth.

—Matthew 25:14-30 (NIV)
(A talent was worth more than a thousand dollars.)

as contrasted with the relative safety of money in the bank. It has to do with the nature of the investment.

In the Kingdom of God, the investment is in relationships. Jesus is the investor. First of all, He staked everything on relationship, His relationship with His Father, and then, with His Father as His backer, He invested everything in us who believe. He is after relationships, lots of them. Jesus's Father is looking for fellowship. When the Greeks wanted to meet Jesus, He went away and left the job to us.

By His death, He made a deposit in us, and the Spirit continues to bring us even more of Him. Jesus is looking for a return on His investment. He knows what it is to risk rejection and be rejected.[2] He expects us to take the same risk and invest ourselves in others.

As I was working on the chapter, I had an increasing sense that I was violating my original intention, which was to be transparent and vulnerable. Then I realized that I was increasingly using the Scriptures to support what I was sharing, and the reason I was doing this was so that I could hide behind the Scriptures. I was hiding behind the Scriptures because of the fear of rejection. Jesus was despised and rejected. I didn't want to be despised and rejected. I wanted to be esteemed and accepted. Talk about "Who do you think you are?"

Recently, Tim (my son) and I were talking, and I found myself wondering about Jesus' style of ministry, wondering if He had used the Scriptures as I was using them. I have not had the

---

[2]Isaiah 53:3.

opportunity to make a thorough investigation, but it is now my impression that this is not at all the way Jesus ministered.

In his skirmish with the Devil, he used the Scriptures to defend himself, but that was war. Jesus is the Prince of Peace. In the beatitudes, He repeatedly said, "It is written..." but then went on to say, "But I tell you...." When confronted by the Pharisees, He quoted Scripture, but, again, that was war. The Scripture is a weapon, our only offensive weapon. We only need weapons when we are at war. When we are at peace, we can be vulnerable. If I am making love, I don't have to come on with all guns blazing. For years I have joked about wearing pink to leaders' meetings to keep them from being too threatened. I don't want to be seen as a threat, but as a lover.

Jesus may have "only said the things His father said," but it did not come out of Him in the form of Bible verses. We use the phrase, "What I am saying is... ," and we go on to say what we have already said, but in different words. This, I believe, is who Jesus was: He was what the Father was saying, but in different words. If challenged, He could use the Scripture to explain Himself well enough, but He did not come to us as Scripture, He came to us as love and life. If only we too could go forth in tears, to the end that we might enter into His laughter. If only we too could be like Him in His death, that we too might attain to the resurrection of the dead.

More and more in recent months, I have found myself saying what the Father is saying, but in different words, and without conscious effort. It's awesome, and it's terrifying all at once. A person could get hurt doing this sort of thing.

It is at the point of relationship that this becomes particularly problematic. Jesus said of those that the Father had given Him that He "kept" them while He was in the world.[3] That's my Father's heart, His heart and my heart. My heart is increasingly broken as I think of inviting others into this same vulnerability. It is one thing to have faith that He can save and protect me. It is a bit more of a stretch to have faith that He will save and protect those whom He has made mine from the fallout of my humiliation.

As I recently wrote to a friend, my own children are still damaged by the rejection I have experienced—and we as a family have experienced—from the church back in Connecticut. As you know, when the church meets in your home, the transparency

---

[3]John 17:12.

and vulnerability are greatly increased, People who were like older brothers and sisters, aunts and uncles, even second parents walked away, because of pressure coming from the institutionalized leaders and saints around us; they just could not understand and are gun shy to this day. I do take some comfort, however, in knowing that no one is going to sell them any snake oil in the name of the Lord.

But it was not just my flesh and blood children, it was my spiritual children as well. At this point, just about all of them have come back in the Spirit, but in between then and now, there were many years of alienation and estrangement. In a recent exchange with a local "pastor," I am looking down the same gun barrel once again. It breaks my heart to see my children hurt so. For this reason, I make every effort to maintain "the unity of the Spirit in the bond of peace,…" and as for my part, to "be at peace with all men."

Perhaps that's enough to give you some sense of what I was feeling at that point. I am wrestling with going back over what I have written, and getting rid of most, if not all, the references and footnotes. The problem is, that the religious will see the passion and the intimacy that I have experienced, and into which I am inviting others, that the religious will see this as illegal. That's what happened to Jesus. When the leadership got in His face about it, He nuked them with the Scripture. At least, tonight, that is the way it looks to me.

Here's the chapter I was talking about.

Chapter 17

Getting Personal

"I grieve for you, Jonathan my brother;
you were very dear to me. Your love for me was wonderful,
more wonderful than the love of women."
—2 Samuel 1:26

Perhaps I can share about relationships from God, in a little more intimate and personal way. I have waited until the end to share at this depth, hoping by now there has been enough explanation and revelation so that what follows does not appear to be illegal. My hope is that the testimony of this chapter will reveal the passion which has accomplished what has gone before.

I believe that the love between David and Jonathan was mutual, so that we can read our opening verse in the following sense, "the love we shared was, to me, wonderful…."

Just how much love, and how much intimacy is ours in the Lord Jesus Christ? Paul prayed: "...that [we], being rooted and established in love, may have power, together with all the saints, to grasp how wide and long and high and deep is the love of Christ, and to know this love that surpasses knowledge—that [we] may be filled to the measure of all the fullness of God." (Ephesians 3:17–19)

Peter writes: "Above all, love each other deeply, because love covers over a multitude of sins." (1 Peter 4:8)

It is so easy to just read the ink, be mere talkers, paying lip service to love, but without passion: "...from such turn away." (2 Timothy 3:5 KJV)

Divine Encounters Anointed by Love

One evening quite some years ago now, I was sharing a fresh insight about relationships that come from God. When I was through sharing, I asked everyone, "Well, who do you think you are?" The question was asked in a very gentle and loving way, not in the dishonoring sense in which it is normally asked. Those present became like children on a Christmas morning, thinking about who the Lord had made them to each other, and to others who, though not present, had been made special to them by The Lord. The implications of the question went far beyond that room, but for some, who were there, came the discovery of who they were to others in the room. There were lots of hugs and tears, many very precious conversations.

One man, about my age, then mid-forties, with whom I had felt a close bond for some time, was very quiet, however. I approached him and asked the question once more, "Well, who do you think you are?" He started to respond, tears flooded his eyes, and he choked up, turned on his heel, and left.

Several days later, he appeared at my office, I jumped up to hug his neck, and he waved me off, saying that he had the flu but had to come by. He went on to explain that I had asked him a question, and the question deserved an answer. He also said that he had known a lot of rejection in his life, and had great difficulty risking rejection once again, but then went on to say, "I think that you are my dad." That was all I had to hear. I leaped over the desk, landed in his lap, hugging and kissing him. We sat there and wept like a couple of babies. I prayed over him, as I had my arms around him. The Lord healed him on the spot, and he went off to find his oldest son to take them to the winter Olympics, which were in Lake Placid New York that year. We have been very close ever since that day.

On another occasion I was overseas, where I had spoken to a church through a translator whom I had barely met. Afterward he came up to me with tears in his eyes and said: "I want to tell you how important it is for me that you are here, but I do not understand why."

I wonder if you can guess how this made me feel. I responded, "I think I understand; we need to talk." By then, I also was in tears. We went to lunch together, he, his wife, their little girl, and me. It was very precious.

Then there was the first time that I was overwhelmed with feeling for a complete stranger. I met him in Detroit, in the early seventies. It was at a men's conference on evangelism sponsored by a denominational church. We were knit together immediately. It felt like "love at first sight." I had no understanding of the Scripture that could account for it at the time. I felt like I had been emotionally violated. The feeling was so strong it was as though God had physically altered my heart and mind. It was sovereign. It felt illegal, it felt weird, but it did feel.

21

We continue to relate in the grace of that relationship right up to this very day. I didn't understand it at the time. It happened before either of us had even had a chance to speak at all, let alone with one another. But, afterward, it was certainly confirmed as being mutual—and now, validated over time. In this case, I had been given an older brother.

At the time, my understanding of relationship was limited to the "brother-hood of all believers." It was the Lord's mercy that my first experience with His sovereignty in relationship was with a brother.

It was some years later before I discovered that the Lord could also put spiritual fathers in my heart. When this first happened, and I shared the sense that I had with each one of them, in each case, the expression of my own heart's content toward them brought tears to their eyes. In two cases, they were men who had ministered for many years, but had interacted with others more in the context of doctrine and ministry than in the reality of relationship.

More and more, I found myself risking transparency. More and more I found the Kingdom of God increasing. More and more I was willing to take risks for the sake of relationship.

I well remember the first time I had these special feelings in my heart for a woman other than my wife. I was tormented by the feelings, I was sure that they were illegal, I was sure that it had to be lust. Internally, I was running away from someone I later discovered the Lord had given into my life as a spiritual daughter.

When I finally stopped to look at the old creation long enough to discover what life had to teach me about relationships, I realized that I was never up all night when someone else's child was sick, but I was up all night when my own children were sick. The old creation taught me that there is room for special feelings toward other women. I am the father of two daughters. We know who we are to each other, so we can be very close with no problem. In fact some-thing would be terribly wrong if we were not very close. Now I have daughters in the Lord with whom I am also very close, and it is wonderful.

I have a mother in the Lord as well; she has long since gone on to be with the Father, but the crafty woman got me into the place where I first came to know the Lord and looked after my spiritual welfare for quite a while after that. The mother of Rufus was a spiritual mother to Paul also. (Romans 16:13)

On another occasion, the Lord gave me another spiritual daughter. I had met her years before but, for a number of reasons, said nothing about what I had felt. One day, after more than 6 years, as we were walking together, I put my arm around her and said, "All right, I think I have waited long enough to ask you a question... Who do you think you are in relationship to me?" She answered, "I think I'm your daughter." It was that simple—and that clear. I wonder if you can imagine how I felt. I immediately answered, "Yes! And I could not possibly love you any more if you were my own flesh and blood."

Think about it for a moment, take the kaleidoscope of emotions felt toward a child from the first news of their conception, through birth, and growing up, cram all of that into a single moment in time, and you will understand why I could barely stand, let alone keep walking. In the weeks that followed, as we began to unwrap the gift of relationship that the Lord had given us in each oth-er, and in anticipation of a block of time when we could share at some depth, I was minded to risk saying a number of other things as being foundational to whatever the rest of the conversation might uncover.

First, I repeated something already understood but perhaps not already verbalized, and that is that, because Jesus is Lord of who we are to each other, there would never be anything between us that could not be understood in that light. Second, I would never want to do or say anything that would violate her conscience. This would, in part, be determined by the cultural givens with which she had grown up and with which she was surrounded. Third—and perhaps most vulnerably—I said that, if I was not convinced that Jesus had given her into my life as a daughter, I would be scared to death, because there is no other way I could account for such strong feelings toward her. All of this she heard and immediately understood. It was also understood that care needed to be taken not to fall into an appearance of evil. (1 Thessalonians 5:22)

About a month after getting clear about who we were to each other, she wrote:

> I have to say I was quite overwhelmed by the affirmation of our father-daughter relationship when I stepped in the door last night and saw you. Thinking about the depth of feeling that seized me (and not of my own volition) is very peculiar to me and brings tears to my eyes as I write. It seems almost presumptuous to feel so much like a daughter to you, whom I've known in this way for a relatively short period of time. Nevertheless...I wanted you to know.

> Your daughter

In His prayer in John 17:6-12, Jesus said "I have revealed you to those whom you gave me out of the world. They were yours; you gave them to me.... I gave them the words you gave me and they accepted them. They knew with certainty that I came from you, and they believed that you sent me.... I am not praying for the world, but for those you have given me, for they are yours.... I protected them and kept them safe by that name you gave me...."

I found myself praying that same prayer. I wasn't praying it on purpose, so to speak, but supernaturally. Without even trying, I was saying the things that the Father is saying, loving the ones that the Father had given me. It wasn't me, it was the Spirit alive in me.

Jesus did not try to reproduce by having office hours and making appointments. Rather, He said to those that the Father gave Him, "Come on with me." They had something like three round-the-clock years with each other. It must have been something! That has been our heart for many years now. We have tried to walk it out in such a way that those that the Father has given us can get as close as they want for as long as they want. Quite a few have stayed in our home, some longer than others. There have been 3:00 a.m., desperate, bursting into the house, tearful all-night sessions, lots of house calls; some have been carried, others bandaged, lots of tears—more of laughter than of sorrow—you name it. And all of that while our own flesh and blood children were still with us.

The flesh and blood kids were mostly gone, and here was a new daughter in The Lord. I wanted her to know that we would not likely have the time together that would be the desire of a father's heart, especially a father with a new daughter. If she moved into the house, after three years, I might want a break, but short of that, not to count on it. This to say, that she would have full and complete access, whether in tears or rejoicing, whether in confusion or in clarity, yes, even in sickness and in health.

There are other divine encounters that I could (and might) share, but perhaps enough for now.

This is the Church, as she is revealed on and between the lines of the Scriptures. To the religious she looks like a cult, but to God, she is the light of

His life to people living in darkness. She is the validation of, and expression of, the Love of Christ in the world.

(**The Parable of the Talents** is included here, with the same explanation as earlier [see page 17])

The Fear of Rejection

One more word of testimony: The first time I felt the Spirit in this tangible way, I was heading for a monetary conference. Over the previous ten years I had come to know those who would be attending and speaking. I had come to know and desire their acceptance and respect, but this day, I had a "Jesus button" on my collar. The first person I ran into at the conference told me to take it off, that it would drive these sophisticated people away from me. He said that I would be rejected. After some considerable prayer and soul searching, I left it on, and he was right. People got out of my way for the two days of the conference. No one wanted to be seen even speaking with me. Today, I might make a different decision, but I made the right one for that day. The acceptance of those in attendance meant too much to me, almost more than obeying The Lord. I was baptized in The Spirit prior to making that decision. I needed that power to make the right choice.

It does not require a Ph.D. to tune in to the Spirit. There are many cues. Where relationships are concerned perhaps one of the strongest is found in Luke 24:32: "And they said to one another, 'Were not our hearts burning within us while He spoke to us on the road, while He was explaining the Scriptures to us?'" Where the Lordship of Christ in relationship is concerned, about the closest carnal analogy I can think of is the feeling described as "love at first sight."

Mary, the mother of Jesus, had Jesus inside of her but did not speak the Magnificat until the baby leapt in the womb of Elizabeth. Where a tangible response to Jesus in another person is concerned, John the Baptist was the first, and that while he was still in his mother's womb. Encouraged by John's testimony, Elizabeth took the risk of telling Mary, and Mary had the confirmation she needed for the expression of her heart in her Magnificat. (Luke 1:46–55)

Do not be afraid, your heavenly Father is not a harsh master reaping where He has not sown. He has sown the life of His Son into your heart. Won't you take the risk of investing Him in others? This is the work which God requires, to believe in the one whom He has sent, perhaps the one who is standing right in front of you.

One night I received a very excited call from someone to whom I had sent the chapter, as it appears above, along with this cover note:

"I have not had the opportunity to proof this yet, so be merciful. You have certainly been on my heart as I have written it. If there is anything that I have said that is either in error, a misrepresentation, or a betrayal of our relationship, please tell me. That is the last thing that I would want to do. As for my part I want to be willing to be vulnerable, but I do not want to presume to put you in that position, unless that is where you want to be.

"It is just that it breaks my heart when I think about the emptiness of life and relationship for so many, when the Lord has paid so dear a price to give them both, and more abundantly.

"I have not sent this to anyone yet. I knew that I had to have your input and blessing to do so. If there is any reservation please tell me. I would never want to violate who we are to each other.

Yours, Jay"

I sent the chapter first to her, because, she had the most to lose of those mentioned. It is here in the same rough form in which I sent it to her.

She responded:

"I read the chapter while waiting in the airport. It's good. I was very blessed by your proud description of our relationship! I must admit, however, that I'm not sure I can be very objective or helpful as far as judging its impact on those reading it for the first time (since I am a part of it). But if you wanted my blessing, you've got it! Also, while I continue to appreciate your caution as far as protecting me from others who might not understand our relationship and I respect your intuition resulting from your previous experience along these lines, know that I am a consenting partner in our relationship and, basically, that I WON'T WALK AWAY!"

She went back to school, after the holidays, knowing that there were others there that were special to her, and looking forward to discovering and confirming who they were to each other. She called right after the first of her explicit encounters and related to me the following:

Not quite knowing how to open the subject, she had shared this chapter with her friend, a girl that she thought might be a sister to her in the Spirit. As the other girl read it, she began to weep, finally coming out and telling her of her own feeling about her, even to the point of, sometime in the recent past, trying to make a list of all the things about her that were special to her. She said to her, "I know that I am your sister." The two of them hugged and wept together for the next 30 minutes or so, and she, rejoicing, phoned me right afterward to share what had happened.

While in Connecticut, I shared some of this with my flesh-and-blood daughter. Her hair was a little straight up about the whole thing. She had a general sense of where I was coming from for many years but had never seen it so clearly before. Her reaction was, "But, Dad, how do you know the limits of such a relationship?" I answered with a question to her, "How do I know the limits on my relationship with you?" When you understand the nature of a relationship, the old creation itself will tell you the limits on what is appropriate to that relationship.

Well, Lisa, like I said, that's a little taste.

Sincerely,

Jay

CHAPTER 2

WONDER WOMAN: THEN AND NOW

Dear Jay,

I have to say that I'm quite touched by your vulnerability and your willingness to speak your truth. What you have to say is quite beautiful. It saddens me to know that you must concern yourself with questions of legality and rejection. Yet I know that there is such truth in that—and it sounds like you have experienced it (rejection) in a big way. That you're willing—no, DETERMINED—to keep and show your heart in your writing is evidence to me of the depth of understanding you have about what I believe we're REALLY here for: to learn how to be an expression of love for everyone and everything. (I know that this is oversimplifying—but that is how I strive to live my life—cutting down to the bare bones.)

I was thrilled to hear you talk of speaking "what the Father is saying, but in different words, and without conscious effort." I believe this happens frequently, which makes sense if you are attuned to a living, breathing presence and not just some words in a book (albeit a very GOOD book). I applaud you for allowing yourself to be led and recognizing it for what it is: gifts from God.

Your relationships from God sound precious and alive in love. How could anyone doubt them? If only our hearts could ALWAYS be so open! I'm grateful that you are so willing to share these words of love with me, and (hopefully) many others.

I have to say that I initially felt like pushing you away when I saw you quoting scripture. I think your insight of people using scripture as a weapon is very true—that's been my experience. My feeling is always that I can't trust such people—that they're not being real and I can't get a sense of who they REALLY are and how they really feel and experience the world. I usually get a sense more of what they think they SHOULD be (and what I SHOULD be in the same breath). I think that's what religion does—in its worst sense—reduce people to this SAMENESS out of fear. It is exactly what Jesus encountered and fought.

My own involvement with Christianity and the Bible has been sketchy, at best. I got way more from reading the last section of the Urantia book (about the life of Christ) than I did from what little reading I did of the Bible. I'm sure this has something to do with the format—the Bible seems much more esoteric. (My father introduced me to the Urantia book—his bible—some 25 years ago, and I've heard him passionately discuss it ever since.) I know that spirituality is an unfolding—a "revelation," in your words. I strive to be consciously aware of—and responsive to—all of the spirit world in the moment. I read what I feel led to read, and someday I may return to the Bible. In the meanwhile it is helpful to know people who are firmly grounded in the Bible's teachings, yet are open to take it to a new level—one that is more heartfelt than authoritative. Perhaps this is happening more than I think—I don't have a good feel for it.

Thank you again for sharing yourself so openly and passionately. It's a rare—and very pleasurable—thing.

I may come into the office over the holidays and work on the computer (check e-mails)—I can't figure out how to get my e-mail to work on my computer at home (or maybe I just don't WANT to check my e-mails at home).

Anyway, I look forward to hearing from you again.

Sincerely,

Lisa

On the same day, Jay responded:

Lisa wrote: *I have to say that I'm quite touched by your vulnerability and your willingness to speak your truth. What you have to say is quite beautiful. It saddens me to know that you must concern yourself with questions of legality and rejection....*

Dear Lisa,

Thank you so much for your very thoughtful consideration and response. I felt I needed to write again right after sending the last, just to say that I had written that chapter to "Christians."

For that reason, I wrote it in their language. The reason that "the church" is as divided as it is, is because most Christians understand Jesus Christ to be some kind of religious add-on. This is the reason for all of the legalism and all the rejection. It might be better called "church-going," rather than Christianity.

...Yet I know that there is such truth in that—and it sounds like you have experienced it (rejection) in a big way. That you're willing— no, DETERMINED—to keep and show your heart in your writing is evidence to me of the depth of understanding you have about what I believe we're REALLY here for: to learn how to be an expression of love for everyone and everything. (I know that this is oversimplifying—...

Actually, what you have just written is very close to the bottom line: 1 John 4:8 says: "Whoever does not love does not know God, because God is love."

Elsewhere it is written: "Dear friends, now we are children of God, and what we will be has not yet been made known. But we know that when he appears, we shall be like him, for we shall see him as he is."[1] If you combine both thoughts, then we will be love for we shall see love as it is.

...but that is how I strive to live my life—cutting down to the bare bones.)

As we have already discussed, it comes more by seeing than by striving.

I was thrilled to hear you talk of speaking "what the Father is saying, but in different words, and without conscious effort." I believe this happens frequently, which makes sense if you are attuned to a living, breathing presence and not just some words in a book (albeit a very GOOD book). I applaud you for allowing yourself to be led and recognizing it for what it is: gifts from God.

Your relationships from God sound precious and alive in love. How could anyone doubt them? If only our hearts could ALWAYS be so open!...

In following Jesus, we eventually come to a cup. It's not a nice cup, not a cup that anyone would volunteer to drink. In a sense, it is a cup full of hazardous waste. It is a cup full of garbage, full of abomination,[2] a cup of wrath,[3] a cup of heartbreak.

---

[1] 1 John 3;2 (NIV).
[2] Revelation 17:4, 18:6; Ezekiel 23:31–33; Habakkuk 2:15–16.
[3] Revelation 15:10, 16:19; Psalms 75:8; Jeremiah 25:15, 17, 28; Jeremiah 49:12, Jeremiah 51; Lamentations 4:21; Zechariah 12:2.

Jesus came to a place in His ministry when he had to drink this cup,[4] but He was not the only one who would drink from it; there would be others.[5]

And what shall we say? It was in the matter of this cup that we first see a difference in wills between Jesus and His Father. For the first time from eternity past, there is a difference between them. It was the Father's will that Jesus should drink of this cup. It was the Son's will that it might pass from Him. In the Garden of Gethsemane, Jesus was locked into a conflict of wills, a conflict that would not pass until His Father's will prevailed. The conflict was so great that Jesus asked His closest friends to come and pray with Him, but they fell asleep in the midst of it and didn't wake up until it was over.

In a sense, this matter had already been settled from before the foundation of the world, but none of us should be too quick to think that we can drink from this cup. When the moment of truth finally comes, we too may sweat blood over the matter. We may not be called to drink the cup for everyone, but we may be called to drink the cup for those we love, if we are going to love them to the end.

There were those in Babylon that the Father loved. He wanted them out of there. But the only way to get them out was to dispose of the cup from which they had been drinking. It was a cup in the hands of a MYSTERY.[6] Once again, Jesus asked, "O my Father, if this cup may not pass away from me, except I drink it, thy will be done."[7] Jesus knew that this cup had to be disposed of. He wanted another way to get rid of it, but there was none. Perhaps someone else to stand in the gap, but there was none.[8]

In order to make it possible for us, the ones who were captive in Babylon, to be intimate with Him, He had to drink the cup of our abomination and, with it, the desolation. In order to love me, He had to take the worst of me into Himself.

Would that were the end of it. In loving one another, there is a cup that we also must drink. Otherwise, we will break faith with one another.[9]

Are we prepared to do whatever is necessary to get the objects of God's affection out of Babylon, and Babylon out of the objects of God's affection?

---

[4]Matthew 20:22 and 26:39, 42; Mark 10:38 and 14:36; Luke 22:42; John 18:11.
[5]Matthew 20:23; Mark 10:39.
[6]Revelation 17:4.   [7]Matthew 26:42.
[8]Ezekiel 22.:30.   [9]Malachi 2:10–16.

"Is it nothing to you, all you that pass by? Look around and see, Is any suffering like my suffering that was inflicted on me, that the LORD brought on me in the day of his fierce anger?"[10]

...I'm grateful that you are so willing to share these words of love with me, and (hopefully) many others.

I don't want to give you the impression that my life is full of rejection and its attendant pain. Actually, having discovered what is possible in relationships, gender neutral, I have been very blessed with many very precious relationships, relationships experienced in shadow form in what I call "old creation families," but much deeper than that in "new creation" or "spiritual families." This is to say, brothers, sisters, mothers, fathers, sons and daughters. In all these relationships it is possible to be much more intimate in the Spirit than it is in the flesh.

I have to say that I initially felt like pushing you away when I saw you quoting scripture. I think your insight of people using scripture as a weapon is very true—that's been my experience....

I certainly understand and very much appreciate your openness to giving me a fair hearing.

...My feeling is always that I can't trust such people—that they're not being real and I can't get a sense of who they REALLY are and how they really feel and experience the world. I usually get a sense more of what they think they SHOULD be (and what I SHOULD be in the same breath). I think that's what religion does—in its worst sense—reduce people to this SAMENESS out of fear. It is exactly what Jesus encountered and fought.

In that connection, I suggest you read (or re-read) the story of Jesus's encounter with the Samaritan woman at the well, found in John 4:4–27. My guess is you'll especially appreciate the following:

—Close encounters of the marvelous kind (verse 27)
—Conceptions and preconceptions (verse 9)
—Here's a quarter, kid, get lost (verse 8)
—The Bridal Paradigm (John 3:29)
—The paradigm shift

It is very difficult to know what to call what I'm about to say. It is difficult, because I know, or think I do, what the preconceptions are. This is a favorite sermon text. It would be difficult to

---

[10]Lamentations 1:12 (NIV).

count how many times I've heard it preached, generally with the same emphasis, the same preconceptions. I would like to try to get beyond the preconceptions, but when we get beyond preconceptions, we are likely to be "reckoned among the transgressors."

Jesus was very aware of the problem, even in the preconceptions of His disciples. In saying what I'm about to say, I have to hope that there is some deeper understanding of what, by now, Jesus Christ has done for us, to us, and in us. But just in case, I want to place the passage in context just a little bit.

In John 3, beginning at about verse 22, we get a fresh perspective from John the Baptist, a perspective on who John is, who Jesus is, and who we are. As is typical, a certain kind of rivalry surfaced. John had been baptizing, and still was, and now Jesus' disciples were baptizing. This bothered John's "...disciples and the Jews...." John 3:25, 26.

When they brought their concern to John, he said, "A man can receive only what is given him from heaven. You yourselves can testify that I said, 'I am not the Christ but that am sent ahead of him.' The BRIDE belongs to the BRIDEGROOM. The friend who attends the BRIDEGROOM waits and listens for him, and is full of joy when he hears the BRIDEGROOM's voice. That joy is mine, and it is now complete." (John 3:27-29, NIV) [Capitalization added.]

Clearly, John had seen and understood, at least in part, the great mystery that Paul speaks about in Ephesians 5:31,32: "'For this reason a man will leave his father and mother and be united to his wife, and the two will become one flesh.' This is a profound mystery—but I am talking about Christ and the church."

John knew that a wedding was coming down. He also knew that he was one of the attendants. He himself was neither the Bridegroom nor the bride. He was a friend of the Bridegroom. John's role was limited. As a friend of the Bridegroom he had been privileged to attend to both the bride and the Groom, but all the while he knew that the bride belonged to the Bridegroom. This was a fairly radical understanding of what was happening. It violated, and to this day, continues to violate our preconceptions.

In his role as the friend of the Bridegroom, John has an ear for the Bridegroom. He is so looking forward to hearing the Bridegroom that he is filled with joy at the hearing of His voice, and by the time of his explanation, he had heard His voice and could see, even by the complaint of his disciples, that the bride and the Bridegroom had found each other. John's joy was complete.[11]

---

[11] John 3:29–30 (NIV).

Now, rather than a preconception, a new conception was taking place.

John, the apostle, has already told us about Jesus' encounter with Nicodemus, and we ought to know that even a new birth requires a conception. The greatest enemy of a conception is a preconception.

Perhaps enough said; now to the text. Jesus was heading to Samaria. We know from all those sermons, that this was already a problem. When He came to Sychar, He knew that he would have a conversation with a woman. How often have we heard an emphasis on what kind of a woman she was, and not altogether without some justification, ("...for the Jews have no dealings with the Samaritans") but, having heard enough about that, I would like to overlook that preconception and focus on another—I think not without some justification. In John 4:27, we read, "And upon this came his disciples, and marvelled that he talked with the woman: yet no man said, What seekest thou? or, Why talkest thou with her?" Isn't that the way we are when our preconceptions get violated? We get surprised, but we're afraid to ask. The answer might damage our preconceptions. Perhaps I should add that this is a particular problem for males. Asking questions of this kind is just too vulnerable for most of us men.

The focus of what I want to share is not the conversation that went on between Jesus and the woman. I am quite willing to take the word of the woman that it was substantial and quite intimate: "Come, see a man who told me everything I ever did...."[12]

Rather, my focus for present purposes is on the fact that the conversation happened, and on what it took to make such a conversation possible. Jesus had to go to a place where Jews do not go, sit with a person whom

The Samaritan Woman at the Well—John 4:1–29

The Pharisees heard that Jesus was gaining and baptizing more disciples than John, although in fact it was not Jesus who baptized, but his disciples. When the Lord learned of this, he left Judea and went back once more to Galilee.

Now he had to go through Samaria. So he came to a town in Samaria called Sychar, near the plot of ground Jacob had given to his son Joseph. Jacob's well was there, and Jesus, tired as he was from the journey, sat down by the well. It was about the sixth hour.

When a Samaritan woman came to draw water, Jesus said to her, "Will you give me a drink?" (His disciples had gone into the town to buy food.)

The Samaritan woman said to him, "you are a Jew and I am a Samaritan woman. How can you ask me for a drink?" (For Jews do not associate with Samaritans.)

Jesus answered her, "If you knew the gift of God and who it is that asks you for a drink, you would have asked him and he would have given you living water."

"Sir," the woman said, "you have nothing to draw with and the well is deep. Where can you get this living wa-

---

[12]John 4:29 (NIV).

33

ter? Are you greater than our father Jacob, who gave us the well and drank from it himself, as did also his sons and his flocks and herds?"

Jesus answered, "Everyone who drinks this water will be thirsty again, but whoever drinks the water I give him will never thirst. Indeed, the water I give him will become in him a spring of water welling up to eternal life."

The woman said to him, "Sir, give me this water so that I won't get thirsty and have to keep coming here to draw water."

He told her, "Go, call your husband and come back."

"I have no husband," she replied.

Jesus said to her, "You are right when you say you have no husband. The fact is, you have had five husbands, and the man you now have is not your husband. What you have just said is quite true."

"Sir," the woman said, "I can see that you are a prophet. Our fathers worshiped on this mountain, but you Jews claim that the place where we must worship is in Jerusalem."

Jesus declared, "Believe me, woman, a time is coming when you will worship the Father neither on this mountain nor in Jerusalem. You Samaritans worship what you do not know; we worship what we do know, for salvation is from the Jews. Yet a time is coming and has now come when the true worshipers will worship the Father in spirit and truth, for they are the kind of worshipers the Father seeks. God is spirit, and his worshipers must worship in spirit and truth."

The woman said, "I know that Messiah" (called Christ) "is coming. When he comes, he will explain everything to us."

Then Jesus declared, "I who speak to you am he."

Just then his disciples returned and were surprised to find him talking with a woman. But no one asked, "What do you want?" or "Why are you talking with her?"

Then, leaving her water jar, the woman went back to the town and said to the people, "Come, see a man who told me everything I ever did. Could this be the Christ?"

Jews do not sit with, and talk with a woman whom Jews do not talk to.

We had a saying when I was growing up, "Here kids, here's a quarter, why don't you go to a movie." The price of admission might be giving away my age, but the point is, everyone understood what this meant: parents wanted some time alone together.

Jesus needed some time alone in order to do something that the kids were not ready to handle. This is the same Jesus who is about to be presented to us as the one who has the power to do wonderful things for lunch.[13] So when John tells us, "His disciples had gone into the town to buy food," it becomes particularly significant that they were not there for the conversation. Especially since he also informs us that, on their return, they are surprised to see him talking to a woman. There is nothing in the text to indicate that she is a particular kind of a woman, other than that she is a Samaritan. The word used for "woman" is the same as that used elsewhere to refer to Jesus mother, so there is no indication that she is particularly "fallen," other than in the conversation which they were not there for. They were just plain surprised that he was talking to a woman.

The Bridegroom was courting His bride. But it was still a great mystery. Jesus knew it, John the Baptist might have understood it,

---

[13]John 6:11.

but the religious did not understand and were afraid to ask. Things really haven't changed so much, where the religious are concerned. Women are beginning to be recognized as people among the religious, but this is not the fault of the religious. The change is being forced on the church, because the very stones are crying out. It's beginning to look like Jesus will have his BRIDE after all.

My own involvement with Christianity and the Bible has been sketchy, at best. I got way more from reading the last section of the Urantia book (about the life of Christ) than I did from what little reading I did of the Bible. I'm sure this has something to do with the format—the Bible seems much more esoteric....

I wonder if I could suggest **The Message** version of the Bible, by Eugene Peterson. Peterson is very tuned in to relationships, and so his version is excellent in that connection. He may be a little weak in other areas, but not enough to take away from this very readable and insightful version.

...(My father introduced me to the Urantia book—his bible— some 25 years ago, and I've heard him passionately discuss it ever since.)...

I think that was also the time frame of my exposure to the Urantia book as well. I had already done most of my research for the money book by then, so I was not influenced away from the validity of the Bible. I had become aware of some of the translation problems, but I was convinced from my study that only God Himself could have written the original version.

...I know that spirituality is an unfolding—a "revelation," in your words. I strive to be consciously aware of—and responsive to—all of the spirit world in the moment. I read what I feel led to read, and someday I may return to the Bible. In the meanwhile it is helpful to know people who are firmly grounded in the Bible's teachings, yet are open to take it to a new level—one that is more heartfelt than authoritative. Perhaps this is happening more than I think—I don't have a good feel for it.

I'm guessing your "feel for it" is just about right. Unfortunately the Bible is more in the hands of the religious than in the hands of those who have been set free. I would like to think that there are an increasing number of freedom fighters, however. Learning how to communicate is very important. In a sense, it is very much the same as learning how to be lovers. Careless or inept lovers shut down, rather than open up. I think this is truly gender neutral, but I don't think that discussion of the problem has been gender neutral in my lifetime. It has hardly begun in "the church."

Thank you again for sharing yourself so openly and passionately. It's a rare—and very pleasurable—thing.

I also appreciate your openness. It is very helpful for me, and I hope it can continue to the end that both of us will find some better answers.

I may come into the office over the holidays and work on the computer (check emails)—I can't figure out how to get my email to work on my computer at home (or maybe I just don't WANT to check my emails at home).
Anyway, I look forward to hearing from you again.

Well here I am again, I hope not as a pest. If there is something of specific interest that you might like to discuss, I would be happy to try to share a Biblical perspective on the subject. It is my impression that we have not discovered any problem, either in nature or in depth, for which the Bible does not have the answers, if only we approach it in the same Spirit in which it was written. Your "WANT" has not gone unnoticed. If I have read you correctly, perhaps I can help some in that area, and from a rather different perspective than you are likely to find in the DD list. I think it would need a rather in-depth discussion, however. As for my part, I am open.

May your Holidays be very blessed!

Jay

On Friday, December 26, 2003, Lisa wrote:

Dear Jay,

I'm sitting here at work, the day after Christmas, deep in thought about what we've written, where I am in life, what my deepest wishes are.

Truthfully, I could not wait to get here and read what you might have written. There is a huge hunger inside me that is being fed by what you say, and the spirit in which you say it. But it's more than just the words—although it is satisfying to have to "wrap my brain around" what you say and let the deeper meaning seep into me. It's also about what you very first talked about—the need for intimacy and the need to express oneself—fully—without the fear of rejection. I like that we have established that we are in really different places—although perhaps not so different—and still have the desire to continue to communicate, using our own means and methods of doing so.

After reading your last e-mail I reached down into my heart to see what I was feeling and cried. I cried for the deepness of my "WANT" and the pain of having to acknowledge my avoiding it. There's fear for not knowing how to proceed in life. It hurts that I have such a need to be heard, validated, and guided by people who don't even know me. It touches me that you are so willing to guide me while remaining vulnerable and open. The beauty and depth of your heart inspires me. And your stories of the bliss and anguish—of Jesus, yourself, and all mankind—at once move and exasperate me. It's all so rich—I wouldn't want to be anywhere but here in this moment.

I was enticed to pull out my Bible (I remembered that I had one here at work) with your discussion of "close encounters of the marvelous kind."

Funny, when the feminine is introduced I become enthralled. What intrigues me the most about Jesus—besides what he did for mankind as a whole—was his desire for and expression of relationship. His sincere interest in each individual and their experience in the world. The encouragement of their individuality and how that manifested in their relationship with him and with God. He was—is—truly personal and personable. I love that about him.

*Thank you for telling me about **The Message**. I'll look for it. Perhaps you could tell me more about what a "freedom fighter" is. Also, could I ask what led you to the Deida web site? I'm very curious. What do you think about his philosophy?*

You're not like any minister that I would have ever imagined (if, indeed, you are one). Or perhaps that's just my own preconception of what a minister "looks like." My most sincere apologies. I would love to hear more about your journey. You need to know that even though I don't respond to each point that you make in your emails, I'm taking it all in fully and am very enlivened by your words. Please feel free to send me your "journal entries" anytime. I know how cathartic it can be. It's very interesting to me how email lends itself to such depth and intimacy in relationships—very quickly. I'm able to say so much more about who I am than when I'm talking face to face—although nothing really compares to face-to-face talking.

I would very much like to hear your perspective on my "want." You seem to be insightful, sincere, open to talking about just about anything, non-judgmental and "coming from a higher place" while tending to the more "human" aspects of ourselves. (Correct me if I'm wrong—please! Also realize that I don't expect perfection, even though I really, really want it!) You mentioned needing an in-depth discussion—I'm ready whenever you are. My preference would be to have it via email because it allows me time to contemplate—and I assume I'm going to need to do some digging. Of course, a verbal discussion may be helpful at some point, too. How would you suggest that we proceed?

It's amazing how long this little bit of verbiage has taken me to construct. You seem so much more prolific—yet I imagine your entries are time-consuming, too. Thank you for taking the time and for caring.

Sincerely,
Lisa

PS: I'm going out of town tomorrow until Monday. I'll probably come by here Monday afternoon to check my email. Talk to you soon!

On Monday, December 29, 2003, Jay responded:

Lisa wrote: *After reading your last e-mail I reached down into my heart to see what I was feeling and cried. I cried for the deepness of my "WANT" and the pain of having to acknowledge my avoiding it. There's fear for not knowing how to proceed in life. It hurts that I have such a need to be heard, validated, and guided by people who don't even know me. It touches me that you are so willing to guide me while remaining vulnerable and open. The beauty and depth of your heart inspires me. And your stories of the bliss and anguish—of Jesus, yourself, and all mankind—at once move and exasperate me. It's all so rich—I wouldn't want to be anywhere but here in this moment.*

Dear Lisa,

Thank you once more for your very sensitive and open response to what I have tried to share! I have read over what you have written a number of times now, and the weekend has given me the opportunity to give a lot of thought to how I might respond. This paragraph above is certainly very profound—and perhaps the most important, revealing as it does your most foundational need/"WANT." For that reason, I would like to leave it until later in my response. I think responding to the rest of what you have written here will be helpful in digesting what you have said and clarifying what I need to answer.

I was enticed to pull out my Bible (I remembered that I had one here at work) with your discussion of "close encounters of the marvelous kind."

Funny, when the feminine is introduced I become enthralled....

I feel badly, pulling you so quickly into my comfort zone, but I am very encouraged by your willingness to enter it. If I can share with you some of the comfort I have found in the Bible, perhaps it might become a place of comfort for you as well. It's quite an amazing book really, once it is rescued from the hands of the terminally religious. In light of what you have said here, perhaps I can share a little more concerning its/my appreciation of the feminine. Let's call it "Wonder Woman."

"And there appeared a great wonder in heaven… "[14]

With age I am less amused by—and more amazed by—female communication and interaction. For the most part, the subject is discussed by males, even otherwise serious males, more with amusement than with insight. John sees a "great wonder in heaven; a woman… " I have become convinced that this revelation is more for our instruction than our amusement, particularly where the church is concerned. For all the references to a "new man"[15] and the "full measure of the stature of Christ,"[16] the Church in her highest revelation comes to us more as a woman than a man.

If we are ever going to see the Church from God's perspective, aside from "fixing our eyes on Jesus," we need to take another look at women, and less for aesthetic reasons than for lessons in human interaction and intimacy. In short, for those who have eyes to see, women are a window on "… a great wonder in heaven …"

By now it has become clear that males are task-oriented and females are relationship-oriented. Clearly, she "…has chosen what is better."[17] But the downside is, because she is so relational, she is more vulnerable to deep relational wounding than her male counterpart. Because of their task orientation, and in order to "get on with it," men get over wounded relationships, or at least seem to, easier than women do.

This is not to say that men don't get wounded in relationship to others, but their/our vulnerability is different. Our vulnerability has to do with the preeminence and vulnerability of the male ego. It seems to me that women are much more confrontational

---

[14]Revelation 12:1.   [15]Ephesians 2:15
[16]Ephesians 4:13.   [17]Luke 10:42.

in their communication. They will easily wade into subjects that men find very threatening. They will "get in your face" seemingly without giving it a second thought. Again, male conversation has more to do with tasks than relationships. From a male perspective, the content of female conversation seems unimportant, perhaps even illogical, and maybe it is, but I think, from a female perspective, the content does not have to be important, or even logical, it is the interaction, the relationship, the intimacy, that matters. Lisa, I'm wondering if you have seen **Shadowlands** with Anthony Hopkins, the 1997 version. If not, or if it was some time ago, I can't encourage you strongly enough to get hold of it. It goes to the core of the problem and does so with great insight and sensitivity. Be sure and have plenty of Kleenex on hand.

With some time off recently—it's been a couple of years now—I had the opportunity to watch at length, and with much repetition, the coverage of the war in the Balkans. On the fourth day of watching, I saw an interview with former Congresswoman Pat Schroeder, along with the ambassador from Macedonia, also a female. The interaction between the two was heart-warming to watch, particularly the reaction of the ambassador to the words of encouragement coming from Pat Schroeder. I should also say that, after watching days of dumb questions, inane observations, and contentious attitudes on the part of the media, Schroeder's comments and insights were both profound and succinct.

This interview stood out in another very important way. Watching so intently for such a length of time also revealed something else. The females who were interviewed, and those doing the interviewing, were clearly trying to look like men in their style and posturing. For me, it was very unbecoming. The ambassador in the Schroeder interview began in the same posture but, bathed in the encouragement of Schroeder, turned back into a woman. The transformation was wonderful to behold. I couldn't help but be struck by the thought that God is not after women who behave like men so much as men who behave like women, at least, in their relationship to others.

During that time away, Carleen and I also stopped by a bookstore. The sign out front read, "Giant Book Sale." While browsing inside, I came across a little illustrated book, a sort of commentary on the book of Revelation. In Revelation 12:1-6, it seemed to suggest that "the woman" has been removed from the scene while the dragon, through man—the wrong man—runs roughshod over everything for 1,260 days, whatever that means. It is clear that this is not the reign of the right man, but the wrong man. In any case, by the time we get to the end of Chapter 13, there are two males and one female. Ultimately the "man child" will rule, but, for the present, it appears that the crowns are on the beast, an unredeemed and unredeeming man.

The church of today is more an auditorium for male ego gratification than it is a sanctuary in time and space for divine relationship. Or, in the words of Liza Doolittle, "Words, words, words, we get words all day through, first from them, now from you. Is that all you blighters can do?"

> A great and wondrous sign appeared in heaven: a woman clothed with the sun, with the moon under her feet and a crown of twelve stars on her head. She was pregnant and cried out in pain as she was about to give birth. Then another sign appeared in heaven: an enormous red dragon with seven heads and ten horns and seven crowns on his heads. His tail swept a third of the stars out of the sky and flung them to the earth. The dragon stood in front of the woman who was about to give birth, so that he might devour her child the moment it was born. She gave birth to a son, a male child, who will rule all the nations with an iron scepter. And her child was snatched up to God and to his throne. The woman fled into the desert to a placed prepared for her by God, where she might be taken care of for 1,260 days.
>
> **—Revelation 12:1-6 (NIV)**

Seventeen hundred years of show business ought to be enough. When Jesus demonstrated what it was to be a servant, it wasn't by preaching at His disciples. Male preaching for the most part has preempted the time during which the church is gathered and might otherwise be getting to know itself—and the Christ who is her source, and life. To be truly cleansing, "... the washing of water by the word," Ephesians 5:25-32 needs to be interactive. As we read in 1 Corinthians 14:26, "What then shall we say, brothers? When you come together, everyone has...."

Males want to do things, their own things. Females want to be related: "...Your desire will be for your husband...."[18] To see the church from God's perspective, we must first see a woman. When we look at the church as it is in the present, about all we can see is a man, and he doesn't look much like Jesus, not even Jesus in the flesh. The Book of Revelation not only reveals Jesus but in some sense indicates what it's going to take to get the wrong man off the throne, "...the removing of what can be shaken ..."[19]

...What intrigues me the most about Jesus—besides what he did for mankind as a whole—was his desire for and expression of relationship. His sincere interest in each individual and their experience in the world. The encouragement of their individuality and how that manifested in their relationship with him and with God. He was—is—truly personal and personable. I love that about him.

---

[18]Genesis 3:16.

[19]Hebrews 12:25–29.

What a wonderful insight and focus on the essential Jesus.

*Thank you for telling me about **The Message**. I'll look for it....*

It is published by Nav Press, and they have a **New Testament in Paper.** I believe that the New Testament is the best where Peterson is concerned, because of his sensitivity to relationships. That sensitivity is perhaps better expressed there than in the Old Testament.

...Perhaps you could tell me more about what a "freedom fighter" is....

In 1993, we moved to Golden Valley, North Carolina, from the shoreline of Connecticut. I had been involved at Yale, but it became clear that it was a losing battle. The problem is something I call "manhandling." It is choking just about all aspects of human life and has been doing so in the church for close to 2,000 years. The challenge is to escape the "manhandling."[20]

We moved to the mountains of North Carolina. One of the reasons was so that I could concentrate on writing, but there was something else, another aspect of our relocation. Part of the vision was to set up a kind of "guerilla base camp" for spiritual warfare. This had to do with being in a place where we might come to better understand how to set people free from the things that rob us of fulfilling life. It wasn't so much a place of escape, as a place to regroup, in the hope of becoming more effective. Meanwhile, if we are going to talk about life, we ought to be living it ourselves, don't you think? And so we do. We are in life with others here in this place, but because relationships easily transcend geography, we are in life with others in other places as well. Most people are unable and/or unwilling to be free. It's just too frightening. This has to do with the first of your paragraphs included above. So I'll come back to it.

...Also, could I ask what led you to the Deida web site? I'm very curious. What do you think about his philosophy?

I'm still trying to get up to speed on "his philosophy." I think it's still a little too early for me to make a judgment.

In the chapter I sent, "Getting Personal," I mentioned a spiritual daughter, the one who was helping me with the relationship book. (Perhaps I should mention at this point, that writing a book about intimacy is a kind of oxymoron. When you "go public" with intimacy, it is no longer intimate. This is a real problem. If you are intimate with a view to writing about it, it tends to defile

---

[20]Galations 4:21–5:1, 13; II Corinthians 3:6–18.

the intimacy. The intimacy is conflicted. Perhaps we could call this the "kiss-and-tell problem." I'm not talking about physical kissing, although it might certainly be included.) About a month ago, she called to chat with Carleen and me, and in that conversation, she told me about a CD called "On Sacred Intimacy," by David Deida. I had never heard of either. Yesterday she dropped by and dropped off two CDs by David. She had listened to part of one of them and wanted my impressions. A neighbor friend in her apartment building had given them to her.

Meanwhile I had jumped the gun, gone looking for David Deida on the web, and found his web site and the discussion list. I have long felt that intimacy is the most important thing, and I am not closed to the experience and thoughts of anyone who is serious in their pursuit of the idea and especially the reality.

"Institutional Christianity" is closed to intimacy. In a sense, intimacy is the alternative to institution. Life tells me that, if we grow up in an institution, it's because something went wrong. "God puts the solitary in families...."[21]

You're not like any minister that I would have ever imagined (if, indeed, you are one). Or perhaps that's just my own preconception of what a minister "looks like." My most sincere apologies. I would love to hear more about your journey....

I think your "preconceptions" are about right. When we moved south, I was urged to become involved with something called Shepherds of Charlotte. This was a group of pastors who have been meeting there for over 30 years now. We were in Golden Valley for about four years before I was finally dragged off to Charlotte and began to meet with them.

In the beginning, they wanted to know where my "church" was, and where I "pastored." When I answered that I had no "church," and that I pastored relationally, not geographically, they went away scratching their heads, wondering what I was doing there. After about a year of sharing with them, some of them began to wonder what they were doing there. In short, I have been given an open door to share with them. Truth be known, most "ministers" are very desperate people. More often than not, they are insecure and lonely and crave center stage for fulfillment in the absence of intimacy. (Again, watch **Shadowlands**. It nails the problem.)

---

[21] Psalms 68:6.

Recently I sent the following to a "minister" who has asked for my help in dismantling "his church." He wants to see the congregation move from institutional to relational, and he is willing to give up his position to see that happen. This is quite rare, and I am looking forward to hearing from him again soon. In any case, by way of answering your question, at least in part, here's what I sent to him:

...My faith is that the compiling of the Scripture is, and has to be, as much a matter of Divine guidance as its writing. As between the Catholic compilation, and the KJV, my faith is that the KJV compilation is the better choice. Except for convenience, I put no stock in the chapter and verse divisions, and I'm not so sure about the order in which the letters are placed. As with the rest of our understanding, I believe that these things are spiritually discerned, and that the compilation is 'close enough for government work.'

...As I have experienced it, my relationship with the Word of God is such that, by whatever means, the Word comes to me; reading, hearing, sharing, all this on a more or less constant basis, although it has not been my bent to have special times set aside for such. I should say that I've been rather more seasonal in all those approaches to dining. Then there is the digestion process. This for me has come from the doing of the Word, sometimes consciously, and sometimes not—perhaps more often not. In that process, the Word becomes liquid. Until that happens, my sharing on any particular text tends to be a little gritty and indigestible, even harmful. Once liquid, however, it finds the right proportion of content, vehicle, and delivery, and comes out of my heart like rivers of living water, rather than the sandblasting of dead letters. By now, my mind works kind of like CNN; split screen, with the Word scrolling across the bottom, as I go through my day. Every now and then, what I'm doing or experiencing lines up with the scrolling Word. In those moments I come to new understanding.

...In addition, I wanted to share something about my understanding concerning the 'Who do you think you are?' question. I suppose you could call this my 'doctrinal statement.' Living a reproducible life has been—and continues to be—very important for me. I never went anywhere and did anything in order to be somebody. I am who I am by the grace of God. I try to avoid being something or someone on any other basis. This is what I teach, and this is what I try to model. At root, I believe that the basic growth kit for a Christian is the Holy Spirit and the Bible. It helps a lot if God sets the person in a spiritual family. Paul had no one like Timothy, and Timothy was his true son in the faith. For me, it remains to be seen how much of Paul would have reached all the way to us, if it had not been for Timothy. I'm not into monasteries, seminaries, Bible schools, training centers, or any other kind of special buildings for the salvation or maturation of the saints. I can love the people in those places, but I have no desire to validate geographical or earthbound structural places as a necessary precondition for producing the 'Real Thing.' In other words, I have pro-actively avoided all that. If that makes me a negative legalist, as Ralph seems to maintain, then so be it. I just think that if neither circumcision nor uncircumcision means anything,[22] but faith expressing itself by love in a new creation, then that is where I would like to invest my life.

Perhaps that's enough on the "minister" subject for now.

---

[22]Galatians 5:6, 6:15.

...You need to know that even though I don't respond to each point that you make in your emails, I'm taking it all in fully and am very enlivened by your words....

Thank you for your sensitivity in sharing that.

...Please feel free to send me your "journal entries" anytime....

And again, thank you for this liberty as well.

...I know how cathartic it can be. It's very interesting to me how email lends itself to such depth and intimacy in relationships—very quickly. I'm able to say so much more about who I am than when I'm talking face to face—although nothing really compares to face-to-face talking.

Yes, email is a wonderful way of communicating. It is so much faster and more interactive than snail mail but also much less vulnerable to careless words than phone conversations. It gives us just a little more time to think before responding and leaves a trail by which misunderstandings can be cleared up and cleaned up, if only there is the desire to do so.

...I would very much like to hear your perspective on my "want."...

I hear your "WANT" expressed in that opening paragraph included above, and I too "want" to go there.

... You seem to be insightful, sincere, open to talking about just about anything, non-judgmental and "coming from a higher place" while tending to the more "human" aspects of ourselves. (Correct me if I'm wrong—please! Also realize that I don't expect perfection, even though I really, really want it!) You mentioned needing an in-depth discussion—I'm ready whenever you are....

I'm ready. I have also learned to be careful not to go too fast. Physical intimacy is a parable of spiritual intimacy, and much can be learned from both that can—and ought to—be applied to the other. As someone who is, in a sense, doing research on the subject, as well as living in it, I tend to push the envelope. Being aware of this, I try not to take people further and faster than they are prepared to go. For that reason, I want to be very sensitive to where you are, as well as your needs, and "wants."

I have already spoken about the matter of circumcision, that it is a priority need before intimacy. Circumcision became gender neutral at the cross of Christ.[23] Again, this has to do with the first paragraph.

…My preference would be to have it via email because it allows me time to contemplate—and I assume I'm going to need to do some digging.…

Yes, I think this is wisdom.

…Of course, a verbal discussion may be helpful at some point, too.…

Yes. It would be my hope that it would come to that at some point. As a kind of preview of that possibility, I have a couple of tapes that come to mind. One is to a "church." The title is "Unoffendable Love." The other is to a small Bible study group. They had been studying together for many years. They were very mature Christians but were no place horizontally. The host or leader of the group asked me to come and take them horizontal. He taped it, and that tape is called "Getting Horizontal." If at some point you would like to listen to either, let me know, and I'll send you a copy.[24]

…How would you suggest that we proceed?

I think we are already doing great, and "all systems are go."

It's amazing how long this little bit of verbiage has taken me to construct.…

I understand; it takes me over two hours to answer an email of this length.

…You seem so much more prolific—yet I imagine your entries are time-consuming, too. Thank you for taking the time and for caring.

The thanks are mutual.

I think, at this point, before responding to your paragraph included at the beginning, I will send this off to you, give it some more thought, and wait for possible further clarification or focus from you. If that should not be forth-coming, I will dig in at my earliest opportunity. For now, I'm heading back to bed for a few more winks before facing my day.

Yours with much appreciation,
Jay

---

[23]Colossians 2:8–15; Philippians 3:3.
[24]Information as to where and how to obtain these tapes can be found at www.notleftbehind.net.

On Monday, December 29, 2003, Lisa wrote:

Dear Jay,

I am taking copies of our communications home to read over and consider.

I know that there is so much here for me to glean, and it does not seem coincidental that you have entered my life. I don't have time to respond today, but will return on Wednesday to write more. Thank you again for all you have shared.

I would very much like to hear both of the tapes you mentioned. I'll give you my address. Looking forward to more.

Sincerely,

Lisa

On the same day, Jay responded:

Lisa wrote: *I would very much like to hear both of the tapes you mentioned. I'll give you my address.*

I'll send them along. More later.

Jay

NOT LEFT BEHIND

CHAPTER 3

THE LOVE PATENT

Dear Jay,

Thank you for sending the tapes. I look forward to listening to them. I'm going to look for **Shadowlands** *today for viewing over the next few days. It feels that these next few days will be spent more in quiet introspection, which I find somewhat frightening. I'm much more comfortable in the chaos. I think I have a belief that the true life "force"—with all the highs and lows that I crave—is bound to the chaos. And that without this whirling of movement, life will become dull and lifeless. I've had to gently push myself to be willing to go to stillness and ask what part of me has to die in order to return—re-newed and enlivened—into the cycle of chaos. I'm still bucking some, with moments of clarity in between.*

And so it's been with the question of the WANT. Cycles of crying, quietness, going inward, talking with my husband (Kurtis): trying to figure it out, surrendering to being clueless, giving it up, delving it up again. I've considered what I need to do to communicate where I am with you—what would be most valuable. At first it was some information about my history—how I got from point A to point B. Then it was information about my marriage—all of its strengths and weaknesses. But all of that seemed to miss the mark somehow. More mire to wade thru.

So I just stayed with the nature of the want. What did it feel like? Where did it want to go? Nothing earth shattering here—I think the nature of the want is at the root of every human's soul. To live freely and abundantly—as you've stated—absolutely. What would that look like? For me it's to feel ALIVE and pulsing with life's energy at all times. To fully feel all sensations—bodily, spiritually, energetically—without shutting down. To be wide open as an expression of love—my heart open, vulnerable, accessible. To love and be loved so tenderly that I cry, and with such wild abandonment that I explode and dissolve, over and over again. To commune with others who have this same heart openness and to be a light for others who desire it. (I'm sure there's much more—for now this is good.)

I would say that I've evolved—somewhat—from a place of neediness to one of desire. From here I feel ready—and have started the wheels in motion—to come from a place of demanding. I've had a taste of life's treasures—this abundance of love—and will not settle for less. As I write this I feel somewhat self conscious of appearing selfish—perhaps even delusional. But I'm really beyond caring about how I sound at this point in my life.

The question for discernment is in the how. What—if anything—needs to happen in order to fully realize this want? There seems to be some sense of urgency that I don't fully trust—perhaps related to my age (47) and the sense that I need to get on with it. My desire and desirability perhaps might lessen (although, in truth, I have never felt more desirable). I don't fully trust my husband to have the depth and sensitivity to commune with me at the level I desire. I don't fully trust any one religion, philosophy or practice, either, to take me to these depths. I don't fully trust my own capacity to stand fully open in love. (It appears, from reading this, that "trust" is a big issue for me!)

For now what I've been doing is feeling for my truth, speaking it, asking for guidance (mostly from spiritual sources), asking for and experiencing energy moving thru my body—keeping me open, and experiencing feelings as fully as possible while keeping my heart open. I am willing to move mountains, if necessary, for this want.

And so, dear Jay, perhaps you have some insights to share with me. I'm sure that none of this is new to you. And you may have more questions—I welcome them. It feels good to be talking about all of this. I hope it is not tedious for you—certainly let me know if it ever becomes so.

I'll be back to work on Monday. Don't see checking my e-mail until then.

My very best to you.
Lisa

Lisa wrote: ...*I don't fully trust my own capacity to stand fully open in love. (It appears, from reading this, that "trust" is a big issue for me!)*

Dear Lisa,

I had started another email to you, which I will doubtless send along in the near future, but after this that you have just written, I am reminded to send something else first.

It has to do with a revelation I received while in a patent office in Düsseldorf, Germany in 1987. It was one of those life-changing paradigm-shift moments that I will never forget. At the time I had the very strong impression that whenever I was to speak in a new place, it was the first thing I was to share. I was just reminded of that strong impression by what you have written here.

That said, I shall begin with your mention of the issue of trust, and then come back to the rest of what you have written.

Perhaps some time in the future, I can share my experience with you in a longer and much more complete written form. It is perhaps said better on the two tapes that I mailed out to you yesterday, but just in case they might be delayed, I'll send it now.

It has to do with a quality of love and trust. I call it, "The Love Patent."[1] For now, here it is in brief:

If I said today, "Greater love than this has no man but that he lay down his life for his friends," it wouldn't be true. It was true when Jesus said it, but it's not true any longer, because the One who said it laid down His life for His enemies. That was—and is—a greater love. That is the love of the Gospel.

When I realized this I had been a Christian for some time. Long enough so that there were days when I didn't feel like the Lord's friend. Even this side of my salvation, I needed—and continue to need—a gospel that is not limited to friends. In fact I need the Gospel most on those days when I feel like the Lord's enemy.

I had already discovered that my own expectations were my greatest problem, especially where loving others was concerned. Every time they didn't live up to my expectations, I became part of the problem. When The Lord revealed to me that He died for me, not on my best day, but on my worst day, I asked Him, "How

---

[1]The entire text of "The Love Patent" is included in Appendix A.

is this possible?" He responded by saying, "The day I said 'I love you,' I nailed my expectations to the tree."

After a moment's pause, He continued, "… and if you are going to love the way I love, you will have to do the same thing: you will have to nail your expectations to the tree."

He went on to show me that trust is nothing more than fulfilled expectations. And if I tried to build relationships with others based on trust, I was bound to be defeated in every relationship. You see, the unique thing about God's kind of love is that it is able to love those who are bad, and, if they can believe it, it changes their lives, it makes them good.

Perhaps enough said about that for now.

Sincerely,

Jay

P.S. I am very encouraged to hear that you are actively looking for **Shadowlands**. Just curl up with a big box of Kleenex and enjoy.

> On Friday, January 2, 2004, Jay responds further to Lisa's e-mail of Wednesday, December 31, 2003:

Lisa wrote:

…It feels that these next few days will be spent more in quiet introspection, which I find somewhat frightening.…

I'll be back to work on Monday. Don't see checking my e-mail until then.

Dear Lisa,

I have wanted to return to what you last wrote, because time constraints related to holiday houseguests kept me from being able to respond in anything like the depth that what you have written here deserves. I think it is a wonderful frame of reference for our further discussion of the pursuit of intimacy/being alive, not just for you, but for anyone who has or is awakening to the same desire and, with it, the same hidden reefs that prevent anything meaningful from moving in the right direction.

However, I'm not sure if I can begin a detailed response as yet, because I want to avoid carelessness or even the appearance of carelessness resulting from our rather brief exposure to one another.

What I did want to express is that I am encouraged by and care deeply about what you have written here, and don't want to lose it by moving too quickly on to further emails. I think you will have a better idea of where I am coming from after listening to the tapes I sent. I am also hopeful that your impression will be positive so that your response will not only give me a better idea of where you/we are, but it will also be a good place to continue at greater depth.

I have a good friend in his 70s. He is what is known as a "Messianic Jew": this is someone of Jewish background who has accepted Jesus as the Messiah. He is the deepest well on the Internet that I know, where the Bible is concerned. He has been teaching ancient Greek and Hebrew for many years. We are a kind of "Odd Couple," Bill being deeply scholarly and me being kind of a "wing nut." I prefer to send and receive in the Spirit, whereas Bill is more an objective Word man.

I think the relationship has been very good for both of us. I say all this to introduce something I would like to share with you, which would be a bit much even for a dedicated theologian to swallow in one bite. To follow much that Bill writes requires the time and patience of a linguistic rocket scientist, so I have tried to send just the key points so that you will be able to understand my response to him.

I think my response to Bill is important because it will help you to understand my wanting to get to know you better as we begin to go deeper in communication, because only by knowing each other, can we understand each other. I don't think either of us wants to be misunderstood or to misunderstand. For that reason I send the following exchange:

I look forward to our continuing conversation even if from time to time it might require some "buddy breathing."

Bill wrote concerning the various levels of difficulty in coming to make decisions about the objective meaning of the Scriptures. He contrasted our own personal experience with five levels of decision-making that stood between present translations and what had been originally spoken. He describes his concern as the conflict between "scripture and experience,"[2] and he ends with:

… Perhaps someone will claim regarding this level five that the Holy Spirit has given you exact answers on some or all of the questions. That could terminate the discussion or divert it to other avenues.

---

[2]The entire text of Bill's e-mail, "Scripture and Experience," has been included in Appendix B. An explanation of who Jannes and Jambres are can also be found there.

What could one say? Several choices seem open. One could deny that He has. Another could claim a different revelation from the Holy Spirit, if it seemed so. Another may even claim that you have been deceived by a demon, if that seemed like a valid discernment. Why, trudging down that lane, [we] could end up pitted against each other like Jannes plus Jambres versus Moses, right? Or it could be more like Jannes versus Jambres... ."

I responded:

Dear Bill,

I guess I'll have to leave it to you to decide if I'm Jannes, Jambres, both, or neither.

Once again, I am inclined to oversimplify. Perhaps it will save you the trouble of going to level 6 and above.

(By the way, did you see **Shadowlands** yet? "That's the deal" is an expression that Joy[3] uses to sum things up pretty nicely. To C.S. Lewis, who is at that point completely in love with her, yet wanting to protect himself from the pain of her suffering, she says, "The pain then is part of the happiness now. That's the deal.")

So "here's the deal."

Suppose you and I have a talk. I happen to catch you on a particularly lucid day, and you are satisfied that you have accurately spoken to me the honest content of your heart. You could even send it to me in writing if you prefer.

I then walk away from the conversation thinking I have understood what you said, and I put it in writing myself or I actually pass along to someone else what you said or wrote, exactly as you said it or wrote it. Will that make either their perception or my perception of the content of your heart any less subjective than the problem we are having with the Scriptures?

The problem, as I understand it is that, communication, as distinct from communion, tends to be more subjective, because with true communion you get to do the truth. Since the Truth turns out to be Jesus, we have to do Jesus to understand Jesus. As the song says, "... He's your Feller and you love Him, and all the rest is talk." The song is from **Carousel**, and the song title is "What's The Use of Wondering."

Yours in Christ,
Jay

Lisa, lest I should seem a pest, I will leave it there for now, and hope to be in touch again soon.

Sincerely,
Jay

On Sunday, January 4, 2004, Lisa wrote to Jay:

Dear Jay,

I received your tapes on Friday—thank you very much! I've been listening to them—letting your meaning soak in. I'm so taken with

---

[3]Joy Gresham, the Jewish American woman who met and later married C.S. Lewis.

your desire to love so intensely—in this horizontal way. To love and be loved on a level few will allow themselves to go. I feel my heart there with you, encouraging you to stay with it, go deeper, speak the unspeakable, go where few dare to go. Isn't it surprising how many are open, hungry to hear your truth—it feeds them on such a deep level—while others just don't know what to do with it (or with you)? I will certainly have much more to say about your perceptions and your messages.

For now I'm about "written out" having just completed the attached. I send it to you out of a desire to be vulnerable and share a part of myself where few have gone. I hope you can read it in that spirit. (It also gives you an opportunity to better see "what you're getting into" and assess if you really want to go there!)

It's attached in both Word Perfect and Word. Please let me know if you can't access it.

I'm also processing your last two emails and hear very clearly your concern about communication—going too fast, not understanding clearly or checking out, having different conceptions about the same words or experiences. I understand that, and being that I am also a person who desires deep intimacy—and has fear of rejection—I share your concern. My general commitment to the few that I've dared intimacy with is to acknowledge the intent of love, however clumsily stated, in all communications. I believe I can trust that's true for you, too. (As much as any of us are truly trustworthy.) I don't know where we're going, Jay, but I'm enjoying the process immensely.

I watched **Shadowlands** *and was moved by the power of it. The pain and pleasure of allowing ourselves to truly live—"that's the deal." Loved that. And watching the expressions in Anthony's[4] eyes—true beauty. Thanks for referring it.*

Also got a copy of **The Message**. *Will begin reading it soon.*

I talked with Kurtis about our communications—which honestly I've put off doing till now because it felt uncomfortable disclosing, "Hey, I met this guy on the internet and we've been having some very intimate conversations." He's already feeling backstage to all that's been occurring lately in my life, and somewhat insecure, so I wanted to handle it with sensitivity and finesse. He has cautiously given me the green light. I'm curious just how far he can stretch—so far I've been pleasantly surprised.

As you can imagine, questions of religion and Christianity have been on my mind. It occurs to me that I'm not sure how one might

---

[4]Anthony Hopkins, who plays C.S. Lewis, author of **The Chronicles of Narnia**, **The Screwtape Letters**, and numerous other Christian-based works, in the movie.

define Christianity—just what is a Christian? I'm trying to define for myself just what I am, religion-wise. I know that I am a child of God, and I believe that Jesus is the son of God and he came here to teach us to love ourselves and each other and God as God loves us. Beyond that things seem to get bogged down. There are very few people that I would want to ask this question of—with you, I feel, I won't get a "patent answer."

Thank you in advance.

All for now. Take all the breathing time you need.

Lisa

Lisa attached the following to her e-mail:

I was reading from the book, **The Power of Now**[5] and was struck by the brief description the author uses as an introduction to his "spiritual enlightenment." He talks about a moment where he experiences extreme emotion, in his case despair, and then becomes aware in a split second that there were "two of him" in his head—the part that was the thought about the despair, and the part that was conscious of the thought. This awareness was such a shock to his system that the "thoughts" ended, and he experienced a very interesting phenomenon—where he "heard" to resist nothing and he felt [he was] being sucked into an energetic vortex and falling into a void. When he awoke from this state, he was a changed man. Peaceful, blissful. Vibrating at a higher frequency. And much more—I recommend the book.

I read another description of such phenomena in a book, **The Journey**, by Brandon Bays.[6] She was in a similar place of deep emotion and was led to follow a process where she felt the full intensity of the emotion, dropped to the level of emotion under that (i.e.: fear to anger), and continued the process until there were no more emotions and then she fell into a void. At the end of the experience she, too, was a changed person—full of light and love—expansiveness. She described it as being and living from "her essence."

I had a similar experience in July of 2003. I've spent much of the time since this experience assimilating it, trying to put it into some sort of context, trying to get back to the intensity of the moment, afraid of the intensity of the moment. Reading others' encounters validates my experience and raises a bigger question—how many other people are having this experience and what does it mean? What am I supposed to "do" with this gift?

I am going to describe the event and some details leading up to the event—mainly because I haven't put it all in writing and I want a record for examination. My understanding of the significance has changed somewhat over the last six months and I'm sure will alter as much again in the next six months.

---

[5]**The Power of Now: A Guide to Spiritual Enlightment**, by Eckhart Tolle, published by New World Library, 1999.

[6]**The Journey: A Road Map to the Soul**, by Brandon Bays, published by Simon & Schuster Adult Publishing Group, in 2001.

My experience involved another person—although now I'm not sure how much significance that had. At the time I thought it was very significant—that perhaps somehow he "did it to me" and that the only way I could get back to that higher frequency would be thru him or someone with abilities such as his. I've since come to believe that his role was significant, although not in the way that I first thought. Perhaps a good place to start would be to talk some about John—the healer—and our relationship.

John first came to me in 2001 as a referral for massage (something that I "do" part time in the evenings out of my house). We ended up trading a few sessions—he's a psychic—and he did this "other thing" which he referred to as "shamanic healing." At the time I don't think I had a clue what that entailed but thought I'd give it a try. I had a fibroid tumor that I had been trying—unsuccessfully thru acupuncture and other techniques—to shrink. Over the course of that year it had more than doubled—so that it was now more than 11 times the size of my uterus—and I had already scheduled surgery to remove the fibroid, and my uterus. The surgery was scheduled for the end of November.

When I went for the healing—it was probably in September or October—I was feeling pretty blocked energetically from the waist down. I don't remember too much about what John did; in fact I went to sleep. But when I awoke I felt a current running thru my body—from head to toe—that I had never experienced before. It felt strong, but very pleasant, somewhat like an electrical current. I was amazed and at the same time dumbfounded and fearful. Something had happened to me here—I had experienced something—that I had no context for. I put the experience aside and went ahead with the surgery and recovery.

Then, around June of 2003, I was talking with my therapist about what my "purpose" might be—my life work. She asked me what my interests were and I listed them. Then she asked what was interesting but at the same time a little scary. I immediately came up with "energy work."

I continue to be amazed at the number of and effectiveness of energy techniques that I've become aware of in the last few years. I've experienced immediate shifts—from anxiety to peace—using EMDR[7] and a technique called "Emotional Freedom Technique" (EFT), which involves tapping on endpoints of meridians. I think of acupuncture and even massage as energy work—removing obstacles from the free flow of energy thru the body. What really intrigues me about this day and age is that there is so much available to anybody—much of it at little or no cost (EFT technique is available at no cost thru their web site[8]). I have a desire to help people become aware of these processes and of the knowledge that they don't have to live in the state of anxiety and fear.

The scary part around energy work was the image it conjured up in my mind: people who did this work were a little "out there" and pulling the wool over our heads, so to speak. In short, I didn't want to be affiliated with anything lacking in integrity. Before my initial healing experience with John, I had received "energy work" and felt nothing. Of course, I know that it's not always necessary to feel anything in order for something to be happening. But for someone like me, and I suppose a lot of people out there, it helps to feel something palpable—to help make it tangible. Working with John made me realize that, yeah, there are many people out there doing "energy work" who are a little out there, and some who

---

[7]EMDR = Eye Movement Desensitization and Reprocessing, a complex psychological methodology, used to accelerate the treatment of a wide range of pathologies and self-esteem issues related to upsetting past events.

[8]The EFT website is at www.emofree.com.

are just "going thru the motions"—with no integrity; but there are also some out there doing really powerful, healing work.

So when my therapist gave me the assignment to talk to people in this "field," I immediately thought of John and called him for a lunch appointment. It turned out that he was planning to move to North Carolina in about four months, but he was willing to work with me intensively both for healing and to teach me what he knew about healing.

My experience of John was complex. On the one hand there was a love quality and gentleness that came thru him that took my breath away. And there was the human side that was most exasperating—distant, critical, judgmental. His energy/personality reminded me a lot of my Dad, and I ultimately worked with that energy to do a lot of healing around my Dad.

John can move energy better than anyone I've ever encountered. But what makes him a "shamanic healer" is his ability to contact the spirit world and see, hear, and intuit messages from beings "on the other side." During his "healings," he essentially sits on some pillows until he gets a message of what to do. What makes him unique is his willingness to do whatever he's told to do—no matter how silly, absurd, or irrelevant it might seem. Sometimes he talked to me or to "energy forms" attached to my body that were blocking me. Other times he would run energy thru me—often while amplifying various chakras with various stones. Sometimes he would shake a rattle, beat a drum, make strange intonations with his voice, or use some other instrument to shake up or shift my energy in some way. Sometimes it appeared he was doing nothing but sitting on his pillow—waiting for a message. He had a very simple way of "clearing" himself before and after each healing, and he communicated with the "spirit guides" before each healing to work with him in a very specific way—only those guides that knew what healing the person needed and how to achieve that healing and could work 100% compatibly with him—in the highest good of the person—were invited to participate. For his part, John spent many hours every day "clearing himself"—with the help of his spirit guides—in order to be a clear vessel for healing to occur thru.

As strange as all of this sounds, and yes, it sounded strange to me, too, there was something that said "go with it—trust it—completely surrender to this process of healing." And so I did.

The first couple of healings were, I think in hindsight, to "prime" me. The unblocking of energies—which can be stored in the body as beliefs and memories—gave me plenty to work with. I began journaling and sharing with John my experience of the healings and their aftermath. It was very cathartic and I enjoyed the intimacy that I felt between us.

I had a premonition that the third healing was going to be life changing. My massage therapist, a woman whom I have deep love for, also had this feeling and told me, "Ground yourself in love and you will be fine." At the time I wondered just how would I do that—ground myself in love—and it occurred to me to ask the spirit guides of the most loving person I know (my dearest friend, Jann) to come—along with my own guides (whom I include along with God and Jesus and my own spirit)—to ground me in love during this healing.

When I arrived for the healing, I was in a very excited state of mind. It was all I could do to contain myself and to remain present. I laid down on the table, asked for my and Jann's guides to ground me in love and to guide John, opened my heart and soul to be completely willing and receptive to whatever healing was to occur, and focused on my breathing while waiting.

Nothing happened for about 15 minutes. John said later, "I don't know what they were doing over there [the spirits with me], but they didn't want me to participate for a while." (I believe they were communicating with each other and preparing me in some way.) The experience that followed sounds very much like the experiences I mentioned at the beginning of this journal—of Eckhart Tolle and Brandon Bays.

John went into his "altered state"—began talking in his "Indian talk" (I guess a "spiritual language") and at some point told me to "let go and fall, fall, fall." He accentuated all of this with his rattle—his voice becoming very excited and enthusiastic as I did just that—I let go—I could feel a release in my body and just did a free fall. This went on for some time—I had no concept of time. At the end of the session he had to help me off the table. I felt literally sick—nauseous and very "high." Completely altered. I processed with him some and finally talked myself into being ready to drive home. I probably should not have been driving. The feelings of delirium intensified over the next several hours—along with paranoia. Later that night I finally concluded that the sickness that I felt was the same feeling I felt when I was on drugs in the hospital after my surgery two years before! John had been working on opening my second chakra—the area just over my scar. I was "detoxing" the medicine in my system from the surgery.

In hindsight, I believe that this sickness was absolutely necessary for me to receive the full impact of this healing (which I have still yet to fully comprehend). It was physical, tangible. No way to deny it—it was a happening thing. This detox lasted three days. I couldn't believe the intensity of the experience. I was so full of sensation—sickness, but an equally if not stronger vibration of energy—that I could barely function. I went to work those three days—relieved beyond words that I didn't have to accomplish anything substantial—and literally just sat at my desk and felt these sensations. I had difficulty doing even the smallest tasks. This was incomprehensible to me. I was always someone who made sure that all of my tasks were done—efficiently and in a timely manner. I made lists and checked things off. I derived satisfaction from knowing that I was capable and got things done.

So here I was—barely capable of functioning—and totally in bliss! Aside from the sickness of detoxing, which gradually gave way, I was so euphoric and present—it's difficult to even put into words. I felt expanded, connected, flowing, high, loving, loved ... absolutely no cares for anything in this world. I spent many hours just experiencing energy flowing thru my body, feeling my body vibrating at a higher level—almost like a fluorescent light buzzing over my head.

After the third day, I received a message—I actually "heard" a voice in my head. Not like the ticker-tape of endless verbiage that kind of flows horizontally thru the mind. This was like a vertical message—it came in thru the top of my head. What I heard was that I have three extraordinary gifts—they are beauty, sensuality, and passion. I have been given these gifts—have had them all along—but where I've erred is in not fully receiving them. My job now is to fully receive them, own them, not judge them—get to know them and love and honor them. Then—and only then—I got not to hurry this process—I would know how to share these gifts with others. I heard that these are gifts—they are not my power. That true power is not something that you own. True power comes thru you and is available anytime, but it's not YOU. True power is love and compassion.

Then I went thru a ceremony of receiving each gift and feeling the energy of the particular gift, thanking for receiving it—saying that I will honor and cherish it—for each gift. I felt the energies of each gift in different parts of my body. The beauty energy (I never knew that beauty was an energy!) was in my heart, the sensuality was in the first and second chakras, and the passion was in my throat.

I spent time receiving and feeling the energies of each of these gifts over the next several days. It became a kind of homework. I also began receiving communication from the spirit of Jann's brother, Shawn, who died about four years ago. (Apparently he was at "the healing.") Since that time, I've experienced communication with a number of spiritual entities through words, visions, and intuitions.

All of this has been truly amazing to me, and I would not believe it all—really—if it had not happened to me. To this day I am altered, and I suspect that is permanent. The intensity has lessened, but I continue to feel a higher vibration, the flowing of energies through my body, a feeling of well-being and blissfulness, more love and connectedness to everything, a desire to express myself and share, a non-concern about "worldly" matters—I have no desire to watch TV or engage in idle conversation. Food has little interest to me and I eat intuitively. I don't worry about "things" and am amazed at how little time and energy I spend thinking about the things I "need to accomplish" and how blissfully the things that need to be done get done. I feel worthy and confident, not as concerned about whether I "measure up" or how I sound—although I don't share my experiences with everybody—I leave that for discernment. Many relationships that I already had have deepened tremendously, and some very special, deep, loving relationships are beginning. I am open and willing to experience every aspect of life in whatever way it is presented to me. And I'm learning and experiencing a lot of new and exciting things.

Before John left—and he is now wandering, I presume, in the mountains of North Carolina with his wife—looking for a place to settle (I hope to hear from him in the near future)—we had a final session where he gave me some communication from my guides. They said that I was entering a very powerful period in my life. That my life will be so changed and exciting that they could not tell me about it because I don't yet have the language to understand it. As if life is not exciting enough already.

On Monday, January 5, 2004, Jay responded to Lisa's e-mail:

Lisa wrote:

I received your tapes on Friday—thank you very much! I've been listening to them—letting your meaning soak in....

Dear Lisa,

You caught me by surprise, I didn't expect to hear from you again until Monday. I'm happy to hear that you received the tapes and have found the time to listen to them.

...I'm so taken with your desire to love so intensely—in this horizontal way....

---

[9] 1 John 4:19.

We love, because He first loved us.[9] This probably includes the love we used to have for friends, but I believe that the focus is the kind of love that is made possible by, and is revealed at, the cross. This is to say, it is not in me to initiate love. I can only truly love in response to His.

…To love and be loved on a level few will allow themselves to go.…

The "make-believe love" of "make believers" isn't good enough, and probably does more harm than good. Whip lash.

…I feel my heart there with you, encouraging you to stay with it, go deeper, speak the unspeakable, go where few dare to go.…

Thank you for the encouragement.

…Isn't it surprising how many are open, hungry to hear your truth—it feeds them on such a deep level—while others just don't know what to do with it (or with you)?…

Lovers are very threatening. They invite you by example to go to scary places, places where "few dare to go."

…I will certainly have much more to say about your perceptions and your messages.

I look forward to your further response.

For now I'm about "written out," having just completed the attached.…

You are certainly a gifted and sensitive writer, and I can well understand how you might be "written out."

…I send it to you out of a desire to be vulnerable and share a part of myself where few have gone. I hope you can read it in that spirit. (It also gives you an opportunity to better see "what you're getting into" and assess if you really want to go there!)

I really appreciate your openness! It was not fast reading for me, and I hope to have some greater feel for all that you have said, after sleeping on it. At first blush, you have spoken a language in your attachment, and by a paradigm, which, for me, are both "less traveled by." I hope to make the brain adjustment by morning.

I'm also processing your last two emails and hear very clearly your concern about communication—going too fast, not understanding clearly or checking out, having different conceptions about the same words or experiences. I understand that, and being that I am also a person who desires deep intimacy—and has fear of rejection, I share your concern....

Thank you, I had hoped you would understand and not be put off by my word of caution.

...My general commitment to the few that I've dared intimacy is to acknowledge the intent of love, however clumsily stated, in all communications. I believe I can trust that's true for you, too. (As much as any of us are truly trustworthy.) I don't know where we're going, Jay, but I'm enjoying the process immensely.

Again, thanks for the encouragement, and the green light. Our communication is also on my front burner, which I thought was already quite full. Somewhere further down the road, I think it will be fun for both of us to share some of the early tangential impressions, which for the present might be too distracting.

*I watched **Shadowlands** and was moved by the power of it. The pain and pleasure of allowing ourselves to truly live—"that's the deal." Loved that. And watching the expressions in Anthony's eyes—true beauty. Thanks for referring it.*

Again, I'm glad that you also found it to be precious.

*Also got a copy of **The Message**. Will begin reading it soon.*

Colossians 3:12-14 is particularly good in **The Message**. Through a very painful experience, it became a revelation to me that this passage was describing the proper garment to wear to a wedding feast. More about that later.

I talked with Kurtis about our communications—which honestly I've put off doing till now because it felt uncomfortable disclosing, "Hey, I met this guy on the internet and we've been having some very intimate conversations." ...

I understand completely, and I am glad that you were able to share with him and that you received his "blessing" to continue our conversation. I look forward to a point when he might be included, and, in some sense, I might be replaced. (I don't go away easily, but I hope I have learned when it's time to leave. I'm not speaking here about rejection of any kind, but simply out of respect for your need for intimacy with him.)

...He's already feeling backstage to all that's been occurring lately in my life, and somewhat insecure, so I wanted to handle it with sensitivity and finesse....

I am so glad that you succeeded in doing that.

...He has cautiously given me the green light. I'm curious just how far he can stretch—so far I've been pleasantly surprised.

My hope is that his grace will be rewarded, really rewarded, and in ways that perhaps none of us might guess at the moment.

As you can imagine, questions of religion and Christianity have been on my mind....

I can and have imagined. I think you have done really well so far!

...It occurs to me that I'm not sure how one might define Christianity—just what is a Christian?...

When the word was first used, it wasn't the "Christians" who used it. Acts 11:26: "... And the disciples were called Christians first in Antioch." I believe that it is significant that it is not written that, "They first called themselves ... " I think it is best to let others decide what to call you. Others are in a better position to tell whether we look like "little Christs" or not. "Little Christ" is the core meaning of the word "Christian." I'm not trying to duck out on your question, just thinking definitions will clarify in our subsequent conversation.

...I'm trying to define for myself just what I am—religion-wise....

If I find out, I'll let you know. [:-)]

...I know that I am a child of God and I believe that Jesus is the son of God and he came here to teach us to love ourselves and each other and God as God loves us....

It's much better than that!

...Beyond that things seem to get bogged down....

Yes, sadly they seem to get bogged down there for most "Christians."

...There are very few people that I would want to ask this question of—with you, I feel, I won't get a "patent answer."

Thank you in advance.

I hope I haven't disappointed you.

All for now. Take all the breathing time you need.

Thanks, I'll hope to see you again soon.

Jay

> On Tuesday, January 6, 2004, Lisa wrote:

Dear Jay,

I've been somewhat reluctant to write to you too quickly—after telling you to take as much breathing time as you need. But I can't resist just touching base. I was surprised and relieved to see a response so quickly from you after my last email—I really didn't know how you would respond. I'm still somewhat nervous about being accepted—although your compassion seems much bigger than my nervousness. (Okay, I'm moved to tears here—so I guess my nervousness is greater than I thought.) I believe that I'm starting to get twinges that the fruits of our relationship will be far greater than anything I could ever imagine—and I don't want to do anything to mess that up. On the other hand, I have to be completely truthful. And so you get the best and worst of me. I like that you don't go away easily. I hope that's a promise.

You didn't disappoint me at all with your definition of Christianity. It's somehow reassuring that you don't have any quick answers and, as you've said, it's all about revelation. I do like the part about "little Christs"—it gives a great visual.

I did forget to mention that I absolutely believe in the "Christ deposit" in each of us and am aware of its energy and aliveness much of the time. It feels much stronger now than it ever has.

I'm listening to your tapes whenever I go somewhere (in the car)—which is a little challenging due to the noise factor. But with repetition I'm deciphering more, and my heart is opened a little more each time. And I read some from **The Message** *last night—starting with the passage you referenced.[10] You refer a lot to the Bridegroom and Bride, a wedding and a wedding feast. I'm one of the multitudes that struggles with parables. It appears you're talking about Christ and his followers (church)—which includes the feminine. Is the wed-*

---

[10]Colossians 3:12–14.

ding feast a sort of perpetual celebration of that union? Am I way off here? And the idea of horizontal relationship—bringing the feminine (intimacy & relationship) into a type of ministering—this, too, is part of the feast?

All for now. I really don't want to overwhelm you—I hear that your plate is quite full. Thanks for caring so much.

Lisa

On Wednesday, January 7, 2004, Jay responded:

Lisa wrote: *I've been somewhat reluctant to write to you too quickly—after telling you to take as much breathing time as you need....*

Dear Lisa,

Again, thank you so much for your encouraging note.

I mentioned "breathing" twice that I can recall. Once was in my email that spoke of the possible need for "buddy breathing." The other was in my "Getting Horizontal" tape, concerning "heavy breathing." Does your use of the word have anything to do with either of those references? I ask, only so that I might clarify my own use of the word, if necessary.

...But I can't resist just touching base....

In this case, I'm glad about your low resistance. I had not meant to put you off by anything that I might have written; on the contrary, I was waiting for your promised continuation:

"I will certainly have much more to say about your perceptions and your messages. For now I'm about 'written out' having just completed the attached." [taken from Lisa's e-mail on 12/31/03]

...I was surprised and relieved to see a response so quickly from you after my last email—...

I think it's called the "golden rule." "Do unto others as you would have them do unto you."

...I really didn't know how you would respond. I'm still somewhat nervous about being accepted—although your compassion seems much bigger than my nervousness. (Okay, I'm moved to tears here—so I guess my nervousness is greater than I thought.)...

However I might have responded, or might yet respond, your "nervousness" confirms to me that I should already have given you reassurance from a much greater source than I could ever be. Except for time constraints, I almost sent a follow-up before receiving this latest. I wanted to tell you that you are the unique object of God's love. You have been and are "accepted" in His love. Your identity does not consist of the garbage which has caused your nervousness. Your identity is found by looking into the eyes of the One who loved you so much that He gave His life for you on your worst day. The best I could ever hope to do is to agree with His assessment of who you are to Him. "That's the deal." That means that I don't get to go away, not even on your worst day.

...I believe that I'm starting to get twinges that the fruits of our relationship will be far greater than anything I could ever imagine—and I don't want to do anything to mess that up....

By now, we already have enough history so that I can ask if those "fruits" might possibly include "the stars of the sky"?

...On the other hand, I have to be completely truthful. And so you get the best and worst of me. I like that you don't go away easily. I hope that's a promise.

And I hope it turns out to be a reality.

You didn't disappoint me at all with your definition of Christianity. It's somehow reassuring that you don't have any quick answers and, as you've said, it's all about revelation. I do like the part about "little Christs"—it gives a great visual.

"... It's all about revelation." I was referring to my understanding of Matthew 16:13-20: "When Jesus came into the coasts of Caesarea Philippi, he asked his disciples, saying, Whom do men say that I the Son of man am? And they said, Some say that thou art John the Baptist: some, Elias; and others, Jeremias, or one of the prophets. He saith unto them, But whom say ye that I am? And Simon Peter answered and said, Thou art the Christ, the Son of the living God. And Jesus answered and said unto him, Blessed art thou, Simon Barjona: for flesh and blood hath not revealed it unto thee, but my Father which is in heaven. And I say also unto thee, That thou art Peter, and upon this rock I will build my church; and the gates of hell shall not prevail against it. And I will give unto thee the keys of the kingdom of heaven: and whatsoever thou shalt bind on earth shall be bound in heaven: and whatsoever thou shalt loose on earth shall be loosed in heaven. Then charged he his disciples that they should tell no man that he was Jesus the Christ."

I have used the King James Version of the Bible here, only because it is the only one I have on my hard drive, so I can search for things easily there. I seem to have misplaced my Message version.

In any case, I quoted the larger context, only to make an observation about, "… and upon this rock I will build my church." I understand this to be the rock of revelation that Peter had received from above. Only what is built upon that rock can stand in the storms of life. (Actually, not only the source of the revelation is instructive for us, but the content as well. Peter identified Jesus as the "Son of the living God." This was a new understanding. It went beyond the identity of the Messiah for whom the Jews were waiting. It was the Jewish understanding of this claim, that Jesus was the Son of God, that got Jesus into so much trouble. The Messiah was one thing, but "the Son of God" was the same as being God Himself. That was too much, and got Jesus crucified.[11]

I did forget to mention that I absolutely believe in the "Christ deposit" in each of us and am aware of its energy and aliveness much of the time. It feels much stronger now than it ever has.

I took the time to elaborate on the rock of revelation, as a prelude for what I would like to share in response to what you have written here, "Christ deposit."

"Seeing ye have purified your souls in obeying the truth through the Spirit unto unfeigned love of the brethren, see that ye love one another with a pure heart fervently: Being born again, not of corruptible seed, but of incorruptible, by the word of God, which liveth and abideth for ever."[12] In the original, the word for the "Christ deposit" is "sperma."

In this 1 Peter context, "obeying the truth" is not referring to obedience to law, in the sense of external constraint, but rather responding to the truth of God's love as it is revealed at the cross. If we are open to the expression of His love, then he comes into us with the "deposit" or "sperma" of His own life and nature. "He that believeth on the Son of God hath the witness in himself: he that believeth not God hath made him a liar; because he believeth

---

[11]Mark 14:61–64. [12]1 Peter 1:22–23.
[13]1 John 5:10–12.

not the record that God gave of his Son. And this is the record, that God hath given to us eternal life, and this life is in his Son. He that hath the Son hath life; and he that hath not the Son of God hath not life."[13]

I didn't say that. The Bible says that, but I have come to agree with what the Bible says. On that basis, my impression is that it is the life of God's Son that is now kicking "stronger" in you than ever. If this is true, then you are alive with the life of Christ. If you can receive that, then I can receive you as one of His, and therefore one of mine, in the sense that those who belong to Christ also belong to each other. That said, who we might be to each other, in a more specific sense, is yet to be discovered.

I'm listening to your tapes whenever I go somewhere (in the car)—which is a little challenging due to the noise factor. But with repetition I'm deciphering more, and my heart is opened a little more each time....

Tuesday is the day I meet with "leaders" in Charlotte. Charlotte is about an hour and a half drive one way. I listened to the tapes yesterday as I went back and forth. I wanted to hear them through your ears, as I had come to know you. Things have a very different sound, depending on the ears or paradigms of those who are listening. I have to confess, I was very happy to hear what I had said through your ears, and I am encouraged to have your confirmation of that perception.

*...And I read some from **The Message** last night—starting with the passage you referenced. You refer a lot to the Bridegroom and Bride, a wedding and a wedding feast. I'm one of the multitudes that struggles with parables....*

That is perhaps the greatest, and the most pervasive parable of the Bible, as well as the creation. It begins in Genesis 1:27 and ends with Revelation 22:17.

...It appears you're talking about Christ and his followers (church)—which includes the feminine....

Yes!

---

[14]Hebrews 11:1—*New International Version.* (I have a few books of the *New International Version* [NIV] of the Bible on my hard drive, and Hebrews is one of them. While I'm here, I should say that the NIV is an excellent contemporary translation, very nice to read and quote, and also good enough for in-depth study. For all of that, I still believe that **The Message** has a better grasp on the Spirit where relationship—and intimacy—are concerned,)

...Is the wedding feast a sort of perpetual celebration of that union? Am I way off here?...

I believe that you are "right on" here. The great tragedy of the "church" is that those who are part of it are mostly waiting for the wedding feast to come later. I don't deny the fullness of the later wedding feast, a fulfillment of all things, but I believe in a faith that is able to reach into the future and make it substantial now, "Now faith is being sure of what we hope for and certain of what we do not see."[14]

...And the idea of horizontal relationship—bringing the feminine (intimacy & relationship) into a type of ministering—this, too, is part of the feast?

I am so blessed by your quickness to ask the right questions!!!

One of the drawbacks of our understanding of male and female is that it tends to see two more than one. In the beginning, both were in one body, the first Adam.[15] In the end, both will be in one body again.[16] Those of us who have the Son are not only the "bride of Christ," but we are also the "body of Christ." The old creation provides us with some male-female graphics so that we can better understand both the how and the implication of two becoming one. As intimate as those graphics are, they still fall short of the graphics of the one body that results. If the male-female connection results in one flesh or body, how much more the parts of the body.[17]

We who are already parts of His body are therefore already in intimate relationship with one another, because of intimacy with Him.

Generally, "ministering" is thought to be the work of the body. It was for the sake of the work that the woman was removed.[18]

Hebrews 4:9-11 makes it clear that the goal is not work, but "rest." Work is what we do, but the most important way of understanding who we are is when we know who we are when we are at rest. This identification is not based on what we do, but on relationship or intimacy. The question is who are we when we are not doing anything at all. It is this that we discover in the eyes of Jesus on the cross. It is this that ought to be confirmed in the eyes of one another in His love.

---

[15]Genesis 2:21–22.
[17]1 Corinthians 12:1–13.

[16]Ephesians 5:31–32.
[18]Genesis 2:20–21.

So I would have to say that I understand the wedding feast to be the "rest" we experience in and by His love. We are called—and empowered—to enter that rest together even now. This is the invitation of the gospel. I have extended it to you, and by all appearances you have said yes. Have I read you right?

All for now. I really don't want to overwhelm you—...

Being overwhelmed by His love in one another, "that's the deal."

...I hear that your plate is quite full....

My prayer is that you might be part of that fullness.

...Thanks for caring so much.

That is my joy, but, actually, you can thank Him who first loved me. It's all His doing.

Has your understanding reached the point of acknowledging that you belong to Him?

The answer to this question is foundational for life in the new and everlasting creation.

Sincerely,
Jay

CHAPTER 4

BREATHING LESSONS

On Wednesday, January 7, 2004, Lisa wrote to Jay:

Dear Jay,

I'm hoping that this message gets thru to you—our system at work has been down, and I may not be able to send this until tomorrow. Funny, how [this happened] on the one day that I wanted to get back to you as soon as possible.

I have to respond to you and your questions only as I'm moved in my heart—I really can't think about them, because I think the mind—with all its fears and doubts—is false. My heart, on the other hand, is jumping all around and saying yes, yes, yes! So, to answer your question, "Has my understanding reached the point of acknowledging that I belong to him?" I would have to go with my heart and say YES!!! I'm just sitting here now feeling a sense of celebration taking place inside me—it's amazing!

I have to tell you that your description of Christ's love and also your description of relationships are what helped me reach an understanding.

I have begun to see the power of his love in a different way. When you talk about how he loved us so much that he gave his life for us—as enemies—on our worst days—it struck me differently than I had ever known. I have always identified with Christ as like an icon—some sort of deity in flesh—who appeared to us to perform a function (which, of course, he could do because he's OF GOD). Oddly, what I've gotten from talking from you (I say oddly because I'm not sure you intended this) is a realization of Christ as the MAN—who had all of the experiences of the flesh—who still chose to go along with the deity. That has brought the significance of what he did much closer to home. I still don't know the full impact of my understanding of this, but it feels real.

And this notion of "knowing who you belong to" has struck me as well.

There have been very few people who have really "grabbed my heart"—where I've felt a deep and amazingly loving connection—of the spirit. I haven't been able to sustain those relationships at that level—my garbage gets in the way. But I can see that living thru the Christ consciousness—asking for and allowing everything and every relationship to be filtered thru that—could change that dynamic. And allow for the intimacy and love that I want so badly. And so I'm making that choice.

As far as our relationship—you already have "grabbed my heart"—which is very scary to say and yet true. As far as "the stars and the sky"—if that means like a father/daughter relationship—I could see that's possible. I even talked with my therapist about that this morning—wanting to be sure that I'm not projecting some unmet needs that I didn't receive from my "dad." I don't think so—this feels much different.

As far as breathing goes—my reference to "breathing time" was more in response to "buddy breathing"—which for me means a little time out for assimilation and/or life. "Heavy breathing" refers more to the state I'm in now.

I don't know what else I believe at this point but will let you know when I know.

My deepest gratitude,

Lisa

On Wednesday, January 7, 2004, Jay responded:

Lisa wrote:

…I have to respond to you and your questions only as I'm moved in my heart—I really can't think about them, because I think the mind—with all its fears and doubts—is false….

…I still don't know the full impact of my understanding of this, but it feels real.

Dear Lisa,

To this point you have every hair on my body standing on end. You have just described it as well as or better than I have ever heard it said!

And this notion of "knowing who you belong to" has struck me as well.

There have been very few people who have really "grabbed my heart"—where I've felt a deep and amazingly loving connection—of the spirit. I haven't been able to sustain those relationships at that level—my garbage gets in the way. But I can see that living thru the Christ consciousness—asking for and allowing everything and every relationship to be filtered thru that—could change that dynamic. And allow for the intimacy and love that I want so badly. And so I'm making that choice.

Tears!

As far as our relationship—you already have "grabbed my heart"—which is very scary to say and yet true. As far as "the stars of the sky"—if that means like a father/daughter relationship—I could see that's possible. I even talked with my therapist about that this morning—wanting to be sure that I'm not projecting some unmet needs that I didn't receive from my "dad." I don't think so—this feels much different.

As far as breathing goes—my reference to "breathing time" was more in response to "buddy breathing"—which for me means a little time out for assimilation and/or life. "Heavy breathing" refers more to the state I'm in now.

When I spoke of "buddy breathing," I was referring to what happens in a deep dive when one of the two divers gets into trouble with their respirator. In times like that, you have to be able to breath from the same respirator, the same oxygen supply. It's more a matter of helping each other to breath than it is of giving a person space to breath on his or her own. Sometimes at depth, it's possible to get so tangled up in the garbage that your mask is torn off and you are in danger of drowning. It is that that I was speaking about.

I don't know what else I believe at this point but will let you know when I know.

You have made a wonderful beginning; perhaps we can both discover more together.

Right now words fail me. I need some time to marinate in what you have said here. I will be back to you soon.

Yours in Christ,

Jay

On Thursday, January 8, 2004, Jay replied again to Lisa's e-mail of the previous day:

Lisa wrote:

I have to respond to you and your questions only as I'm moved in my heart—I really can't think about them, because I think the mind—with all its fears and doubts—is false....

Dear Lisa,

I'm ready to be a little better communicator than at the first moment of reading what you wrote.

There's time enough for thinking; right now I am celebrating what you are experiencing in your heart!

...My heart, on the other hand, is jumping all around and saying yes, yes, yes! So, to answer your question, "Has my understanding reached the point of acknowledging that I belong to him?" I would have to go with my heart and say YES!!! I'm just sitting here now feeling a sense of celebration taking place inside me—it's amazing!

Not to tarnish the celebration by inviting you back into your mind, I need to tell you that my heart and mind are full of things to share with you, as you are ready to receive them. The first of those things, which I'll focus on later in this e-mail, is meant for your protection against the mental/spiritual battles that soon follow the experience that you are now enjoying. For the present, perhaps it's enough to say: I'm ready when you are.

I have to tell you that your description of Christ's love and also your description of relationships are what helped me reach an understanding.

Right from the beginning, it was His love expressed in close relationships with those that the Father had given Him that helped them to understand as well. The moment of truth had to await the experience of the cross.

I have begun to see the power of his love in a different way. When you talk about how he loved us so much that he gave his life for us—as enemies—on our worst days—it struck me differently than I had ever known. I have always identified with Christ as like an icon—some sort of deity in flesh—who appeared to us to perform a function (which, of course he could do because he's OF GOD). Oddly, what I've gotten from talking from you (I say oddly because I'm not sure you intended this) is a realization of Christ as the MAN—who had all of the experiences of the flesh—who still chose to go along with the deity. That has brought the significance of what he did much closer to home. I still don't know the full impact of my understanding of this, but it feels real.

Lisa, thank you so much for your feedback. So often we say things and yet don't know if we have really communicated what was in our hearts. You have heard what was, and is, in my heart, more and better than the words I used to try to express it. That for me is a sign of very strong connection, not just between us but between you and the Spirit of God.

And this notion of "knowing who you belong to" has struck me as well.

There have been very few people who have really "grabbed my heart"—where I've felt a deep and amazingly loving connection—of the spirit....

I am so encouraged to hear that. Around these parts I have been called "the fastest gun in the Bible belt." I tend to be a little tough on those who posture as "Christian leaders."

...I haven't been able to sustain those relationships at that level—my garbage gets in the way....

I guess that had been my impression from the time I first saw your note to the Deida list. My heart is to keep reminding you that your garbage has been taken away. It was nailed to the cross. When you look there to find it, my prayer is that you will always be graced to look just a little higher, and see the look of love in Jesus' eyes. That look is at you, and for you, and for all who will open to Him.[1]

...But I can see that living thru the Christ consciousness—asking for and allowing everything and every relationship to be filtered thru

---

[1] Revelation 3:10.

that—could change that dynamic. And allow for the intimacy and love that I want so badly. And so I'm making that choice.

"That's the deal."[2]

As far as our relationship—you already have "grabbed my heart"—which is very scary to say and yet true....

I pray that I have not put my hand in the cookie jar. It's all about Him, and I am trusting that it is He who has "grabbed your heart." Otherwise, I will have "grabbed in vain." It's less scary when it's He in us Who does the "grabbing."

...As far as "the stars of the sky"—if that means like a father/ daughter relationship—I could see that's possible. I even talked with my therapist about that this morning—wanting to be sure that I'm not projecting some unmet needs that I didn't receive from my "dad." I don't think so—this feels much different.

I'm so glad that you shared this, because getting clear about it is so important as a strong foundation for what might be possible between us. You had written:

"I believe that I'm starting to get twinges that the fruits of our relationship will be far greater than anything I could ever imagine— and I don't want to do anything to mess that up." [From an earlier message Lisa sent on January 6; see page 64.]

...and I had responded:

"By now, we already have enough history so that I can ask if those 'fruits' might possibly include 'the stars of the sky'?"

The focus of my question was primarily as a point of contact, and understanding between us concerning the "stars of the sky" for you. I wasn't, in the moment of my asking the question, presuming you or your "fruits" to be the "stars of my sky." Let me very quickly add, however, that I was not excluding that possibility either. My question was directed primarily to your heritage, your stars. I just wondered if you had made the connection between what you had described as "fruits" and the "stars of the sky" as I had spoken of them in the "Getting Horizontal" tape.

It was probably the furthest thing from your mind that I might possibly have my hand in the cookie jar where you are concerned, but I wanted to be clear about this in any case, because it is bound to surface as one of the spiritual battles you will face

[2]Philippians 2:1–13.

in the near future. You see, "church people" have mostly missed Jesus' promise in Mark 10:29–30. They tend to use words very loosely, which results in trivializing the most foundational spiritual relationships that God offers us in the Person of His Son. For the present, true and substantial father-daughter relationships in the spirit are considered illegal by most "church goers." Sooner or later you will run into this reaction, and probably more sooner than later, especially if you are graced to remain in your state of "heavy breathing" (new love).[3]

So far, I have shared with you in the Love of Christ in a way that I consider to be normal to what God is after in those of us who believe in His Son. I am not suggesting that the exchange between us has been normal by the standards of anything I have ever seen described as "evangelism." This to say that, while there may, and I hope, has been, a great deal of the loving Spirit of your heavenly Father in what and how I have shared with you, I have not shared with the conscious intention of spiritually fathering you myself. (Again I am not ruling out that possibility, just wanting to be clear about who we might be to one another.) I'm reminded of the song, "Nice 'n' Easy." (Sinatra does it the best, and, if this were eye to eye, I might be tempted to sing it to you myself.)

How I might share with you based on a clear understanding of who we are to each other, would be, and perhaps, will be, very different than my way with you to this point. In this connection, perhaps I should elaborate on my understanding of spiritual relationships just a little more than I have on the tapes I sent or in anything I might have written to date.

Even though there is great resistance to the idea of spiritual fathers in the "Christian community (Catholics excepted)," there is openness to the possibility of spiritual mothers. This is because of something that Jesus said that has been understood out of context. "... Do not call anyone on earth 'father,' for you have one Father, and He is in heaven."[4] Jesus never said, "Call no woman mother." As a result there is openness to the possibility of spiritual mothers but not to fathers. That said, for now, I direct your attention to 1 Corinthians 4:15, 1 Timothy 1:2, 2 Timothy 1:2, Titus 1:4, 1 Peter, 5:13, 1 John 2:1, of course, Mark 10:29–30, and I could offer many more places where you could find who we might be to one another in the Spirit.

---

[3]Revelation 2:4.

My point here, however, is that, even though there is a greater acceptance of the possibility of spiritual mothers, in fact, there are even fewer spiritual mothers available than there are fathers. This is tragic. Women have been non-people in the church for so long, that "believers" have been terribly un-mothered. I spent some time on this problem in the "Getting Horizontal" tape.[5] This to say that, in the absence of spiritual mothers, should it be that The Lord has made or is making you a daughter to me, you might even find the content of a mother's heart coming from me on occasion.

Several years back, in a conversation with my flesh-and-blood daughter, Heather (this occurred close to the beginning of a twelve-hour non-stop conversation—and I mean non-stop— even when she went to the john, she left the door open so as not to break the flow of the conversation), she said to me, "Dad, we can't have this conversation. This is a conversation that should only happen between a mother and a daughter." I responded by saying, "If you can find a mother with whom you can have this conversation, then find one. Meanwhile, if you think I am going to leave the formation of your sexuality to **Cosmo** magazine, you had better guess again," or words to that effect. I went on to explain that, because in Christ there is neither male nor female, I had no problem taking off my father hat, and putting on my mother hat. The conversation began with Heather announcing to me that "sex is the most important thing there is." I touched on this in the "Horizontal" tape without going into the details.

All of this to say, if you turn out to be a spiritual daughter to me, both of us will probably have to fasten our seat belts. Having said that, because of the great diversity that is possible in people and in life relationships, there is no telling what the content might be, but it is quite likely that it would be something that neither of us have experienced before, at least, where the specifics are concerned. Once more, before leaving this aspect of the subject, one thing that is always true, if things are healthy and working right: the content between a father and a daughter changes rather drastically when the daughter marries. This may be a little sad for both, but it is normal, and healthy, and this applies to spiritual parenting as well.

Because things seem to be somewhat shut down right now between you and Kurtis, there might be a need to do some catch-up spiritual fathering, but my heart would be that it always be di-

---

[4]Matthew 23:9   [5]Galatians 3:28.

rected to the end of your having a vital and fulfilling relationship with your husband. That is my hope, and prayer for you.

In that connection, lest I put some kind of bondage on you, I need to mention what both Jesus and Paul said. First, Jesus, in Matthew 10:34-39, and then Paul in 1 Corinthians 7:15. I mention this last, not as an easy escape, but only to be balanced in expressing both the high regard in which marriage is held in the purposes of God and also the higher calling we have in the "liberty wherewith Christ has set us free."[6]

Finally, now that you are in God's family, it remains to be seen who you are, and who you belong to in particular in His family. I look forward to exploring that with you to the end that you might not only discover who you are, but who you are in relationship to others, even including myself. It's the Christmas morning I spoke about in the tape I sent. I, for one, am looking forward to opening the package. :-)

As far as breathing goes—my reference to "breathing time" was more in response to "buddy breathing"—which for me means a little time out for assimilation and/or life. "Heavy breathing" refers more to the state I'm in now.

I guess I already covered the breathing question.

I don't know what else I believe at this point but will let you know when I know.

And so we begin to unwrap the package. Merry Christmas!!!

Yours in Christ,

Jay

---

[6]Galatians 5:1–14.

NOT LEFT BEHIND

CHAPTER 5

LOOKING FOR
A PLACE TO LIVE

The next day, Thursday, January 8, 2004, things took a "seren-dipitous" turn. Here's how Jay explains what happened:

When Lisa said "Yes," as she did so resoundingly [see page 71], I suddenly realized she was going to need Jesus with skin on. (That's the church, by the way, "His body."[1]) My brain went on "scram." (I think that's what they call it when something goes seriously wrong or there is an emergency in a nuclear power plant.) I remembered something called "housechurch.org" and I went there. People who are doing "house church" or looking for a "house church" can register there. There was a listing for Austin, Texas, where Lisa lives, with an e-mail address, a phone number, and a physical address. The e-mail address, which began "tnfdale," meant nothing to me.

I sent an e-mail, and it came back "Delivery Failure." Being a bad loser, I called the phone number, still with no idea about who might be at the other end. Lo and behold, it was a man by the name of Tony Dale—and I knew him! My wife, Carleen, and I had met Tony and Felicity, his wife, along with their son Jon, at a "house church" conference two years earlier. We had had supper with them twice, I believe, and some really good sharing. For my part, I had a real sense of connection with them, which was confirmed over the months that followed, and I would get an e-mail of encouragement every now and then in connection with things I was attempting to share with "house church" leadership world-wide.

---

[1] Ephesians 1:22–23.

I don't know who was more surprised to find the other on the other end of the line, Tony or me. Certainly, neither of us was expecting to hear from the other. In fact, it was the first time we were ever in touch by phone—and it was an "accident."

When I told Tony what had happened and shared a little of the correspondence, he immediately appreciated the implications of what had happened. By "accident," I had found Tony and Felicity, whom I consider the finest couple in leadership in the "house church" movement around the world, and there they were in Austin! The rest, as they say, is history. In our case, it led to the e-mail that follows.

On Thursday, January 8, 2004, Jay e-mailed the Dales in Austin:

Dear Tony and Felicity,

What a delightful serendipity!!

I'll give you Lisa's address in this e-mail. I don't have her number and have not spoken to her except by tape.

I am taking the liberty of sending the most recent e-mail exchange including hers of yesterday, and my first post-conversion response to her, sent this morning. My hope is that this will give you some insight into where she is, and how she has understood the gospel as I have shared it with her to date. I am a total ignoramus where New Age is concerned, but, that said, to date, I have tried to speak her language, and let the Lord clean up the lingo later.

If you would like the rest of the exchange. Let me know, and I'll send it along.

I'll also give you my number here, which is where I spend most of my days writing. I will try to get copies of the two tapes that I sent to Lisa off to you by tomorrow.

Bless You Both. I'm still on cloud 9 after our conversation.

Yours in Christ,
Jay

On the same day, Tony Dale responded to Jay's e-mail:

Jay,

It is a delight to see the way that the Lord is working here. I will certainly look forward to hearing from Lisa, and Felicity and I will seek to see her and her husband drawn into the life of one of the house churches here.

Every blessing,
Tony

Dear Jay,

Thank you for celebrating with me and for walking with me at this moment. It is such a gift.

I thought of (or "felt") some things to communicate with you—both last night and after reading this latest. When I write I do best to go "off the cuff"—actually bypassing the brain in some respects. I'm allowing the content of what I say to come "through" me—my brain only participates to give it structure. So, in that light, I would say that it really is "spirit driven," and I can see why you would feel the connection. It is the same way I feel when I listen to you. That is why you "grab my heart." I feel the "spirit-drivenness" of your words. That is what I respond to with you.

You talk about how, when a door opens in a spiritual relation-ship, you go thru it. I feel certain that God has led me to some doors and I've peeked thru. This is not the first time I've been called into relationship with Jesus. I would say that what I've done here is recom-mit—on a whole new level. I have been very aware of his presence in my heart most of my life. But I wouldn't say I've been willing to be intimate with him, just as I haven't been willing to walk thru those doors he's led me to and to be intimate with the people he's sent me. I believe you can have the Christ consciousness within you, and go about doing a "good life" with love and compassion, and still feel empty. This could be for a lot of reasons: one could be because it's a choice—this living thru Christ—that you have to make on a constant basis. And it's because the mind—which I believe to be our greatest enemy (or perhaps you might refer to it as the garbage)—puts up barriers. And I also think that unless there is some relationship—as you would say, on the horizontal—where you are connected and can feel and express this spirit, then you're not experiencing the fullness or completeness of his love.

You have to love other people, and more importantly, you have to commune with people who are "spirit-driven" to enliven and feel the full intensity. I believe that you and I have been led to each other, not of our own volition, but thru spirit, and this is a door that I choose to go through. You've spoken in a language of relationship and intimacy, and these are the areas in which my spirit is leading me to grow. I believe that your spirit has been led before me in these areas and that you have an understanding and a way of communicating this understanding that I can hear.

In another context, I believe that I've been living relationships much as I've looked at Jesus—in some sort of "icon" sense. I weave through my life and various relationships—relating on this and that issue. But like I haven't really "felt" the realness of Jesus, I haven't really "felt" the realness of these people. Perhaps it's the same in reverse—I am well aware of their "humanness" but not of their divinity. And I suppose that is what intimacy is about—the allowance and acceptance of both. Without expectations—on any of our parts.

I'm looking thru your email now and am so moved by the following:

"My heart is to keep reminding you that your garbage has been taken away. It was nailed to the cross. When you look there to find it, my prayer is that you will always be graced to look just a little higher, and see the look of love in Jesus' eyes. That look is at you, and for you, and for all who will open to Him."

Such beauty and grace! This has filled my heart—it's the essence of love—the totality of love. I feel overwhelmed. Thank you for saying this.

*I'm so glad I saw the movie [**Shadowlands**] so that we can begin to share little one-liners: "That's the deal." Precious. I watched the movie again last night (I had it rented for the week) and was moved by the transformation in each of their lives by love. I'm glad I watched it again.*

And finally, on the issue of relationship. My heart goes out to you—you put a lot of thought into this one! As you can see, I have a tendency to move rather quickly myself. Sometimes—I would say frequently—I move from a feeling in my heart and not with the caution of my mind, and it probably has gotten me into trouble many times. I can be very child-like in that respect—so I appreciate a word of caution, so to speak.

I'm hoping that what I wrote above gives you a little better understanding of what your relationship means to me. I am not wanting YOU, so to speak, but I'm wanting more of an understanding of your understanding of Christ's love, relationship, and intimacy—and to experience Christ's love through you. The structure—the "how"—we adopt to accomplish this is an unknown—and may not be as important to me as the "what." I'm taken by the description of relationships in the spirit that you talk about—and I long for the experience of this. I'm not looking for relationships to replace what I already have in spirit—or my relationship with Kurtis—but rather to enhance it. For now I would say calling ourselves "friends in Christ" would probably be a good description. I think you obviously have a much better feel for how these relationships go—having been in a number of them yourself. And it sounds like you've had to suffer thru the repercussions of what these relationships have brought up for the observers as well as the participants. Having never experienced the "whole enchilada" (as we Texans might say), I probably am much freer in my enthusiasm and expression of that enthusiasm. Please forgive my naivety—and I hope I didn't make you too uncomfortable.

I am reminded also of a couple of things you have said—on the horizontal tape (my favorite)—which I'll probably misquote, but the content has to do with going to certain places within ourselves, where we've never been, with another person—otherwise the experience wouldn't be the same. The other thing is something like you can't love by yourself—there has to be another person. These, I think, relate directly to what I've been talking about above in "feeling the full intensity" of the love of Christ. So, in that sense, I would say that I would want and need YOU—and/or other spirit-driven people that I connect with—to be able to realize what I think I hear you talking about. So, are we back to square one?

I appreciate your sensitivity to my relationship with my husband. It is my desire that he and I grow and have a vital and fulfilling relationship as well. I would say that in many ways it already is. This is really more about "going for broke."

Is it the nature of ALL spiritual relationships that they change drastically when one of the parties get married? Is marriage, somehow, supposed to take the place of other spiritual relationships?

My first challenge: how to talk with Kurtis about my experiences in a way that doesn't "turn him off." It may not be a big deal to him at this point—he knows the content of what we've been talking about—and he's seen me get excited about Christianity before. He just has his own garbage around it and has never had the experience of Jesus' love (that he's aware of or is able to admit). And he's distanced himself from me in the past over this.

At the same time, we've been talking for some time about attending a church that we've been to a few times over the years that is Christian and very non-denominational. There are many people who attend this church that I care for deeply—including our "ex-therapists" (we did therapy with a couple for six years many years ago—mainly based on "Imago therapy"—developed by Harville Hendrix). The man of this couple is who we worked with most, and he is one of the few who "grabbed me spiritually" over the years. I believe Kurtis and I would both benefit from attending and we've agreed to go there this Sunday.

Any thoughts?

So, I think this is all for now. I look forward to hearing from you soon.

Lisa

On Friday, January 9, 2004, Jay responded to Lisa's e-mail:

Lisa wrote:

Dear Jay,

Thank you for celebrating with me and for walking with me at this moment. It is such a gift.

Dear Lisa,

It is such a gift for me to be able to walk with you at this moment. Thank you so much for sharing it with me!

I thought of (or "felt") some things to communicate with you—both last night and after reading this latest. When I write I do best to go "off the cuff"—actually bypassing the brain in some respects. I'm allowing the content of what I say to come "through" me—my brain only participates to give it structure. So, in that light, I would say that it really is "spirit driven," and I can see why you would feel the connection. It is the same way I feel when I listen to you. That is why you "grab my heart." I feel the "spirit-drivenness" of your words. That is what I respond to with you.

I am very taken with the fresh way that you express eternal truth. Jesus said: "It is the spirit that quickeneth; the flesh profiteth nothing: the words that I speak unto you, they are spirit, and they are life."[2]

You talk about how, when a door opens in a spiritual relationship, you go thru it. I feel certain that God has led me to some doors and I've peeked thru....

Somehow "peeking" just doesn't do it: "Now the Lord is that Spirit: and where the Spirit of the Lord is, there is liberty. But we all, with open face beholding as in a glass the glory of the Lord,

---

[2]John 6:63.

are changed into the same image from glory to glory, even as by the Spirit of the Lord."[3]

... This is not the first time I've been called into relationship with Jesus. I would say that what I've done here is recommit—on a whole new level. I have been very aware of his presence in my heart most of my life. But I wouldn't say I've been willing to be intimate with him, just as I haven't been willing to walk thru those doors he's led me to and to be intimate with the people he's sent me. I believe you can have the Christ consciousness within you, and go about doing a "good life" with love and compassion, and still feel empty. This could be for a lot of reasons: one could be because it's a choice—this living thru Christ—that you have to make on a constant basis. And it's because the mind—which I believe to be our greatest enemy (or perhaps you might refer to it as the garbage)—puts up barriers. And I also think that unless there is some relationship—as you would say, on the horizontal—where you are connected and can feel and express this spirit, then you're not experiencing the fullness or completeness of his love.

You have to love other people, and more importantly, you have to commune with people who are "spirit-driven" to enliven and feel the full intensity. I believe that you and I have been led to each other, not of our own volition, but thru spirit, and this is a door that I choose to go through....

It is wonderful that you can both see and express the truth of this so beautifully.

... You've spoken in a language of relationship and intimacy, and these are the areas in which my spirit is leading me to grow. I believe that your spirit has been led before me in these areas and that you have an understanding and a way of communicating this understanding that I can hear.

Perhaps this is the reason that The Lord has saved you from "church." Those who spend a lot of time there are generally immunized against relationships.

In another context, I believe that I've been living relationships much as I've looked at Jesus—in some sort of "icon" sense....

Yes, I understand, that's the sense which "church goers" see as legal.

---

[3]2 Corinthians 3:17–18.

In February of 2000, I had the following conversation with a local pastor with whom I was very close. I had asked him if he was prepared for today, and he answered, "I think so, a Valentine's Day message from John 3:16." He went on to explain a little bit. When he was done, I asked him if I could throw him a curve ball, without messing up his mind too much, and he said "Come on." I then shared a Valentine's message that the Lord had given me: it came out of Song of Songs. (Peterson's translation is quite good, but has a couple of problems, which I would be glad to share at another time.)

"They all hold swords, being expert in war: every man hath his sword upon his thigh because of fear in the night."[4]

I had already seen Luke 22:36-38. "Then said he unto them, 'But now, he that hath a purse, let him take it and likewise his scrip: and he that hath no sword, let him sell his garment, and buy one. For I say unto you, that this that is written must yet be accomplished in me, "And he was reckoned among the transgressors"; for the things concerning me have an end.' And they said, 'Lord, behold, here are two swords.' And he said unto them, 'It is enough.'"

This is why Peter was armed in the garden of Gethsemane. It was for fear in the night, fear that he would be "reckoned among the transgressors," and rejected.

It is in Genesis 3:24 that we are first introduced to swords, and in light of our understanding that the flaming sword was for the purpose of keeping the way, rather than obstructing it, it appears to me that: one, Jesus is the way, and more specifically, the way was opened through His flesh, when He was beaten and crucified. Remember, "... by abolishing in his flesh, the law which stood against us and was opposed to us, He took it away, nailing it to the cross" or words to that effect; two, the way back into the garden is through the cross. In instructing his disciples to get swords, Jesus' purpose was to fulfill the Scriptures that He might be "reckoned among the transgressors." The swords were not for the purpose of keeping Jesus from being crucified, (Peter's heart) but for ensuring that he was crucified. The way back into the garden is through the crucifixion of Jesus. The swords were "to keep the way."

What was in the garden? Intimacy with God and each other.

In Luke 9, it is written: "And it came to pass, when the time was come that he should be received up, he steadfastly set his face to go to Jerusalem." I believe that this way of expressing it was to fulfill the passage in Isaiah 50:7: "For the Lord God will help me; therefore shall I not be confounded: therefore have I set my face like a flint, and I know that I shall not be ashamed."

Hebrews 2:2 says: "despising, or having no regard for the shame of the cross, Jesus sat down at the right hand of God." It was Joy in his heart that made that possible. He was beaten beyond human recognition, stripped naked, and hung up on a stick like a piece of meat, and he was not ashamed. He won back what was lost in the Fall, nakedness without shame.

I ended by saying: "Fred, This was the first time since the fall that a man was naked before the one he loved, but without shame." I said, "Fred, since that time God has been looking for those who would receive His Valentine. The problem is that the Love of God is so great that unbelievers think that it's not

---

[4]Song of Songs 3:8.

possible, and believers think that it's illegal." By that time Fred was wiping away tears.

...I weave through my life and various relationships—relating on this and that issue. But like I haven't really "felt" the realness of Jesus, I haven't really "felt" the realness of these people. Perhaps it's the same in reverse—I am well aware of their "humanness" but not of their divinity. And I suppose that is what intimacy is about—the allowance and acceptance of both. Without expectations—on any of our parts.

Most of us are governed by our expectations. The main thing is what we have done with our own. If we can get our own nailed to the tree, then we are in a position to be redemptive when the expectations of others make them unattractive. (And I cleaned that one up. :-))

I'm looking thru your email now and am so moved by the following:

"My heart is to keep reminding you that your garbage has been taken away. It was nailed to the cross. When you look there to find it, my prayer is that you will always be graced to look just a little higher, and see the look of love in Jesus' eyes. That look is at you, and for you, and for all who will open to Him."

Such beauty and grace! This has filled my heart—it's the essence of love—the totality of love. I feel overwhelmed. Thank you for saying this.

I am so filled with joy by your ability to hear, and see.

*I'm so glad I saw the movie [**Shadowlands**] so that we can begin to share little one-liners: "That's the deal." Precious. I watched the movie again last night (I had it rented for the week) and was moved by the transformation in each of their lives by love. I'm glad I watched it again.*

Again, I'm so glad that you could see in it the value that blessed me. I have another one for you. Have you seen **Tuesdays with Morrie**? If not get yourself some more Kleenex, rent the film, and enjoy. It's pure Bible without being religious. Jack Lemmon's last, and perhaps finest, performance.

And finally, on the issue of relationship. My heart goes out to you—you put a lot of thought into this one! As you can see, I have a tendency to move rather quickly myself. Sometimes—I would say frequently—I move from a feeling in my heart and not with the caution of my mind, and it probably has gotten me into trouble many times. I can be very child-like in that respect—so I appreciate a word of caution, so to speak.

I had not said what I said in this connection, so much out of fear or even a need for caution, although you are right about experience with the pain that can and does accompany relationships. My concern was rather more directed toward the need for clarity from the Lord. I also am inclined to move too fast. The problem comes when I move faster than the clarity needed to see where I am going. Where you are concerned, my desire is that who we are be very clear to both of us, before we try to go someplace together in the Spirit where we are not yet equipped to go.

I'm hoping that what I wrote above gives you a little better understanding of what your relationship means to me. I am not wanting YOU, so to speak, but I'm wanting more of an understanding of your understanding of Christ's love, relationship, and intimacy—and to experience Christ's love through you....

I can hear that, and appreciate it. The most important thing is experiencing Christ's Love. The means by which we experience it, while still important, are more secondary. I say this being well aware of what Paul says to the Thessalonians, 1 Thessalonians 2: 19–20, and to the Philippians, 4:1.

...The structure—the "how"—we adopt to accomplish this is an unknown—and may not be as important to me as the "what."...

Yes. It's been almost 2000 years since anyone has seen an authentic church.

...I'm taken by the description of relationships in the spirit that you talk about—and I long for the experience of this....

I long for this with you and for you.

...I'm not looking for relationships to replace what I already have in spirit—or my relationship with Kurtis—but rather to enhance it. For now I would say calling ourselves "friends in Christ" would probably be a good description. I think you obviously have a much better feel for how these relationships go—having been in a number of them yourself. And it sounds like you've had to suffer thru the repercussions of what these relationships have brought up for the observers as well as the participants. Having never experienced the "whole enchilada"

(as we Texans might say), I probably am much freer in my enthusiasm and expression of that enthusiasm....

I'm not so sure about this, I tend to be a very "up" and enthusiastic person. (Did I say "optimist"?)

...Please forgive my naivety—and I hope I didn't make you too uncomfortable.

I have not read you as naive, and you have made me very comfortable. All things considered, I have tried to make you comfortable as well.

I am reminded also of a couple of things you have said—on the horizontal tape (my favorite)—which I'll probably misquote, but the content has to do with going to certain places within ourselves, where we've never been, with another person—otherwise the experience wouldn't be the same....

You got that right!

...The other thing is something like you can't love by yourself—there has to be another person. These, I think, relate directly to what I've been talking about above in "feeling the full intensity" of the love of Christ. So, in that sense, I would say that I would want and need YOU—and/or other spirit-driven people that I connect with—to be able to realize what I think I hear you talking about. So, are we back to square one?

I had not intended to go back, and anyway, what happened to square one? Where was it? I think I lost it somewhere in the pile of discarded giftwrappings.

I appreciate your sensitivity to my relationship with my husband. It is my desire that he and I grow and have a vital and fulfilling relationship as well. I would say that in many ways it already is. This is really more about "going for broke."

Thank you for that appreciation. I was not trying to put distance between the two of us, but only to be sensitive to where you are.

Is it the nature of ALL spiritual relationships that they change drastically when one of the parties get married? Is marriage, somehow, supposed to take the place of other spiritual relationships?

I don't think so. There is a wonderful book on the subject by a good friend, Joanne Krupp. The title of the book is, **Woman:**

God's Plan, Not Man's Tradition.[5] It is the best book on women in the economy of God that I have seen. Your question brings it to mind, because, in the book Joanne discusses the meaning of "headship."[6] She points out that the word used for "head" has the same sense as the "headwaters" of a river, the source of the river. So it has to do with source.

When we are young, parents are our source. If it's working right, we find a new source in marriage. It is the content of source that transfers, or ought to transfer, from a father to a husband. If the source stays pure, many other tributaries can flow in without polluting the river. If the source is polluted, the other sources can dilute the pollution, but the best is when things are cleaned up at the source.

That's pretty much off the top, but I think it could be pursued at some greater depth, and still hold up.

My first challenge: how to talk with Kurtis about my experiences in a way that doesn't "turn him off." It may not be a big deal to him at this point—he knows the content of what we've been talking about—and he's seen me get excited about Christianity before. He just has his own garbage around it and has never had the experience of Jesus' love (that he's aware of or is able to admit). And he's distanced himself from me in the past over this.

This is a difficulty that Peter addresses.[7] It is not so easy to bridge the paradigm gaps between then and now, but I believe it contains great wisdom. Words are a very poor substitute for a life lived. If there is anything I might be able to do to help, please do not hesitate to ask.

At the same time, we've been talking for some time about attending a church that we've been to a few times over the years that is Christian and very non-denominational. There are many people who attend this church that I care for deeply—...

I am so glad to hear that. Actually, after writing to you yesterday morning (I try to respond in time for my email to be on your desk before you get to work in the morning), I checked to see if there might be a good place of fellowship for you in Austin. At that point I was not yet aware that you were an escapee where "church" was concerned. I made a call to a number I didn't recognize, and to my great surprise and delight, Tony Dale picked up the phone.

---

[5]Mentioned previously, page 17.   [6]1 Corinthians 11:3.
[7]1 Peter 3:1–7.

Tony and his wife, Felicity, are among the top 10 leaders and speakers in the "house church movement" world-wide. I'm not into movements, so I put it in quotes. These are people who see the validity, vitality, and necessity of Christians meeting in homes. That was the primary meeting place in the early church.

Tony and Felicity are a couple who glow in the dark. They are very free and very sound in the faith. You are certainly welcome to call them any time that might be good for you.

...including our "ex-therapists" (we did therapy with a couple for six years many years ago—mainly based on "Imago therapy"—developed by Harville Hendrix)....

I think I have heard the name.

...The man of this couple is who we worked with most, and he is one of the few who "grabbed me spiritually" over the years. I believe Kurtis and I would both benefit from attending and we've agreed to go there this Sunday.
Any thoughts?

I guess I have already shared my thoughts. I would only add that, in light of our recent conversation, things might look a little different to you than they did when you were last there. I think that you may perhaps come to see Tony and Felicity as a lifeboat. Tony asked for the tapes that I had sent to you, and I hope to send them to him today. I have shared with them, at some length, my understanding concerning both relationship, and the place of women in the economy of God. They have been very encouraging in their reception of both.

I would guess that they are in their mid-50s, very youthful in their impression, however.

So, I think this is all for now. I look forward to hearing from you soon.

Soon!

Yours in Christ,

Jay

NOT LEFT BEHIND

CHAPTER 6

GETTING
COMFORTABLE

Dear Jay,

Joy, joy, joy!!! I'm feeling so joyful about all that we have shared! Yes, isn't this fun? It's even better than Christmas day! I love the heading here—"getting comfortable." It's a place where I can rest. Thank you!!

Well, I just called Tony Dale (I write these emails over a period of hours during the day) —without having a clue of what I was going to say or what would transpire. I was nervous—it's one thing talking with someone over e-mail—quite different on the phone—and even more so in person. Plus, I don't know how to relate to "Christians" and their lingo. It feels very foreign to me to hear and respond to this language.

My mind gets in the way. I'm not sure how I feel or think about a lot of things around Christianity—and I don't even know many of the questions yet. It was somewhat startling then when Tony asked how Kurtis felt about all of this—I stumbled around and eventually got to, "He seems ok with me exploring but not sure he wants to participate." Then Tony asked if Kurtis and I could come to dinner Saturday night—or coffee at Starbucks if dinner seemed too much. I stumbled around—I don't know how Kurtis would feel (how do I feel?—nervous)—but said I would ask him and get back to Tony. But at least I'll go meet with them—probably for coffee.

And so, I just talked with Kurtis—AND HE AGREED TO GO TO COFFEE! (For me, he says—I'll take what I can get!) So I called Tony back and we're meeting tomorrow at 10 AM. Wow!

So much swirling around now. I really want to respond more to your email, but I have some things I need to do until I leave, so will have to wait. Don't see that I'll get back to you until Monday—should have a lot to tell you then! Take care and thank you again so much.

Lisa

> **On Friday, January 9, 2004, Tony Dale wrote:**

Jay,

Lisa called me yesterday, and today we were able to follow up together on the phone. Felicity and I are meeting with her and her husband tomorrow morning at Starbucks. Pray for us, and let's ask the Lord for this young woman, and then her husband, to grow rapidly in the Lord.

Tony

> **On Saturday, January 10, 2004, Jay wrote:**

Dear Tony and Felicity,

Thank you so much for your note. The following will give you an up-date on my communication with Lisa. The enthusiasm of her last response to me is a reflection of my own. Thank you so much for your caring, your faithfulness, and your ability to see.

Yours in Christ,

Jay

> **Added to the above e-mail is the following:**

I think it was Wednesday, under the subject heading of "among all nations," that I had the following encounter with a church planting web list. It was yesterday morning, and I haven't heard anything back yet. Could it be that they just don't get it?

Someone had written:

"It's getting harder and harder to find a truly "Un-reached" people group."

My [Jay's] response:

Dear _____,

I am very much in harmony with the place you have given to Romans 1 and the things created.

"Over the past couple of days, it has occurred to me that genetic people groups are increasingly scrambled in places like the large nation states. Looking at the yet un-reached more in terms of "paradigm groups" might be more and more helpful. The cultures of people groups become blurred; the boxes in which people think seem more and more to be clarifying.

Since the battle for salvation seems to take place more between the ears than it does in geographical territory, it may be more effective to think in terms of finding the particular spiritual weapons suitable for pulling down particular mental strongholds.

Seen in this light, the Internet becomes an enormous mission field with most of the strongholds already categorized and labeled as to what people are looking for, as well as the fears with which they are struggling. Surfing the net is not so different than wandering around Athens must have been for Paul. Perhaps enough said for now.

I hope no one takes this as an invitation to erect website cathedrals. I was rather thinking more about going out into fiber optics and broadbands, "...to compel them to come in...."

Tony, I have yet to answer Lisa's latest response. But I probably will do so in time for Monday morning. Meanwhile, I can't think of a better response than your time with Lisa and her husband Kurtis this morning. I am very grateful, and you will all certainly be in our prayers.

Please give Lisa a hug for us, and whatever Kurtis might be able to receive as well.

I look forward to our continued pursuit of this great mission field. While the Inter-"net has been cast in front of the evangelists," I'm not so sure it is wisdom for evangelists to "cast their net in front of the birds." I'm still wrestling with the best approach for reaching this "unsaved people group."

Yours in Christ, and with great appreciation,

· Jay

On Saturday, January 10, 2004, Tony wrote:

Jay,

Felicity and I had a wonderful 90 minutes this morning at Starbucks with Lisa and Kurtis. They are joining us tomorrow morning with one of our couples who host a website ministry exploring sexuality and spirituality from a Christian perspective. I think, as this was the nature of the chat room that Lisa was in, it will be fascinating to see what transpires. This couple has been praying for ways to penetrate the "spiritual" scene here in Austin. They view this as a start.

Will let you know how everything goes.

In Christ,

Tony

On Saturday, January 10, 2004, Jay wrote:

Dear Tony,

Thanks so much for the good report!!!
I would really appreciate that, and I'll keep you posted from this end as well.

Again, thank you so much for your faithfulness. Please express my gratefulness to Felicity as well.

Yours in Christ,

Jay

On Sunday, January 11, 2004, Jay responded to Lisa's e-mail of two days earlier::

Lisa wrote: *Joy, joy, joy!!! I'm feeling so joyful about all that we have shared! Yes, isn't this fun? It's even better than Christmas day!...*

Dear Lisa,

I think ***Surprised by Joy*** is the title of one of C.S. Lewis's books.

I am blown away that you have made connection so easily with the Dales. I certainly share your joy, and I pray that your time together has been fruitful, and happily await the next chapter.

...I love the heading here—"getting comfortable." It's a place where I can rest. Thank you!!

Before leaving, Jesus said: "Let not your heart be troubled: ye believe in God, believe also in me. In my Father's house are many mansions: if it were not so, I would have told you. I go to prepare a place for you. And if I go and prepare a place for you, I will come again, and receive you unto myself; that where I am, there ye may be also."[1] Later, The writer of Hebrews said: "… Christ is faithful as a son over God's house. And we are his house, if we hold on to our courage and the hope of which we boast."[2]

This is just to say that I don't believe that Jesus was talking about "pie in the sky by and by," but rather a safe place in the Spirit that he would make for us in his house, in relationship to one another, a place of rest.

Well, I just called Tony Dale (I write these emails over a period of hours during the day) —without having a clue of what I was going to say or what would transpire. I was nervous—it's one thing talking with someone over e-mail—quite different on the phone—and even more so in person. Plus, I don't know how to relate to "Christians" and their lingo. It feels very foreign to me to hear and respond to this language.

My mind gets in the way. I'm not sure how I feel or think about a lot of things around Christianity—and I don't even know many of the questions yet. It was somewhat startling then when Tony asked how Kurtis felt about all of this—I stumbled around and eventually got to, "He seems okay with me exploring but not sure he wants to participate." Then Tony asked if Kurtis and I could come to dinner Saturday night—or coffee at Starbucks if dinner seemed too much. I stumbled around—I don't know how Kurtis would feel (how do I feel?—nervous)—but said I would ask him and get back to Tony. But at least I'll go meet with them—probably for coffee.

And so, I just talked with Kurtis—AND HE AGREED TO GO TO COFFEE! (For me, he says—I'll take what I can get!) So I called Tony back, and we're meeting tomorrow at 10 AM. Wow!

So much swirling around now. I really want to respond more to your email, but have some things I need to do until I leave, so will have to wait. Don't see that I'll get back to you until Monday—should have a lot to tell you then! Take care and thank you again so much.

I understand, and I look forward to hearing how your weekend went when you get the chance to share.

Yours in Christ,
Jay

---

[1]John 14: 1–3.   [2]Hebrews 3:6 (NIV).

On Monday, January 12, 2004, Lisa wrote:

Dear Jay,

So many wonderful things are happening here it's hard to grasp it all. Let me first say that we had a WONDERFUL connection with Tony and Felicity. I think Kurtis is excited, too, in his guarded way. I think, like all of us, he has such fear—and at the same time such hope. I'm just so grateful that he has walked this far and seems willing (and somewhat intrigued) to continue. Our heart connection already seems stronger.

We met with Tony and Felicity Saturday morning and again on Sunday morning with Paul and Lori, a couple who is a part of their church circuit. They have constructed a website, TheMarriageBed.com, about sex and intimacy with more of a Christian influence. I haven't had time to log onto it yet, but will. Isn't that an amazing connection? Both experiences were very comfortable for me. It was really about just getting to know one another in the presence of great love and acceptance.

Just being around these people gives me great hope and fills me with inspiration. The depth of love and the spirit of service—for two strangers—really moves me on a deep level. Tony is a Godsend in the way that he suggests continued meetings. It takes the pressure off me—so I don't seem to be trying to "direct" Kurtis's spiritual life. It allows me the space to just be able to share my experience, but in the context of a group which is there to support the exploration of our spirituality. And in a mature, real, non-threatening, and very loving way.

*This has been pure heaven to me! We are meeting with Paul and Lori on Saturday night (Tony and Felicity are busy this weekend), and I look forward to that. We got Tony and Felicity's book, **Simply Church**,[3] and I read it last night. Fascinating! Such a simple yet powerful concept. I like this idea of Home Church. I'm already ready to give these books to my friends and invite them to come. There's a part of me that says to wait—to let Kurtis read the book and perhaps he will be inspired to talk to the guys in the couples we're friends with about doing this. That would be my desire. It seems that the women are always talking about spiritual matters, while the men talk about flying and engines and such. Wouldn't it be wonderful to have us all talking together about our spiritual lives? Then I just talked to Kurtis, and he said that he had a short conversation with one of his friends,*

---

[3]The book Lisa is refering to is **Simply Church**, by Tony and Felicity Dale, published by Karis Publishing, Inc., in 2002.

where he told him about our weekend—so he's talking about it! I'm so amazed at how our lives unfold!

I talked to my friend and co-worker, Carol, this morning about my experiences. She is from a fundamental Baptist background and very leery about Christianity. But we talked quite a while, and I could see her heart opening. She is interested in the Home Church concept – our conversation got cut off, but she would probably at least like to read the **Simply Church** *book. I'll have to get a supply.*

It feels really good to be able to talk about all of this with my friends. I talked some with some of my girlfriends Saturday night at a get-together. Everyone is very loving and supportive—and I think open to further exploration.

The only scripture that I remember Tony quoting on Sunday morning was something like "all things are made new in the Lord." He suggested that Kurtis and I ask the Lord to make our sexual re-lationship new. I did that in the wee hours of the night on my own (I've been waking up a lot in the night time with all of this on my mind)—I hope to do so with Kurtis soon.

I'm wanting to return to some of the things we were talking about, but I need to get some work done for now! Look forward to hearing from you—as always.

Lisa

On Monday, January 12, 2004, Jay wrote:

Dear Lisa,

I couldn't be happier to hear your wonderful report of your weekend, and the various meaningful connections that you have made in such a short time. I have seen and experienced miracles, but some of the most profound, meaningful, and healing have been miracles of relationship. It sounds to me like you have run headlong into a whole garden full.

I am a little behind on my paper work, and the urgency of cleaning up for the holidays—putting things in all kinds of nooks and crannies—has found me out. Now I am on a search, trying to find where I have put everything. Interesting things happen when you go on this kind of a hunt, however; all kinds of long-lost things show up. This afternoon, I came across a tape that I have been looking for for some time. It is the tape where I was first introduced to the existence of "Storge" love. It is by a grand-mother from New Zealand. If you would be interested, I would be happy to make and send you a copy.[4] I have a feeling about it. I think you, and even Tony and Felicity, and perhaps even Paul and Lori would get a lot from it. I have met very few Christians who have ever heard of "storganos" or "storge." Yet it is the most foundational love.

Have to run now.
God Bless you!
Yours in Christ,

Jay

On Tuesday, January 13, 2004, Lisa wrote:

Dear Jay,

Yes, I'm feeling there's some sort of miraculous things going on here, too. It's almost too hard to believe—and then I remember to go into my heart and just let it be.

I'm very interested in any tapes that you think of along the way. I just told Kurtis today that I've been wanting to give him your tapes but have been getting so much out of listening to them over and over again that it's been hard to give them up. He suggested that we make copies of them (duh!—I forget that we have a machine now that does that—if I can figure out how to do it). So... please send them on and I'll be better about sharing.

I know what you mean about needing to catch up on paperwork—me too. So I think I'll make this short and sweet. Please do keep me in mind as you clean out, though. I have enjoyed all that you've shared so far and am open for much more.

With gratitude—
Lisa

On Wednesday, January 14, 2004, Jay responded:

Lisa wrote: *Yes, I'm feeling there's some sort of miraculous things going on here, too. It's almost too hard to believe—and then I remember to go into my heart and just let it be.*

Dear Lisa,

---

[4]For information as to where and how to obtain this tape, go to www.notleftbehind.net.

"Marinating," that's what it feels like to me.

I'm very interested in any tapes that you think of along the way....

Yesterday was my weekly Charlotte day. I took the Denise Jordan tape on Storge with me. Carleen lets me take her car on Tuesdays. It's a little nicer than my old Toyota. Anyway, she just left for school, and I forgot to take the tape out of her car. So please forgive my forgetfulness. I'll try to make the copy and send it off to you tomorrow.

...I just told Kurtis today that I've been wanting to give him your tapes but have been getting so much out of listening to them over and over again that it's been hard to give them up....

I'm encouraged that you were blessed by them.

...He suggested that we make copies of them (duh!—I forget that we have a machine now that does that—if I can figure out how to do it). So... please send them on and I'll be better about sharing.

Will do. I don't know if Tony and Felicity are familiar with Denise Jordan, so you might want to share her tape with them if I can just remember to get it off to you.

I know what you mean about needing to catch up on paperwork—me too. So I think I'll make this short and sweet. Please do keep me in mind as you clean out, though. I have enjoyed all that you've shared so far and am open for much more.

I have a feeling that there is much more coming! [:-)]
I'm still playing catch-up today, so I have to run for now.
Before I go, I think I need to tell you that you make me feel very comfortable.

Yours in Christ,
Jay

On Wednesday, January 14, 2004, Lisa wrote:

Dear Jay,

It touches me that you feel comfortable with me and that you take the time to talk with me. I'm glad that there is a mutual sense of satisfaction—it feels very promising to me. It occurs to me that we have a lot to learn from each other. There are a lot of people out there like me—who are "this close" to accepting Jesus—but are put off by their concepts of what Christians are and the limiting beliefs that they appear to embrace. There's a lot of bridging that needs to be done. My understanding of what Jesus says is that he's here to free us from our bondage—not add to it. So when "non-Christians" are concerned about whether they will be accepted because maybe they have different views, different experiences, different beliefs—I would say that absolutely they are accepted. Jesus doesn't limit who you are—he ADDS to who you are.

There's a whole host of ways to go about BEING in the world and a lot has been written that helps conceptualize what Jesus was saying. The Christ spirit within us is our guide to truth. None of these experiences, ways of being, or understandings of concepts needs to be in conflict with our faith in Jesus. That faith—who we choose to worship—is a totally separate thing. So with this faith we are free to experience life in whatever way we're guided to and in ways that give us pleasure. If we're truly guided by our spirit, we are free.

I wanted to share something with you "on the horizontal." I have a massage client who has been a wonderful example of Christianity over the last 3 years or so. He is probably around 40, married with 4 adorable kids. Just a loving, sharing, REAL person. He worked for a local company at a higher management level. He lost his job a couple of years ago and broke his back in a skiing accident right after that (no paralysis—thank God—but a slow recovery process). Through it all, he has kept and shared his faith. I talked with him last night—told him about my recent experiences—and thanked him for his influences.

We talked about how special we were to one another. I don't know who he is to me—but I know he was given to me. It is very precious.

No worries about your forgetfulness—it's endearing. And I will figure out how to do the tapes—or die trying!—and share them with Tony and others.

I'm off to bookkeeping land. Did I ever tell you that my other job is as the bookkeeper—amongst other things—at a non-profit mediation center. Wonderful place to work—I'm so blessed. It's where I engage my brain. Massage is where I pour out love—that kind of love that you talked about in your first email. Very satisfying.

Talk to you soon!

You make me very comfortable, too.

Lisa

Lisa wrote: *It touches me that you feel comfortable with me and that you take the time to talk with me....*

...If we're truly guided by our spirit, we are free.

Dear Lisa,

Thank you so much for your note of encouragement. Of course you are so right about what you have written here. However, this paragraph is going to take some time for me to answer in any way that might be at all satisfying to all of us, you, me, and the Lord, so I will have to wait for another time. Very full plate today. Carleen's birthday, and I have to run into town; around here that's at least 1/2 hour, no matter which direction.

I wanted to share something with you "on the horizontal." I have a massage client who has been a wonderful example of Christianity over the last three years or so. He is probably around 40, married with 4 adorable kids. Just a loving, sharing, REAL person. He worked for a local company at a higher management level. He lost his job a couple of years ago and broke his back in a skiing accident right after that (no paralysis—thank God—but a slow recovery process). Through it all, he has kept and shared his faith. I talked with him last night—told him about my recent experiences—and thanked him for his influences.

We talked about how special we were to one another. I don't know who he is to me—but I know he was given to me. It is very precious.

That is very encouraging to hear, and I hope that he can embrace the truth of it as you have.

On several occasions I have gone beyond foot-washing and seen really miraculous results. It is probably a little less scandalous for a woman to do this with a man's feet than it is for a man to do this with a woman's feet. I believe—in fact I know—that both are possible, but you better know who you are to each other, and take care in the latter case, not to usurp the place of a spouse or a romantic partner. In every case what I have experienced is the breakdown of barriers to intimacy. Peter had objected, saying "not my feet." But Jesus responded by saying, "Unless I wash your feet, you can't be one of mine." From experience, I am inclined to paraphrase Peter's after-the-fact response, "Take me: I'm yours."

I have a very precious spiritual brother. After mentioning the prompting to "do" his feet a couple of times, the day finally came when I could follow through without his being embarrassed. I first washed and then oiled his feet. What I had not known was that he had "sugar problems," and his feet were badly swollen, with areas of dead skin and numbness. When I started to take off his sock, he began to weep; by the time I got to the oil, he said to me, through something close to sobbing, "The only people I ever tried to hate were white people." He is a black man in the flesh, but something else altogether in the Spirit. The swelling went away, and the feeling came back. Talk about "male bonding." I envy you your calling. It is one that has great power for destroying strongholds.[5] I have also seen it reduce very hard and wounded women to tears of release.

No worries about your forgetfulness—it's endearing....

Thanks, that's a good sign. "Love covers a multitude of sins."

...And I will figure out how to do the tapes—or die trying!—and share them with Tony and others.

I sent the two tapes that I sent you to Tony, so he should have them by now.

I'm off to bookkeeping land. Did I ever tell you that my other job is as the bookkeeper—amongst other things—~~at~~ a non-profit mediation center....

Did I ever tell you that Carleen has been after me for years to see about getting work in the area of mediation? WOW! Most of the firms so engaged require law degrees. I tend to mediate from another paradigm and have done a lot of it, but for love, not money.

...Wonderful place to work—I'm so blessed....

Again I am envious. By the way do you know the difference between envy and jealousy?

...It's where I engage my brain. Massage is where I pour out love—that kind of love that you talked about in your first email. Very satisfying.

Storge is wonderful, no matter which end you are on.

You make me very comfortable, too.

---

[5] 2 Corinthians 10:3–5.

Thank you, I could feel it.

Yours in Christ,
Jay

Dear Jay,

Happy Birthday to Carleen! I hope you have a very special time together.

I'm very interested to hear what you have to say about the first paragraph I wrote. I really appreciate your thoughtfulness in replying—I know it will be well worth the wait. (No pressure here, huh?) Please know that what I appreciate about your sharing is your vulnerability in saying things like, "I don't have a full understanding of this yet." I don't expect anyone to have all the answers. And anyone who doesn't have ongoing shifts in their perceptions and convictions is not, I believe, "growing in the spirit." So... just wanted you to know how much I appreciate what you share, your willingness to be vulnerable and "transparent," as well as your knowledge and experience, and I don't expect perfection. (I would be leery if you were.)

And I can't wait to hear what you have to say!

I appreciate the thought about not "usurping the place of a spouse or a romantic partner." I'm very much aware of the danger here and will heed your advice. It is certainly not my intention, and I'm certain in this case with my massage client that it was not his intention, either. Even with both of our vulnerabilities, it is clear that what we have is a spiritual connection, and we're both very respectful of our boundaries.

But I will watch for that and seek my inner guidance on intimate relationships—especially with men. (Truthfully, there are very few men in my life that I'm intimate with—for this very reason. We're all so guarded! And, sadly, perhaps necessarily so.) I realize I have a lot to learn about your concept of "horizontal" (and perhaps used the term too loosely in this context) and continue to be interested in hearing more about it.

It's so precious hearing about your spiritual relationships. Thanks for sharing.

I'm sure you're a wonderful mediator. It's a very rewarding thing to do—I especially like working with divorced couples who have children. It's so important for them to work out some civil way of communicating and being with each other so that they don't tear the kids up. I do some volunteer mediating here at the center—all of the mediators are volunteers here, about 100 of them. Such a wonderful, giving group of people. We also train mediators—we do a 40-hour training about five times a year. Sort of our fundraiser. I help with training, too. Think in some ways I'm a better trainer than mediator—putting into practice is much harder—especially when there are aggressive attorneys in the room! Anyway, good stuff.

I would like to hear the difference between envy and jealousy.

All for now. Have fun!

Lisa

On Thursday, January 15, 2004, Jay responded to Lisa:

Lisa wrote: *Happy Birthday to Carleen! I hope you have a very special time together.*

Dear Lisa,

Thank you. I don't know about "special," but it was a very full afternoon and evening, visiting with several couples that we are close to in Christ. We have a wonderful group of people that we are close to and meet with. Actually it's more descriptive to say that we are in life together. One of the couples has two daughters whom they have been more than willing to share with us as spiritual daughters, Meghan, 19, and Kendra, 17. Meghan will be here tonight for her weekly geometry session. The girls have been home schooled, and Meghan is having to finish up with geometry in order to graduate, which otherwise she would have done last year. We only met this family a year ago last August, but it has been a very wonderful relationship to date. Others have since come close as well, some of whom we have known much longer.

I'm very interested to hear what you have to say about the first paragraph I wrote. I really appreciate your thoughtfulness in replying—I know it will be well worth the wait. (No pressure here, huh?)…

Not much! [:-)]

…Please know that what I appreciate about your sharing is your vulnerability in saying things like, "I don't have a full understanding of this yet." I don't expect anyone to have all the answers. And anyone who doesn't have ongoing shifts in their perceptions and convictions is not, I believe, "growing in the spirit." So… just wanted you to know how much I appreciate what you share, your willingness to be vulner-

able and "transparent," as well as your knowledge and experience, and I don't expect perfection. (I would be leery if you were.)

Not much chance of your becoming "leery."

And I can't wait to hear what you have to say!

I have to run out of here this morning for a dentist appointment, but let's see what I might be able to do before leaving:

> Here, Jay responds to Lisa's first paragraph from the previous day's e-mail:

It touches me that you feel comfortable with me and that you take the time to talk with me. I'm glad that there is a mutual sense of satisfaction—it feels very promising to me....

Yes, I also have a very strong sense of connection.

...It occurs to me that we have a lot to learn from each other....

I have to continually check my temptation to run on ahead, where thinking of the possibilities of working together are concerned, and now you have made it even more difficult for me to go slow, because what you talk about below, is exactly in the arena of my own hopes on the subject. This is just to say that, so far, "all systems are 'go.'"

...There are a lot of people out there like me—who are "this close" to accepting Jesus—but are put off by their concepts of what Christians are and the limiting beliefs that they appear to embrace....

Yes, and there are probably just as many who have accepted Him but who have been so beaten up in the "church" that they have thrown out the baby with the bathwater. They are very real parts of the body of Christ, but they are strewn all over the place by the "manhandling" that they have experienced in "church." I have felt for a long time that there are probably more true believers who have quit "going to church" than there are true believers who are still "going to church."

It has been in my heart for many years, to go out and find them, to somehow have a part in healing their wounds and inviting them once more into "Christmas" as I have come to experience it.

...There's a lot of bridging that needs to be done....

The cost of this "bridging" is very high. If it is in your heart to have a part in that, we will have to count the cost together. If that seems good for you, I am very open to having that dialogue.

...My understanding of what Jesus says is that he's here to free us from our bondage—not add to it....

That is my understanding as well. Declaring it is a very high calling, because it requires a life lived in reality, rather than a lot of "Christian information."

...So when "non-Christians" are concerned about whether they will be accepted because maybe they have different views, different experiences, different beliefs—I would say that absolutely they are accepted....

I would say you are right!

...Jesus doesn't limit who you are—he ADDS to who you are.

"The thief cometh not, but for to steal, and to kill, and to destroy: I am come that they might have life, and that they might have it more abundantly."[6]

There's a whole host of ways to go about BEING in the world and a lot has been written that helps conceptualize what Jesus was saying. The Christ spirit within us is our guide to truth. None of these experiences, ways of being, or understandings of concepts needs to be in conflict with our faith in Jesus....

There may be a conflict with some of them: "For the Jews require a sign, and the Greeks seek after wisdom: But we preach Christ crucified, unto the Jews a stumbling block, and unto the Greeks foolishness;"[7]

...That faith—whom we choose to worship—is a totally separate thing. So with this faith we are free to experience life in whatever way we're guided to and in ways that give us pleasure. If we're truly guided by our spirit we are free.

A girl could get stoned for talking like that around religious people—I know Paul did. If this is in your heart, I am more than ready to continue this particular discussion, not to say that I have no interest in the rest that we might learn from one another. I know that this is a very summary response to what you have written here, but, as I already said, I am reluctant to run ahead, so let's

---

[6]John 10:10. [7]1 Corinthians 1:22–23.

just talk it through together in a conversational way, if that seems good to you.

Here, Jay returns to Lisa's later email of yesterday:

I appreciate the thought about not "usurping the place of a spouse or a romantic partner." I'm very much aware of the danger here and will heed your advice....

Actually, it hadn't been in my heart to give you any advice. I was just sharing a little of my own concern for how my body language might be read.

... It is certainly not my intention, and I'm certain in this case with my massage client that it was not his intention, either. Even with both of our vulnerabilities, it is clear that what we have is a spiritual connection, and we're both very respectful of our boundaries.

It was clear to me from what you had written that there was a wonderful connection between the two of you, and what you said gave me no bad vibes concerning the possible transgression of any "boundaries." I'm reminded of something that my spiritual daughter (whom I have already written to you about, in the chapter I sent.) ...something that she said one day, kind of as a sudden and wonderful insight, "You know, where intimacy is concerned, there are no limits, but there are rules." Now that I write it, I think I mentioned it in the Horizontal tape. She said it, not so much to express restriction resulting from the rules, but to express her delight in the limitless possibilities of intimacy that are ours in Christ.

But I will watch for that and seek my inner guidance on intimate relationships—especially with men....

I can't argue with that, I just wanted you to know that what I shared was not out of concern for you so much as to share a point of common experience where physical contact is concerned.

...(Truthfully, there are very few men in my life that I'm intimate with—for this very reason. We're all so guarded! And, sadly, perhaps necessarily so.)...

I hear this loud and clear, This is the tragedy of wasted lives. Lives that are cut off from intimacy, because they haven't gotten the point where gender is concerned. As long as we are still hung up on the plumbing, we can't get very close to more than one person, and even the closeness to that one person is less than it could be if only we could get the point. Both men and women have problems here, but each from their own point of need, with men having a really difficult time with intimacy, beyond the graphics.

...I realize I have a lot to learn about your concept of "horizontal" (and perhaps used the term too loosely in this context) and continue to be interested in hearing more about it.

My impression was rather that you were "right on" in your understanding of what I have been talking about, and that you had picked a good example from your own life and relationships. I didn't feel that you had used anything I might have shared "too loosely."

It's so precious hearing about your spiritual relationships. Thanks for sharing.

I'm glad you enjoy my sharing. That's just the way love is!

I'm sure you're a wonderful mediator....

For sure, we are not always successful, but every now and then we have the joy of seeing relationships restored. One of the downsides that we have experienced over the years is that, after couples that we have been close to spill their guts concerning their marital problems, once they get cleaned up with each other, they don't want to be around us anymore, because they just can't imagine that we are not carrying their garbage. I think this is one of the reasons people go to professional strangers, unload, and pay them for their services. This to me is very sad, because, as I understand it, Jesus has already picked up the tab, so that we can build one another up in love.

We've been working on a relational disaster in Germany for many years now. The revelation in the patent office in 1987 came as a result of this struggle. This past year, it has taken a very interesting turn. The estranged husband and father has, more or less, found himself in a spiritual relationship with the local pastor's wife. He is my former boss and is not yet a believer (a really tough case!). For the past six months, the emails between us going in both directions have copied the pastor's wife. About two months ago he told me on the phone that she and her husband, the pastor, want to come over for a visit. I have come to think of this as my "foreign missions project." Day before yesterday, I received my first email from the pastor's wife.

What I have discovered is that God is outrageous in the lengths to which He will go to accomplish His purposes. There have been so many times when what I thought was a disastrous human failure turned out to be a necessary prelude to an otherwise unimaginable Divine success. So, anyway, I'm still eagerly watching the developments on the eastern front.

...It's a very rewarding thing to do—I especially like working with divorced couples who have children. It's so important for them to work out some civil way of communicating and being with each other so that they don't tear the kids up. I do some volunteer mediating here at the center—all of the mediators are volunteers here, about 100 of them. Such a wonderful, giving group of people. We also train mediators—we do a 40-hour training about five times a year. Sort of our fundraiser. I help with training, too. Think in some ways I'm a better trainer than mediator—putting into practice is much harder—especially when there are aggressive attorneys in the room!...

Yes, the attorneys have always been a problem: "And he said, Woe unto you also, ye lawyers! for ye lade men with burdens grievous to be borne, and ye yourselves touch not the burdens with one of your fingers."[8]

...Anyway, good stuff.

I would like to hear the difference between envy and jealousy.

"Envy" has to do with something or someone who belongs to someone else. "Jealousy" has to do with something or someone who belongs to you. "For thou shalt worship no other god: for the LORD, whose name is Jealous, is a jealous God:"[9] "I charge you, O daughters of Jerusalem, that ye stir not up, nor awake my love, until he please. Who is this that cometh up from the wilderness, leaning upon her beloved? I raised thee up under the apple tree: there thy mother brought thee forth: there she brought thee forth that bare thee. Set me as a seal upon thine heart, as a seal upon thine arm: for love is strong as death; jealousy is cruel as the grave: the coals thereof are coals of fire, which hath a most vehement flame. Many waters cannot quench love, neither can the floods drown it: if a man would give all the substance of his house for love, it would utterly be contemned."[10]

Well, time to head out of here.

Yours in Christ,

---

[8]Luke 11:46. [9]Exodus 34:14.

[10]Song of Songs 8:4–7.

Jay

P.S. The tape copy is made, and I hope to mail it off to you when I go into town.

CHAPTER 7

COUNTING THE COST

On Thursday, January 15, 2004, Lisa wrote:

Dear Jay,

Wow! This is so exciting! I can't get over how the spirit is taking over here—it just blows me away.

Just an aside—I went to the dentist this morning, too, and have lunch with my girlfriends in a bit. I wanted to get something off to you, so this will be much shorter than I want. I do want to let you know that I'm going to be talking with my girlfriends about meeting in my home the weekend of the 24th for "church"—fellowship— whatever you want to call it. I'm excited to just talk about where we are spiritually—especially in regards to our understanding of Jesus and what he means to us. Tony and Felicity—and I hope Paul and Lori—will come to guide us. I'm so excited! I hope my friends will be led to join us.

I absolutely want to continue our conversation about how this "bridging" might work. It's very apparent to me that this is part of the reason that the spirit has put us together. I have absolutely no idea how I might be of help, but the desire is there and there's a tremendous amount of excitement in my heart when I think about it. So—let's talk!

Really have to go now so will send this off. Just want you to know that I'm feeling completely consumed by this spirit—it's practically all I think about—and I feel this aliveness that I've never felt before. I'm totally blown away. Marinating is such a good description—com- bined with combusting!

Talk soon,

Lisa

On Friday, January 16, 2004, Jay responded:

Lisa wrote: *Wow! This is so exciting! I can't get over how the spirit is taking over here—it just blows me away.*

Dear Lisa,

I think I heard about that once before:[1]

Just an aside—I went to the dentist this morning, too, and have lunch with my girlfriends in a bit....

Nice. I hope your dentist is as good as mine!

...I wanted to get something off to you, so this will be much shorter than I want....

I know the problem. I'm still digging out myself.

...I do want to let you know that I'm going to be talking with my girlfriends about meeting in my home the weekend of the 24th for "church"—fellowship—whatever you want to call it....

I will be praying with you for their graced response, and that you will have a really fruitful time together.

...I'm excited to just talk about where we are spiritually—especially in regards to our understanding of Jesus and what he means to us....

Make sure your seat/grace belt is fastened. "Head-ons" can be fatal.

...Tony and Felicity—and I hope Paul and Lori—will come to guide us. I'm so excited! I hope my friends will be led to join us.

Tony and Felicity have already agreed to come??? Wow! This is wonderful news. I rest in the knowledge that you are in good hands.

I absolutely want to continue our conversation about how this "bridging" might work. It's very apparent to me that this is part of the reason that the spirit has put us together....

Wow again!!

I think our conversation needs to begin where Jesus began His in Luke, Chapter 14.

It's best to count the cost before we get started. I have just been through something like this. I tried to take someone where

---
[1]Acts 2:1.

they were not yet equipped to go. The pain was almost terminal. The one I tried to take along is the one who told me about David Deida. She herself had not read or listened to anything he had written or said, but the title of one of David's CDs reminded her of me, "On Sacred Intimacy." That's how I got to the list to see what he was talking about. That's how I met you. She is still healing from the terrible beating that she went through at the hands of the "Christians" in her life. It was worse than anything I had ever seen before, and I have been in some terrible fire fights.

You have a big advantage over her, because you are older, and because the culture of who you are was not formed in a Baptist Church, and in the context of Baptist relatives, and even a Baptist employer. Someone once said, "You can always tell a Baptist, but you can't tell him much." Very, very tough turf. Not impregnable, but very tough. In the present case, we are talking about going after those who have already been offended or have dropped out. That is also very difficult. It is a different problem, but still very difficult. Proverbs 18:19 says: "A brother offended is harder to be won than a strong city: and their contentions are like the bars of a castle."

A better translation of this last part would be "...and arguing only puts bars in their windows/openings." Great care needs to be taken not to only alienate them further from Christ. What happens is that people are offended by or in "church," and they "throw the baby, Christ, out with the bath water, Christian faith and practice." Of course, the Bible is rejected as well. This means that we have to find out where people are, and go to them speaking their language and not our own. In your case, I was led to be quite up front, and, as you said in your first response, you almost rejected me out of hand, except that you heard a certain sound, somewhere behind your offendedness.

The clearest path to understanding the problem that I have yet discovered is the "sexual parable." It is very powerful—and very deep in the truth that is hidden/revealed there.

I am getting a little spacey in my old age, so I am prompted to say something here before I forget it. Women are wooed by love. Men are wooed by honor.

...I have absolutely no idea how I might be of help, but the desire is there and there's a tremendous amount of excitement in my heart when I think about it. So—let's talk!

I'm talking. In my experience, all of the "hows" will surface in our conversation, and even in the outworking of this that is the desire of your heart. More often than not, I discover the "how" after I have been led to say or do the right thing in spite of myself. God has a way of being sovereign like that.

Really have to go now so will send this off. Just want you to know that I'm feeling completely consumed by this spirit—it's practically all I think about—and I feel this aliveness that I've never felt before. I'm totally blown away. Marinating is such a good description—combined with combusting!

There is so much Bible that is confirmed in this expression of the way you are feeling. I pray that you will be able to sustain the Spirit's fire.

Yours in Christ,

Jay

P.S. I mailed the Storge tape to you yesterday. You should get it today or tomorrow. I look forward to your comments.

On Friday, January 16, 2004, Lisa wrote:

Dear Jay,

I've been listening to your tape, "Unoffendable Love," and in light of that and what you shared today, I feel compelled to talk a little about some of my history and understandings.

I was thinking of this offendable love and, having just had a conversation with my friend, Carol, yesterday—the one who was raised fundamentalist Baptist and has rejected the baby and the bathwater—was thinking how grateful I was to not have that to contend with. And also I was struck, listening to her, at how defended she was about love—especially receiving it. She even stated at one point that she could see how I might be fulfilled by the love part—given my history of not receiving it—but that she felt that her life was one where she was to give service; she didn't need the love. My heart just cries for her. She will not receive love because of her offendedness.

Her biggest stumbling block to Christianity is the notion that Jesus is the only way and words like "salvation" are big buzzwords to her. This is huge for a lot of people—isn't there another way to get to God? The exclusivity offends them. I happen to believe that Jesus was the turning point for humanity—that his "gift," in addition to the love that you're able to describe so well, is this Christ deposit in us that guides us in knowing God. I realize that some of my understanding and acceptance of Jesus comes from what I've heard from my Dad over the years and what I've read from the Urantia book, so it's difficult to relate to what a "typical" Christian has been exposed to. My belief and understanding is that this deposit was given to all people—we are becoming "spiritualized" whether we choose to believe in God or Jesus—let's say the capacity to believe and understand is becoming greater whether we're conscious of it or not. But my conviction is that we have to choose to do God's will—in essence be willing to follow him—in order to fully realize not only his spiritual gifts during our time here on earth, but also to continue beyond this world. I also happen to believe that Jesus is "Lord" over people on this planet, that his will is aligned with God's, and that it was set up that he is the "go-between" between us and God. I believe that Jesus didn't come here to set up a religion about himself, but to help us understand the truth about God and his desires and love for us so that we would be more willing to align ourselves with him and reap the benefits. And a whole lot of other stuff, but this is the crux of my beliefs to date. And there's a whole lot that I don't understand and probably will never completely understand, but you have to start somewhere. So is Jesus the only way? I don't know. He certainly points the way distinctly to me, and I feel led to follow his example and learn about this incredible love that he demonstrated. It appears to me, from my limited knowledge, that his is the best way. But I honestly don't know how to answer that question. I think every person has to come to their own conviction. Mine was a strange, cosmic, surreal kind of way to some—but it worked for me. The experience I had with the shamanic healer was a strange, cosmic, surreal kind of way to some—but it worked for me—and it helped to get me to this point where I'm talking with you.

I think one of the differences between me and Carol, and maybe a lot of people, is my current willingness to be led by—and to put a great deal of trust in—this spirit I've come to know as way bigger than me. To really let go of my brain and trust my heart. I obviously don't always do it but am learning to go there more. How does one get from a place of non-trust to trust? From being offended to non-offended? Grace, desire, surrender, understanding? It's a great mystery to me.

My father, who is and has been such a fervent believer in the Urantia book, is one of the most emotionally unavailable men I've ever known. He seems to be afraid of intimacy. I never could reconcile what I saw in him and what I read in the Urantia book. Something was seriously wrong here—where was the love? I listened to him talk about the Urantia book because it was interesting and because it was one of the only areas where we could connect. He was fanatical about the book—frustrated that nobody else seemed to want to know the "truth" as he had come to know it thru the book. I watched him try to reconcile within himself this intense desire to infuse this knowledge and his belief that when we're ready to read the book, we'll be led to read it. I'm grateful for what he did talk to me about, though.

It wasn't until I had this recent experience on my own and was able to hear and better understand this tremendous love that I could accept this faith in Jesus and want to live there. Certainly the foundation was set—the missing ingredient was love.

I grew up in an environment that had a big deficit of love. My mother and father divorced when I was three. My mother drank and was depressed, and my dad appeared uninterested and unavailable. We (I had an older brother and sister) saw him some for a few years, but I always felt distanced from him. Mom was remarried when I was 8 to an explosive man—very angry and in-your-face. We walked on eggshells. I spent as much time as possible away from the house, which seemed to be encouraged—when I was home we were not to be seen. Mom had two more children, who are 10 and 13 years younger than me, and was preoccupied with them and trying to hold this family together. I ended up doing drugs, drinking, having sex. Numbing myself and looking for love.

My stepfather eventually left my mom, my older sister died of colon cancer nine years ago, my older brother drinks and fights depression, and my two younger siblings are struggling. There's more love there now—it's a process. Just very wounded people.

When I was 35, I was talking with my stepmother about why my dad didn't seem to like me. It was always puzzling to me—I always had felt rejected by him and felt like he was angry with me. My dad called me that week and asked me to schedule an appointment with my therapist (it's when Kurtis and I were in Imago therapy). He told me in that session that the reason that I had felt those things from him was because he didn't think he was my father. (We did a DNA test: he's not my father.) He didn't mean to act that way, but he was just so angry about it—still, after all those years he was consumed with bitterness towards my mother that got projected on me. It all made so much more sense to me then! I was stunned, yet not too surprised, and relieved beyond words.

We ended up agreeing to continue in our relationship as father and daughter—in our own limited ways. It was definitely somewhat *of a turning point for me—I could start to heal. I started feeling a sort of "redemptive love." Here was a man who was clearly suffering from his own version of hell, and I had an opportunity to forgive him and love him regardless of his ability to love me. He had one request of me as we were leaving that session—not to tell him that I loved him in front of my stepmother. Because then he felt obligated to tell me that he loved me. It breaks my heart that he is not able to receive love. He's so offended.*

I tell you all of this to let you know that I know a lot about offendedness. It comes in all forms. I've also had some experience with this redemptive love for which I have such gratitude! My marriage would not still be going and as strong as it is—even with its imperfections—if it weren't for this redemptive love and for my lessons in "not having expectations." My interest in helping others does not come from a place of needing to be right or to know the answers or to tell them how to live. It really comes from wanting to end the pain and to help us all grow in love. And I'm convinced that the only way to do that is thru this redemptive kind of love that only comes from God.

I'm going to sit with all of this and all that you have written—I keep it all in a notebook—and see what comes up for me. I'd like to hear more about what experiences you've had doing this work reaching out to people. Tell me what happened to your spiritual daughter. I could learn from your experiences.

In the meanwhile, my lunches with my girlfriends (had another one today) have been quite fruitful in that, when I talk about where I am spiritually and my desire to meet and talk with others about our spirituality and lives, they all seem to want to go there. I'm planning on going tomorrow night to Paul and Lori's—and one of our couple friends might go, too.

I set up "church" at my house for 6 p.m. on the 25th and am inviting people to come. So, we'll see. It feels weird but, so far, within my comfort zone (which is definitely getting stretched).

I'm off work on Monday so you probably won't hear from me until Tuesday.

Time to marinate and pray for guidance. This is really big, important, and life-changing stuff that we're talking about. Your last email had a sobering effect on me, which was necessary. But it didn't shut me down—just a slowing down and a reality test. I welcome that.

Have a good weekend—I'll talk to you soon.

Lisa

Lisa wrote:

Dear Jay,

I've been listening to your tape, "Unoffendable Love," and in light of that and what you shared today, I feel compelled to talk a little about some of my history and understandings.

Dear Lisa,

Thank you for your vulnerability. I am encouraged that you are getting comfortable even as you "count the cost."

I was thinking of this offendable love and, having just had a conversation with my friend, Carol, yesterday—the one who was raised fundamentalist Baptist and has rejected the baby and the bathwater—was thinking how grateful I was to not have that to contend with. And also I was struck, listening to her, at how defended she was about love—especially receiving it. She even stated at one point that she could see how I might be fulfilled by the love part—given my history of not receiving it—but that she felt that her life was one where she was to give service, she didn't need the love. My heart just cries for her. She will not receive love because of her offendedness.

I am reminded of something I had started to write to you, and then hesitated, because I thought it was perhaps too early to share. This has been sitting in my drafts folder since 12/30/03. Perhaps this might be a good time and place to share it:

After reading your last e-mail I reached down into my heart to see what I was feeling and cried. I cried for the deepness of my "WANT" and the pain for having to acknowledge my avoiding it. There's fear for not knowing how to proceed in life. It hurts that I have such a need to be heard, validated, and guided by people who don't even know me. It touches me that you are so willing to guide me while remaining vulnerable and open. The beauty and depth of your heart inspires me. And your stories of the bliss and anguish—of Jesus, yourself, and all mankind—at once move and exasperate me. It's all so rich—I wouldn't want to be anywhere but here in this moment.

Dear Lisa,

The following response from a friend became an opportunity to pursue a revelation concerning the latest space shuttle disaster a bit further than I had first understood it.

My friend wrote:

The tiled surface of the spacecraft also reminds me of "the shield of faith" that will protect us from the fiery darts of the wicked one.[2] Truly God is about to do something very big, and He is giving us many signs if we only have ears to hear.

I wrote back, in part:

I have been exploring in my meditation the possibility that those tiles are a picture of the Love of God that is revealed to us in the cross. That exploration is not so far from your own insight concerning faith, because it is becoming increasingly clear to me that "faith works by love." Without hope, faith has no raw material: "Now faith is being sure of what we hope for..."[3] It is foundational that we have hope. And without love, our faith is bound to fail: "Love never faileth..:"[4]

I am thinking about the kind of love that is able to take the heat: "Set me as a seal upon thine heart, as a seal upon thine arm: for love is strong as death; jealousy is cruel as the grave: the coals thereof are coals of fire, which hath a most vehement flame."[5]

A love that is only good for friends is not good for re-entry: "A brother offended is harder to be won than a strong city: and their contentions are like the bars of a castle."[6]

That kind of re-entry requires a love that is good for enemies: "For if, when we were enemies, we were reconciled to God by the death of his Son, much more, being reconciled, we shall be saved by his life."[7]

The "institutional church" is mostly built on the kind of love that was made obsolete at the cross. My very strong impression is that this is why it continues to break up on re-entry.

It is also my very strong impression that those who preside over the "institutional church" are in as much denial about the problem as those who preside at NASA. "O Jerusalem, Jerusalem, thou that killest the prophets, and stonest them which are sent unto thee, how often would I have gathered thy children together, even as a hen gathereth her chickens under her wings, and ye would not!"[8]

Vested interest in the status quo is a veil of great darkness that stands between those armed with information, and the revelation of Divine Life. Reality is found only in Christ. Man-made religion keeps us from seeing it/Him.

Yours in Christ,

Jay

---

[2]Ephesians 6:16.
[4]1 Corinthians 13:8a.
[6]Proverbs 18:19.
[8]Matthew 23:37.

[3]Hebrews 11:1a.
[5]Song of Songs 8:6.
[7]Romans 5:10.

At this point Jay shares with Lisa an email exchange with his friend Bill in which he asks for Bill's help in understanding how the first city of Jerusalem was captured. The revelation that Jay received was that this too is part of the sexual parable. The city is a woman, and she was captured by the penetration of her stronghold. For the actual exchange that was sent to Lisa, look in Appendix C under the heading "Getting New Life Into a Woman."

The point here is that this is true for all of us. We hole up behind our paradigms, and these are the strongholds that keep us from really being able to touch each other.

And there appeared a great wonder in heaven: a woman clothed with the sun, and the moon under her feet, and upon her head a crown of twelve stars; ...

—**Revelation 12:1**

And I John saw the holy city, new Jerusalem, coming down from God out of heaven, prepared as a bride adorned for her husband.

—**Revelation 21:2**

"For this cause shall a man leave his father and mother, and shall be joined unto his wife, and they two shall be one flesh." This is a great mystery, but I speak concerning Christ and the church;... .

—**Ephesians 5:31-32**

Looking at this through another paradigm, the paradigm I call the "sexual parable," the city is a woman. I don't think I need to site the many references for this, except perhaps the following: Revelation 12:1, Revelation 21:2, and Ephesians 5:31–32. These are doors into our understanding of the "sexual parable."

The question is, how do you get new life into a polluted woman? The answer is, you wait for the right time, you go in through the "gutter," the place where the pollution comes out, and you plant a seed. The name of the "mighty man" who did this for David was Joab.[9] According to Strong's, his name means: "Jehovah fathered."[10]

This is to say that, in "testing everything," this revelation passes the "sexual parable" test.

What I see is that the stronghold is not pulled down with regulations, laws, condemnation, programs, or manipulation, but with the planting of a seed, an incorruptible seed, even Christ.

This raises the question of where, how, and to what end are our lives going to be planted. Keep in mind what is written: "Except a corn of wheat be cast into the ground and die..." The

---

[9] 2 Samuel 5:6–10.

[10] **The Strongest Strong's Exhaustive Concordance of the Bible**, rev. edition, by James Strong, LL.D., S.T.D., fully revised and corrected by John R. Kohlenberger III and James A. Swanson, published by Zondervan Publishing Company, in 2001.

dying and the planting are a package deal. In contemplation of His own death, Jesus prayed: "…O my Father, if this cup may not pass away from me, except I drink it, thy will be done."[11]

Some time back, I wrote a little piece called "The Cup." I don't recall right now if I already sent it to you. I know I mentioned the thought on the "Getting Horizontal" tape. Let me know, and I will send it to you if you like.

Today, I would put it still a little differently: Do we have the love required for re-entry? Do we have the love required to enter the stronghold, having no regard for the pollution we may encounter in the process? Do we have what it takes to pull down the strongholds presently held captive by thoughts that are not part of the mind of Christ?

If we don't, our mission is doomed from the start. It's critically important what happens on "lift off." Are we armed with the kind of love that "covers a multitude of sins"?

Before going further I have been meaning to share with you a little bit about the reaction to the two tapes I sent at the time that they were recorded.

The "Getting Horizontal" gathering became increasingly interactive as the tape ran out. After about two hours, a young woman who was there, a young mother in her early 30s I would guess, began to sob, really sob. I waited to see how those in the group who knew her might comfort her. After about a minute, a rather long sobbing silence in the circumstances, no one had made a move or said a thing. I got up, crossed the circle, knelt down, put my arms around her, and whispered words of encouragement to her. I whispered, "Thank you for your heart's cry. Thank you for this very appropriate and prophetic response to what I have shared." She felt comforted and began to regain her composure, and I returned to my place beside the host. When I sat down, he leaned over to me and asked in a whisper, "Why didn't I do that?" I said, "Perhaps you were afraid what others might think. Perhaps you were afraid what that young woman might think or what your wife might think." True worship doesn't care what others think.

As she got back her composure, she shared that she had never experienced a love like I was talking about, not even in her own mother's heart toward her children. Two weeks later, I called the host to see if there had been any fall-out from the gathering. He was very excited as he shared with me that the woman had been so transformed by the message that her family wanted to know

---

[11]Matthew 26:42b.

what had happened to her. The result was that he had been asked to teach—and was now teaching—what looked to be two Bible studies a month just for her relatives.

At the end of the "Unoffendable Love" meeting, two women came up to me (separately) and said, "You just saved my marriage today. Thank you." It wasn't me. It's the power of God's kind of love. I'm just a dumb ox who stumbled into it.

Her biggest stumbling block to Christianity is the notion that Jesus is the only way and words like salvation are big buzzwords to her....

Yes, these are big stumbling blocks, especially in the way that they have been presented.

...This is huge for a lot of people—isn't there another way to get to God? The exclusivity offends them....

This is a real problem requiring great sensitivity.

...I happen to believe that Jesus was the turning point for humanity—that his "gift," in addition to the love that you're able to describe so well, is this Christ deposit in us that guides us in knowing God. I realize that some of my understanding and acceptance of Jesus comes from what I've heard from my dad over the years and what I've read from the Urantia book so it's difficult to relate to what a "typical" Christian has been exposed to....

You got that right.

...My belief and understanding is that this deposit was given to all people—we are becoming "spiritualized" whether we choose to believe in God or Jesus—let's say the capacity to believe and understand is becoming greater whether we're conscious of it or not....

Most Christians/church-goers would have a problem with this. In such a case, it's probably not the best approach to gaining entry.

...But my conviction is that we have to choose to do God's will—in essence be willing to follow him—in order to fully realize not only his spiritual gifts during our time here on earth, but also to continue beyond this world. I also happen to believe that Jesus is "Lord" over people on this planet, that his will is aligned with God's, and that it was set up that he is the "go-between" between us and God....

This would be accepted in any "church" I have ever known.

...I believe that Jesus didn't come here to set up a religion about himself,...

Most would also agree with your statement, even if it's completely ignored in practice.

...but to help us understand the truth about God and his desires and love for us so that we would be more willing to align ourselves with him and reap the benefits. And a whole lot of other stuff, but this is the crux of my beliefs to date....

You are in much better shape than I might have guessed! :-)

...And there's a whole lot that I don't understand and probably will never completely understand, but you have to start somewhere....

With an outlook like that you are bound to go very far.

...So is Jesus the only way? I don't know....

I'm hesitant to try to answer the question at this point because Who and What Jesus is is a very big subject, bigger than any of us can wrap our minds around. The size, scope, and sparkle of the many facets of Jesus make the word "only" a bit of a problem.

...He certainly points the way distinctly to me, and I feel led to follow his example and learn about this incredible love that he demonstrated. It appears to me, from my limited knowledge, that his is the best way. But I honestly don't know how to answer that question....

I think the reason is what I have just mentioned.

...I think every person has to come to their own conviction. Mine was a strange, cosmic, surreal kind of way to some—but it worked for me. The experience I had with the shamanic healer was a strange, cosmic, surreal kind of way to some—but it worked for me—and it helped to get me to this point where I'm talking with you.

Among other things, Jesus is outrageous, especially to the terminally religious.

I think one of the differences between me and Carol, and maybe a lot of people, is my current willingness to be led by—and to put a great deal of trust in—this spirit I've come to know as way bigger than me. To really let go of my brain and trust my heart. I obviously don't always do it, but I am learning to go there more. How does one get from a place of non-trust to trust? From being offended to non-of-

fended? Grace, desire, surrender, understanding? It's a great mystery to me.

For me the look of love in Jesus's eyes makes the rest of it go away. To find that look in our own eyes is "joy unspeakable and full of glory."

My father, who is and has been such a fervent believer in the Urantia book, is one of the most emotionally unavailable men I've ever known. He seems to be afraid of intimacy. I never could reconcile what I saw in him and what I read in the Urantia book. Something was seriously wrong here—where was the love? I listened to him talk about the Urantia book because it was interesting and because it was one of the only areas where we could connect....

My dear spiritual brother, whom I mentioned to you in connection with foot washing/massage, told me that he had tried to become a Muslim, but he couldn't find a copy of the Quran. I think it was probably the result of the same offendedness that drove your father to the Urantia book. He wanted no part of what he saw as the white man's religion, the white man's Jesus, and the white man's Bible. He had been so offended by what was calling itself "church" and "Christianity." This is at the root of our present world struggle with terrorism. I'm guessing that for your father it wasn't a racial issue, so much as a war of ideas. As it has been displayed so far, "Christianity" just does not look like a good idea. I Corinthians 13 could be understood to anticipate this problem.

...He was fanatical about the book—frustrated that nobody else seemed to want to know the "truth" as he had come to know it thru the book....

"Religious fundamentalism": it's not a pretty sight, certainly not very attractive.

...I watched him try to reconcile within himself this intense desire to infuse this knowledge and his belief that when we're ready to read the book, we'll be led to read it....

That's where the "manhandling" comes on the scene.

...I'm grateful for what he did talk to me about, though.

It wasn't until I had this recent experience on my own and was able to hear and better understand this tremendous love that I could accept this faith in Jesus and want to live there. Certainly the foundation was set—the missing ingredient was love.

As you already know, that is a very big "missing ingredient."

I grew up in an environment that had a big deficit of love. My mother and father divorced when I was three. My mother drank and was depressed, and my dad appeared uninterested and unavailable. We (I had an older brother and sister) saw him some for a few years, but I always felt distanced from him. Mom was remarried when I was 8 to an explosive man—very angry and in-your-face. We walked on eggshells. I spent as much time as possible away from the house, which seemed to be encouraged—when I was home we were not to be seen. Mom had two more children, who are 10 and 13 years younger than me, and was preoccupied with them and trying to hold this family together. I ended up doing drugs, drinking, having sex. Numbing myself and looking for love.

I think you are really going to appreciate the "Storge" love tape. I think I mentioned on the "Getting Horizontal" tape what Denise does not mention on hers, and that is that Spiritual Storge has been made legal in Romans 12:10. This means that I can transfuse love into you by look and tone and touch. I can tell you what God wants you to know, I love you! This is doing what the Father is doing, and what the Father is saying. That's all that Jesus ever did. If I were there in person, you would be getting lots of hugs.

My stepfather eventually left my mom, my older sister died of colon cancer 9 years ago, my older brother drinks and fights depression, and my two younger siblings are struggling. There's more love there now—it's a process. Just very wounded people.

Again, I am so sorry but so grateful for our connection. Did I mention that Jesus is our connection? :-)

When I was 35, I was talking with my stepmother about why my dad didn't seem to like me. It was always puzzling to me—I always had felt rejected by him and felt like he was angry with me. My dad called me that week and asked me to schedule an appointment with my therapist (it's when Kurtis and I were in Imago therapy)....

I'm not familiar with that "therapy." Was your father participating with you in it?

...He told me in that session that the reason that I had felt those things from him was because he didn't think he was my father....

It sounds like he was in the session. That's a big hit!

…(We did a DNA test: he's not my father.)…

WOW!!

…He didn't mean to act that way, but he was just so angry about it—still, after all those years he was consumed with bitterness towards my mother that got projected on me. It all made so much more sense to me then! I was stunned, yet not too surprised, and relieved beyond words.

Things are pretty rough when that kind of news becomes a big relief.

We ended up agreeing to continue in our relationship as father and daughter—in our own limited ways. It was definitely somewhat of a turning point for me—I could start to heal. I started feeling a sort of "redemptive love." Here was a man who was clearly suffering from his own version of hell, and I had an opportunity to forgive him and love him regardless of his ability to love me. He had one request of me as we were leaving that session—not to tell him that I loved him in front of my stepmother. Because then he felt obligated to tell me that he loved me. It breaks my heart that he is not able to receive love. He's so offended.

This leaves me a little short of words.

I tell you all of this to let you know that I know a lot about offendedness. It comes in all forms. I've also had some experience with this redemptive love for which I have such gratitude! My marriage would not still be going and as strong as it is—even with its imperfections—if it weren't for this redemptive love and for my lessons in "not having expectations." My interest in helping others does not come from a place of needing to be right or to know the answers or to tell them how to live. It really comes from wanting to end the pain and to help us all grow in love. And I'm convinced that the only way to do that is thru this redemptive kind of love that only comes from God.

I'm listening.

I'm going to sit with all of this and all that you have written—I keep it all in a notebook—and see what comes up for me. I'd like to hear more about what experiences you've had doing this work reaching out to people. Tell me what happened to your spiritual daughter. I could learn from your experiences.

Have you seen **Legends of the Fall**? Her story has that kind of sweep and intensity. The spiritual cinematography is breathtaking. It is ongoing, and right now it is in a very hopeful chapter. I say chapter, not because it's so easy to put it in a book, but because, early on, she had said that she would help me with my book on relationships. I think perhaps I already mentioned that it wasn't long before it became clear that writing a book about intimacy is kind of an oxymoron. I don't know a book that needs more to be lived, written, and read, but it requires a tremendous commitment and willingness for self-disclosure. Intimacy with the intention of going public is seriously compromised. For instance, if we continued to probe what you have written here, the depth of the impact it may have had on who you are and what you have done and experienced, say, about a thousand pages worth, perhaps you can imagine what a self-revelation that would be.

This is to say that your request for me to tell the story is "spot on," as the Brits would say. Interesting: when the storm hit, she acknowledged that I had tried to warn her but said she had no place to put my warning because she could not have imagined how bad it could be. We had a long and very clear conversation about the possibilities, as early on as could be thought appropriate, so much so that she asked me to stop insisting that she count the cost, lest I make her paranoid. In short I was persuaded that I had said enough, and that she had heard. Her subsequent confession that she "had no place to put it" was a painful lesson all by itself. It's one thing to realize that "bad things happen to good people"; it's something else to lead them into places of great vulnerability. As a result, I made the mistake of taking her to a place where she was not prepared to go, and one that I myself did not anticipate.

Lest any of this be read as negative toward her, I need to quickly say that she has been awesome in the circumstances. For now perhaps it is enough to share with you that it was a crisis in her life that finally triggered the connection. She had lost her voice. Her life's direction, almost from before she could talk, was to be a singer; then in the summer between her junior and senior years of college, music/voice major, 4.0, first in her class, she developed cysts on one of her vocal cords and for most of her senior year was only able to communicate using either a chalk board or a voice synthesizer. Finally it became clear exactly what it was and that it would require surgery to correct the problem, if it could be corrected. Julie Andrews had undergone the same surgery, and, in her case, it didn't work, and her singing career was ended.

In **this** case it worked, but it was a very difficult and dark night of the soul for her. As it turned out, that was the easy part.

She recently had the starring role in an opera in Charlotte. Perhaps one day this side of heaven the two of you will meet.

In the meanwhile, my lunches with my girlfriends (had another one today) have been quite fruitful in that, when I talk about where I am spiritually and my desire to meet and talk with others about our spirituality and lives, they all seem to want to go there. I'm planning on going tomorrow night to Paul and Lori's—and one of our couple friends might go, too.

I set up "church" at my house for 6 p.m. on the 25th and am inviting people to come....

I could only wish that there were some way for me to be there. In any case, I am certainly looking forward to how things develop and to hearing all about it.

...So, we'll see. It feels weird, but, so far, within my comfort zone (which is definitely getting stretched).

You were very much in my thoughts and prayers last night, Saturday, and through this weekend. I look forward to hearing how everything went. I know that Tony and Felicity also have a kind of mini-conference going on this weekend as well. Perhaps there will have been some connection there that surfaces, before the weekend is over.

I'm off work on Monday so you probably won't hear from me until Tuesday.

Time to marinate and pray for guidance. This is really big, important, and life-changing stuff that we're talking about....

Yes. As a good friend of mine, a very anointed brother from Nigeria and a professor at Yale at the time, said to me, "Jesus is the only game in town."

...Your last email had a sobering effect on me, which was necessary. But it didn't shut me down—just a slowing down and a reality test. I welcome that.

Then perhaps I have been able to serve you well.

Yours in Christ,
Jay

CHAPTER 8

A TIME-SHARE
IN ETERNITY

Dear Jay,

*Thank you for your thoughtful reply—it was very affirming. Also I'm blown away by the "Storge" tape. I listened to it twice and both times became a puddle. Her prayer at the end was maybe the most powerful prayer I've ever heard. I'm making copies of it and your tapes for anyone who wants them... could take a while. (But I did figure it out.) While I'm thinking of it, thanks for telling me about **Tuesdays With Morrie**. Watched it twice last week. It was so moving!*

I spent all weekend in contemplation—especially yesterday when I read thru some of your emails. Wasn't able to get thru all of them. The subject matter is so deep and extensive. It feels like a lifetime of work that you've presented, and I'm having to absorb it all. I'm reading it with "spiritual ears," which is, I realize, the only way to understand any of it. I'm amazed at the level of detail with which you decipher these passages, and I love the way you have gone thru the Bible and pulled passages on themes. Thank you for that compilation—it reflects, as you said, years of research.

I find myself having to limit my doses—otherwise it becomes a little overwhelming. Are you always this intense? I'm not asking this as a criticism—in fact, it's a quality I value a great deal. I've been known to be rather intense myself. I'm just trying to gage what I'm getting into here.

There's a deep sense of urgency that comes thru in your writing that I find somewhat unsettling. It sounds like war and a fear that "we're" losing. This seems in conflict to me with the strongest message I've heard you offer—the one of redemptive love. Just listening to you at times makes my heart speed up and my palms a little sweaty—kind of a "fight or flight" response. It could be just a response that I have to intellectualism—I always have my doubts that I fully understand really complex thought processes. My tendency is to oversimplify so that I can understand it. But even more than this is a momentous, outraged, almost explosive striking out against something that is seemingly impenetrable.

Even as I say that I realize that it is penetrable—if each of us does our part against our own strongholds. I guess I wonder what your perceived stronghold is. To what extent are you going and what are your weapons? From where I stand, walking in your wake feels like a tidal wave coming. I hope that none of this is offensive to you. I realize that it may sound presumptuous of me. I certainly don't want to trivialize anything that you think or feel. I think it is an important topic to discuss, however. I, for one, don't want to bite off more than I can chew. On the other hand, I don't want to avoid doing what I can out of fear.

Part of what I "got" this weekend is more of an understanding of this trust in God. If I listen to my own inner guidance—from God—I will be able to handle anything he puts in my path. So I guess that one of my biggest challenges at this point is to be able to listen to and understand my guidance, my path. I could see how I could be easily swayed by people such as yourself, or Tony and Felicity, in your combined passions. I could adopt any number of beliefs in a desire to please and conform. It's important to me to be clear about what is true and what is creating more barriers to my peace. The issues we're discussing are so huge that sometimes it's difficult to determine whether what I'm consumed with is a barrier to peace or if it's just something that needs to be thought out. I'm guessing that only time can tell and I'm hoping that we have an eternity to figure all this out! (I'm hoping at this point that any of this makes sense).

Another concept that chewed on me was this concept of church. Are the "body of Christ," the "kingdom of God," the "Holy Ghost," and the "Christ deposit" the same as church? So that when we talk of church we're talking about this one big spiritual entity that embodies everyone (or, at least to some people, every Christian)?

I have to go for now. We start one of our mediation trainings tomorrow so things will be rather pressed around here thru next Wednesday. I'm going to spend more time reflecting on what we've written.

Thank you again for your affirmation of God's love. I can feel your hugs.

Lisa

Lisa wrote:

Dear Jay,

Thank you for your thoughtful reply—it was very affirming. Also I'm blown away by the "Storge" tape. I listened to it twice and both times became a puddle. Her prayer at the end was maybe the most powerful prayer I've ever heard. I'm making copies of it and your tapes for anyone who wants them… could take a while. (But I did figure it out.) While I'm thinking of it, thanks for telling me about **Tuesdays With Morrie**. *Watched it twice last week. It was so moving!*

Dear Lisa,

Thank you for your note. I'm so glad that you enjoyed both the "Storge" tape and **Tuesdays with Morrie**. I seem to have misplaced my copy of the latter. Seems like favorites are the ones that we lend the most, and eventually they don't come back. With my memory, I can never remember whom I lend things to.

I spent all weekend in contemplation—especially yesterday when I read thru some of your emails.…

Does that mean that you didn't meet with the others on Saturday night, and on Sunday morning?

…Wasn't able to get thru all of them. The subject matter is so deep and extensive. It feels like a lifetime of work that you've presented, and I'm having to absorb it all. I'm reading it with "spiritual ears" which is, I realize, the only way to understand any of it. I'm amazed at the level of detail with which you decipher these passages, and I love the way you have gone thru the Bible and pulled passages on themes. Thank you for that compilation—it reflects, as you said, years of research.
I find myself having to limit my doses—otherwise it becomes a little overwhelming.…

I'm still trying to get a sense of what your needs, desires, and capacities might be, so please don't feel pressured if I have sent too much too soon. I had only wanted to be responsive to your desire to go after those who had been offended by their exposure of what has been calling itself "church," and to give you a little heads up with regard to the cost.

…Are you always this intense?…

I try to adjust my output, and intensity to the comfort zone of those around me but don't always succeed. I have an aversion to patronizing people. It is so dishonoring. Perhaps for that reason, I try to err on the side of thinking of others as equal to or higher than myself.

…I'm not asking this as a criticism—in fact, it's a quality I value a great deal. I've been known to be rather intense myself….

I think I appreciate both your not being critical, and your own intensity.

…I'm just trying to gage what I'm getting into here.

Thank you for sharing with me.

There's a deep sense of urgency that comes thru in your writing that I find somewhat unsettling….

I had not meant to "unsettle" you, only to encourage and caution you concerning the inclination of your heart. As for me, where I am coming from and what I may have been called to do is not something that you should feel pressured about. We all have different gifts, callings, and loads to carry. Please don't ever take on any more than Jesus Himself puts on you. He said, "Take my yoke upon you, for my yoke is easy and my burden is light."[1] He knows what we can carry better than we do. I have learned to get rid of even the things that I might have put on myself. I have also learned to be very careful not to let others do a number on me.[2]

…It sounds like war and a fear that "we're" losing….

The war is between two kinds of love. One is the love in the heart of a merchant, and the other is the love in the heart of Christ. In His love, we are more than conquerors.[3] "Don't leave home without it."

In this connection, a couple of days ago I wrote Tony about a revelation that came to me while I was in Mexico last year. It was in the midst of the most outrageously pretentious time-share presentation I have ever experienced. The contrast in value systems was so glaringly apparent that I couldn't miss it. I found myself in the midst of a parable. It was so clear. This was the time-share version of the rich fool.

---

[1]Matthew 11:30. [2]Revelation 13:16–18, 14:9–11.
[3]Romans 8:35-39.

The time-share sales gal was a **Legally Blonde** wannabe. She was about 20 years past her prime but, with some surgical help, was making a good effort. She was all in pink with a contrasting pink pocket book and the right walk; I didn't get a chance to see her "bend and snap," although I was tempted to show her mine. Lots of attitude. She pretty much sensed I was the enemy right from the gitgo. Ah, but such a loving enemy.

I tried to share another kind of time-share—let's call it 'eternity-share'—but it was clear that she would not be able to hear it without being completely destroyed in everything she presently valued and understood. She asked me about the cost. I told her that it was within her reach, but that it would cost her everything she had.

> ... The ground of a certain rich man produced a good crop. He thought to himself, "What shall I do? I have no place to store my crops."
>
> Then he said, "This is what I'll do. I will tear down my barns and build bigger ones, and there I will store all my grain and my goods. And I'll say to myself, "You have plenty of good things laid up for many years. Take life easy; eat, drink and be merry."
>
> But God said to him, "You fool! This very night your life will be demanded from you. Then who will get what you have prepared for yourself?"
>
> This is how it will be with anyone who stores up things for himself but is not rich toward God.
>
> **—Luke 12: 16–21 (NIV)**

NO SALE!

In the end she was hostile, because we were unwilling to pay $119,000 for the four-week time-share she offered us. In fairness to her, however, we gave her three hours to make her presentation. At one point, she even offered to take an old time-share as a trade-in.

With a very few words I could have burned down everything that was of value to her, but that would hardly have been love if I could not have offered her a better place to live.

Instead, what happened was that I got greater clarity concerning the timing and nature of the burning of "Babylon the Great."[4] When I see something in Christ like this, my internalized Bible software immediately begins to scan all that He has already made mine, to see if the latest revelation computes. Among other places, a passage that came to mind was that of Peter's response at the "Gate Beautiful:" "Silver and gold have I none; but such as I have give I thee: In the name of Jesus Christ of Nazareth rise up and walk."[5]

Here's a portion of what I wrote to Tony about the experience:

---

[4]Revelation 17:16.   [5]Acts 3:6.

For me, the presentation resulted in an opening of my understanding in connection with a choice between two kinds of "time-shares," two places of rest, two places to live, even a choice between two kingdoms. How can we leave the one, without entering the other? This to say that getting out of Babylon seems to be a call to everyone of us, but where are we to go, if we are given no alternative? What kind of life is it for us to be consigned to some kind of mental holding pattern until Jesus comes back? Why should the people living in darkness want a piece of that action?

Paul wanted to go where the gospel had not been preached, and no wonder: as things are now, a great deal of demolition work needs to be done on the half-way houses that we have offered in the name of The Lord. Otherwise people haven't the faintest idea of what we're talking about. The people living in darkness need very badly to know that there is another place to live. If I understand it right, we are to be a demonstration in their midst of that other place. "Oh well, maybe next time..".

... NOT!

We need to live in the Spirit's alternative to Babylon; we need to live there now, and my experience tells me that this is well within the grasp of the faith once delivered to the saints and still available even in our own day. What we are presently calling 'church' isn't fooling anyone except perhaps ourselves.

I found myself wanting to share about the work of the cross, as a remedy for sin, even in spiritual urban renewal. This certainly requires revelation, preaching, faith, and the power of the Holy Spirit, to live in what we say we believe.

She didn't give me a minute to share what was in my heart.

In that sense, it was a lot like "going to church." What Jesus has to offer is bad for business, any business: "...To what then shall I compare the men of this generation, and what are they like? They are like children who sit in the market place..."[6]

The Book of Revelation is a strange kind of a letter. It messes up our tenses. I believe that the beast will burn Babylon when he appears in the future, The problem seems to be that we are so locked into our futureness that we are missing the burning that is going on in the present, This burning is the result of the fire Jesus kindled at the cross. This is to say that we don't have to wait until the eleventh hour to get out of the burning tower. Fact is, the fire Jesus set at the cross has already gutted the building.

> At this point, Jay contrasts two economic systems, the familiar system of buying and selling in a marketplace, where the gospel has been up to the new covenant, the other a system that is based on love and requires no "trip to the marketplace" at all. The entire text of this e-mail can be found in Appendix D, entitled "Burning Babylon."

The mind of Christ is already out of Babylon. For the people of God to be called out of Babylon is for them to be called into a new place, a new way of thinking. It is to be called into the mind of Christ.[7] This is the mark of Christ.

---

[6]Luke 7:30–32.

[7]Romans 12:2; Philippians 2:5.

In the end the only alternative is the mark of the antichrist, the mark of the beast.

Right from Pentecost to the end of the age, the gospel is calling people out of their old place, their old way of thinking, and into a new place, a place which only became available on the day of Pentecost. What began that day is still available to us who believe. The call still goes out, "Come out of her, my people, that you may not participate in her sins and that you may not receive of her plagues."[8]

Babylon was first set on fire at the cross, and another place to live was made available in the first resurrection. This is the new birth.

The question now is, "Will we live the life that it promises?" Somehow our minds have to be changed. How can we come out of Babylon unless we have another place to go, unless we have another place to live? We can live in the Kingdom of God. It has an economy that is wholly other, one with no merchants and no market place.

It does not matter what else we are doing: until the world sees the fruits of this new economy in our midst, they will not believe in the One Whom God has sent.

"Silver and gold have I none, but such as I have give I thee ..." The New Jerusalem is also a "great city." It is presented to us as a city that comes down from above.[9] Let's call it the "new way," the "heavenly new way."

> I saw the Holy City, the new Jerusalem, coming down out of heaven from God, prepared as a bride beautifully dressed for her husband.
>
> **—Revelation 21:2 (NIV)**

In Revelation 17, we have a city that doesn't "come down," but rather "comes up." Let's call it a "bad deal." Let's call it "the old deal," the "earthly old deal." What we need is not "Let's make a deal." What we need is "No Deal." In me there dwelleth no good thing, I have nothing with which to make a "good deal." I have nothing to bring to the table of God's provision. I need grace, even more abundant grace. Access to that grace was opened up at the cross.

The Gospel offers us a new medium of exchange. Our new medium of exchange is the Love of Christ. "Don't leave home without it!" We cannot participate in the economy of God without first having received His love. The currency exchange is the cross. In exchange for our sin, we got His righteousness. In exchange for our fallenness, we got His risenness.

The implications of this transaction are enormous even in this present age.

The question is, "Do we believe it?" Clearly, at least, by the days of the "beast," God does not want His people still "buying and selling."[10] Hello!

This is not just the matter of the medium of exchange rather than barter, it is "NO MORE DEALS!!!" In that day we will be among those shouting, "...GRACE, GRACE..."[11]

Is this just a human-interest story, or is this some kind of call to action? The gospel coin has two sides to it. One side says, "Come in!" The other side says, "Come out!"

So, Lisa, as I see it, the war is between two kinds of love. One is the love in the heart of a merchant, and the other is the love in the heart of Christ.

---

[8]Revelation 18:4.
[10]Revelation 14:9–10.

[9]Revelation 21:2.
[11]Zechariah 4:7.

...This seems in conflict to me with the strongest message I've heard you offer—the one of redemptive love. Just listening to you at times makes my heart speed up and my palms a little sweaty—kind of a "fight or flight" response....

For our part, we are to be lovers, not fighters. That said, however, there is a fight going on. Paul writes about it in Galatians 4: 16-31.

...It could be just a response that I have to intellectualism—I always have my doubts that I fully understand really complex thought processes....

I hope I'm not being intellectual with you. That is not my intention. As for your own capacity to understand, it is my impression that you have more than your share of bites on your hard drive.

...My tendency is to oversimplify so that I can understand it....

Getting to the core truth is really important, because then you can draw upon it in a great variety of circumstances. II Corinthians 11:3 speaks about the simplicity that is ours in Christ and cautions us not to be drawn away from that simplicity. Again, it is in the context of the sexual parable or bridal paradigm.

...But even more than this is a momentous, outraged, almost explosive striking out against something that is seemingly impenetrable. Even as I say that I realize that it is penetrable —if each of us does our part against our own strongholds. I guess I wonder what your perceived stronghold is.

I think I like your spirit here. It is much like Paul's. It was a quality in Paul that Jesus harnessed with His love. The harnessing took approximately 3 and 1/2 years in the Arabian Desert.

To what extent are you going and what are your weapons?...

My heart is to go all the way, that is, to go as far as faith might take me in this present age, and, in the age to come, to arrive in the city to which those of faith are headed.[12] As for the weapons, I am still in the process of discovery of what might be available. In any case, they only work when operated in the Spirit. Quite often this happens without my knowledge or understanding.

One day I had some business with the president of a small company. He had been very helpful in trying to find parts I need-

---

[12]Hebrews 11:8–12:29.

ed for some equipment I was working on. I mentioned the equipment in the "Getting Horizontal" tape. It was in that time frame when I met with this man. While I was seated on the other side of his desk, he was on the phone trying to locate what I needed, and I felt The Lord prompting me to share Him with this man.

I was in very beat-up work clothes. It was winter, and I had done a lot of welding in these clothes. They were full of grease stains and welding burns. In short, I didn't feel very presentable, as the Lord's best representative. The Lord gave me no peace, however. In my inner conversation, I finally said, "O.K. Lord, but if that's going to happen, You are going to have to give me some very clear sign."

We finished our business, his not having been able to locate what I needed but promising to pursue it and get back to me. I got up to leave, with only the closing amenities left unsaid, and his phone rang. He excused himself to pick it up. After a moment, he held the phone away from his ear with a very troubled look on his face. I couldn't hear the voice on the other end of the phone, but, leaning against the door of his office, I was prompted to say, "Oh my people, women rule over them, and children oppress them."[13]

He reacted as if I had hit him with a baseball bat. He said something very harshly, quickly cutting the phone conversation short, turned to me and said, "Why did you say that? Where did that come from? Do you know who was on the phone? That was my wife! She and my daughter are having an argument, and trying to involve me. Why did you say that?" He hardly took a breath. I responded by saying where it had come from, Isaiah. He said, "But how did you know it, and why did you say it?" I explained that I had come across the verse when I was studying about the monetary implications of the Bible. (At the time, I was still working on what became my first book.)

He said, "Please come, and sit down and tell me all about this." He didn't have to ask twice. I had not gotten very far, when he interrupted, asking, "Would you be willing to speak to my group?" I had no idea that he had a group or what that group might be, but I said, "I would be happy to do that." Our conversation eventually ended. He did finally succeed in finding the part that I needed, but there was no further mention of the conversation that had taken place between us. Then about 6 months later, I got a call. He explained that he was president of the local

---

[13]Isaiah 3:12.

Chamber of Commerce and had been charged with the responsibility of getting the speaker for their annual dinner. Would I be willing to come?

It was quite a lavish affair. Carleen and I were very blessed to be there, the supper was wonderful, and the atmosphere electric. I spoke for about 45 minutes and sat down. They wouldn't let me off that easy, however, and a question and answer session began that lasted for another hour.

All of this is just to say that, where weapons are concerned, most of my best work has been done when I didn't have any idea what I was doing. They really are "spiritual weapons."

I'm not sure I understand your question about my "perceived stronghold," so I'll wait for further clarification from you before attempting to answer that question.

...From where I stand, walking in your wake feels like a tidal wave coming. I hope that none of this is offensive to you....

No, but honestly I had not intended on taking you water-skiing. I had only hoped to be responsive to the expressed desires of your own heart. I am more than willing to throttle back.

...I realize that it may sound presumptuous of me. I certainly don't want to trivialize anything that you think or feel....

I have not read you as either presumptuous or trivializing.

...I think it is an important topic to discuss, however....

Very, and I'm grateful, lest any misunderstanding come between us.

...I, for one, don't want to bite off more than I can chew....

This is wisdom!!

...On the other hand, I don't want to avoid doing what I can out of fear.

This also is wisdom, even realizing that "perfect love casts out fear."

Part of what I "got" this weekend is more of an understanding of this trust in God. If I listen to my own inner guidance—from God— I will be able to handle anything he puts in my path. So I guess that one of my biggest challenges at this point is to be able to listen to and understand my guidance, my path....

Yes, this is very important. "Salvation" is personal and intimate. God wants to have a relationship with you personally. There are treasures in the Word of God that I would never be able to get for myself, treasures that are yours. Of course, if you wanted to share some of them with me, that would be wonderful, but the main thing is not to let anyone, myself included, get between you and God.[14]

...I could see how I could be easily swayed by people such as yourself, or Tony and Felicity, in your combined passions....

That's a lot of fireworks to take in all at once.

...I could adopt any number of beliefs in a desire to please and conform. It's important to me to be clear about what is true and what is creating more barriers to my peace....

Yes.

...The issues we're discussing are so huge that sometimes it's difficult to determine whether what I'm consumed with is a barrier to peace or if it's just something that needs to be thought out. I'm guessing that only time can tell, and I'm hoping that we have an eternity to figure all this out! (I'm hoping at this point that any of this makes sense).

It not only makes sense, it is very well expressed!

Another concept that chewed on me was this concept of church. Are the "body of Christ," the "kingdom of God," the "Holy Ghost," and the "Christ deposit" the same as church? So that when we talk of church we're talking about this one big spiritual entity that embodies everyone (or, at least to some people, every Christian)?

You sure know how to ask some doozeys! After your problems with intensity already expressed, I'm somewhat hesitant to wade in. Perhaps it would be better to let Tony and Felicity answer that question for the present. I am not wanting to put you off. It's just that I am very intense and passionate on the subject of the "Church," and I don't want to bury you under my passion.

While I'm on the subject of putting you off, it has occurred to me that perhaps I should give you our phone number, just in case you get in a jam, but more than that, because all of my kids have our number, and even some of our friends. [:-)] I'm here most all the time, because of my writing, and Carleen is usually home by

---

[14] I John 2:26–29.

5:00. I know she would be delighted to talk with you as well, so feel free to call any time. While our friends tend to not call after 10:00 PM, Carleen's bed time, (she has to get up and out of here by 7:00 AM for school), our kids, both flesh-and-blood and spiritual, know that they can call any time as needed, night and day.

I have to go for now. We start one of our mediation trainings tomorrow so things will be rather pressed around here thru next Wednesday. I'm going to spend more time reflecting on what we've written.

Thank you again for your affirmation of God's love. I can feel your hugs.

I'm glad. Bless you in your reflections!

Jay

On Wednesday, January 21, 2004, Tony wrote to Jay:

Jay,

By the way, it was great to hear from Nate and Joanne that you have invited them over to NC. I am sure that you will have a wonderful time with them.

Every blessing,

Tony

On the same day, Jay wrote back to Tony:

Dear Tony,

Nate has been a very precious older brother to me in the Lord for over 30 years. Carleen and I are really looking forward to our time with them both. Please keep the Shepherds Meeting in prayer. These ministers are mostly institutional in their thinking, but many are coming to an end of themselves, and I am very hopeful that this is a very pregnant season.

Yours in Christ,
Jay

CHAPTER 9

UNPACKING

Dear Jay,

I wonder if I've expressed enough to you how happy I am to be talking with you. These interactions and the subsequent revelations and actions have become a light in my life beyond comparison. I feel so blessed! In that light, don't you dare curtail your intensity! I'm not put off by it—really. And I've learned so much! I think more than anything it was my feeling of needing to be free and not penned in by my own worries of being swept away. I just needed to know that you know and understand. So please continue to send any and all information with as much intensity as you can muster! I'll deal with my own stuff around it.

Thank you also for sharing your phone number and invitation to call. I've thought of calling you a number of times—not just because I'm in a jam, but to have that connection. It's heart warming to be put in the context of a kid or a friend. So kind! I'll give you my numbers, and I would love to hear from you anytime.

I haven't really talked much with Tony and Felicity although I hope that our friendship will grow. They seem quite busy, and so far Tony's communications have been brief and to the point. It's really too soon to tell what might transpire. I'm just very grateful that we've made a connection and that they've been so gracious and willing to help. As far as having in-depth conversations about "church," I've been somewhat hesitant about doing that with anyone (although I have way more than ever before). The timing hasn't seemed right yet—I'm still assimilating. I've told my friends little other than the very basic concept of "coming together to talk about our spiritual lives and to support one another in living them," when inviting them to my house next Sunday. (I wish you could be there, too!) It's funny to watch my thought processes about what I need to say or do with this group of people. I've given up on planning anything and am trusting that what happens will be just right.

You asked about last weekend—we met with Lori and Paul at their house last Saturday—nothing on Sunday (that's at our house this Sunday). It was a more in-depth "getting to know you" meeting. They talked more about the home church concept and their experiences—and their website. They are having a "leadership" of home churches meeting tomorrow night at their house and I'm planning to attend. Just to listen in. I think Tony's son and daughter-in-law will be there.

Thank you for the communication you sent Tony. More to ponder. Just amazing insights!

My comment about intellectualism was more a comment about myself than you. (More explanation later.) On the contrary. While I find what you write extremely intellectually stimulating and demanding, there is none of the "one-upsmanship" that I encountered growing up around my step-father and his professor friends (he was a Ph.D. in music theory—pretty esoteric all in itself). I felt very discounted as a child in my intellectual abilities—so it's an area that I'm especially sensitive to—I would say easily offended. You are inviting in your writing and oh so sharing and caring—I enjoy going along with you. Big difference.

Speaking of offendedness, I had some big insights last night while massaging (a really great place to have big insights). It did not escape me that you invited me to look at my experiences of being offended and of redemptive love. The comment, "I'm listening," seemed like an invitation to go deeper—be more intimate. It struck me as a little strange, since I'd just poured out some very intimate details of my life. I put it on the back burner.

Then, last night, I started thinking about my response to you yesterday. And it occurred to me that couched in my comments were some of the things you were asking about—my offendedness. Words like "intellectual" and "intense" and "overwhelmed" and "unsettling." I laughed at myself for not realizing what was happening in the moment. The invitation to "get real," be intimate, is at the core of what we've been talking about from day one. And yet the invitation, as gentle as it was, seemed threatening. What I wrote yesterday had a certain "backlash" feel to it—like a cornered animal. So I started thinking about this offendedness and just how subtle—and blatant—it can be and how it shows up in my life.

I thought a good place to start would be with my offendedness around "Christianity," since that seems to be most on point. In the moment I can think of the following things I have experienced being offended at (some of which I've couched as "other peoples' concerns" in previous emails):

—exclusivity
—quoting scripture
—feeling stupid about not getting the message
—not having an owner's manual with clear instructions
—"being saved" and the "unsaved"
—"the Lord"
—"amens" and "Alleluias"
—prayer
—"Jesus is the way"
—thinking I don't fit in
—not wanting to be told
—not getting to be "special"

I'm sure this is just a partial list, but you get the message. Better yet, I'm getting the message. What you've written, compounded by the fact that I'm already out there inviting people to enter this spiritual realm with me, makes it imperative that I realize and acknowledge my offendedness. How can I be of any use to myself or to others if I don't? I realize that when I get offended I "go away." Many times I'm able to "come back" quickly, but not always. What if I'm talking to someone and they say something that is offensive to me and I go away? What if they can see in my eyes suspicion or guardedness? How can they feel comfortable*—much less loved—in that situation? If I'm not aware of and acknowledging my offendedness, what keeps me from projecting that onto the person I'm talking to?*

It's not easy to acknowledge these things. It's part of the "garbage." And then I remember the image that you described so beautifully— the look of love in Jesus' eyes—and I remember that by my faith in him, I'm already forgiven. And it occurs to me that if I keep my eyes on his eyes when talking to people about Christianity, church, faith, whatever—that I can keep my heart open while talking and listening. That even as the offendedness comes up—if I keep my eyes there—it will melt away even as it is occurring. I think this is what you mean about redemptive love—the love that comes at and thru you from Je-

sus. It occurred to me that my life "story" is not the issue here. Things happen that might be good, bad, hard. It's the "attitude"—this of-fendedness—about it that kills you. And you have to be willing to watch for it, acknowledge it for what it is and then let it go—sur-render it—to be at peace.

After "getting" these insights I've felt much more at peace. I feel better prepared to hear spiritual truths—and perhaps some grappling with all of this—while staying present. I feel much closer to Jesus, too. How can you look at that look of love in his eyes and not feel closer?

One other question before signing off—the information about the cup. (And yes, I'd like your writing on this as well as more of your pas-sionate discourse on the church when you're so moved.) Is what we're talking about—acknowledging and letting go of our own and other's offendedness—the same as drinking from the cup? Is there more?

Thanks—I'm getting excited again!

Lisa

PS: Thanks for sharing about your spiritual daughter. I would love to meet both her and you at some point. Singing has been some-what of a passion in my life, too—although very informally. A gift my mother shared—she actually studied it and got her master's in voice. I'm glad her operation was successful.

On Thursday, January 22, 2004, Jay responded:

Lisa wrote:

I wonder if I've expressed enough to you how happy I am to be talking with you. These interactions and the subsequent revelations and actions have become a light in my life beyond comparison. I feel so blessed!...

Dear Lisa,

I'm so glad that you are blessed by our interaction. It has been a breath of fresh air for me as well.

...In that light, don't you dare curtail your intensity! I'm not put off by it—really. And I've learned so much!...

I guess, then, I'll just have to keep on being me.

...I think more than anything it was my feeling of needing to be free and not penned in by my own worries of being swept away. I just needed to know that you know and understand....

You have been very helpful to me in your willingness to be transparent. I think it will help me to be better at knowing what to look for. If I get the impression that you are being swept away, I will reach out and grab you by the life jacket. There may come a time or a season that you are swept away from me, and that would surely be a very sad time for me, but I will do everything in my power to keep you from being swept away from Christ.

...So please continue to send any and all information with as much intensity as you can muster! I'll deal with my own stuff around it.

I'm reminded of the introductions that a pastor friend of mine would make. This was back when fax machines were the leading house-to-house technology. He would introduce me and say, "Just don't give him your fax number." I really don't think I was that bad, but I could run a person out of fax paper pretty quickly, if they seemed to be interested in anything I might have to say.

Thank you also for sharing your phone number and invitation to call. I've thought of calling you a number of times—not just because I'm in a jam, but to have that connection. It's heart warming to be put in the context of a kid or a friend. So kind! I would love to hear from you anytime.

A couple of weeks ago now, as I was heading for my Tuesday meeting in Charlotte (about an hour and a half drive, one way), I found myself wondering, what must I look like to you. Immediately a passage from Isaiah 53, verse 2, came to my mind: "For he shall grow up before him as a tender plant, and as a root out of a dry ground: he hath no form nor comeliness; and when we shall see him, there is no beauty that we should desire him." As I pondered this, the Lord gave me a new understanding about it. It's not that Jesus was ugly; it's just that his attractiveness is spiritual, not external or superficial. It is with our inner eye that we must see him. If we can only speak the things that the Spirit wants to say through us; if, like Jesus, we only say the things the Father is saying, then the connection or comprehension is on a spiritual level. There is an inner hearing.

Being just a little "intense," I pushed the matter further. I still wondered, if that is the inner **hearing**, what is the inner **seeing**? If I have somehow managed to say the things that the Father wanted me to say to Lisa, and she has heard them with spiritual ears, what must I look like to her inner eyes?

The answer came. "She isn't seeing you, she is seeing the 'desire of all nations'": "And I will shake all nations, and the desire of all nations shall come: and I will fill this house with glory, saith the LORD of hosts."[1] Jesus is the desire of all nations, the desire of everyone. He is the personification of the inner longing of every heart for intimacy. As such, external appearances only get in the way, because intimacy is so personal that each of us experiences our own facets of it.

I was bowled over considering the possibility that I might have been privileged to be included in the loop of such a Divine transaction. You see, I have never related, sight unseen, at this depth to anyone before, so the Lord is using you to give me understanding about Him.

All of this is to say, beyond confession, I am feeling somewhat conflicted about becoming personally more apparent to you in an external sense. Even a phone call gives me pause. While you have heard my voice by tape and somehow survived, my flesh might become more apparent on the phone than it is on the tape. (While I'm here, one of the tests of relationship is something Jesus said: "My sheep hear my voice.") The voice that all of us need to hear, and the face that all of us need to see, is His voice, and His face. You had asked, "What is the church?" Here's one indication of the answer: "And hath put all things under his feet, and gave him to be the head over all things to the church, Which is his body, the fullness of him that filleth all in all."[2]

What I have found is that I don't hear Jesus's voice through everyone, and most people don't hear Jesus's voice through me. This doesn't mean that either of us are disqualified from Jesus speaking through us, it only means that we are limited in those to whom we can speak and be heard. For instance, it would be kind of a dirty trick to give us parents we could not understand or children who couldn't hear our voice. Not all the kids in the neighborhood can hear and understand me, but mine can. There are still other kids in the neighborhood, and they have equally valid parents of their own. That's just the way life is, and, in the final analysis, Jesus is the life.[3]

If you can't hear Jesus through someone, it doesn't mean that Jesus is not in them, it only means that Jesus is not in them for you. He may certainly be in them for others. Knowing this helps to get the grace to love and accept those we don't understand very

---

[1]Haggai 2:7. [2]Ephesians 1:22–23.
[3]John 1:4.

well or who may even be offensive to us. They may be altogether lovely to someone else.

Some years ago now, I asked Jesus how He did this, and He said, "It is done by my blood."[4] Perhaps enough said for now on that subject. My concern is that you be neither offended nor in relational bondage to those who may not be yours in the present season of your life.

I haven't really talked much with Tony and Felicity although I hope that our friendship will grow. They seem quite busy and so far Tony's communications have been brief and to the point. It's really too soon to tell what might transpire. I'm just very grateful that we've made a connection and that they've been so gracious and willing to help....

I am feeling the same way. When we first began walking together in our connection, it hadn't yet occurred to me that if you heard what I was saying and describing, very soon you would have to experience it in person. I had no idea where you lived. (The Lord did.) I had no idea that Tony and Felicity lived in Austin, TX. (The Lord did.) I had no idea how to make a connection for you there. (The Lord did.) Lisa, I know of very few who have the understanding and experience of relationships that I have enjoyed, and you have responded to, at least, in writing. I have done seminars on the subject, and to a much lesser extent, have shared some with Tony and Felicity about my understanding of our relational inheritance in Christ. I don't know how much they have been able to receive. But, all that aside, I know of no other couple that I could have greater peace about your being in fellowship with. To date, our connection is filled with "signs and wonders."

...As far as having in-depth conversations about "church," I've been somewhat hesitant about doing that with anyone (although I have way more than ever before). The timing hasn't seemed right yet—I'm still assimilating....

I believe that this is the Lord's wisdom in you.

...I've told my friends little other than the very basic concept of "coming together to talk about our spiritual lives and to support one another in living them," when inviting them to my house next Sunday....

---

[4]Ephesians 2:13.

The word "church" translated is "ekklesia." It is literally "gathered together out of." For me the best way to think about the "church" is to see it as a "new creation," a creation of and in the Spirit, and superimposed on the old creation. By understanding it this way, you don't have to go to beginner's classes to find out what it's all about. All you have to do is look at the old creation. It is God's flannel board designed by Him to teach us what it/He is all about.[5]

...(I wish you could be there, too!)...

I can't tell you the number of times I have imagined myself showing up in disguise, just so I could take it all in. Our connection is so strong I think it would have to be a very good disguise. If I could afford to be there I would. Carleen and I have talked about this, delighting in the prospect. [:-)]

...It's funny to watch my thought processes about what I need to say or do with this group of people. I've given up on planning anything and am trusting that what happens will be just right.

You are obviously a much quicker study than I was. It took me quite a few years before I learned to keep my hands out of the cookie jar. I've learned that I would much rather go to meetings that He does than the ones that I do. I would much prefer that He has His way with me, than for me to have my way with Him.

You asked about last weekend—we met with Lori and Paul at their house last Saturday—nothing on Sunday (that's at our house this Sunday). It was a more in-depth "getting to know you" meeting....

Nice. We meet with about 18 when we are all able to be there. Most of us have known the Lord for many years, except for the kids, Kendra, 17; and Meghan, 19; and to some degree, all of us, even they, have been through the fire of "church." No one wants to be in charge. This is very nice, because Jesus is very polite. He doesn't do "date rape." Unfortunately, many men, and increasingly even women, do. So we just come together with no agenda, and let Jesus have his way with us. In over 30 years of meeting in homes, mostly our own, this is the most free ongoing gathering Carleen and I have yet experienced. Beyond the gathering, we are also in life together the rest of the week. As "teachable moments" surface for you, I will be happy to share more about our experience with this dimension of our inheritance in Jesus.

---

[5]Romans 1:19–20.

...They talked more about the home church concept and their experiences—and their website. They are having a "leadership" of home churches meeting tomorrow night at their house and I'm planning to attend. Just to listen in. I think Tony's son and daughter-in-law will be there.

As long as you stay armed with the knowledge that the old creation is your best teacher on the subject of how God does life, you will be fairly safe from the trap of becoming programmatic in your understanding and practice. Jesus didn't come to bring us a method He came "that we might have life."

Thank you for the communication you sent Tony. More to ponder. Just amazing insights!

My comment about intellectualism was more a comment about myself than you. (More explanation later.) On the contrary. While I find what you write extremely intellectually stimulating and demanding, there is none of the "one-upsmanship" that I encountered growing up around my step-father and his professor friends (he was a Ph.D. in music theory—pretty esoteric all in itself). I felt very discounted as a child in my intellectual abilities—so it's an area that I'm especially sensitive to—I would say easily offended. You are inviting in your writing and oh so sharing and caring—I enjoy going along with you. Big difference.

Thank you for your sensitivity and encouragement.

Speaking of offendedness, I had some big insights last night while massaging (a really great place to have big insights)....

Yes, as we plumb the depths of intimacy, we find ourselves immersed in great revelation. (As long as we are not hung up on the plumbing.)

...It did not escape me that you invited me to look at my experiences of being offended and of redemptive love. The comment, "I'm listening," seemed like an invitation to go deeper—be more intimate....

Yes.

...It struck me as a little strange, since I'd just poured out some very intimate details of my life. I put it on the back burner.

One of the things I have come to see is that relationships in the flesh are very limited by considerations of the flesh, The Bible puts it this way: "The flesh warreth against the spirit, and the spirit against the flesh."[6] The result is that it is much easier to be intimate at very deep levels in the spirit, than it is in the flesh. The precondition of such intimacy, however, is the "circumcision of the cross."[7] (You really must be a quick study if you can take in all that I'm writing. I've had years to assimilate and digest what I'm sharing. For me, it is no longer a matter of theory: it has been cooked in the fire.[8] Beware of those who try to serve you raw Christ, those who try to serve you their theories.)

Then, last night, I started thinking about my response to you yesterday. And it occurred to me that couched in my comments were some of the things you were asking about—my offendedness. Words like "intellectual" and "intense" and "overwhelmed" and "unsettling." I laughed at myself for not realizing what was happening in the moment. The invitation to "get real," be intimate, is at the core of what we've been talking about from day one. And yet the invitation, as gentle as it was, seemed threatening. What I wrote yesterday had a certain "backlash" feel to it—like a cornered animal. So I started thinking about this offendedness and just how subtle—and blatant—it can be and how it shows up in my life.

The miracle of faith is the power to believe in a love that doesn't go away on your worst day. The test and the challenge of the reality of that love in our lives is what happens when we begin to drink the cup of the worst days of those who have been given to us in Him.

I thought a good place to start would be with my offendedness around "Christianity," since that seems to be most on point. In the moment I can think of the following things I have experienced being offended at (some of which I've couched as "other peoples' concerns" in previous emails):

—exclusivity
—quoting scripture
—feeling stupid about not getting the message
—not having an owner's manual with clear instructions
—"being saved" and the "unsaved"
—"the Lord"
—"amens" and "Alleluias"
—prayer
—"Jesus is the way"

---

[6]Galatians 5:17.   [7]Colossians 2:11–15.
[8]Exodus 12:9.

—thinking I don't fit in
—not wanting to be told
—not getting to be "special"

I'm sure this is just a partial list, but you get the message....

Yes, "partial," but wonderful, and very helpful. Rather than tackling it head on, perhaps we can just look in on it now and then as we walk together.

...Better yet, I'm getting the message. What you've written, compounded by the fact that I'm already out there inviting people to enter this spiritual realm with me, makes it imperative that I realize and acknowledge my offendedness....

When I shared about this on the "Unoffendable Love" tape, my body language was to turn my back on those who were there, look up as though I was standing at the foot of the cross, and cry out, "Do I have to put up with this?" It's in those moments so pregnant with the possibility of being offended that we are forced into the eyes of Jesus, even as He is still nailed there, marred beyond human recognition, by the things that I have done.[9] I can still hear Him crying out, "Father forgive them for they know not what they do."

...How can I be of any use to myself or to others if I don't?...

That's a bull's eye.

...I realize that when I get offended I "go away."...

Yes, I weep as I read and think about it.

...Many times I'm able to "come back" quickly, but not always....

Looks to me like it's a growth process.

...What if I'm talking to someone and they say something that is offensive to me and I go away? What if they can see in my eyes suspicion or guardedness? How can they feel comfortable—much less loved—in that situation? If I'm not aware of and acknowledging my offendedness, what keeps me from projecting that onto the person I'm talking to?

This is the cry of "GRACE" that I mentioned in what I sent to Tony. The place to get it is in the opening passage I read in the "Unoffendable Love" tape.[10]

[9] Isaiah 52:13–53:8. [10] Hebrews 10:19–25.

It's not easy to acknowledge these things. It's part of the "garbage."…

Yep.

…And then I remember the image that you described so beautifully—the look of love in Jesus' eyes—and I remember that, by my faith in him, I'm already forgiven. And it occurs to me that—if I keep my eyes on his eyes when talking to people about Christianity, church, faith, whatever—I can keep my heart open while talking and listening. That even as the offendedness comes up—if I keep my eyes there—it will melt away even as it is occurring. I think this is what you mean about redemptive love—the love that comes at and thru you from Jesus.…

It is so encouraging to know that words that you have said or written have been heard and understood!

…It occurred to me that my life "story" is not the issue here. Things happen that might be good, bad, hard. It's the "attitude"—this offendedness—about it that kills you. And you have to be willing to watch for it, acknowledge it for what it is, and then let it go—surrender it—to be at peace.

This is what happened in the Garden of Gethsemane. This is where the conflict of wills between Jesus and His Father was resolved. Before or after a crucifixion, there must be this garden encounter.[11] Otherwise we are only left with bitterness. This is what shuts us down.

After "getting" these insights I've felt much more at peace. I feel better prepared to hear spiritual truths—and perhaps some grappling with all of this—while staying present. I feel much closer to Jesus, too. How can you look at that look of love in his eyes and not feel closer?

Beats me.

(And yes, I'd like your writing on more of your passionate discourse on the church when you're so moved.)…

Perhaps I've already said enough about that for one email. [:-)]

…Is what we're talking about—acknowledging and letting go of our own and other's offendedness—the same as drinking from the cup? Is there more?

---

[11] Gene Edwards is the first one I heard make this very clear in his book **Crucified by Christians**, published by Seedsowers, in 1994 (and now titled **Exquisite Agony**).

Yes, there's more, but perhaps this is enough for now. I don't want to give you chest pains again.

Thanks—I'm getting excited again!

That sounds like just the right temperature. [:-)]

Lisa

PS: Thanks for sharing about your spiritual daughter. I would love to meet both her and you at some point. Singing has been somewhat of a passion in my life, too—although very informally. A gift my mother shared—she actually studied it and got her masters' in voice. I'm glad her operation was successful.

She called yesterday morning. It was the best (most intimate) conversation that we have had in almost three years. This is the part I was speaking about above when I mentioned allowing someone to be "swept away from me, but not from Christ." It was very, very painful at the time, but I had to let her go. I shared the following with her in that conversation, but in connection with a relationship about which she was still in great pain. (She is such a quick study, however, I doubt that she missed the significance in connection with what I had experienced when she had to distance herself from me.)

Jesus said, "I am the vine, and you are the branches. If you abide in me, and I in you, you will bear much fruit. My Father is the husbandman. Branches that bear no fruit are cut off and thrown into the fire. (OUCH!) The branches that bear fruit, He prunes, (OUCH again!) that they might bear more fruit."[12] Perhaps that's enough to make my point. Just because people walk away, it doesn't necessarily mean that you failed.

Lisa, keep this in mind even as you consider the outcome of your upcoming meeting. Perhaps not all will seem to respond favorably. That doesn't mean that you have been a failure or did not hear God. Often times all He allows us to do is plant a seed or perhaps water seeds that someone else has planted. The results of our labors in Him quite often take a long time to become apparent. Sometimes I am minded to think of it this way. When you vaccinate someone, they may not like it, they may even deny that the vaccination took, but they have been vaccinated, whether they like it or not, whether they admit it at the time or not. This to say, be careful to guard your heart and not take people's reactions

---

[12]John 15:1–17.

personally. It is our heavenly Father's business to change hearts, not ours.[13]

So I shared with her that, when He seems to "prune us clean," it is not necessarily that we have failed. It may be that we have been fruitful, and He just wants to strengthen and make room for more fruit on our branch. The important thing is to guard our hearts, so that, "as for our part we are at peace with all men." This way, the door to our own heart is kept open, should those who have left ever want to return. Fact is, we can't force our own love or even Christ's love, on someone else; it is enough if we can keep it new in our own hearts so that we are always a safe place for those we love, even if for a season, they should choose to walk away. I have seen this time and again. He is faithful that promised.[14]

Well, I have to run!

I love you!

In Him,

Jay

---

[13]Proverbs 21:1

[14]Isaiah 53:9–12.

CHAPTER 10

"WE WOULD SEE JESUS"

Dear Jay,

I'm almost at a loss for words to describe how I'm feeling. That last email was so real and loving. The love I'm feeling is so huge that it almost hurts. In fact, tears have come to my eyes several times today. Not sad tears: perhaps it's overjoy. I know I'm a changed person to be able to experience this feeling and let it inhabit me. This must be grace.

It's interesting that you mentioned hesitating getting to know me better "in the flesh." I've had those thoughts, too. It's another filter to deal with—what we have now seems so pure. I have even thought of you as "the voice of God"—my own personal voice. Perhaps voice of Jesus would be more appropriate, as you were describing. Not that you are taking the place of either of them, and I know you're only human. But the voice I hear from you really does seem other-worldly, of the spirit. For now it seems appropriate that I don't have the flesh and blood experience of you.

I have attributed some physical qualities to you, which might amuse you.

I think it's because it was the first movie you recommended and because you remind me of him some in your speaking patterns (and because we always think of movie stars!)—but I visualize you look- ing like Anthony Hopkins. So, if you come in disguise, don't come as him!

That reminds me—Kurtis has listened to both of your tapes now and he seems engaged. He said he could see why I "had to listen to them several times." He also has talked to a couple of the guys that I

159

invited to church—as a personal invitation. I am quite thrilled about it!

He says you sound like Gene Hackman!

I wanted to share an experience I had this morning before signing off (time limitation). I was in mediation training—we break the participants into groups and "coach" role plays of the various stages of mediation. I find coaching to be extremely challenging—listening, processing, affirming, giving feedback, managing dynamics, and explaining complex and sometimes unanswerable questions—in a short and pressured time frame. I've been doing it for years and cut back in recent years to just segments of the training because it was too challenging. Of course, all of my insecurities about my mental abilities are up in the air every time I participate—I just grind thru it. With rewards, but I'm sweating blood regardless.

Today, with these stars in my eyes, I was in a group and was about halfway thru the exercise when I realized that I was doing it wrong—I was on the wrong "stage" of mediation—had given them the wrong information and feedback. Normally this would have caused me deep humiliation and fear of rejection by the trainers. But today, I fixed my eyes on Jesus' eyes (I'm fortunate that I'm a very visual person) and just acknowledged the mistake and that was that. Even "reporting" the incident to the trainers didn't trigger a fear response. More grace!

Sorry this is short. I'm in a really good place, though.

I think you need to know that I love you too. It's difficult to separate out the love I feel—what part is for whom. But you're definitely in there!

Lisa

On Friday, January 23, 2004, Jay responded:

Lisa wrote: *I'm almost at a loss for words to describe how I'm feeling. That last email was so real and loving. The love I'm feeling is so huge that it almost hurts. In fact, tears have come to my eyes several times today. Not sad tears: perhaps it's overjoy. I know I'm a changed person to be able to experience this feeling and let it inhabit me. This must be grace.*

Dear Lisa,
This sounds like an answer to prayer.[1]

---

[1] Ephesians 3:14–21.

...I visualize you looking like Anthony Hopkins. So, if you come in disguise, don't come as him!

Ouch, I'm pretty close to a dead ringer.

That reminds me—Kurtis has listened to both of your tapes now and he seems engaged. He said he could see why I "had to listen to them several times." He also has talked to a couple of the guys that I invited to church—as a personal invitation. I am quite thrilled about it!

I am so encouraged to hear of Kurtis's response. Please feel free to give him my very best, and let him know that, should he ever want to be in touch, I would welcome that.

He says you sound like Gene Hackman!

That possibility never occurred to me, although there was a time when I identified with his driving.

...[Here, Lisa describes the point during mediation training when she discovered she was presenting material out of sequence.] Normally this would have caused me deep humiliation and fear of rejection by the trainers. But today, I fixed my eyes on Jesus' eyes (I'm fortunate that I'm a very visual person) and just acknowledged the mistake and that was that. Even "reporting" the incident to the trainers didn't trigger a fear response. More grace!

Sorry this is short. I'm in a really good place, though.

You bring me great joy in how you are doing!!

I know that your time is limited, but noting your encouragement to keep it coming, I had thought a number of times to send you something I saw after 9/11. It came to mind in connection with what you shared about your family life. So, if you are ready to do a little deep-sea diving, I'll share it with you. You will need a wet suit, and perhaps an extra oxygen bottle.

First, though, some background: Our youngest son, Tim, is an underwater construction/welder/salvage guy, and so diving looms a little large for me as a word picture for intimate sharing. Tim is a real trip!!! Perhaps while I'm on the subject I could take a moment and share a little about him. He was "baptized in the Spirit" a couple of years ago now, and plowed up the whole area where we live to a radius of about 25 miles.

In that time frame, we had had some prophets at our home for the weekend. Kind of a prophetic demolition derby. On Saturday morning, Tim came in (We have a separate garage apartment where Tim was living at the time), sat down, and listened for about a half hour. The subject of discussion was—you guessed it: intimacy. Then Tim broke in, a little bit like Joy broke into C.S. Lewis's ivory tower,[2] and said, "You know, where intimacy is concerned, the more intimate you are with a leader, the less able they are to lead you, but the more intimate you are with a father, the better they are able to father you."

That pretty well shut things down. He was absolutely correct of course. Problem is that most Christian leaders have been trained "not to be intimate with their people."

On another occasion, Tim had been invited to go to a college play, "No Exit."[3] It had been assigned to the philosophy classes. Tim did not know about that part of "the deal." So afterward, the classes convened to debrief about the play. Tim had not gone to college. He was just sitting there as they went through their mental gymnastics until the question was asked, "How do you suppose the idea of an eternal Hell with eternal suffering ever got started and managed to continue to this day?" (Did I mention that it was a Baptist college?) No one seemed to want to answer the question. After a long silence, Tim spoke up, saying, "That's easy." The professor, with a patronizing tone, responded, "Oh yes? Won't you share the answer with the rest of us." Tim responded, "It keeps the pews full and the money coming in." ... Dead silence. I've taken him to "leaders" meetings with me. He has a gift for seeing through things, sizing them up, and taking a meeting to the mat with just a short observation. Again, much like Joy in Lewis's office.

At this point Jay shared something he had written previously concerning "The Mark of Cain," which can be found as Appendix E. What Jay shared was the result of thinking about the terror attack on the Twin Towers on September 11, 2001. Aware of the religious, and even the genetic background of the terrorists, Jay was reminded of Ishmael, and the terrible rejection he had suffered as an oldest child being sent away in favor of a younger brother. What Jay shared had to do with what happens to first children when the second or subsequent children come along. They are displaced from center stage

[2]Referring again to the movie, **Shadowlands.**
[3]A one-act play by Jean-Paul Sartre, published in 1943 and first performed in Paris in May 1944, just before the liberation of that city.

before their source people. In the content of their heart, this results in "Abba" being replaced by "Uh Oh!" This is often our first wounding and carries marks with it late into adult life. And very often into the heritage of the generations to come.

Yours in process,
Jay

On Friday, January 23, 2004, Lisa wrote:

Dear Jay,

Tim sounds like a trip! I'm sure I like him already.

That reminds me about Jon, Tony's son. I met him and his wife, Amy, and their two kids, along with Penny (Tony's mother) last night at that home church "leadership" meeting. (Tony and Felicity were there, too. It was good seeing them and talking more.) John was so casual—laying flat on the couch with his feet on the coffee table, joking and kidding. Very much in command, even at his young age. He has an energy and a sense of deep commitment along with total unpretentiousness. Very refreshing! I marvel at the straight-forward-ness and conviction of some youth. Even if they're not always right, the energy is contagious.

I felt an immediate connection with Penny. She seems very active and somewhat feisty (we were talking about where she lives—right around the corner from where I work—next to a restaurant that I have frequented. She asked if I had been to the restaurant—I said oh yes, have you? She said, oh no—I don't eat at restaurants—it's a waste of money! I knew right then and there that I liked her—and could learn a lot from her!) We're planning on having lunch—I've got to call her.

The meeting was very casual—mainly a place to catch up, plan, and pray. Paul seems to be the reluctant "herder"—keeping on track to cover details. I got to see more of his sense of humor. He's very sharp.

This is a really quick response—really short time today. Am planning to spend much time over the weekend making tapes, reading, and doing some follow-up calls for "church." Tony suggested, since it's a pot luck, to call from the regard of arranging food (in lieu of RSVP). So far I don't have any definites. Your previous email was very comforting in regards to this. Thanks.

A quick read thru of your current email lets me know that it will take some time to process. So add that to the list!

I'm off to Pilates—a "core strengthening" type of exercise using all sorts of pulleys and what not. Started after the hysterectomy and am a weekly diehard. It is taught at Austin Ballet by relentless ballet dancers turned Pilates instructors. Try surrendering your body to that!

Have a wonderful weekend. I'm sure I'll have lots to say on Monday!

Lisa

P.S. One other thing—I have a girlfriend in Colorado who is interested in reading some of our emails. How do you feel about that? They are quite intimate—I haven't wanted to share them with anyone to date. Just wanted to see if you had any reservations.

In that light, it has occurred to me that you have probably shared or wanted to share some or all of this with Carleen and perhaps a select few. I think that's fine with me—in the spirit of sharing and learning.

Thanks,
Lisa

On Friday, January 23, 2004, Jay responded:

Lisa wrote: *P.S. One other thing—I have a girlfriend in Colorado who is interested in reading some of our emails. How do you feel about that? They are quite intimate—I haven't wanted to share them with anyone to date. Just wanted to see if you had any reservations.*

Dear Lisa,

Please feel free to share whatever might be helpful where ever, and whenever you are led to do so.

In that light, it has occurred to me that you have probably shared or wanted to share some or all of this with Carleen and perhaps a select few. I think that's fine with me—in the spirit of sharing and learning.

Thanks, I appreciate having that freedom also. Any time you note "confidential," you can rest assured that an email so marked won't go beyond me. If I sense that you may have shared something much too personal to be shared with someone outside of our conversation, I will also keep that in confidence, just in case you have forgotten to say "confidential." That way you won't have to switch to the other side of your brain, when you are in the midst of plumbing the depths.

Your emails are a great encouragement to me!!
Have a wonderful weekend!

Love,

Jay

P.S. Where your meeting is concerned you can perhaps rest in the knowledge that the fewer there are the more intimacy is possible. There is a kind of Newton's law of intimacy. It is directly proportional to the felt love of Christ and, more often than not, inversely proportional to the square of the number of people who are present.

On Sunday, January 25, 2004, Jay wrote:

Dear Lisa,

The goings-on in your house and in your heart have been much on my heart this weekend. I look forward to hearing how it went, and how it goes with you.

Yours in Christ,
Jay

CHAPTER 11

OPENING DOORS

Dear Jay,

Thank you for keeping me in your heart and for all of your encouraging words. I carried you in my heart as well.

The weekend really did go "just perfect." Many poignant moments. Like the telephone call I made to Yin, the daughter-in-law of my friend, Abigail. Yin and Darrell (Abigail's son) got married last July. She moved here just previous to that from China—Tian Jin, to be exact. When I saw Yin at a New Year's party, she was clearly suffering while trying to maintain a stiff upper lip. She misses her girlfriends, her family. She can't find a job. She is just learning to drive and has been pretty isolated. When I called her Friday to invite her and Darrell on Sunday, she jumped at the chance to come be with a bunch of old fuddy-duddies. I thought this sounded pretty desperate. So I started thinking.

I'd just met Tony's mother, Penny, Thursday night at the leader's meeting. Having lived in China (and she even speaks Mandarin), she has a vested interest in the Chinese population. She talked about how she has been involved in a local Chinese Christian church. I called her up and asked her thoughts about Yin.

Penny managed to arrange her schedule so that she could attend our meeting last night. I think she was a great comfort to Yin (who had expressed a desire to meet Penny and some of her Chinese friends) and they exchanged information. I'm not sure if Darrell and Yin will return to our meetings, but I feel there was some divine intervention there. I'll keep up with their goings on.

I had one friend call and tell me that she and her husband talked about it and they weren't "into it." She wanted to make sure that I wasn't hurt. She wanted to be supportive. I let her know that I didn't have any expectations and that I was glad that she was able to talk to me about it. She said she might come "snoop around" (she didn't). I know she's intensely curious—and searching. Just not ready, for whatever reason.

Karen called Friday and said that she and her husband, Richard, were coming. She said that they were quite committed to going to their church (their 14-year-old is adamant about wanting to attend this church and the youth programs—quite appropriately, I think). But they were curious and also wanted to be supportive.

Abigail (who is probably closest to my heart of the friends I have in Austin) called Saturday, and she and her husband, John (the most "Zen" guy I know), were coming. They seemed excited about the whole idea. Abigail is always ready to "get high on God."

*So I prepared the house, made copies of tapes (I handed out the "Storge" and "Getting Horizontal" tapes—along with Tony's book; unfortunately Tony left in a hurry—had another meeting at 9—and I forgot to give him a copy of the "Storge" tape; next time), went to the store, and cooked. All the while thinking that that was all I was supposed to do. The rest was beyond me. Kurtis and I talked throughout the weekend, wondering how it would be, making logistical plans. He was very loving and supportive. And shared some on a deeper level than customary. I interspersed reading some of your emails and some from **The Message** and meditating on Jesus' eyes in my activities to help calm me. I knew I had to wear love at the meeting, and it was going to have to come thru me.*

So when people started showing up I was in a good place—peaceful and surrendered. In addition to the three couples mentioned above, Tony and Felicity, Penny, and Paul and Lori were there.

Paul and Lori arrived first and left last. They were especially supportive and loving. Afterwards, they said they have been praying about having a new group to meet with—theirs is disbanding—and that they felt comfortable with our friends (and I guess, us!) and they want to continue meeting with us. This is really encouraging. And I'm growing to love them more each time. It's interesting to note that they found this group refreshing—not fixed in stale Christian modes.

We all had a wonderful meal—pot luck. I did a pot roast which lent a certain anticipatory feeling all day as we were reminded by the smells. It's always interesting to watch how the people group—as is typical, the men (for the most part) went to the coffee table setting (probably out of politeness since it was seating on pillows—leaving the table and chairs for the women) and the women sat together. Lots of getting to know you and bridging of conversation. Allowing for some pregnant silences and subsequent divergent conversation.

After eating, we put the chairs in a circle—in meeting style. I could see a little discomfort in the room—(was this sermon time?). Richard had already approached Kurtis asking what the format for the evening was (Kurtis had turned to me and said "I don't think there's a rule book."). So I looked at Tony and Tony looked at me and said that perhaps I would like to start by talking about why I called the meeting.

I just started talking—letting it flow—however it went. I ended up briefly describing my experience last July with the healer—what I now believe to be a type of "spiritual conversion" where the holy spirit took over. I talked about the journey since then—trying to conceptualize what had happened and the subsequent events and people (you, Tony and Felicity, Paul and Lori) that had been put into my life. And how it was in my heart to become more intimate on a spiritual level with particularly them—the people in my life that I love.

Tony talked about his journey some and his concept of home church. Felicity added some. (They're so cool!) Then we opened up to the group.

Most everyone shared some about their spiritual journeys and seemed open and transparent. It was quite wonderful to hear my friends talk on this level. It was exactly what I had hoped for. By the end, there was a definite feeling of warmth and camaraderie in the room. People seemed genuinely touched by the sharing.

Afterward Kurtis and I just sat and talked some about the experience. We were both somewhat in awe—just taking it in.

We talked with the group briefly about meeting next week—we're all checking our schedules and agreed to contact by email. I offered hosting again. There are some other people I invited who couldn't make it yesterday who said they were interested in maybe meeting next week. So we'll see. I hear what you say about intimacy and small groups. There were times when I was inviting people when I wondered "would this person get along with that person"—would people allow themselves to go deep in this mix of cultures and personalities. Would the group be too large and eclectic. But then I would listen to the inner voice that said, "God is no respecter of persons," and it would become clear to invite the person. I'm just doing what I'm told.

So… wanted to get this off to you—have another busy day. Want to bask in the experience of the weekend for a while before deep sea diving into your last email. But it is on my mind.

Thanks again and much love to you,

Lisa

Lisa wrote: *Thank you for keeping me in your heart and for all of your encouraging words. I carried you in my heart as well.*

The weekend really did go "just perfect." …

Dear Lisa,

What a wonderful report!!!

…Many poignant moments. Like the telephone call I made to Yin, the daughter-in-law of my friend, Abigail….

…I'm not sure if Darrell and Yin will return to our meetings, but I feel there was some divine intervention there. I'll keep up with their goings on.

How amazed, and blessed I am to hear of your China connection.

You probably have never heard of Watchman Nee. I would say that he was probably the leading apostle of the 20th century. He only wrote one book, **The Spiritual Man**,[1] but many books have been published in his name, these based on the notes of his students. One of those books that is very highly esteemed has the title, **Sit, Walk, Stand**.[2] It is Nee's commentary on Ephesians. I would be very surprised if it is not available in Mandarin Chinese. You may want to see if you can find a copy for Yin. I would also be very surprised if Penny does not know of this book. It is just a little booklet, but very foundational, and very powerful. I highly recommend it for you and Kurtis as well.

I had one friend call and tell me that she and her husband talked about it and they weren't "into it." …

---

[1] **The Spiritual Man**, by Watchman Nee (3-volume set), published by Living Stream Ministry, in 1998.
[2] **Sit, Walk, Stand**, by Watchman Nee, published by Tyndale House Publishers, in 1977.

Paul and Lori arrived first and left last. They were especially supportive and loving. Afterwards, they said they have been praying about having a new group to meet with—theirs is disbanding—...

(Like I said above, honeymoons are easy. It's marriage that is a little more challenging. [:-)])

...and that they felt comfortable with our friends (and I guess, us!) and they want to continue meeting with us. This is really encouraging. And I'm growing to love them more each time. It's interesting to note that they found this group refreshing—not fixed in stale Christian modes.

Lisa, Carleen and I are tickled to the bone!

We all had a wonderful meal—pot luck. I did a pot roast which lent a certain anticipatory feeling all day as we were reminded by the smells. It's always interesting to watch how the people group—as is typical, the men (for the most part) went to the coffee table setting (probably out of politeness since it was seating on pillows—leaving the table and chairs for the women) and the women sat together....

It took the early Church a long time in the upper room, "together with the women and children," before they were together in one accord.[3]

...Lots of getting to know you and bridging of conversation. Allowing for some pregnant silences and subsequent divergent conversation.

Making love gender-neutral takes time and patience.

After eating, we put the chairs in a circle—in meeting style. I could see a little discomfort in the room—(was this sermon time?). Richard had already approached Kurtis asking what the format for the evening was (Kurtis had turned to me and said "I don't think there's a rule book."). So I looked at Tony and Tony looked at me and said that perhaps I would like to start by talking about why I called the meeting.

I just started talking—letting it flow—however it went. I ended up briefly describing my experience last July with the healer—what I now believe to be a type of "spiritual conversion" where the holy spirit took over. I talked about the journey since then—trying to conceptualize what had happened and the subsequent events and people (you, Tony and Felicity, Paul and Lori) that had been put into my life.

---

[3]Acts 2:1.

And how it was in my heart to become more intimate on a spiritual level with particularly them—the people in my life that I love.

Wow! I am so proud of you, in the best sense of the word.

Tony talked about his journey some and his concept of home church. Felicity added some. (They're so cool!) ...

I am so glad that you made that connection!

...Then we opened up to the group.

Most everyone shared some about their spiritual journeys and seemed open and transparent. It was quite wonderful to hear my friends talk on this level. It was exactly what I had hoped for. By the end, there was a definite feeling of warmth and camaraderie in the room. People seemed genuinely touched by the sharing.

Afterward Kurtis and I just sat and talked some about the experience. We were both somewhat in awe—just taking it in.

I'm blown away!! [:-)]

We talked with the group briefly about meeting next week—we're all checking our schedules and agreed to contact by email. I offered hosting again. There are some other people I invited who couldn't make it yesterday who said they were interested in maybe meeting next week. So we'll see. I hear what you say about intimacy and small groups. There were times when I was inviting people when I wondered "would this person get along with that person"—would people allow themselves to go deep in this mix of cultures and personalities. Would the group be too large and eclectic. But then I would listen to the inner voice that said, "God is no respecter of persons," and it would become clear to invite the person. I'm just doing what I'm told.

That's the secret. That and not letting men do a number on you.

So...wanted to get this off to you—have another busy day. Want to bask in the experience of the weekend for a while before deep sea diving into your last email. But it is on my mind.

You are doing great!!

In Him,
Jay

On Tuesday, January 27, 2004, Lisa wrote:

Dear Jay,

I look forward so much to every day these days—and these daily messages are such a part of it! So, even if there's not a lot going on (which doesn't seem to be happening much lately), you'll probably get some sort of communication.

Today's event (so far) totally took me by surprise. I needed my "other sister's" address (my dad and stepmother had a daughter who lives in LA—she's 33 and we have a strong connection) to send her a birthday card. I called my stepmother to get it. I was feeling a little rushed, thinking I wanted to get the card in the mail today—and the thought of calling her put me off a little because I knew we would talk a while. But I went ahead and called. While we were talking I heard to tell her about my experiences. I haven't been ready to talk to her or to my dad about any of this—and just a bit of it to my sister. I haven't really even been able to put words around it until just recently.

Anyway, we talked well over an hour, sharing thoughts and experiences. I got to see a side of her that I've never fully appreciated. It was wonderful! I told her about the healing all the way up thru the church meeting. She told me about how she's heard "other worldly—indescribable" music on a couple of occasions while in a state of grace.

We talked about the Bible, the Urantia book, prayer, living from the spiritual realm—lots of stuff. It was the best conversation I've ever had with her! I'm sure my dad is next—we'll be talking soon. I'm sure all sorts of healing will follow—some has already occurred on some levels just with this conversation. It feels so good to be able to share on this level! Awesome!

There's another friend whom I've grown closer to over the years (we're REALLY different—she grew up in a missionary family and she is a little fireball), whom I've opened up to. I'm beginning to see her through different eyes, too, and suspect we will become much closer—which I never would have guessed.

What a day!

Thanks for the "Chinese connection"—very interesting. I'm really so ignorant as to what's going on around the world. (I tend to avoid the media.) Tony has talked some about Christianity in other countries—fascinating! I'll certainly look for the book for Yin and us. Penny wrote a book on their adventures in China[4]—she promised me a copy (would you like one, too?).

---

[4]**Ten Sacks of Rice: Our Way to China**, by Penelope Dale, published by Karis Publishing, Inc., in 2002.

Still cooking on the Cain piece. Am focused on the part about if you wish you don't have to deal with someone, you're already murdering them. Ouch! Where have I done that?…

All for now—really should get more work done. Thanks for listening.

Love,

Lisa

On Wednesday, January 28, 2004, Jay responded:

Lisa wrote: *I look forward so much to every day these days—and these daily messages are such a part of it! So, even if there's not a lot going on (which doesn't seem to be happening much lately), you'll probably get some sort of communication.*

Dear Lisa,

Thanks so much!! You are blessing my socks off, and what you have shared below is no exception!

Today's event (so far) totally took me by surprise. I needed my "other sister's" address (my dad and stepmother had a daughter who lives in LA—she's 33 and we have a strong connection) to send her a birthday card. I called my stepmother to get it. I was feeling a little rushed, thinking I wanted to get the card in the mail today—and the thought of calling her put me off a little because I knew we would talk a while. But I went ahead and called. While we were talking I heard to tell her about my experiences. I haven't been ready to talk to her or to my dad about any of this—and just a bit of it to my sister. I haven't really even been able to put words around it until just recently.

Anyway, we talked well over an hour, sharing thoughts and experiences. I got to see a side of her that I've never fully appreciated. It was wonderful! I told her about the healing all the way up thru the church meeting. She told me about how she's heard "other worldly—indescribable" music on a couple of occasions while in a state of grace. We talked about the Bible, the Urantia book, prayer, living from the spiritual realm—lots of stuff. It was the best conversation I've ever had with her!…

[:-)] [:-)] [:-)]

…I'm sure my dad is next—we'll be talking soon. I'm sure all sorts of healing will follow—some has already occurred on some levels

just with this conversation. It feels so good to be able to share on this level! Awesome!

It's amazing what happens when we are looking in the right direction! You are such a delight to me!!

There's another friend whom I've grown closer to over the years (we're REALLY different—she grew up in a missionary family and she is a little fireball), whom I've opened up to. I'm beginning to see her through different eyes, too, and suspect we will become much closer—which I never would have guessed.

What a day!

WOW!!!

Thanks for the "Chinese connection"—very interesting. I'm really so ignorant as to what's going on around the world. (I tend to avoid the media.)...

This has nothing to do with ignorance on the part of either of us; it has to do with the Lord's pleasure and leading in connection with connection.

...Tony has talked some about Christianity in other countries—fascinating! I'll certainly look for the book for Yin and us. Penny wrote a book on their adventures in China—she promised me a copy (would you like one, too?)

If that would be possible without imposing, that would be very nice. Thank you/Penny.

Still cooking on the Cain piece. Am focused on the part about if you wish you don't have to deal with someone, you're already murdering them. Ouch! Where have I done that?...

All for now—really should get more work done. Thanks for listening.

A pleasure always.

One of these days I'll have to share with you what's going on at my end. It's mind boggling. I can barely take it all in. I think you are part of it or perhaps soon will be. A number of things have happened that I may need your help with.

I'll keep you posted if you like.

The snow has cancelled school once again tomorrow, so Carleen and I get another bonus day together. These days have been wonderfully full. Time for Carleen and I to get caught up with each other; rich correspondence, good progress on my money book rewrite, and good things happening in Charlotte with the "leaders" there.

Well, I have to run. I got a rather challenging answer to an email that I sent to my daughter Heather. Heather is 35, lives in New Haven, CT, and works at Yale. I sent her a little piece from today's Dr. Phil show. Carleen and I happened to catch it this morning, and there was an exchange between Phil and a woman on the show that was excellence of communication if ever I have seen it. I went to his web site, and ordered the transcription, as well as the video. I'll send it to you if you like.

Yours in Christ,
Jay

P.S. Here it is as I sent it to Heather:

The following is a clip from today's Dr. Phil show. Mom is snowed out of school, so we are enjoying our second bonus day together, and just watched his show. The exchange, including the following snip, was amazing in a number of ways. Let me know what you think, Perhaps we can talk about it some. The video is available on his web site. The other two women on the show also had addictions, but they were drug-related. In any case, what he had to say to the third woman, a victim of long-term childhood sexual molestation, had tremendous relevance to the addictions of all three. What he shared, and the way he shared it was core!

I love you!

Dad

Dr. Phil says, "Anne's past abuse has been one of the defining moments in her life. At a very young age, they were writing on a blank slate: 'This is where you are, this is what you do, this is what you're good for …' It has nothing to do with sex. It has to do with the feeling of power because somebody early in your life took your self-esteem, your innocence, your value, and they wadded it up and threw it away."

"Anne says she's angry because it caused her to lose so much in her life. 'It's just been a nightmare,' she says.

"You've never developed relationship skills. And the relationship that you develop that's more important than any other is your relationship with yourself. You don't know Anne. You've never met her for real. You don't recognize her true worth and value as one of God's creatures. You just don't get that or you wouldn't sell her down the river," Dr. Phil says.

He tells her that he's worried for her safety as well. Anne promises she will do everything she can to get to know herself, and Dr. Phil arranges for counseling in her town.

Dear Jay,

I'm so glad when you share what's going on with you. I can't wait to hear more details! And I'm curious as to how I might be able to help.

I've never asked you about your book—is it still in print? What's the title? It must be mind boggling to try to write something that will reach a wide audience. I would think that you must get information passed thru to you about what to say and how to say it. The portion that you sent to me was a study—I can't imagine a whole book like that. Please keep me posted on how you're coming along and if there's a way I can possibly help.

Sounds like your life is very full and rich right now. So glad!

Please do send info about the Dr. Phil show. He's pretty provocative, isn't he? I haven't really watched TV over the last 6 months, but enjoyed watching his show from time to time in the past. We even studied some of his work (my girlfriends and I—we've studied a lot over the years). I like the way he gets to the core of things and doesn't mince words.

Today I'm buried. It's the last day of the training, so things should calm down a little bit here. Still have end-of-the-month finance push. One thing I like about this finance job is that, while it's ongoing, at least it's pretty predictable. It helps to stabilize the "unpredictability" of the rest of my life!

Looking forward to hearing more about what's going on in your life!

Love,
Lisa

Lisa wrote: *I'm so glad when you share what's going on with you. I can't wait to hear more details! And I'm curious as to how I might be able to help.*

Dear Lisa,

Thanks again for your note. Actually, what I was thinking about was something we have already discussed: going after those who have been offended by what they have seen in those who call themselves "Christians," and what they are doing, and calling "church." We don't have to start with bin Laden, but neither do I rule him out. Certainly there are plenty out there, so we wouldn't have to worry about unemployment, and it looks to me like we can reach them through the internet, so the price of gas doesn't much matter either. [:-)]

I've never asked you about your book—is it still in print?...

No. It has been out of print for quite a few years now.

...What's the title?...

It was published under the title, **Inflation: The Ultimate Graven Image**. It hasn't been decided yet what the new title will be for the new edition. One possibility that has occurred to me is, **For Love Or Money**.

...It must be mind boggling to try to write something that will reach a wide audience....

Yes, "it must," not exactly my strong suit. I already know that I need a translator when I share in Germany. Problem is, friends and family tell me I need a translator when I share here.

...I would think that you must get information passed thru to you about what to say and how to say it....

I have a fairly low-profile life, and life style, so not much "gets passed through to me." What does find me here, in the bushes of the South Mountains, is quite amazing however. The present publisher, for instance found me here because of an email exchange I had had with a Kariate Jew from Wall Street. This Jewish man is very well connected, and one day he sent an email to some one with about five copies to others. I was one of the others. The email was so far into my yard, that I sent him back an answer with copies to those who had received his. I knew none of them. One wrote me to ask a question about what I had sent. I responded with a brief explanation, quoting the **Inflation** book. He wanted to know about the book. I had one copy left other than my own personal one that Carleen had leather-bound for me. I sent him the copy, about a month went by, and I received a very excited email to call him. He never knew that the Bible supported what he considered to be the only moral monetary system. You can check out his website if you like:

http://www.FAME.org

…The portion that you sent to me was a study—I can't imagine a whole book like that.…

I think what I sent you was the chapter from the manuscript on relationships. The following contains a testimony, summary, and taste from the **Inflation** book: I should say that it was written about 25 years ago, but for the most part, it still reflects my understanding.[5]

…Please keep me posted on how you're coming along and if there's a way I can possibly help.

Well, the publisher has asked me to find people who will proofread it for me, point out obvious errors, typos, etc., and let me know when they hit areas that are difficult to understand. The publisher is also an excellent editor, but he does not have the time to do that himself. If this would be of interest to you, let me know, and I'll send it to you by email in small bites, about the size of that above. Please understand this is not to be a pressure on you. I'm just sharing one of the kinds of help that I may need in the present season of my life.

Sounds like your life is very full and rich right now. So glad!

Very full, and very rich, spiritually! As I have confessed for many years now, "One day at a time, I am a spoiled brat. The only way I can keep that from being the case is by borrowing trouble from tomorrow."

Please do send info about the Dr. Phil show. He's pretty provocative, isn't he? I haven't really watched TV over the last 6 months, but enjoyed watching his show from time to time in the past. We even studied some of his work (my girlfriends and I—we've studied a lot over the years). I like the way he gets to the core of things and doesn't mince words.

Exactly. I'll send it when I get it.

Today I'm buried. It's the last day of the training, so things should calm down a little bit here. Still have end-of-the-month finance push.

---

[5]This material is presented as Appendix F, "Inflation: The Ultimate Graven Image."

One thing I like about this finance job is that, while it's ongoing, at least it's pretty predictable. It helps to stabilize the "unpredictability" of the rest of my life!

Looking forward to hearing more about what's going on in your life!

Well, I guess that ought to be a big enough slice of my life for one email.

I love you!

Jay

On Thursday, January 29, 2004, Lisa wrote:

Dear Jay,

I have to say that, after a quick read of your overview, I'm so excited that it made sense to me! I suppose it's not coincidental that my dad is extremely interested in the economy (I think he has his master's in it) and, I believe, in the spiritual connections, and he has long talked about the implications of inflation—even to the extent of writing his own booklet. I can't remember the title, but it was something to do with following the Pied Piper. I will look for a copy and send it to you, if you'd like. Dad is totally against the credit system—hasn't had a credit card since the 70s (which is also when he wrote his book). You two would probably have a lot to talk about. I wonder if he would be interested in being one of your "proofers"? He's got the time and certainly the interest. I'd be happy to send him this excerpt and get his response if you would like me to pursue it.

Kurtis also has an intense interest in economics—and a growing interest in the spiritual. I'll give this to him to read as well. Another person came to mind— my client that I told you about that I have such a strong connection with. He has talked about this topic—what the Bible says about money—in the past. I'm having lunch with him on Monday—I could take a copy of this to him as well, if you don't mind.

And, of course, I would be happy to read and give comments. It's not my area of "expertise," but you need just some normal people reading it for clarity as well.

This is very exciting—thanks so much for sharing with me! And I particularly liked hearing about the pieces of your personal spiritual journey within the overview. Precious!

I'm still very much interested in looking at reaching people who are on the fence spiritually. It feels like there's a whole bunch right here in my back yard—coming to my house on Sundays right now. So very apropos. I believe we left off on counting the cost. I'll spend time with that email tonight and see what comes up.

Still catching up! All for now...

Love,
Lisa

PS: I've put my other books aside to read thru **The Message.** *I've read bits and pieces—going along with references you've made in the emails. But I thought, particularly if we're going to introduce the Bible in our church meetings, that I should at least be somewhat familiar with it—so I'm starting at the beginning and reading thru it. I like how Peterson gives a little contextual background information before each "chapter." So far, so good!*

At some point, I'd like to hear more about your take on how "man" has messed with the Bible. I'm sure it will come up—big time—in our meetings. I have read some thru the Urantia book, and my Dad has talked some about it (and a book that's popular right now—the Mona Lisa (?) book addresses some, I hear[6]), in fact, it seems that everyone talks about it. I realize that the basic messages still come thru—and I really want to focus more on those. I think all this other can be major detractors. But I feel that in order to be "real" about something, you have to be open to an awareness of all of it. So when the time seems right....

On Thursday, January 29, 2004, Jay responded:

Lisa wrote: *I have to say that after a quick read of your overview, I'm so excited that it made sense to me! I suppose it's not coincidental that my dad is extremely interested in the economy (I think he has his master's in it) and, I believe, in the spiritual connections, and he has long talked about the implications of inflation—even to the extent of writing his own booklet. I can't remember the title, but it was something to do with following the Pied Piper. I will look for a copy and send it to you, if you'd like. Dad is totally against the credit system—hasn't had a credit card since the 70s (which is also when he wrote his book). You two would probably have a lot to talk about. I wonder if he would be interested in being one of your "proofers"? He's got the time and certainly the interest. I'd be happy to send him this excerpt and get his response if you would like me to pursue it.*

---

[6]Lisa is referring to **The Da Vinci Code,** by Dan Brown, published by Doubleday in 2003.

Kurtis also has an intense interest in economics—and a growing interest in the spiritual. I'll give this to him to read as well. Another person came to mind—my client that I told you about that I have such a strong connection with. He has talked this topic—what the Bible says about money—in the past. I'm having lunch with him on Monday—I could take a copy of this to him as well, if you don't mind.

Dear Lisa,

The connective miracles just keep coming!

And, of course, I would be happy to read and give comments. It's not my area of "expertise," but you need just some normal people reading it for clarity as well.

Let me see if I have this right: Lisa…"normal"… Not! [:-)] In any case I did think you might help me not to get too obtuse.

This is very exciting—thanks so much for sharing with me! And I particularly liked hearing about the pieces of your personal spiritual journey within the overview. Precious!

I'm still very much interested in looking at reaching people who are on the fence spiritually. It feels like there's a whole bunch right here in my back yard—coming to my house on Sundays right now. So very apropos. I believe we left off on counting the cost. I'll spend time with that email tonight and see what comes up.

Still catching up!…

Like I said, "No unemployment in sight for either of us."

*PS: I've put my other books aside to read thru **The Message**. I've read bits and pieces—going along with references you've made in the emails. But I thought, particularly if we're going to introduce the Bible in our church meetings, that I should at least be somewhat familiar with it—so I'm starting at the beginning and reading thru it. I like how Peterson gives a little contextual background information before each "chapter." So far, so good!*

That's really good news!

At some point, I'd like to hear more about your take on how "man" has messed with the Bible. I'm sure it will come up—big time—in our meetings. I have read some thru the Urantia book, and my Dad has talked some about it (and a book that's popular right now—the Mona Lisa (?) book addresses some, I hear), in fact, it seems that everyone talks about it. I realize that the basic messages still come thru—and I really want to focus more on those. I think all this other can be major detractors. But I feel that in order to be "real" about something, you have to be open to an awareness of all of it. So when the time seems right....

For now, perhaps it's enough to say, there is a war, an increasingly intense war, being waged against The Word of God. It is difficult to tell where the greatest losses are coming from, "friendly fire" or the detractors. In both cases, I think a big reason for the war is the lack of spiritual understanding of what the Bible is actually saying in the Spirit.

More later.

You are such a delight to me!!
Jay

CHAPTER 12

STRAIGHT TALK

Dear Jay,

HA! You got me on that normal thing. What was the first clue? Glad you love me anyway!

Gearing up for the weekend. Having lunch in a few minutes with one girlfriend who came last Sunday and one who didn't. This was a last minute call, probably in response to an email I sent out yesterday making arrangements for this Sunday. I'm a little nervous—more ex- cited really—wondering what the spirit will prompt me to say.

Had a wonderful connection with my sister Traci yesterday. She's really suffering—long story—and I invited her to come Sunday. She's coming and bringing my niece, who turns 10 on Wednesday. I think this group will be really comforting to her.

There's a Chinese friend who grew up in Panama (speaks fluent Spanish—no Chinese! Freaks people out). I told him about the church meeting and asked him to come. He's coming even though he said, "I don't think I'm very spiritual." (My assurance was that I thought he was extremely spiritual and that he appeared to be searching and that this might be a good place to explore.)

There's another couple—the woman is a client of mine who also went to that shamanic healer—who are coming. She seems excited.

*I have another friend, who is an ardent **Course in Miracles**[1] believer (she's the only person I know who seems to really understand what it says!) who is coming.*

---

[1] **A Course in Miracles**, 2nd edition, published by the Foundation for Inner Peace, in 1992.

And the woman who cleans my house, a black woman whom I have had a special connection with for over 10 years now, is coming.

And John and Abigail, Yin and Darrell, Paul & Lori, Tony & Felicity & me and Kurtis. Think that's all—subject to change!

Gotta run! Love you!!

Lisa

On Friday, January 30, 2004, Jay responded:

Lisa wrote:

And John and Abigail, Yin and Darrell, Paul & Lori, Tony & Felicity & me and Kurtis. Think that's all—subject to change!

Dear Lisa,

Gotta love it!
Thanks for keeping me in the loop.

P.S. I have a confession to make. I don't know if you're still getting the Deida list emails, but after getting about 60 of them yesterday, and last night, I had to take a shot. Did you see "Hunt For Red October"? This morning I surfaced for the first time on the list, and sent "one ping only."

I may need your help before this encounter is over.

I can smell the fragrance of Jesus all over you, even through the fiber optics!

Love,
Jay

On Monday, February 2, 2004, Lisa wrote:

Dear Jay,

Wow! Things are moving so fast around here it's making me dizzy! I'm very grateful that I don't have any massages scheduled tonight so I can just "steep."

It's funny you mentioned the Deida list. Yes, I'm still getting the list and quickly look thru most of them. There's some pretty amazingly deep things being said. Real searching. I'd say extremely fertile ground—and I wouldn't be surprised if several are already Christian—just looking for deep experiences and connection. I was deleting a lot last week with barely a glance—what did yours say? Did you get any responses? I hate it that I missed it!

I have been somewhat connected with the "Deida community," though. I had asked the list (before Christmas) if there was a local women's group that practiced some of what David talks about. The guy who runs "Plexus"—the web site and e-mail list—lives here in Austin—forwarded my request to a woman who was starting a woman's group. They have all "studied" with David for years.

I met with two of the women to check each other out and see if we had compatible goals. They were a little mystical, but that has never put me off. I liked that they were putting together a group of women who were interested in learning to be more intimate, open, and loving. I decided to go to the first group and see how it felt.

That was last Tuesday. It was a beautiful group of women, and we did a lot of experiential things to tune into each other and help each other move thru blocks to being more open and intimate. These women were going for it—I was genuinely impressed. I talked about my faith (we all shared our "intentions" for what we wanted out of the group experience) and how I wanted to grow in my intimacy with God, Jesus, and other people and how I wanted to learn, feel, and allow to come thru me this amazing love of Jesus. There was another woman in the group who had a late-term miscarriage last month who had recently broken thru with what I recognized as a "spirit-driven" awakening and who, like me, was having difficulty putting words around it. I felt an immediate connection with her. Actually, I felt a pretty deep connection with all of the women by the end of the evening. We're meeting once a month.

Saturday night a friend, Pat (she came to church last night—she's the one into **The Course in Miracles**) *and I went to see one of the women from this group (who's about 25 and bowls me over!) in a play that she wrote and acted all of 19 characters. She's from England where she was trained and has won all sorts of acting awards. Really talented. I'm going to enjoy getting to know her better!*

So, you never know. I'm glad I didn't rule this group out as "mystical non-Christians" (actually some were Christians). This is what I meant when I said there's lots of ways to "be" in the world—lots of experiences to engage in—that can experientially increase my connection with God, Jesus, and others. It's all in the intention that I enter into the experience with.

Church was great last night! There were 3 things that Tony "led" us thru—one was sharing any "God" events that happened in the last week. Then we started reading John's Gospel (Tony brought a bunch of bibles—contemporary) and discussing it (didn't get very far or spend a lot of time on this—I think it was a good introduction), and in the end we broke into small groups and talked about an area in our lives that we wanted God to be more present and prayed about it.

I have to tell you about where I am on prayer. The whole concept is somewhat foreign to me. It feels really awkward doing it. I remember my Dad's voice, "there's no need to pray for anything—the Father knows your needs and what's in your heart." What I'm "getting" now is that prayer is what leads to intimacy.

My hairdresser, who I just found out this week "just loves Jesus" (she wants to come to church with her fiancé soon), brought me a little book, Prayer of Jabez, (sp?) which I read Friday night. It really got me thinking—wow! If I'm already feeling so high, without prayer, just how much more powerful could this spiritual life be WITH prayer (kinda scary thought). So I've been doing that little prayer every day and trying to remember to talk to God and Jesus more—just for that intimacy.

I looked around some for my Dad's booklet—I think it's in a box in the shed. Could be a while before I locate it. In the meanwhile, I'm planning on sending that overview to him today with a request of perhaps mailing me another copy, which I'll make a copy of for you. I'll also send you Penny's book—got a copy last night.

I read thru your email on "counting the costs." Maybe it's because I'm older, have done a lot of therapy in establishing "boundaries" and in not taking on other peoples' "stuff," and maybe because I don't have a whole community of relationships that are extremely rigid—but I don't have a lot of fear about what the "costs" might be for me. My experience so far has been whatever fear I have in my head—particularly what people might think of me or if I'm capable of handling what's coming so fast—is dispelled again and again when I just focus on what I'm doing in the moment—the conversation, the email, the preparation—and say what's on my heart. The moment-to-moment experience is generally peaceful and exciting as long as I stay in my heart and not my head. So, I'm probably doing this from a very naive place—but I'm doing this pretty low key. No big threatening religious leaders or communities in my face yet. What am I missing?

Hope you're doing well. Keep me posted on what you're doing—please! Also, please give my love to Carleen. I was thinking this week about how generous she is in allowing you to spend so much time with other people (me!). Many thanks.

Talk soon!

Love,
Lisa

Lisa wrote: *Wow! Things are moving so fast around here it's making me dizzy! I'm very grateful that I don't have any massages scheduled tonight so I can just "steep."*

Dear Lisa,

I know the feeling. The gathering here at our house yesterday, was mind blowing, from 9:30 AM when the first one showed up, to about 3:00 PM when the last ones left.

It's funny you mentioned the Deida list. Yes, I'm still getting the list and quickly look thru most of them. There are some pretty amazingly deep things being said. Real searching. I'd say extremely fertile ground—and I wouldn't be surprised if several are already Christian—just looking for deep experiences and connection. I was deleting a lot last week with barely a glance—what did yours say? Did you get any responses? I hate it that I missed it!

It probably went out with the trash. It was in the same time frame of the night when there was such a high level of activity on the list. As you may have noticed, one of the subjects being discussed was that of trying to define "love." Finally I sent the following in response to what was sent in, and included just below my response:

Love is defined by demonstration. "I love you so much I would give my life for you even if it was you who was taking my life." That much is talk. It becomes reality when someone takes your talk to the bank, and the look of love does not leave your eye.

Jay

One person on the list wrote:

In the film, the last samurai, katsumoto asks algren—do you think a man can change his destiny? and algren replies I believe a man can do what he can, and his destiny is revealed to him. To me this seems the same as not waiting to love.

Another wrote:

Everyone is waiting to love
Waiting for the other to turn up
Before we reveal our heart

That was my first and only time, to date, that I sent in anything to the list. I received the following response, the only one I received. It also came into the list:

"Jay Jay...Jay this is fierce and romantic (in the best sense of the word). I would add that as always a good quote reads you, not you it. So someone caught in the romantic addictions of our culture may interpret this pathologically. Not much we can do about that in terms of clarifying the language—would lose its poetic power. the portugese say if you tell me a lie your lie would become my truth, if you shoot me, a rose of blood would bloom in my heart—yeah that's gittin pathological I suppose....but what I like in your idea, and the portugese one, what we get attarcted to I guess, is the 100% commitment in the words/action,

"if we 'third stage –ise' this commitment then perhaps its a commitment to the Moment, and what it demands, rather than to a person although sometimes they would merge......

Stage 1 and 3 do they both have passion?"

I have not yet responded. I'm hoping to get a little better feel for where people are, before I "go public" again. I have a conversation of sorts going with someone else on the list, however, It is also in private. He is another who has been turned off by what is calling itself "Christianity." I was very direct with him when I saw that his posturing on the list was not consistent with what I was seeing in private. I've been hanging around "church" too long not to spot that kind of thing very quickly. He had come back to me after my very straight talk to him, but right at the moment the ball is in his court.

Here's the "straight talk" I sent him:

Yesterday as I continued to think about our private exchange while observing the various contributions to the list, yours included, I thought about how I might best respond to what you had last written to me.

My path has been somewhat narrower than that of most on the list, including your own. Perhaps that's the reason I don't seem to be getting it. What I am seeing so far is a three-stage caste system, where upward mobility, if that's the right phrase for it, consists of mastering the lingo and the "buzz names."

The object appears to be alienation from our own thoughts and words. This makes it just a little difficult to figure out where the real person is based on the words they are using. (Key word, "using.")

That has given me pause where my next communication with you is concerned. It had not been my desire to respond to your words, but to you, if only I could find you. I'm not at all sure that I have, but I will risk the following. For me it's more than words.

What grabs me by the throat is the profound sense that my answer needs to be more than disconnected information. To have any credibility with you at all, I must search my own heart to be sure I own what I am about to share, to be sure it exists for me, to me, and in me, before I dare to answer.

Here's the core of my problem. It's my garbage. Call it "Kinks" if you want to, but I don't really think that does it justice on the down side. It's all the things that make me so unlovable, most of them issuing out of old wounds, rejections, abuses, insecurities, unmet desires, unmet needs, all of things that tend to fill a person with hidden agendas, and touchy expectations, all of the things that tend to shut me, and those around me, down. Somehow all of that garbage boils down to the fear of rejection. What I want is intimacy, but the fear of rejection makes it impossible to get there. You see, at root, I'm unqualified for love, the kind that is good for friends, that is, but then one day I discovered another kind of love, a love that's good for enemies, a love that's good for those who don't "deserve" it. I ran to the head of the line. I finally qualified!!

In 1987 I was in a patent office in Düsseldorf, Germany. There was a fairly substantial meeting going on. My German was not good enough to pay much attention to what was being said, and, anyway, I was in a rather desperate place at the time. I had already learned that my expectations were my greatest enemy. Every time they weren't lived up to I became part of the problem.

I had heard a "Gospel" that "Jesus laid His life down for His friends," but that wasn't doing me much good.

As I sat there in the patent office, a verse out of the Bible kept cycling through my not quite consciousness, "Perfect love casts out fear."[2] When I became conscious of it (you know, kind of like the moment you become conscious of a melody which continually recycles in your mind even before you're aware of it.), my awareness took the form of, "That's interesting, love casts out fear." Suddenly I felt inwardly rebuked, "NO! Love creates fear! Perfect love casts out fear!"

As I sat there, "perfect love" was explained to me in the context of a patent. I don't know if you know anything about patents or what is needed to get one, but, in general, a couple of things are required. The first thing is to describe what is called "the state of the art." This is the prior art, this is what is already known, this is "as good as it gets," or perhaps more accurately, "as good as it has gotten," the "prior art." That is "the state of the art." Next, comes a description of what the applicant thinks he has that's new, something never done or practiced before. This is called the "abstract." The clincher is the reduction to practice or the "demonstration."

What I heard in my inner man was, "NO! That was not the good news, 'Gospel,' when I said that. That was just the 'state of the art.' " It was as though Jesus was saying to me. "I said that before I died, but when I died, I demonstrated another kind of love, a love that had never been seen before, a love that is good for enemies."

My mind was racing! Suddenly my internal software came to rest at another verse from the Bible. (Perhaps I should explain that back in the late 70s I spent seven years researching and writing a book on the monetary implications of the Bible. It was published under the title, **Inflation: The Ultimate Graven Image.** For present purposes I mention it only by way of explaining how I became familiar with the Bible.) "For when we were yet without strength, in due time [When we didn't 'deserve it'] Christ died for the ungodly. For scarcely for a righteous man will one die: yet peradventure for a good man [for a friend] some would even dare to die. But God commendeth ['demonstrated'] his love toward us, in that, while we were yet sinners, Christ died for us. Much more then, being now justified by his blood, we shall be saved from wrath through him. For if, when we were enemies, we were reconciled to God by the death of his Son, much more, being reconciled, we shall be saved by his life."[3]

I was blown away. All at once I saw that the "good news" was that Jesus died for his enemies. That's what I was! I was qualified! I was qualified, not because I deserved his love, but because I didn't! I never would have thought of that. Jesus died for me, not on my best day, but on my worst day! I had never seen anything like that before, and I had to ask the question, "How is

---

[2] 1 John 4:18. [3] Romans 5:6–10.

that possible????" Then I heard His voice once more, "The day I said I love you I nailed my expectations to the tree..." My mind was still racing. This time it came to rest at another passage from the Bible, "And you, being dead in your sins ['kinks'] and the uncircumcision of your flesh, hath he quickened together with him, having forgiven you all trespasses; blotting out the handwriting of ordinances that was against us, which was contrary to us, and took it out of the way, nailing it to his cross."[4] In that patent office, Jesus went on to say, "...And if you are going to love like I love, you are going to have to nail your expectations to the tree."

From what you have written, I'm guessing that you have mostly seen, and been on the receiving end of, the kind of love that's only good for friends. Where the Love of God is concerned, that is make-believe love. What has been calling itself "church" is full of it. It is the kind that is demonstrated by make believers. But there is another kind of love: "Hereby perceive we the love of God, because he laid down his life for us: and we ought to lay down our lives for the brethren."—"This is how we know what love is, Jesus Christ laid down His life for us, and we ought to lay down our lives for each other."[5] It gets really tricky when we have to do so on our worst days, especially the worst days of those we claim to love.

Lest I forget to mention the garbage, it was all nailed the tree. Fact is there is no other place to put our garbage. It's the garbage disposal that makes true lovers out of us. Once you/we have a place to put our garbage, our "kinks," you/we can go places together. True intimacy becomes possible without the "kinks" making the love go away.

Where "taking a bullet" as a definition of love is concerned, Jesus said, "Greater love hath no man than this, that a man lay down his life for his friends."[6] That was a love that was demonstrated by dying, and Jesus talked about it before He died. Presumably Jesus was talking about a love that was good for those who deserved it, a love that was good for friends. That's not yet what I am talking about, however, because it was a love that was only good for friends.

I always had a problem with that kind of love. When I need love the most, I don't feel much like anyone's friend. On my worst days, I just didn't feel much like I "deserved to be loved." In fact I felt rather more like the enemy of love.

Jay

I have been somewhat connected with the "Deida community," *though. I had asked the list (before Christmas) if there was a local* *women's group that practiced some of what David talks about. The* *guy who runs "Plexus"—the web site and e-mail list—lives here* *in Austin—forwarded my request to a woman who was starting a* *woman's group. They have all "studied" with David for years.*

Yes, I was monitoring the list in the time frame of that discussion.

I met with two of the women to check each other out and see if we *had compatible goals. They were a little mystical, but that has never*

---

[4]Colossians 2:13–14.   [5]1 John 3:16.
[6]John 15:13.

put me off. I liked that they were putting together a group of women who were interested in learning to be more intimate, open, and loving. I decided to go to the first group and see how it felt.

This might be a good time to share a little insight I received back in the late 70s:

NEW COVENANT PEARLS[7]

Pearls to pigs

Matthew 7:1-6 [Jesus is speaking here] "Do not judge, or you too will be judged. For in the same way you judge others, you will be judged, and with the measure you use, it will be measured to you.

"Why do you look at the speck of sawdust in your brother's eye and pay no attention to the plank in your own eye? How can you say to your brother, 'Let me take the speck out of your eye,' when all the time there is a plank in your own eye? You hypocrite, first take the plank out of your own eye, and then you will see clearly to remove the speck from your brother's eye.

"Do not give dogs what is sacred; do not throw your pearls to pigs. If you do, they may trample them under their feet, and then turn and tear you to pieces."

To understand about pearls, let's be oysters for a minute or so, and let's look at how the pearls get started. They begin as foreign objects, usually sand. The sand is painful or aggravating to the oysters, much the same as sin is to us. We're not designed to be hospitable to sin. However, where the oyster takes the aggravating sand and makes a pearl of it, in the end, the sand—the sin—will kill us.

Viewed from that perspective, then, we could understand it this way: Sand came and brought death.

Romans 5:12-14 Therefore, just as sin entered the world through one man, and death through sin, and in this way death came to all men, because all sinned—for before the law was given, sin was in the world. But sin is not taken into account when there is no law. Nevertheless, death reigned from the time of Adam to the time of Moses, even over those who did not sin by breaking a command, as did Adam, who was a pattern of the one to come.

After that, the judgment:

1 Peter 4:17 For it is time for judgment to begin with the family of God; and if it begins with us, what will the outcome be for those who do not obey the gospel of God?

Utterly sandy:

Romans 7:7-12 What shall we say, then? Is the law sin? Certainly not! Indeed I would not have known what sin was except through the law. For I would not have known what coveting really was if the law had not said, "Do not covet." But sin, seizing the opportunity afforded by the commandment, produced in me every kind of covetous desire. For apart from law, sin is dead. Once I was alive apart from law; but when the commandment came, sin sprang to life and I died. I found that the very commandment that was intended to bring life actually brought death. For sin, seizing the opportunity afforded by the commandment, deceived me, and through the commandment put me to death. So then, the law is holy, and the commandment is holy, righteous and good.

[7]All Bible references are from the NIV.

Sand everywhere

Isaiah 6:5 (NIV) "Woe to me!" I cried. "I am ruined! For I am a man of unclean lips, and I live among a people of unclean lips, and my eyes have seen the King, the Lord Almighty."

There seems to be no escape.

Romans 7:21-23 So I find this law at work: When I want to do good, evil is right there with me. For in my inner being I delight in God's law; but I see another law at work in the members of my body, waging war against the law of my mind and making me a prisoner of the law of sin at work within my members.

A wretched oyster.

Romans 7:24a What a wretched man I am!

How do I escape?

Romans 7:24b Who will rescue me from this body of death?

Jesus is the answer.

Romans 7:25 Thanks be to God—through Jesus Christ our Lord! So then, I myself in my mind am a slave to God's law, but in the sinful nature a slave to the law of sin.

Hope for the whole oyster bed.

Isaiah 9:2,6 The people walking in darkness have seen a great light; on those living in the land of the shadow of death a light has dawned....For to us a child is born, to us a son is given, and the government will be on his shoulders. And he will be called Wonderful Counselor, Mighty God, Everlasting Father, Prince of Peace.

Transformation

2 Corinthians 5:21 God made him who had no sin to be sin for us, so that in him we might become the righteousness of God.

The source of Grace

John 1:17 For the law was given through Moses; grace and truth came through Jesus Christ.

More Grace than sand

Romans 5:20,21 The law was added so that the trespass might increase. But where sin increased, grace increased all the more, so that, just as sin reigned in death, so also might grace reign through righteousness to bring eternal life through Jesus Christ our Lord.

Grace is not a license.

Romans 6:1 What shall we say, then? Shall we go on sinning so that grace may increase?

Gates of Grace

Revelation 21:10-12,21 And he carried me away in the Spirit to a mountain great and high, and showed me the Holy City, Jerusalem, coming down out of heaven from God. It shone with the glory of God, and its brilliance was like that of a very precious jewel, like a jasper, clear as crystal. It had a great, high wall with twelve gates, and with twelve angels at the gates. On the gates were written the names of the twelve tribes of Israel. The twelve gates were twelve pearls, each gate made of a single pearl. The great street of the city was of pure gold, like transparent glass.

The way to Glory

Revelation 21:23-27 The city does not need the sun or the moon to shine on it, for the glory of God gives it light, and the Lamb is its lamp. The nations will walk by its light, and the kings of the earth will bring their splendor into it. On no day will its gates ever be shut, for there will be no night there. The glory and honor of the nations will be brought into it. Nothing impure will ever enter it, nor will anyone who does what is shameful or deceitful, but only those whose names are written in the Lamb's book of life.

Sand from the accuser, Grace from The Lord.

2 Corinthians 12:7-9 To keep me from becoming conceited because of these surpassingly great revelations, there was given me a thorn in my flesh, a messenger of Satan, to torment me. Three times I pleaded with the Lord to take it away from me. But he said to me, "My grace is sufficient for you, for my power is made perfect in weakness." Therefore I will boast all the more gladly about my weaknesses, so that Christ's power may rest on me.

Our weakness, His strength

2 Corinthians 12:10 That is why, for Christ's sake, I delight in weaknesses, in insults, in hardships, in persecutions, in difficulties. For when I am weak, then I am strong.

Help wanted—full employment?

Romans 3:23,24 ... for all have sinned and fall short of the glory of God, and are justified freely by his grace through the redemption that came by Christ Jesus.

Help each other in the work.

Hebrews 12:15 See to it that no one misses the grace of God and that no bitter root grows up to cause trouble and defile many.

The Pearl of great price

Matthew 13:44-46 [Jesus is speaking here] "The kingdom of heaven is like treasure hidden in a field. When a man found it, he hid it again, and then in his joy went and sold all he had and bought that field.

"Again, the kingdom of heaven is like a merchant looking for fine pearls. When he found one of great value, he went away and sold everything he had and bought it."

Grace is God's kind of love.

1 Peter 4:8 Above all, love each other deeply, because love covers over a multitude of sins.

In short, a pearl is very different in its composition than every other kind of jewel. A pearl begins with an irritation, and is made out of it. In the end, the beautiful part is much bigger then the irritation.

In sharing our pearls with others (when we are intimate), sharing our garbage is part of the pearl. If the person is unclean toward us, they are likely to only pick up on the bad part and use the information to tear us to pieces. In other words, we shouldn't think we can be intimate with everyone.

That was last Tuesday. It was a beautiful group of women and we did a lot of experiential things to tune into each other and help each other move thru blocks to being more open and intimate. These women were going for it—I was genuinely impressed. I talked about my faith (we all shared our "intentions" for what we wanted out of the group experience) and how I wanted to grow in my intimacy with God, Jesus, and other people and how I wanted to learn, feel, and allow to come thru me this amazing love of Jesus. There was another woman in the group who had a late-term miscarriage last month who had recently broken thru with what I recognized as a "spirit-driven" awakening and who, like me, was having difficulty putting words around it. I felt an immediate connection with her. Actually, I felt a pretty deep connection with all of the women by the end of the evening. We're meeting once a month.

You are a busy girl!!

*Saturday night a friend, Pat (she came to church last night—she's the one into **The Course in Miracles**) and I went to see one of the women of this group (who's about 25 and bowls me over!) in a play that she wrote and acted all of 19 characters. She's from England where she was trained and has won all sorts of acting awards. Really talented. I'm going to enjoy getting to know her better!*

Nice! Yesterday, the first one to arrive at our weekly gathering, which was held here this week, was a 15-year-old that Carleen had spoken with at school last week on a teacher's workday. It was quite a conversation to hear Carleen tell it, and from the fast response, I guess it must have been so from Holly's viewpoint as well. The meeting was very powerful. Part of the power was a strong encouraging prophetic word that one of the older ones brought to Holly. He got up, stood before her, and prophesied over her for about 15 minutes. He really read her mail. She had never seen or experienced anything like that before. When Carleen took her home afterward, that was the first thing she asked about. It was the first time that I had ever met her, and I think she went home with a testimony to her mother that looked a lot like 1 John 1:1-4.

So, you never know. I'm glad I didn't rule this group out as "mystical non-Christians" (actually some were Christians). This is what I meant when I said there's lots of ways to "be" in the world—lots of experiences to engage in—that can experientially increase my connection with God, Jesus and others. It's all in the intention that I enter into the experience with.

Great grace is upon you!! Someone who Tony knows quite well is known to say, "It is either all grace or it is no grace at all."[8]

Church was great last night! There were three things that Tony "led" us thru—one was sharing any "God" events that happened in the last week....

That's nice to hear. It is so important that people are encouraged to share what God is doing in their lives. Too often, when there is no place to share it, it is not even noticed.

...Then we started reading John's Gospel (Tony brought a bunch of bibles—contemporary)...

I'm guessing they might have been the New International Version.

...and discussing it (didn't get very far or spend a lot of time on this—I think it was a good introduction), and in the end we broke into small groups and talked about an area in our lives that we wanted God to be more present and prayed about it.

Nice!

I have to tell you about where I am on prayer. The whole concept is somewhat foreign to me. It feels really awkward doing it. I remember my Dad's voice, "there's no need to pray for anything—the Father knows your needs and what's in your heart." What I'm "getting" now is that prayer is what leads to intimacy.

Every now and then, the Lord puts me in a place of very self-conscious intentional prayer. Most of the time I consider prayer to be the vertical dimension of "speaking the truth in love."[9] This is to say that prayer is a kind of ongoing conversation with the Lord. The flow of communication goes in both directions, and we experience it with Him as we go about the business of our daily lives. "Prayer meetings" tend to be too contrived, and too often people use them to demonstrate how spiritual or knowledgeable they are. There are some in the New Testament, but those that are there do not look much like what is going on in most of the prayer meetings that I ever attended. In short, I think I'm on your father's side on this one, but for a different reason.

My hairdresser, who I just found out this week "just loves Jesus" (she wants to come to church with her fiancé soon) brought me a little

---

[8]Gene Edwards.   [9]Ephesians 4:15.

197

*book, **Prayer of Jabez**,[10] (sp?) which I read Friday night. It really got me thinking—wow! If I'm already feeling so high, without prayer, just how much more powerful could this spiritual life be WITH prayer (kinda scary thought). So I've been doing that little prayer every day and trying to remember to talk to God and Jesus more—just for that intimacy.*

That book made quite a splash a couple of years ago now.

I looked around some for my Dad's booklet—I think it's in a box in the shed. Could be a while before I locate it. In the meanwhile, I'm planning on sending that overview to him today with a request of perhaps mailing me another copy, which I'll make a copy of for you. I'll also send you Penny's book—got a copy last night.

I read thru your email on "counting the costs." Maybe it's because I'm older, have done a lot of therapy in establishing "boundaries" and in not taking on other peoples' "stuff," and maybe because I don't have a whole community of relationships that are extremely rigid—but I don't have a lot of fear about what the "costs" might be for me. My experience so far has been whatever fear I have in my head—particularly what people might think of me or if I'm capable of handling what's coming so fast—is dispelled again and again when I just focus on what I'm doing in the moment—the conversation, the email, the preparation—and say what's on my heart. The moment-to-moment experience is generally peaceful and exciting as long as I stay in my heart and not my head. So, I'm probably doing this from a very naive place—but I'm doing this pretty low key. No big threatening religious leaders or communities in my face yet. What am I missing?

I have a wonderful peace that I said enough to you about this. I am very happy to hear that you are at peace in this connection as well!

Hope you're doing well. Keep me posted on what you're doing—please!...

As it happens, I'm working on the rewrite of the **Inflation** book, as well as another book that sets out my perspective on the Scriptures and how best to understand them. I think it might be timely to share some of the latter with you now.

---

[10]**The Prayer of Jabez: Breaking Through to the Blessed Life**, by Dr. Bruce Wilkinson, published by Multnomah, in 2000.

THE WORD

"In the beginning God created the heaven and the earth."[11] "In the beginning was the Word, and the Word was with God, and the Word was God."[12]

Before proceeding any further, it may be helpful to share some thoughts concerning the Scriptures, and the study of the Scriptures. It is our understanding that the Bible is the inspired Word of God, and inerrant in its original communication to men. Every word in the original was put there for a reason; we cannot pick and choose between what seems reasonable to us and what does not; the Bible must be studied as a whole, and while God used men whose individual styles are apparent, the content of their writing accurately reflects God's message to us and the truth of history.

While translations may be more or less accurate, each having its own difficulties, the only translation, which is fully accurate in any case, according to Jesus Himself, is the one which is written in the human heart by the Holy Spirit. It is our belief that, just as salvation is personal, rather than institutional, the communication of God through His Word is also personal, albeit for the good of all. This is to say that you, by virtue of your background and experience may well see something in a given passage of Scripture, which I have not been equipped to see. Our conclusion must be that we should not allow anyone to come between ourselves and the Word of God: "You need not that any man teach you, but as the same anointing teacheth you of all things, and is truth, and is no lie, and even as it hath taught you, ye shall abide in him."[13]

In this same connection, I should also say that there are many who go into the Scriptures looking for principles to live by. Certainly there are many and good principles to be found there, but if we come out of the Bible with nothing more than principles we have missed the essential point. Jesus said, "... search the Scriptures, and in them ye think ye have eternal life: and these are they which testify of me."[14] God's intention was, and is that we should come out of the Scriptures not with principles, but with life, the life of His Son, even the Son Himself. The Scriptures themselves are like the DNA of God "Whereby are given unto us exceeding great and precious promises: that by these ye might be partakers of the divine nature,.."[15] Today, as in Jesus' day, there is a great deal of squabbling that goes on among us as to literal versus figurative or allegorical interpretation of the scripture, This is not the real issue however. The real issue is, do we see Christ in the Scriptures. The most important thing about the story of Jonah and the whale is its revelation of Jesus Christ. Jesus Christ is "the Truth."[16] The issue then, is not whether we see the Scripture literally or figuratively, but whether we see the Scriptures Christocentricly.

Another insight that I have found helpful over the years is that the Scriptures reveal truth in both principle and personification. Jesus, for instance is "The Truth" He is The Truth in personification. He is The Truth in its fullness. The principles of the Scriptures reveal The Truth in part. The partial revelation preceded the full revelation.

Another example would be "Little children, it is the last time: and as ye have heard that antichrist [personification], shall come, even now there are many antichrists [principle]; whereby we know that it is the last time."[17] Please permit me to take this a step further as it works itself out in practice. You have

---

[11]Genesis 1:1.　　　　　[12]John 1:1.
[13]1 John 2:27.　　　　　[14]John 5:39.
[15]1 Peter 1:4.　　　　　[16]John 14:6.
[17]1 John 2:18

heard that the mark of the beast is coming; even now many beasts have come, many marks have come. Paul had "... fought wild beasts at Ephesus."[18] What is important here is that the principle has application in our lives now, the personification may only be important later on or to a later generation. If the church is preoccupied with the identification of a person, it may well be, and we believe, has already been deceived in the principle. Protestantism has been pointing fingers at the Pope, at least, since Martin Luther, and has missed the point where its own man handling is concerned.

The wisdom of the Bible is not something that can be exhausted by any one man or even a history of men. And something fundamentally new happens when you get together with the Word of God. There are things in the Bible that are uniquely yours, because you are unique. In addition, and by the same token, this is a new day, and it gives us the benefit of a hindsight that no one else in history has ever had before. The events of history clarify the meaning of certain passages that, when written, were yet to be fulfilled.

I should also mention that this book is not meant to be an exposition of the obvious or central message of the Bible, though it may be such in certain parts. Nor is there any thought to ignore or neglect the obvious meaning, but rather to look beneath, if possible to catch a glimpse of the "unsearchable riches of Christ,"[19] in the hope that the obvious meaning will take on even greater significance to burn all the brighter in our daily lives.

The next important principle...is this: to study the creation without reference to the word of God is to be confused about nature, and the nature of things. To study the Scriptures without reference to the creation, is to come out religious. There needs to be balance.

For me, the first time through the Bible was a labor of love. Time and again, I found myself turning the pages and only reading the ink. But since the individual parts are to be understood in the context of the whole, the Bible itself being its own best interpreter, there was no great understanding on first reading of any part. The foundation was not yet there. The second time through, however, interesting things began to happen. First, by then I had a closer relationship with the author, and second, I also had an overview of the entire context. (Perhaps I should quickly add that I did not develop the relationship or anything else for that matter. The Lord did it all.) In this same connection, It is a truism that the Old Testament is understood in light of the Gospels, Matthew, Mark, Luke and John, and the Gospels are understood in the light of the Epistles.

I also took a major interest of my life into the Word of God with me in order to see what God had to say about it. Because of that interest, I had a greater motivation to listen and learn than would have been the case if I had just been aimlessly wandering through. This can be true for anyone each time they go through the Bible, no matter what the major interest is, good or bad. You will pay better attention if you have a felt desire to do so, and your major interest can help you to have that desire.

...Also, please give my love to Carleen....

I'll do that!

...I was thinking this week about how generous she is in allowing you to spend so much time with other people (me!). Many thanks.

---

[18]1 Corinthians 15:32.   [19]Ephesians 3:8.

Carleen is amazing in this way. One of the greatest obstacles to intimacy that exists in Christian leaders is that their spouses will not allow them to lay down their lives for others. This is a very big problem. It ranks very close to not knowing who you are in relationship to others.

Have a great day!!!

Yours in Christ,
Jay

CHAPTER 13

ADOPTION AND
NEW BIRTH

Dear Jay,

Well, today has been an emotional day. Saw this coming yesterday when I felt a need to "escape" from it all and went to a fairly depressing movie, "Mystic River." The movie was good, but it seemed to compound the feeling. Life just doesn't make sense sometimes.

You'll get the flavor of the feeling from the following correspondence I had with Tony today:

Hi Tony—

I enjoyed our second meeting—I was much less nervous preparing for it. Hopefully eventually the nervousness will completely give way and I'll just be able to enjoy! I'm happy with the structure—the simplicity of it. It was awesome how you introduced the Bible and prayer in the meeting. Do you expect that we would just pick up where we left off each week in the Bible—or would it be more free flowing? I don't have a feel for this group—their desire to study the Bible. But it makes sense to me to establish some sort of core to the meetings. I'm encouraged that even though Kurtis feels "weird" reading the Bible in a group, he thinks it makes sense to do it. It must be interesting to you to be working with someone who professes faith in Jesus and God and feels shaky introducing studying the Bible to a group of friends. It's just that my experience in faith has not yet jelled with what I see "Christians" doing—meeting together, studying the Bible, spreading the Word, having a hand in other peoples' faith choices. So, even though I feel I can talk about my experience and somewhat about my faith and invite people to explore with me, I feel that I fall short in other areas. I guess that's why you get to come. I'm feeling pretty tender here so I'm guessing that I really needed to put this on the table.

How many books are in a box? I think I would like a box[1]—if I could pay you in "installments." Do I make the check out to Tony Dale?

---

[1] Lisa is referring to Tony and Felicity Dale's book, **Simply Church**, first mentioned on page 100.

Felicity mentioned coming to your house for the Baptism on Sunday—which I would be interested in doing if I can make it work out logistically and still be ready for our meeting. I don't have her email address—perhaps it would be best if she and I worked out those details—could you send it to me please?

I'll be sending a group email out tomorrow about next Sunday.

Thanks,

Lisa

Tony wrote back:

Hi Lisa,

Great to hear from you as always. Felicity and I really enjoyed the time on Sunday also. You have such a great bunch of friends. The warmth from all of them is such a blessing. I'm glad that you felt comfortable with the way that I introduced some Bible study and prayer. We have found working with many different types of groups that people value a little structure. Not that dictates how a time is "allowed" to go, but rather provides a skeleton on which one can hang whatever is going to happen anyway.

In our experience, as one learns to let the Holy Spirit gently guide what goes on in any meeting, you will find that most meetings have in them part or all of the elements mentioned in Acts 2:42 where it says, "And they devoted themselves to the apostles' teaching (Bible study) and to fellowship (we're all good at that one), to the breaking of bread (meals together remembering that Jesus is at the center of all we do) and prayer." We find that it is useful in the Bible study portion to plan to gently go through a planned section of the Bible, but to be ready to drop it for whatever else the Holy Spirit might lead one to during the meeting. For example, if someone began opening up about a relationship need, then I would drop the plan to "carry on where we left off last week" in the Bible study, and go to a passage that might directly address their need. Of course, to do this one needs someone around who knows their Bible fairly well. That is another very good reason to typically stick with slowly but steadily working one's way through certain sections of the Bible. It is amazing (see Isaiah 55: about verses 10-12) how "God's word will not return to Him void, but will accomplish what He pleases." You will be amazed at how the Lord will find a way to speak to people through whatever we study together.

If you ever feel that Felicity and I are moving things too fast or not being sensitive to the needs of the group, do let us know. We want to respond to your tender touch as you are the one that the Lord has used to bring the group together.

It would be super if you can get down to our place for the baptisms on Sunday. We would love you and Kurtis to be at our place and enjoy some of the good things that the Lord is doing with this younger group whom we have been meeting with over the past few months. The baptism is scheduled for 3 pm (meaning we will start around 3:30) and you could easily be away by 4:30, having had lots of chance to meet and talk with various folk.

You asked about the books. Just take whatever you need rather than feeling any obligation to a whole box. I'll bring you another 5 or 10 if you are finding them useful, and as I said, just pay us what you can afford. Make any check payable to House 2 House. Our goal is just to help get out the good news of what Jesus can do in our lives.

Give our love to Kurtis,

Tony

Hi Tony,

Thank you for your sweet reply. I don't know what happened to me—I've been tender and crying ever since writing that. I think I needed encouragement, so I'm grateful that you were in town and replied. Yes, I think people value some structure, too. And I think you're being very sensitive. This is just some of my "garbage," as Jay would call it. I have to learn to trust that this is God's word and that He works thru it—like you said.

I talked with Kurtis, too, and he was encouraging. He said to tell you that he's been thinking of you all week and praying for you. He says that you are the kind of person that he would like to do business with, and he thinks your meeting will go well. We think we will be able to be there on Sunday—we'll make it a motorcycle trip weather permitting! If you or Felicity could send us directions. Do we need to bring anything? And yes, 10 more books would be great—we can pick them up then.

Lisa

Regarding your last email, I was quite impressed with the timing of some of it, like the "New Covenant Pearls." Karen, my girlfriend who attended our first meeting (has the 14-year-old—said they enjoyed talking with couples about spiritual stuff but were a little put off by what they perceived as "putting down of churches"—they invited us to their church), called for a last-minute lunch with a group of girlfriends. After I said yes, I wrote the above email to Tony and promptly started crying. So, on the way over I was thinking of what you sent—the New Covenant Pearls—and about my current weak feeling—and realized that I was going to have a tough time getting thru this lunch because I couldn't stop crying and I didn't feel safe being intimate. I decided that I would just focus on them and try not to talk. I got there and waited 20 minutes—nobody showed up—ate lunch and went back to work (I'm one of the few people left in the world that doesn't have a cell phone). When I got back to work, I called them and it appears that I heard the wrong restaurant. God's way of protecting me. And I heard your message loud and clear.

I really appreciate what you said about prayer. That sounds much more comfortable to me to just talk to God. My dad says that prayer isn't necessary, but he "communes" with God regularly. He says to each day choose whom to serve—God or yourself—and to invite Him into my heart. This is what I've been doing for many years. I will often give thanks for my many blessings, but I don't "pray" for much else.

I would love to hear more about what you do for six hours in your gatherings on Sundays! Amazing! And I'd like to hear more about the older one who prophesied over Holly. I don't think I've ever witnessed anything like that! I wonder how Holly is handling it—kind of strange for a 15-year-old.

And, lastly, the part about the Deida list. What a cool thing you said on the list! Short and sweet and to the point. It appears that I've been excluded somehow from the list—haven't received anything since Friday. (I wrote the list administrator to get back on—haven't heard anything yet. So don't know if there's been any recent discussion about this.)

I think you nailed it on the head with the fellow from the Deida list—so much of what of I hear on the list seems to be "cookbook" with some theatrics thrown in. It is hard to get a feel for who these people really are. I think he is a key person to address here—he seems to have far-reaching influence. And his purpose—to take someone to God every day—sounds noble. He sounds more grounded than most—although a little "know it all"—and also seemingly in a very vulnerable place with his grieving process. I loved hearing how you shared with him. You are so awesome! It's helpful hearing you deliver your message from a little different angle. Your love patent message is so powerful I can't imagine that people wouldn't be stirred up on some level. Please keep me posted!
Gotta go!

Love,
Lisa

On Wednesday, February 4, 2004, Jay responded:

Lisa wrote: ...*Regarding your last email, I was quite impressed with the timing of some of it. Like the "New Covenant Pearls." Karen, my girlfriend who attended our first meeting (has the 14-year-old—said they enjoyed talking with couples about spiritual stuff but were a little put off by what they perceived as "putting down of churches"—...*

Dear Lisa,

This is always a problem in house groups. Generally Christians meet in homes because they are dissatisfied in some way with Sunday morning institutional Church. Generally it gets better with the passage of time. The institutional wounds don't loom as large, and the more positive content of the group becomes more important, at least, until those in the group begin to wound one another in the greater intimacy of the small group. Institutional wounds are painful. House group wounds are often terminal where further fellowship is concerned.

I hadn't thought about the possibility of your becoming a "house group leader" so quickly, and I'm feeling like there is a lot

I need to share with you in that connection, and sooner rather than later.

...they invited us to their church) called for a last minute lunch with a group of girlfriends. After I said yes, I wrote the above email to Tony and promptly started crying. So, on the way over I was thinking of what you sent—the New Covenant Pearls—and about my current weak feeling—and realized that I was going to have a tough time getting thru this lunch because I couldn't stop crying and I didn't feel safe being intimate. I decided that I would just focus on them and try not to talk....

For the most part, those in the "house church movement" suffer from alienation. This is not Christ. Jesus was never alienated. He was always redemptive. If you have the grace to fellowship across the "church" barrier, that is wonderful. The challenge is to remain loving toward those who are alienated, as well as those who are still within the system.

...I got there and waited 20 minutes—nobody showed up—ate lunch and went back to work (I'm one of the few people left in the world that doesn't have a cell phone)....

Same here. There is no cell phone service in Golden Valley.

... When I got back to work, I called them and it appears that I heard the wrong restaurant. God's way of protecting me. And I heard your message loud and clear.

It is amazing the lengths to which the Lord will often go to protect us from ourselves.

I really appreciate what you said about prayer. That sounds much more comfortable to me to just talk to God. My dad says that prayer isn't necessary, but he "communes" with God regularly. He says to each day choose whom to serve—God or yourself—and to invite Him into my heart. This is what I've been doing for many years. I will often give thanks for my many blessings, but I don't "pray" for much else.

I already mentioned my "CNN split-screen mind." That for me makes for wonderful fellowship throughout my days.

I would love to hear more about what you do for six hours in your gatherings on Sundays!...

We come together never knowing what is going to happen. In over 30 years of meeting in homes, mostly ours, there have been seasons of Bible study, but so far, that has not been necessary in this group. Just about all who come are already cooked, and very familiar with the Scriptures. This does not mean that the Bible is not an important part of our time together. It's just that it is brought in as part of our interactive sharing, and not as systematic teaching.

...Amazing! And I'd like to hear more about the older one who prophesied over Holly. I don't think I've ever witnessed anything like that! I wonder how Holly is handling it—kind of strange for a 15-year-old.

Carleen and I were also concerned that very likely Holly had never been exposed to anything like that. Our eyes were riveted on her as Lloyd spoke to her, prophesied over her, and anointed her head with oil. Her face was radiant. She didn't blink an eye the whole time. I think she went away feeling very much encouraged and empowered by the experience.

We will doubtless know more when we see her again this Sunday.

Have to run now. More later.

Jay

On Wednesday, February 4, 2004, Lisa wrote:

Dear Jay,

You are such a Godsend! It is very comforting to be reassured that this is a process and that it will take some time—and some uncomfortableness. The last read of your email gave me hope—I'm beginning to understand your sexual parable better. I look forward to spending more time with it tonight, although I have a busy evening scheduled with two massages. (I spend about 2-1/2 hours with each person).

I don't have a lot of time, but I especially want to tell you how the strength of your faith has redirected me again and again. I only hope to some day have that much strength and faith!

I had lunch with Penny today. She is a delight and not much gets past her. I talked openly with her about my confusion about the Bible and about the premise that seems to separate the Christians from the people who believe in God and that Jesus was his son—and that to me is this issue of salvation. Bottom line, at least from what I'm deciphering, is this belief that Jesus died to save us from our sins. Why is that a stumbling block for me? I don't have any problem with you talking about Jesus taking away the garbage; I don't have a problem with understanding that I do and have done many things that separate me from God (my definition of sin); I have the experience of peace and oneness with the Holy Spirit on a regular basis; I feel led by Jesus and ask Him regularly to take away my garbage. So why is it so difficult for me to say, "I accept Jesus as my Savior—He is Lord"? Why is it difficult for me to call myself a "Christian"? Is this the slaughtering or the fear of being slaughtered? I groan in my weakness.

I have to go now. I finally got to a place last night where I could see the look of love from Jesus—he graced me so that I could sleep. I'm in a better place today and feeling supported and encouraged by you, Tony, Penny, and Kurtis. Thank you for your kindness, love and ongoing support!

Love,
Lisa

On Thursday, February 5, 2004, Jay responded to Lisa's Tuesday e-mail:

Lisa wrote:

And, lastly, the part about the Deida list. What a cool thing you said on the list! Short and sweet and to the point. It appears that I've been excluded somehow from the list—haven't received anything since Friday. (I wrote to the list administrator to get back on—haven't heard anything yet). So don't know if there's been any recent discussion about this.

Dear Lisa,

Perhaps by now you got the little flurry of activity of yesterday afternoon. Other than that, there hasn't been much on the list since Friday, so perhaps you are still ok.

…Your love patent message is so powerful I can't imagine that people wouldn't be stirred up on some level. Please keep me posted!

Nothing so far. I'll let you know when I hear something. I'm beginning to feel a leading to respond to the "Jay, Jay…Jay" email. I'll send you a copy if and when I do. It will be off list.

Jay continues in response to Lisa's later e-mail of February 4:

Dear Jay,

You are such a Godsend! It is very comforting to be reassured that this is a process and that it will take some time—and some uncomfortableness. The last read of your email gave me hope—I'm beginning to understand your sexual parable better...

I'm very glad if I can be of some encouragement to you!

...I look forward to spending more time with it tonight, although I have a busy evening scheduled with two massages. (I spend about 2-1/2 hours with each person)....

Nice.

My first experience with massage was when a man (about my age) who had been coming to the gathering at our house for a number of years showed up late one afternoon with a pan, towels, and ointments. He said that the Lord told him to come and do my feet. He said resistance is futile.

I've gotten better about going with the flow in my old age. After about 30 minutes, I was a limp noodle. I told him I felt like 30 seconds the other side of a climax. He did that on one other occasion, and on one occasion he brought his folding massage table and gave me the full body version. Wow. The Lord really used him to teach me some very important lessons. Prior to that time I had been a little gun shy about getting physical with people. Afterward I knew that this was part of our inheritance in Christ. Of all the things that were done for Jesus, it was the woman with the nard[2] that He said would be remembered for what she had done. I encourage you in what you are doing; keep up the good work. People need Jesus with skin on.

I don't have a lot of time, but I especially want to tell you how the strength of your faith has redirected me again and again. I only hope to some day have that much strength and faith!

I'm a bad loser. I have no intention of letting you go. While I have breath, I will be there to encourage you. And after that, I suspect that I will still be running my mouth in your behalf. That's one of the nice things about hanging around Jesus, you get to do it forever.

Perhaps while I'm at it, I should also tell you that, in your present circle of fellowship, my primary relational connection is with you. While I am available to Tony and Felicity, should they

[2]An aromatic ointment.

ever want to contact me for any reason, the confirmed life line is with you, and, in that connection, The Lord has made me a safe place for you. What you are seeing and sensing there is priority communication where I'm concerned.

I don't have a "ministry." As a result, having nothing to lose, I tend to talk very straight with "leaders." I have a very strong bond with some, "dead men walking," but with most I am seen as very threatening, even though in Charlotte they have nicknamed me "Agape Man."

I had lunch with Penny today. She is a delight and not much gets past her.... .

I'm so glad to hear that. I'm guessing she has been pretty well cooked.

...I talked openly with her about my confusion about the Bible and about the premise that seems to separate the Christians from the people who believe in God and that Jesus was his son—and that to me is this issue of salvation. Bottom line, at least from what I'm deciphering, is this belief that Jesus died to save us from our sins. Why is that a stumbling block for me? I don't have any problem with you talking about Jesus taking away the garbage; I don't have a problem with understanding that I do and have done many things that separate me from God (my definition of sin); I have the experience of peace and oneness with the Holy Spirit on a regular basis; I feel led by Jesus and ask Him regularly to take away my garbage. So why is it so difficult for me to say, "I accept Jesus as my Savior—He is Lord"? Why is it difficult for me to call myself a "Christian"? Is this the slaughtering or the fear of being slaughtered? I groan in my weakness.

Your question is a real mouthful, and I think it is going to take an even bigger mouthful to answer it. This will not be a sermonette for a christianette. What I am about to share is not a widely understood perspective on "salvation." It is, however, the understanding that I hear the Spirit groaning in your heart. If you once "knew the Lord" (Christian lingo for being saved), and came back or only finally came to "know Him" in the context of our meeting and conversation, then, in either case, I have to believe that your point of reentry or entry was quite different than what most experience in evangelism crusades, "going to church" or pat "witnessing" formats. You have come in, and, at least at this point, opened up at a much deeper level of penetration.

In short, you have not gained entry or tried to gain entry by what I would call a "Confession formula": "Repeat after me"; "Say this prayer"; "Come to the altar"; "And now, while the lights are dim, and every head is bowed, if you accept Jesus, slip up your hand"; "Yes, I see that hand"; etc.

You have come to him with all eyes open in the full light of day. Take a look at John Chapter 3. It's the story of Jesus' encounter with Nicodemus. About 20 years ago now, I met a man who was really well-cooked. He had done it all where "Christian religion" and "ministry" is concerned. He put it this way. "Nicodemus represents religion at its best. Religion at its best only comes to Jesus after dark, and when it gets there, it hasn't the faintest idea of what He is talking about."[3] This is the passage where Jesus introduces the "new birth."

With that as introduction, perhaps I could share about the "new birth" at a depth which is closer to the groaning I hear coming from your heart. I share this not to alienate you from others or what is going on in the name of the Lord, but just to give you an understanding so that you will not give in to the pressure to be conformed to formula Christianity. Neither am I saying that those who have come in by that route are not "saved." I think you have already noticed that Jesus has a way of saving us with or without our understanding. In some sense, Paul's letter to the Galatians has this matter as its primary focus of concern. That is a letter well worth your reading, sooner rather than later. Just don't let the religious explain it away.

By way of opening you to what I am about to share, I will begin by asking you a couple of questions:

Is there a difference between "birth" and "adoption"?

What is the difference?

Do you think God knows about it?

At this point, Jay shares a number of emails that he had sent to his friend Bill, which discuss the difference between adoption and birth, as it relates to the application of these two ways of relating to the spiritual truth of relationship in Christ. This correspondence can be found in Appendix G, "Adoption and Birth." Later, Jay shared this correspondence with his daughter, Heather (Heather is a research associate at Yale, working

---

[3] Warren Litzman.

on a project aimed at reducing AIDS among Hispanic women in the vicinity of Yale.) She asked some questions about it.

Jay's responses to Heather's questions are presented below. To help in understanding her questions, several paragraphs from the original correspondence to Bill are provided first.

...Adoption is a legal matter; a new birth is a matter of impregnation. We had been "under the law." Under the law, it would have been illegal for God, the Father, to adopt us, so Jesus took care of the legal obstacle to our adoption, so that God the Father could legally adopt us. That was a necessary precondition to our adoption. That having been taken care of, and we having availed ourselves of that provision by faith in Jesus Christ, His blood, and His righteousness, we were adopted.

The fact is we were not competent to be part of God's household, and adoption did not empower us for change. In my case, it was as though God had adopted a person wholly incompetent to live in His house. God was looking at me through the blood of His Son, so it was okay for me to be in His house, but for my part, I was still incompatible.

Now, some otherwise incompatible people are quite good at doing imitations, even imitations of Christ, but Christianity was to be built not on imitations, but on the reality of Christ.

Having adopted me, however, and because I was a consenting recipient to my legal adoption, God then poured out His Spirit into my heart, so that I was able to cry out in Spirit and in truth, by a brand new nature, "Abba." Everything to that point was the drawing of the Father to receive the Son, but at that moment I became born again by an incorruptible Seed....

Heather wrote to Jay, her dad:

Could you explain to me the following as if I were a 12-year-old?

If under the law it would have been illegal for God to adopt us because we had all sinned and come short of the right, then how did God adopt those that lived before Christ died on the cross, those who lived before the Pentecost? You say that they were His before the Pentecost even if only adopted...or were they not even adopted before the Pentecost?...In which case, what exactly was the relationship of God with his people before the Pentecost?...

DAD: This is a very good question!

As I understand it, no one gets into the Father's house except by the blood of Jesus. Jesus said, "I am the way, the truth, and the life; no one comes to the Father except through me." Those who lived and died before Jesus, lived, and died, and were saved by their faith in the revelation of Christ that was available to them at the time. They were looking forward to the cross, before it had yet become clear. Those of us who have lived since the cross and have heard about it are saved by looking back on it.

Does that mean that those who have lived since the cross and never heard about it are lost? No, but that is another question and one that is somewhat more complex to answer. I will address it in another email if you would like, but I will finesse it for this one.

Peter wrote: "For Christ also hath once suffered for sins, the just for the unjust, that he might bring us to God, being put to death in the flesh, but quickened by the Spirit: By which also he went and preached unto the spirits in prison; Which sometime were disobedient, when once the long-suffering of God waited in the days of Noah, while the ark was a preparing, wherein few, that is, eight souls were saved by water. The like figure whereunto even baptism doth also now save us (not the putting away of the filth of the flesh, but the answer of a good conscience toward God,) by the resurrection of Jesus Christ:..."[4]

As I understand this passage, those who died before Christ got a chance to receive Him while held captive in the prison of death. He went to them there and preached the good news to them: "By which also he went and preached unto the spirits in prison."

Continuing:

Well, here goes my attempt at further explanation according to your observations and questions in the attachment you sent. I should say that this is my second run-through, as my Netscape software couldn't handle your Apple script, and erased the whole thing when I stored it.

First there was only the seed of Eve, and God watched over that seed all through human history making sure it never died until it died in Jesus. The seed was always passed along prior to the death of its carrier. Finally the seed gave birth to Jesus, and in Him it died.

HEATHER: This was the seed of Eve????

DAD: Yes. In Genesis, God said to the serpent in the presence of Eve, "And I will put enmity between thee and the woman, and between thy seed and her seed; it shall bruise thy head, and thou shalt bruise his heel."[5]

A little later God spoke to Eve's seed when it was in Abraham: "Now to Abraham and his seed were the promises made. He saith not, And to seeds, as of many; but as of one, And to thy seed, which is Christ."[6]

One more: "And no matter how many promises God has made, they are 'Yes' in Christ. And so through him the 'Amen' is spoken by us to the glory of God. Now it is God who makes both us and you stand firm in Christ. He anointed us, set his seal of ownership on us, and put his Spirit in our hearts as a deposit, guaranteeing what is to come."[7]

HEATHER: Is the seed Christ's spirit?

DAD: Yes, God is Spirit, and therefore His Seed is Spirit.

HEATHER: The nature of God: wouldn't that be the DNA or the chromosomes of God?

DAD: Yes, Peter puts it this way: "According as his divine power hath given unto us all things that pertain unto life and godliness, through the knowledge of him that hath called us to glory and virtue: Whereby are given unto us exceeding great and precious promises: that by these ye might be partakers of the divine nature, having escaped the corruption that is in the world through lust. "[8]

HEATHER: Wouldn't seed be sperm?

---

[4] 1 Peter 3:18–21.
[6] Galatians 3:16.
[8] 2 Peter 1:3–4.

[5] Genesis 3:15.
[7] 2 Corinthians 1:20–22.

DAD: Yes, in the Greek it is "sperma."

HEATHER: Wouldn't Eve have the egg???

DAD: Yes, the egg contains her sperm, but also the material necessary for the foundational nurture of life.

HEATHER: How was the seed fertilized?

DAD: I believe Mary's experience is a kind of benchmark, but to really get into it, I will have to explain the sexual parable in some greater detail.

"And the angel answered and said unto her, The Holy Ghost shall come upon thee, and the power of the Highest shall overshadow thee: therefore also that holy thing which shall be born of thee shall be called the Son of God."[9]

HEATHER: Before his death Jesus was the last Adam carrying the one seed?

DAD: Yes, but not only carrying the one seed; He himself was the one seed. Again, I quote Galatians: "...And to thy seed, which is Christ."

The seed, which is Christ, cycled through death and came up out of the ground as new life, the fruit. Jesus's resurrection was the first fruit of the dead. It is through the fruit of Christ's resurrected life that the seed of God was disseminated to the hearts of men or made available to the Father for dissemination into the hearts of men.

Jesus's resurrection and ascension provided God, the Father, with the Seed He needed to keep His promise. His promise was to disseminate Christ into the hearts of human beings.

"For since by man came death, by man came also the resurrection of the dead. For as in Adam all die, even so in Christ shall all be made alive."

HEATHER: We who receive his seed are Christ's at his coming?

DAD: Yes!

HEATHER: No man can receive Christ or become a son of God unless God draws him (her?) in?

DAD: Yes.

HEATHER: The drawing process can take time, short in some, long in others. Often during this period people believe that they have been born again because they have confessed, or been baptized prematurely. Because of this the courtship/drawing/receiving of Christ is cut short and the seed is terminated before conception?

DAD: Yes except that, rather than say that our seed is terminated, I should say that it does not come to conception.

HEATHER: (It never reaches the egg? What is our metaphor for the egg and for the womb?) A birth cannot be achieved without a seed and an egg, which together are the conception of the zygote.

DAD: Another really good question. Going back to your terminated-seed word picture, I would have to say that the manifestation of a terminated seed is menstruation.

Isaiah expresses this best: "But we are all as an unclean thing, and all our righteousnesses are as filthy [original—periodic] rags; and we all do fade as a leaf; and our iniquities, like the wind, have taken us away."[10]

---

[9]Luke 1:35.　　　　　[10]Isaiah 64:6

With the emphasis on the periodic aspect of menstruation, I would have to say that, time and again, the drawing of God brings us to a place of spiritual readiness to be impregnated with Christ. If the drawing of God's love is not interrupted, that drawing will come to a climax in us. If we are not spiritually infertile, then that climax results in Christ in us. According to Romans Chapter 9, some are spiritually infertile. Others are barren going into their old age. I should add that this preparation of our spirits to receive Christ tends to be a periodic condition. In other words, we have many opportunities to have that kind of intimacy with the Father that can result in conception. Outward religious righteousness, which does not have its source in Christ, is simply a cover up for our lack of fruitful intimacy with God. Hence menstruous rags. "Get away from me, you evil doers, I never knew you (we were never intimate)."

I believe that the egg is our human spirit. Into our human spirit comes the life-giving Spirit, Christ, the "sperma" of God. Also the "Holy Spirit" comes to us and nurtures this Christ, who is now our life, into our soul, mind, will, and emotions. Christ is our new identity, and the Holy Spirit is the one who teaches us this Christ, who is now our life.

In John, Chapter 14:16-18, you will see that not only is there the promise of another comforter, the Holy Spirit, but Jesus promised that He Himself would come to us.

The "zygote" is the new life within us. At the border of that life is a warfare that is ongoing between our old person, and our new person, Christ. In Christ, the war is over, for the Bible tells us that the Kingdom of God, that is Christ, is "...righteousness, peace and joy in the Holy Spirit."[11] The Kingdom of God is a place in the Spirit.

HEATHER: In order to truly receive Christ we must be baptized in the Holy Spirit. This too is God drawing to receive the son (me/ or Christ within me)?

DAD: In John 7 we read: "In the last day, that great day of the feast, Jesus stood and cried, saying, 'If any man thirst, let him come unto me, and drink. He that believeth on me, as the scripture hath said, out of his belly shall flow rivers of living water.' (But this spake he of the Spirit, which they that believe on him should receive: for the Holy Ghost was not yet given; because that Jesus was not yet glorified.)"[12]

It is clear from the context of the whole Scripture that Jesus was speaking in a very specific and limited sense of the Holy Spirit. He was speaking about an experience of the Holy Spirit that humanity had never known before, because Christ had not yet been glorified/crucified.

Perhaps this is as good a place as any to get back into the sexual parable: Another good word for glorified is "expressed." In its highest comprehension an ejaculation is the expression of life. I believe that Jesus's death on the cross is that highest expression. That is the moment when the seed, which was His life was cast into the ground to die. In the highest sense, He was "spent."

The old creation teaches me that between that moment and the moment of conception there can be a rather considerable passage of time. In Jesus's case, there even had to be an intervening fruit stage, whereby the one seed became the many.

HEATHER: Without baptism by the Holy Spirit we can only be adopted by God, we cannot be reborn as a child of God?

---

[11]Romans 14:17.   [12]John 7:37-39.

DAD: Not in this life.

HEATHER: What is the difference between the Holy Ghost and the Holy Spirit?

DAD: They are one, but they may come to us in various expressions. For instance, speaking of Christ, Paul tells us: "...The first man Adam was made a living soul; the last Adam was made a quickening spirit."[13] I don't believe that the Holy Spirit was eliminated at that point, rather that God the Father continues to express himself both as the life-giving Spirit of His Son and also the Holy Spirit who had already been available to mankind. This is the Holy Spirit who, in the beginning of creation, "...moved upon the face of the deep."[14] That work of the Spirit is as necessary for the new creation as it was for the first one.

HEATHER: Receiving Christ gives us the power to become sons (daughters) of God. This too is God's drawing us to receive the son (me/or Christ within me?) Christ enables us to become sons (daughters?) of God by redeeming us who are under the law, that we might receive the "adoption" of sons (daughters)?

DAD: Under the law it would have been illegal for God to adopt us, because we have all sinned and come short of the right to live in the Father's house. We were reconciled to God by the death of His Son, by the blood of Christ. We are adopted by our faith in Christ and His sacrifice for us.

When we are fully adopted sons (daughters?), God sends forth the spirit of Christ into our heart. Without this spirit in our heart there is no supernatural heart's cry of "Abba, Father."

HEATHER: Receiving the very nature of God and receiving the spirit of Christ is one and the same at this moment?

DAD: Yes!

HEATHER: When God sends the spirit of Christ into my heart and I receive it, at that moment I have become born again by an incorruptible seed.

DAD: Yes!

HEATHER: The heart's cry only happens at the moment of the new birth, when we actually become partakers of the divine nature. In this way we are actually born from above by the incorruptible seed (and egg)?

DAD: Again, the egg is our human spirit. The new birth does not annihilate our uniqueness as an individual.

HEATHER: Does this mean that everyone born before Christ died were merely God's adopted incompatibles? So, would that mean the Jewish?

DAD: It includes them if they are among those who received Christ prior to His death. Without Christ, we are all incompatible with God.

The writer of Hebrews puts it this way: "All these people were still living by faith when they died. They did not receive the things promised; they only saw them and welcomed them from a distance. And they admitted that they were aliens and strangers on earth. People who say such things show that they are looking for a country of their own. If they had been thinking of the country they had left, they would have had opportunity to return. Instead, they were longing for a better country--a heavenly one. Therefore God is not ashamed to be called their God, for he has prepared a city for them.... These were all commended for their faith, yet none of them received what had been promised. God

---

[13] 1 Corinthians 15:45. [14] Genesis 1:2.

had planned something better for us so that only together with us would they be made perfect."[15]

HEATHER: That is pretty harsh.

DAD: If you think that's harsh, you should take the time to read all of Hebrews 11.

HEATHER: Can I be under the law and receive Christ?

DAD: Well, not exactly because, as Paul explains to the Romans: "Know ye not, brethren, (for I speak to them that know the law,) how that the law hath dominion over a man as long as he liveth? For the woman which hath an husband is bound by the law to her husband so long as he liveth; but if the husband be dead, she is loosed from the law of her husband. So then if, while her husband liveth, she be married to another man, she shall be called an adulteress: but if her husband be dead, she is free from that law; so that she is no adulteress, though she be married to another man. Wherefore, my brethren, ye also are become dead to the law by the body of Christ; that ye should be married to another, even to him who is raised from the dead, that we should bring forth fruit unto God. "[16]

HEATHER:
Legally Adopted Daughter/incompatible
Here am I under the law
Here am I still under the Law
Here am I ready to receive Christ
Confirming sign: speaking in tongues?

DAD: Perhaps I should also say that I do not believe that "speaking in tongues" is the only confirming sign. I know I was baptized in the Spirit at least a year before I spoke in tongues. In my case, it was tears and a word of wisdom, a very powerful one: "Inflation begins the minute government calls money something else."

HEATHER: Here am I drawn in by God.
Baptized.

I cry Abba! And I am born again by an incorruptible seed/I am no longer incompatible?

DAD: Are you saying you are ready to receive the baptism in the Holy Spirit or have you already received it?

I love you too much to be uncertain about such things,

Dad

I have to go now. I finally got to a place last night where I could see the look of love from Jesus—he graced me so that I could sleep. I'm in a better place today and feeling supported and encouraged by you, Tony, Penny and Kurtis. Thank you for your kindness, love, and ongoing support!

Always: Hebrews 10:25

---

[15]Hebrews 11:13–16, 39–40.   [16]Romans 7:1–4.

I have a feeling I might be taking more than my share of your time at the keyboard, so I'll stop for now. Perhaps it will give you a little more time to respond. I hope this has been helpful for you.

You are so very precious to me,

Jay

NOT LEFT BEHIND

CHAPTER 14

A CHANGE OF SPECIES

On Thursday, February 5, 2004, Jay wrote to Lisa:

Dear Lisa,

I think I need to share a revelation I received back some time ago. It came as a vision. (I don't have many.) But this one was a lulu, and it probably has had the biggest impact on the relationship between Carleen and me of any revelation I have ever had.

It was either 1979 or 1980, as best I can recall. A man who was like a father to me in the Lord (like Paul, I had at least one mother also, Romans 16:13) asked me to go with him to a conference in Dallas, Texas. I was at a desperate place in my walk with the Lord, and I said yes. I had no idea what the conference was to be about, or who would be there. I said yes because he was older, and I thought he needed someone to accompany him. It was the John 17:21 Conference, the first meeting in North America. The conference was called to try to mend the rift in the charismatic renewal, which had resulted from the Shepherding Movement. (This is the conference that I mention on the "Horizontal" tape.)

Nate Krupp was also there. It seemed like everybody I had ever heard of was there. The Lord met me there in a very powerful way, most of which is a subject for another time. I had a very keen sense of the need to bring back everything I had seen and experienced to my wife.

Meanwhile back at the ranch, she had been left with all of the cares of this life, the house, the children, the bill collectors, and even what was left of the "church that met at our house." On my arrival home, our expectations met in collision. She needed to unload all that she was carrying of the cares of this life, and I was trying to download the revelation I had received concerning the life to come. I was so far in the clouds that I was clueless as to the state of her desperation. The more I tried to share, the more frustrated she became.

We found ourselves in the worst communications break down of our 10-year-old marriage. She was flipping back and forth between, "That insensitive jerk, why doesn't he see the needs that I see?... If he doesn't see them, then I'm not going to tell him!!" And on the other hand, "Why isn't he upset by all that is wrong around here? How come he is handling the stress so well?... There must be something wrong with me or my faith!!!"

As for my part, I went back to God, thinking out loud, "And for this cause a man shall leave his father and mother...????... What cause could possibly be worth all this aggravation?" Then it hit me... "What cause?" I couldn't think of the cause! Somehow, I had missed that part. I immediately began a desperate search of the Scriptures, looking for the cause... "For we are members of his body, of his flesh, and of his bones. For this cause shall a man leave his father and mother, and shall be joined unto his wife, and they two shall be one flesh. This is a great mystery: but I speak concerning Christ and the church."[1]

I don't know about you, but, if the cause is there, I couldn't find it. There was still hope, because Paul was quoting Genesis 2: 24: "Therefore shall a man leave his father and his mother, and shall cleave unto his wife: and they shall be one flesh."

I went there, and I still didn't find the cause. There was that "therefore" word, and so I backed up to see what it was there for.

"And the LORD God said, 'It is not good that the man should be alone; I will make him an help meet for him.'... And Adam gave names to all cattle, and to the fowl of the air, and to every beast of the field; but for Adam there was not found an help meet for him. And the LORD God caused a deep sleep to fall upon Adam and he slept: and he took one of his ribs, and closed up the flesh instead thereof; and the rib, which the LORD God had taken from man, made he a woman, and brought her unto the man. And Adam said, 'This is now bone of my bones, and flesh of my flesh: she shall be called Woman, because she was taken out of Man.' Therefore shall a man leave his father and his mother, and shall cleave unto his wife: and they shall be one flesh.

---

[1] Ephesians 5:30–32.

And they were both naked, the man and his wife, and were not ashamed."[2]

As I wrestled with the Lord about this, it came to me that in the beginning there was a two-legged creature naming animals, who was male and female in the image of God.

This is the way I figured it. There was nothing that was done in the first six days, except by God. On the seventh day God rested, and if there was one thing I had learned, even by then, it is that, when God rests, we better rest. So I don't see Adam doing anything on the seventh day either. So, let's say, along comes Monday, and Adam is "up and at 'em" with God, and God has him naming animals. Please note there is no visible woman yet. She's still in the man. She is only called "woman" when, and because, she is taken out of the man. I don't know about you, but I think Bill Cosby has the right spin on all this.[3]

It looks to me like on the seventh day everything was "very good": at least, that was God's opinion. But, once the man was through naming animals, something was "not good" again, in God's opinion.

So God puts him to sleep, and you know what happened, or do you? The KJV says God "took one of his ribs." No big deal, …right? Except that it goes on to say, "…and closed up the flesh instead thereof …." It's hard to imagine that was good English even in King James' day. In the more modern translations it looks more like some kind of skin graft than a matter of stitches.

And there is another clue, …what Adam said: "This is now bone of my bones, and flesh of my flesh." So it was not just a rib that was taken; there was also flesh that was taken. Up to then I had been a "rib man." You know, no big deal, I'm only missing a rib. Well that perception does not make for "living with your wife according to understanding," to paraphrase Peter. And you know what happens when you don't do that: your prayer life is in trouble. "Likewise, ye husbands, dwell with them according to knowledge, giving honour unto the wife, as unto the weaker vessel, and as being heirs together of the grace of life; that your prayers be not hindered."[4] But more about that shortly. I hope you are with me so far.

---

[2]Genesis 2:18,20-25.

[3]In one of his comedy routines, Bill Cosby says that the female got her name because, when Adam took his first look at her, all he could say was, "Wooo, man!"

[4]1 Peter 3:7.

So, a missing "rib" didn't seem to be enough of a cause to justify all this aggravation. Not even a missing rib plus some flesh seemed to be enough of a cause. Then it hit me…my woman was missing. She was in him the first time that man ever entered God's rest, and that was very good, a perfect union. Then, apparently for the sake of the work, she had to be removed. It looked to me like resting was one thing, but working was something else again; after all, who needs a "help meet" when all you have to do is rest?

I was already pretty Christocentric in my thinking and understanding of the scripture, so, revelation by revelation, thought by thought, I was checking all of this against the "great mystery, Christ and the Church." The Christology seemed to be working so far. Jesus even said, "…For the hardness of your heart he wrote you this precept. But from the beginning of the creation God made them male and female. For this cause shall a man leave his father and mother, and cleave to his wife; And they twain shall be one flesh: so then they are no more twain, but one flesh."[5] If I understand Him correctly, God had made them one flesh, male and female, and in such a way that divorce was not an option. The woman had not been removed yet. But I was still unclear about what I was missing, so the Lord helped me out with one of my only visions. (Fortunately I was already a charismatic, so visions were legal.)

I looked and saw a turtle. It was walking along scratching and snapping, when suddenly a big hand came from above, picked up the turtle, and opened it like a cherrystone clam. Having removed the insides, the top and bottom were put back together and the turtle put back on the ground, where it continued to walk, scratch, and snap. Apparently it had been left with enough equipment to keep on scratching and snapping.

Of the inside, the hand made a woman. That was the vision.

The Lord then opened my understanding. He was showing me what I was left with, and what I was missing. What I saw was that I was left with the strong, protective, relatively insensitive part. After all, a sensitive shell would be a contradiction in function. I had enough left to successfully interact with the cold cruel world. What was missing was most of my telecommunications equipment. She got that part. I guess you've noticed how, everything else being equal, women seem to be able to keep track of a lot more things at once than men can. Actually I think I learned

---

[5]Mark 10: 5–8.

since the vision that a lot of left-right brain connections are broken in males before birth. There is actually some physiology to back up the mass media portrayal of men.

There was more than that which I came to understand, but, armed with that much, I went to Carleen and told her what I had seen and come to understand. I explained the Lord had showed me that my woman was missing, and that she had most of the telecommunications equipment that I needed to properly function. I told her that the Lord had showed me that he had left me with the protective—and less sensitive—part. I said that I would try to become more sensitive, but that there was a very good chance that I would never be as sensitive as she was. That the nature of my function was to be more focused for the sake of being task-oriented. I said that the only way I could see it working was for her to be willing to continue to bring to my attention the things that she was concerned with, so I would know where I needed to apply my strength.

Up to then, when she had brought me her concerns, I had found them very threatening and condemning: after all, the wife of a good husband shouldn't have any concerns. The expression of her needs and concerns came at me as criticism, an indication of my failure as a provider. Often, when what I read as her "honey do" list became impossibly long, I would just dump the whole thing back on her head. I apologized for all the times I had been reactive rather than redemptive and promised to try to be better about that. I said that, if she would reopen to me, I would try be better about receiving what she had to say. The whole conversation was very healing for both of us. In the process I discovered that "giving honor to the wife as unto the weaker part" could easily be understood as "unto the more sensitive part."

I soon found out, that I didn't have to try to fix everything that was wrong. All she really needed was a place to put her garbage without getting it dumped back on her head. Next day, she would be clean as a whistle, even though I hadn't made everything better. (My hands might be hanging down and my knees weak, but she was fine.) It was enough for her just to have a place to put her concerns. Going back to my Christology, I saw a whole new meaning for Philippians 4:6,7: "Be careful for nothing; but in every thing by prayer and supplication with thanksgiving let your requests be made known unto God. And the peace of God, which passeth all understanding, shall keep your hearts and minds through Christ Jesus."

Just as Jesus is my garbage man, I'm supposed to be her garbage man. The vineyard can get pretty messed up when wives have no place to put their garbage. That vision probably made the biggest difference in our marriage of any revelation or insight I have received in the Lord. So you see, being head doesn't mean shutting my wife down, it means giving her a safe place to open up. I have found this not only to be true in our marriage, but true in the Church as well.

I should also say that this garbage disposal business is not the exclusive privilege of men. Carleen has had to take away plenty of my garbage over the years. Also, we husbands may be called to be the primary earthly source for our wives, but we make a very poor substitute for Christ as the primary source of our wife. None of us are strong enough for that. Each of us, husbands and wives, has to find our source in Him.

Some years ago now, I was having lunch at the home of a pastor friend of mine. And I shared an observation I had come to after many years of providing hospitality in our home to many couples in "full-time ministry." I said, "Pastors' wives are the loneliest people I know, because they have no one to talk to about their biggest problems." (In general, I think husbands tend to be their wives' biggest problems.) He responded by saying, "That can't be true," and asked his wife, "Who do you talk to?" She answered, "No one."

I'm not suggesting that wives hang their husbands out to dry in the Church, but I am saying there is a problem, and most "ministers" I've met are in denial about it. Whatever the God-given differences between men and women, shutting women down in Church is not the proper response.

Well, Lisa, I had a moment, and just thought I would pass that along. You never know when you might need it—or perhaps you do. :-)

Yours in Christ,

Jay

On Thursday, February 5, 2004, Lisa wrote in response to Jay's lengthy e-mail received earlier that day:

Dear Jay,

You really blew me away with this email! I love the way you personalize what you say with your own experiences, as well as dialogues with others (the ones with Heather are always particularly riveting), as well as how you bring in scripture and your interpretation and pulling together of scripture and concepts. It's like reading little masterpieces—each deserving of loving in-depth study, assimilation, and dissemination. It's such a joy to share these preoccupations with you. I feel so privileged. Agape man ...I like that.

That reminds me—I want to tell you this and then get on with your email. It's interesting that you mentioned in the earlier email about "the older one that prophesied." My second massage was for Barbara, the (black) lady who cleans my house. She has been cleaning for over 10 years and we have a very close connection. She is another that has been an inspiration in her faith—which sounds very similar to what you've described—talking in tongues and all. Her last church left her bruised, and when I told her about this one, she got really excited. This Sunday will be her first—she had planned to go last week but had a family emergency. I'm really excited that she's coming—I know her presence will inspire me. But an added bonus—she is bringing her 87-year-old "spiritual mother" with her (I believe she said her name was Lenora). Lenora insists on coming (Barbara says, "you just never know what she will do—get up and prophesize—evangelize— speak in tongues—just whatever the Holy Spirit moves her to do"), and she's bringing Barbara with her. According to Lenora, Barbara has been "slacking off—and here's this woman who is picking up and running with the Lord [I guess she means me], and it's time for Barbara to jump back in." I'm so excited about having her be there I could just about spit.

Had to tell you about that!

Your devotion to my growth in Christ continues to touch me. How did I get so lucky? I'm so glad that you feel such a strong connection with me and that the Lord has made you a safe place for me. I really feel that. So far you've treated every disparaging thought I've uttered with the utmost thoughtfulness and discernment. Such a gift! Thank you so much! And it's cool that I get to hang out with you forever...

I hope you don't mind—I'm going to attempt to encapsulate what you said in the last email in terms of how it applies to this "groaning in my heart." The concepts seem to be that there is first a "drawing to God" in which He selects us and prepares us via the Holy Spirit to become fertile ground for the "Christ seed" to grow. Then there is an "entry"—disposal of sin—adoption—a legalization in relationship to God. Salvation is guaranteed here, but there's much more to the story. This seems to be the sticky point in the process—and where a lot of people get stuck (is this where I am?)—that unless the seed is nurtured and grown to maturity (which involves death and resurrection of the "old self" and a changing of species)—the "real birth"—and life as Christ intended us to live—will not come to fruition. This is another "drawing by God" process. And the last part involves being "baptized in the spirit"—which, if I hear you right, is not something widely done in "churches." With this baptism in spirit comes gifts and a knowing and living of Christ that most people never realize. Am I anywhere close?

(Sorry again for the oversimplification.)

Wow! Awesome! So how do you know when you're ready to be "baptized in the spirit"—does it just happen? How do you know when it happens? What is this talking in tongues? Did you literally say, "Inflation begins the minute government calls money something else"—in English—out of nowhere? Was that the beginning of your quest for your book? (You said we need to talk about the debate of the "Baptism of the Holy Spirit" whenever I'm ready. I'm ready whenever you are.)

Hope you don't mind all of the questions—it's just a new, fascinating concept—explained in a way I've never heard before. I think growing with you—and in Christ—is going to be quite fun.

Before I go—(I feel like I'm cheating here in the shortness of my reply to your masterpiece)—I want you to know that I'm becoming more comfortable in believing that the Bible is God's word. It occurs to me that in the beginning, at least—until you read and understand enough to where God can convince you—the believing is really based on faith. It is not such a long stretch to have faith that the Bible is the word of God—when you consider that all of this "spiritual stuff" is really based on faith (oh yeah, and that indescribable feeling) and that it makes sense that God would give us some sort of "written manual." I'm ready to extend that faith.

You are so precious to me, too!

Love,

Lisa

On Friday, February 6, 2004, Jay responded:

Lisa wrote [about her friend Barbara's "spiritual mother," Lenora]: ...*I'm so excited about having her be there I could just about spit.*

Dear Lisa,

I have a feeling you are in for a real treat. There aren't too many 87-year-old black lady saints around who don't know who they are. So I'm sure Barbara isn't kidding. Even Tony, Felicity, and Penny may have to fasten their seat belts.

Had to tell you about that!

Thanks. I'm tickled!

Your devotion to my growth in Christ continues to touch me. How did I get so lucky? ...

I think His name is Jesus, not "luck." Actually I was rooming with an old saint at a monetary conference back around 1973. I had wished him "luck," and he informed me that the root of "luck" came from "Lucifer." That's Satan's name before he fell from heaven. I haven't wished anyone "Good luck" since. I'll never forget that man. He told me about a book and then sent me a copy. The book's title is, **On the Release of the Destruction of Life Devoid of Value**.[6] It was the most often-quoted book by the defense at the Nuremberg trials. I still have it.

...I'm so glad that you feel such a strong connection with me and that the Lord has made you a safe place for me. I really feel that....

I am so glad. I like the arrangement. You are a wonderful communicator. Anyone would be very blessed to be on the receiving end of your writing.

...So far you've treated every disparaging thought I've uttered with the utmost thoughtfulness and discernment. Such a gift! Thank you so much! And it's cool that I get to hang out with you forever ...

My pleasure on both counts.

I hope you don't mind—I'm going to attempt to encapsulate what you said in the last email in terms of how it applies to this "groaning in my heart." ...

Thank you. This is a very good way for me to know if you have understood me or not. I may just correct your synopsis line by line as a way of making the understanding clearer [Jay's corrections and additions appear in bold type].

---

[6] **The Release of the Destruction of Life Devoid of Value**, published in Leipzig in 1920, and authored by jurist Karl Binding and psychiatrist Alfred Hoche.

*...The concepts seem to be that there is first a "drawing to God" in which He selects us, **draws us**, and prepares us **by** the Holy Spirit to become fertile ground for the "Christ seed" to **be implanted**....*

*...Then there is an "entry"—disposal of sin—**reconciliation**— adoption—a legalization in relationship to God. **Inclusion in God's house** is guaranteed here, but there's much more to the story....*

Actually, as I understand it, salvation was guaranteed to everyone at the cross. The only question is whether or not everyone will believe it or want it. Perhaps while I'm here I should explain that salvation pertains to this world. We are not "saved to," but rather "saved from." Romans puts it this way: "For with the heart man believeth unto righteousness; and with the mouth confession is made unto salvation."[7]

Eternal life is a matter of inner faith, but salvation is a matter of outer expression. This is also what water baptism is all about. It is a statement we make to the world with our body that we are relocating by death and resurrection from the old creation to the new creation. Baptism is the wedding ceremony of faith in Christ. Except that in baptism we don't say, "I do," but "I am." "I am crucified with Christ." "I am buried with Him in baptism." "I am risen with Him to new and everlasting life." Peter calls it "the pledge of a good conscience toward God."[8] This is like our "I do" statement: it is the pledge of a good conscience toward our spouse. Otherwise we are just living together without commitment.

...This seems to be the sticky point in the process—and where a lot of people get stuck (is this where I am?)

I am usually hesitant to judge another's faith, but, in your case, you have been so transparent with me that I am inclined to render an opinion. I would have to say that you are not only in the house, but probably baptized in the Spirit. I say this last with some reservation, only because while the "fruit of the Spirit" is so strong in your life right now,[9] it is not yet clear what the gifts of the Spirit might be in your life. I suppose if I thought really hard about this, pouring over your emails, I might be able to spot some of your gifting, but right off-hand I am hesitant to risk manhandling you into a wrong direction. In addition, I think you will be even more empowered by the Spirit as you come into greater understanding about the baptism in the Spirit, and the infilling

---

[7]Romans 10:10.   [8]1 Peter 3:21.
[9]Galatians 5:22,23

of the Spirit. Baptism has an aspect of meaning that is introductory. Once you have had that introductory experience,[10] there is a need to keep on being filled with the Spirit.[11]

You are right about a lot of people getting stuck at the point of reconciliation,[12] but then not moving into being "saved by His life." As for you, I would hardly say that you are "stuck." You are amazing. You are just in recovery from the wounds you received in your understanding from what you have seen calling itself "Christianity," "Church," "saved," "receiving Jesus," and a lot of other "Christian lingo" that you have clearly seen was more talk than reality. Aside from that you are very spiritually healthy. Your hard drive is in very good shape, and you are downloading understanding at a very accelerated pace. "Advanced chips," I would guess.

...—that unless the seed is nurtured and grown to maturity (which involves death and resurrection of the "old self" and a changing of species)—the "real birth"—and life as Christ intended us to live—will not come to fruition....

Rather than trying to correct what you have written here, I will try to explain it another way. If you look at Acts 19:1-6, just cited above, you will discover some believers in Jesus who only knew the "baptism of John the Baptist." They had taken a step toward getting rid of their garbage, but they had not yet received their new life in Christ, which was still a mystery to them, and to Apollos.[13] The mystery that had not yet been revealed to Apollos, and to those who received his teaching, was "Christ in you the hope of Glory."[14] This mystery was not revealed until the "Seed" was made available by which Christ could actually live His life in those who believe. This was at the heart of the promise that God had made by implication to Eve when He said to the serpent, "He (the Seed of the woman) shall bruise your head." This is what happened—and always happens—at the cross.[15]

When you move from adoption to the new birth (which can be at the same moment or be delayed by lack of understanding as

---

[10]Acts 19:1–6, Galatians 3:2.   [11]Ephesians 5:18–19.

[12]Romans 5:10.   [13]Acts 18:24–28.   [14]Colossians 1:25-29.

[15]Hebrews 2:8-15 Since writing this, I have been instructed in the way more excellently by Mel Gibson's film "The Passion of the Christ." In his film, he has Christ crushing the head of the serpent in the Garden of Gethsemane, While Hebrews tells us that the devil was destroyed by the death of Jesus, the spiritual battle that settled the matter once and for all was won in the Garden. I believe that "The Passion" has it right. The film contains a great deal of spiritual intelligence.

in the case of the believers in Acts 19:1-6), you become pregnant by an incorruptible Seed.[16] That Seed is Christ in you. Again, I would have to say that you could pass a pregnancy test in a "New York minute." If any of this is still unclear, do not be anxious about it, because the Holy Spirit will make it clear to you, and it is only what you get from Him that counts in eternity. The Spirit is your perfect teacher; I am only His unprofitable servant.

…This is another "drawing by God" process.…

At this point we are two steps beyond the "drawing." We have moved from being drawn to being received, to being filled with the life of Christ Himself. The bad news is that we have this treasure in "earthen vessels."[17] It's the earthen part that remains the problem. That's where our inward groaning goes on. This is the process in us by which Christ develops in us from conception to the final form of the new birth.[18] By faith, it's a done deal. It's done, but it's still in process. This is the mystery of faith.

…And the last part involves being "baptized in the spirit"—…

Yes, I believe that the "new birth" is ours by Spirit. The Spirit that was not available until Christ was glorified.[19]

…which, if I hear you right, is not something widely done in "churches."…

Actually the baptism in the Holy Spirit is quite widely understood by Pentecostals (the Holy Spirit was first poured out on the Church at Pentecost.[20]) and "charismatics." Charismatics are recent arrivals to the experience of Pentecost. Generally they have come on the scene since the 1950s. The Pentecostals got started around the turn of the last century. By now, the Pentecostals have institutionalized themselves, but the Charismatics are only recently beginning to get institutionalized. Initially the Charismatics were institutional Christians who had been set free by the Holy Spirit. Tragically, believers don't do very well at standing firm in the liberty whereby the Holy Spirit has set them free.[21]

…With this baptism in spirit comes gifts and a knowing and living of Christ that most people never realize. Am I anywhere close?…

That one is a bull's eye.

---

[16] 1 Peter 1:23.
[18] Romans 8:14–27.
[20] Acts 2:1–4.

[17] 2 Corinthians 4:6–7.
[19] John 7:39.
[21] Galatians 5:1.

...(Sorry again for the oversimplification.)

Please don't apologize. You are doing great!

Wow! Awesome! ...

Absolutely!!

...So how do you know when you're ready to be "baptized in the spirit"—does it just happen? How do you know when it happens?...

It's kind of like falling in love. When it happens you know it. In the beginning the outward sign that this had happened was most often the speaking in tongues. 1 Corinthians 14 is a good place to go to get an idea of what this is all about. For us in our own day, however, it is good to keep in mind that "tongues" was for a sign to unbelieving Jews. Where there are no unbelieving Jews, I believe there is less likelihood that the sign is limited to tongues. God is very gracious. He is quite willing to meet us where we are. We are the ones who tend to come short of the grace of God.[22]

This is running longer than expected, and I have to get some sleep, so I will try to share a little more completely about "tongues" in the morning.

...What is this talking in tongues? ...

Like I said, in the morning.

...Did you literally say, "Inflation begins the minute government calls money something else"—in English—out of nowhere? ...

My first experience of the thought was written on the inside of my forehead. Then I wrote it down and later spoke it to others. It was a "word of wisdom."[23]

...Was that the beginning of your quest for your book? ...

Yes.

...(You said we need to talk about the debate of the "Baptism of the Holy Spirit" whenever I'm ready. I'm ready whenever you are.)

In the morning.

Hope you don't mind all of the questions—it's just a new, fasci-nating concept—explained in a way I've never heard before. I think growing with you—and in Christ—is going to be quite fun.

---

[22]Hebrews 12:15.   [23]1 Corinthians 12:1–11.

Now you have done it again! I have a confession to make. It has to do with how you have made me feel. Here is how I explained it to a local pastor a several years ago now:

2/15/2000

Dear _____,

I haven't shared this with anyone else, in fact it is not even altogether coherent in my own heart and mind yet, but I thought I might be able to give it expression with you, in the hope that you might be able to understand, kind of, woman to woman.

I could cite a lot of Scripture as foundational to what I'm about to share, but trusting that we are not at war, I would like to try to come at this thing peacefully. In any case, a macho biker dude like yourself might just have to fasten your seat belt.

In the letter to Nate, I talked about "the other words" of God. What God is saying, but "in other words." Jesus shared with his disciples about their having been made clean by the words that He had shared with them. Paul talks about "the washing of water by the word." To come at people with Bible verses is like coming at them with a sand blaster. It may be better than stoning, but it is not as easy to take as washing with water. As I am beginning to understand it, our responsibility, even hunger, in the Lord is to be so exposed to the Scriptures that they become liquid in our hearts, That they come out of us "in other words," like a fountain of life, like a spring of living water, like milk and honey, for others.

Romans 1 has us without excuse if we don't learn about our creator from what he has made, and, in the first instance, what he has made is "male and female." Two simple words, seemingly obvious on the face of it, but each containing a package of information, even revelation that the church has barely touched. The Scriptures, however, draw on their content in many, and amazing ways. That's what I want to do now, not so much an exposition of the Scripture but an expression of my own feeling, understood in the light of the Biblical revelation.

_____, I've been dry for a long time. I came to Golden Valley from an environment where there were those whom I had been feeding for many years. Feeding at a deep and very intimate level. I wasn't here very long before even my milk dried up. I would like to share with you a little bit about that, you know, just one mother to another. I never saw the process in this context before, but recently my milk has come back in, and in such a copious amount that I have been forced to finally understand some of the word pictures in the Scripture.

I don't know how it was around your house—perhaps before your own children were weaned, you were not even in a position to notice—but in my house, when the children were still nursing, the minute they let out the slightest cry to be fed, Carleen would go off like a New York City fire boat. If I was in the same room, and she was not covered, I would get wet. If she tried to take the child to her breast too quickly, they would just about drown. Even after things would settle down some, there was need for periodic "burping."

If, in the midst of this wonderful early nurturing process, the babe is taken away, perhaps due to a permanent loss, the first thing that happens is that the breasts get engorged. If they're not properly relieved, this can be extremely painful. I'm guessing this is what you might suffer if something came between you and those that you are feeding. But when everything is working right, a balance gets established where the stimulation of milk production is just right for the amount needed. As the babe matures, and there is none to take its place, the milk finally dries up, and that phase of nurture is ended.

In and by the Spirit, we are heading into a land flowing with milk and honey. Some of that milk, by the grace of God, and the power of His Spirit, will be flowing out of us, if The Lord is merciful, and we know He is.

Well, if that isn't enough to get me drummed out of the Valley, I don't know what is.[24]

God Bless you today!

Yours in Christ,

Jay

Before I go—(I feel like I'm cheating here in the shortness of my reply to your masterpiece)—I want you to know that I'm becoming more comfortable in believing that the Bible is God's word....

I am very blessed to hear that. Part of the growth process is going from milk to a place where our relationship with the Word of God is strong enough so that we are able to feed ourselves. Too often what happens is that institutionalized believers suffer from institutional retardation, because it suits the finances of the teachers to keep them in pews where interminable offerings can be taken. As for me, I would rather have the stars of the sky. [:-)] I think I see some of mine in you!

...It occurs to me that in the beginning, at least—until you read and understand enough to where God can convince you—the believing is really based on faith. It is not such a long stretch to have faith that the Bible is the word of God—when you consider that all of this "spiritual stuff" is really based on faith (oh yeah, and that indescribable feeling)....

"That indescribable feeling" is what makes me think you have already been baptized in The Spirit. All that is lacking is a little more understanding.

...and that it makes sense that God would give us some sort of "written manual."...

That "written manual" contains the Seed that is able to make us pregnant with new life.

...I'm ready to extend that faith.

"Ready, willing, able"—and well along.

---

[24] 1 Samuel 18:3–4.

I'll be back in the morning, Lord willing.[25]

Sweet dreams,

Jay

On Saturday, February 6, 2004, Jay continued his response to Lisa:

Dear Lisa,

Yesterday I wrote, "I have a feeling you are in for a real treat. There aren't too many 87-year-old black lady saints around who don't know who they are. So I'm sure Barbara isn't kidding. Even Tony, Felicity, and Penny may have to fasten their seat belts."

As I thought about this paragraph, in the context of all that I had sent you, it occurred to me that I should have added that Lenora is probably a Pentecostal. You might want to ask her about it. More than likely she believes that speaking in tongues is the introductory sign of the baptism in the Holy Spirit. That is a position widely held among Pentecostals. By the way, that movement really got started among poor black people. Jesus has a way of going where He will be received.

You had written: "So how do you know when you're ready to be "baptized in the spirit"—does it just happen? How do you know when it happens?"

I wrote:

"It's kind of like falling in love. When it happens you know it. In the beginning the outward sign that this had happened was most often speaking in tongues. 1 Corinthians 14 is a good place to go to get an idea of what this is all about.

For us in our own day, however, it is good to keep in mind that "tongues" was for a sign to unbelieving Jews 1 Corinthians 14:22. Where there are no unbelieving Jews, I believe there is less likelihood that the sign is limited to tongues. God is very gracious. He is quite willing to meet us where we are. We are the ones who tend to come short of the grace of God, Hebrews 12:15."

Then I said:

"This is running longer than expected, and I have to get some sleep, so I will try to share a little more completely about "tongues" in the morning."

---

[25]James 4:15.

Well, it's morning.

I had hoped to find an explanation that I had already written, but after a couple of hours of searching for it in my computer files, I couldn't find it. Perhaps I never wrote it down before. I know I have shared it on tape with a very anti-tongues Baptist pastor.

In any case, I will try to be brief but I hope still understandable.

Also, you had written:

"(You said we need to talk about the debate of the "Baptism of the Holy Spirit" whenever I'm ready. I'm ready whenever you are.)"

I responded similarly to that: "In the morning."

So here goes:

Tongues is a lot of things. I'll try to begin with what I consider to be most core, and work my way out from there.

In Genesis 11:1, everyone on earth is said to have spoken the same language. The result was that they tried to get to heaven on their own steam (Genesis 11:4). God had another way to get to heaven in mind, so he sabotaged their efforts, by scrambling their language so they couldn't understand each other any more. (Genesis 11:7–8).

On the day of Pentecost, God reversed the confusion, by giving the believers a spiritual language by which they could communicate with those who did not speak or understand their earthly language. This was a sign that the other way to heaven had been revealed. It was confirmation that Jesus Christ was the way to heaven. Not only was this a sign to the world, but more specifically in that time frame, it was a sign to the Jews.[26]

On the day of Pentecost there were people of other languages present. They did not speak, but they did hear, and what they heard, they understood in their own languages.[27] There were also those present who heard and didn't understand. They thought those who were speaking were drunk.[28] Peter went on to explain what was happening[29] and really elaborated on what this meant in Acts 2:22-36. The reaction of those present is seen in verses 37-47.

My understanding of it is that God had made an old creation that was destroyed because of unbelief. (It was never meant to work.[30] It was flawed in that it could not make God's kind of

---

[26]Isaiah 28:11–12, 1 Corinthians 14:21.   [27]Acts 2:6–12.
[28]Acts 2:13–15.   [29]Acts 2:16–21.
[30]Romans 8:20.

lovers out of people.[31]) On the day of Pentecost a new and everlasting creation was introduced to our human understanding. It was a creation of, in, and by the Spirit of God. It was a creation of perfect intimacy, and spiritual tongues was its new language or means of communication.

As I understand it—and have experienced it—you should be a natural. Because it is a yielding of your own intellect's sovereignty over what comes out of your mouth or off your tongue. We simply yield our intellect to the Lordship of Jesus by His Spirit. It may well be that you will find out what it sounds like when your friend and her spiritual mother show up on Sunday. Not necessarily, but quite possibly.

In my case, I was probably too intellectually proud to "speak in tongues" for a year after I was baptized in the Holy Spirit with the sign of the word of wisdom I had received, "Inflation begins …" I had not been taught anything on the subject prior to this happening to me, and it was only later on that I found out and came to understand what had happened. However, the word of wisdom was not the only sign in my case. I spent the day in tears, both on the plane to Washington, and later in the lobby of the Washington Hilton, as I finished the book I was reading[32] and waited for the guests to show up for the monetary conference I was there for.

Perhaps because of the tears part, I came to understand something about tongues that might help to explain it in another way, quite possibly one that you can already relate to.

Praying in tongues is like praying in tears. Both are valid expressions of the content of our hearts. Neither is rooted so much in the intellect as in the emotion and in the spirit. Both may need to be interpreted,[33] even for the one who is doing the praying. We don't always understand why we are "feeling weepy." Sometimes it's sadness, sometimes it's joy, sometimes anger or frustration.

Having said that, I should add that speaking in tongues may also bring with it the same inhibitions as many men have about being willing to cry. I'm sure you have heard the expression, "Why don't you have yourself a good cry? It will do you good." This understanding is reflected in 1 Corinthians 14:4. Just as some men need to be taught that it is okay to cry, many need to be taught that

---

[31]Luke 7:36–50.

[32]**Mr. Jones, Meet the Master: Sermons and Prayers of Peter Marshall**, published by Fleming H. Revell Co., in 1982.

[33]1 Corinthians 14:13.

it is okay to speak in tongues. Yielding our tongues to the Spirit is not what most would consider a very "manly" thing to do.

Often a message in tongues serves as a kind of trumpet blast, focusing attention on the interpretation to follow.

All this said, the abuse of tongues is widespread. It is often used as a means of spiritually "showing off." That appears to be the problem that Paul was addressing in 1 Corinthians 14, and it remains a big problem in our own day, now that this gift has been restored to the Church.

One final thing before I come to a close for now, and that is, I believe I received the gift of speaking in tongues when I was first baptized in the Spirit, but through ignorance—and pride—I failed to open the package. I believe that this has been true of the "church" as well for most of Church history.

On the light side, I had almost become a pest to a spiritual daughter, in asking her to let me pray for her to receive the baptism in the Holy Spirit, As a good Baptist girl, she wanted no part of that, even though we are so close. At a critical time I sent her an email with some pretty strong counsel. She got baptized in the Spirit reading it. It made quite an impact on her life, enough so that her friends couldn't miss it. They had asked her what had happened to her. After a very frustrating time trying to explain, she finally said, "This is like trying to explain an orgasm to someone who has never had one."

On that note, I'll give you a break, and close for now.

I hope this helps!

Yours in Christ,
Jay

On Friday, February 6, 2004, Lisa wrote:

Whoa! Jay!

I've been floating on air all day. These last emails have been so confirming to my spirit! I have so much excitement inside of me—it's overflowing.

Since that day of healing in July, I've regularly experienced what I have called "spiritual orgasms"—where I feel a rush of energy thru my body and out of my heart. Sometimes it lasts for 30 seconds or so and sometimes there are "multiple orgasms." It is an amazing feeling! Other times I just feel full, expanded, vibrating, overcome with bliss. It's a state that I'm frequently in—often it makes it difficult to function—or maybe I just don't want to have to move out of that state. Another thing that has happened is this communication thing. Maybe I just never felt that I had anything to write about before, but since July I've been writing pretty constantly, and talking about my experiences in ways that people listen to. There have been other days that I've wept, too. Not because of anything I was conscious of—but something from deep inside.

Is it possible I was "baptized in the spirit" on that healing table? It feels like it to me. Strange and wonderful.

Thank you so much for giving me all of this information and languaging to help me understand what's happening to me! It is such a comfort! So this is what Christ is all about?! I'm so excited about the rest of my life!!!

Time to go celebrate! This should be one glorious weekend!!

You've really been working overtime this week. Wow! You've got to feel that it's been worth it!!

Have a WONDERFUL weekend!

I love you so much!!!
Lisa

On Friday, February 6, 2004, Jay responded:

Lisa wrote: *Whoa! Jay!*

I've been floating on air all day. These last emails have been so confirming to my spirit! I have so much excitement inside of me—it's overflowing.

Since that day of healing in July, I've regularly experienced what I have called "spiritual orgasms"—where I feel a rush of energy thru my body and out of my heart. Sometimes it lasts for 30 seconds or so and sometimes there are "multiple orgasms." It is an amazing feeling! Other times I just feel "full, expanded, vibrating, overcome with bliss." It's a state that I'm frequently in—often it makes it difficult to function—or maybe I just don't want to have to move out of that state....

Dear Lisa,

One thing for sure. It sounds a lot better than hot flashes!!! [:-)]

...Another thing that has happened is this communication thing. Maybe I just never felt that I had anything to write about before, but since July I've been writing pretty constantly. And talking about my

experiences in ways that people listen to. There have been other days that I've wept, too. Not because of anything I was conscious of—but something from deep inside.

Is it possible I was "baptized in the spirit" on that healing table? It feels like it to me. Strange and wonderful.

From what you have told me, I think it is quite possible that Jesus had already taken away your garbage, perhaps without you being aware with full understanding. That would have put you in a position of adoption, and according to Galatians, 4:5-7 that would have made it legal for you to receive the Spirit of God's Son into your heart whereby we cry "Abba," "Father." Paul contrasts the manifestation of the Spirit with that of understanding, so it is possible for you to experience a lot without yet having any understanding of what is happening to you or through you.[34]

Thank you so much for giving me all of this information and languaging to help me understand what's happening to me! It is such a comfort! So this is what Christ is all about?! I'm so excited about the rest of my life!!!

Have a wonderful life, and a wonderful weekend!!!

Time to go celebrate! This should be one glorious weekend!!

I'll be looking forward to a "good report."

You've really been working overtime this week. Wow! You've got to feel that it's been worth it!!

All I had to do to know that you are worth it was to look in Jesus's eyes the day He said "I love you." Like I said on the "Horizontal" tape, after that it's as easy as agreeing with God. Hanging around the cross is a good place because it is there that you get to hang around those He died for. It doesn't get any better than that!!! [:-)]

I love you too, and bless you in that to which the Lord has called you in these very precious days.

Jay

P.S. Did you get the "turtle story"?

On Friday, February 6, 2004, Lisa answered Jay's question:

---

[34]1 Corinthians 14:13,15.

Yep, got the turtle story! It was wonderful—shared it with Kurtis, too. It was a bit of a struggle for him (he's saying, "What's all of this about Christ? Isn't it God that we're talking about?" I told him it was a long story—and at 10:30 last night that was about as good as I could do.) But he read it and got the message. It is very similar to what we learned to do in therapy—just with a whole new, deeper understanding.

Cool vision, too, Jay!

I've got to run to Pilates. A couple of things—I mailed you Penny's book today. Also, I sent your overview to my dad and to my massage client as I told you. Gave them your email address—hope you don't mind—in case they would like to correspond about your work.

Later,
Lisa

On Sunday, February 8, Jay responded:

Lisa wrote:

What's all of this about Christ? Isn't it God that we're talking about?

This is a good question. (While I think of it, have you ever seen "The Power of Myth"? It is a series of interviews that Bill Moyers did with Joseph Campbell. Campbell was the world's foremost expert on mythology. He had given his whole life to the subject. He was a professor at Smith College, I think. Moyers did the interview the year before Campbell died. He was in his 80s.[35]

You can probably find the series in your local library. It is a six-video set, each about an hour long. Moyers interviewed Campbell from a nominally Christian perspective. Campbell was an agnostic at best. The series is very powerful from a truly Christian perspective. Campbell came so close to seeing the truth and yet missed it. It is very sad to see how big an investment someone can make—and still miss it. It is a tremendous presentation on the sovereignty of God. We can only come to Him if He draws us.)

Now to the question, "Why Christ?" All the religions of men are nothing more than head trips. Only impregnation with divine life can result in true intimacy with God. This requires seed, and, in the first instance, that Seed is Christ. The Paradise Lost

---

[35]The series was televised on PBS in 1988 and also became a best-selling book, published in 1989 by Doubleday.

of the Garden of Eden was lost because, as close as Adam and Eve were to God, they had no way of partaking of God's nature. This would only be possible through the Seed of God. It is God's Son, the Christ, the Messiah, The Anointed One, who is the Spiritual Seed of God. It was the wisdom of God to arrange things so that His Seed would not only take care of the garbage of human doing, but would also be the one who would bring to us the very life of God Himself.

Here is my try at the Fatherhood of God.

"If any man be in Christ, he is a new creation; Old things are passed away, behold all things become new."[36]

To paraphrase for the sake of broader and deeper application: If anyone is in Christ, which can only happen if He is in them, then they are a new race, their old race has passed away, and like Paul, they can consider their membership in their old race rubbish. Look and see, everything about you, deriving from your new lineage is new.

To explore why it is important to see and understand God as our Father, I want to get very narrow in focus. There is more to His Fatherhood, than what I want to say here, and by excluding it for the purpose of this present discussion, I don't want to imply that the rest is not very important.

Let me begin by saying that, if we are "created male and female in God's image," then God must be male and female. An image ought to look like what it represents, don't you think? The irreducible significance of male and female is relationship. It was an "us" that said in the beginning "Let us make ..." There is authority in the "let," there is intimacy in the "us," and there is a new creation in the "make."

We don't know what the intimacy of the Godhead must be like in reality, because we are not there yet, but God has made an effort to communicate something of this intimacy by giving us the graphics of our own bodies. It is increasingly apparent to me, however, that the graphics are very limited in possibility when compared to the reality that is hidden in Christ in God.

Here, I want to explore what can be learned from the graphics, however.

God has promised to redeem the race of the first man Adam, by the seed of the first woman Eve. Keep in mind that she began in Adam and was not called woman until she was taken out of

---

[36] 2 Corinthians 5:17.

him. Was she any less for having come out from him? No, rather she was more in some ways than he was. He was "made," she was "formed." In the original, the difference is that He was put together good enough to function. She was formed in the same sense as the creation of a work of art.

Where reproduction is concerned, the man contained seed, she contained more than seed, she contained egg. The egg contains not only the potential for new life, but the environment for the early nurture of new life. Where his seed is concerned, it could not participate in the creation of a new race. It would take God's seed to do that, even Christ. All through the lineage of the human race, God kept track of the egg. Abraham was looking for love in all the wrong places. Love was in the egg of Sarah, and hers only. Look at Tamar: the love was in her, and within the limits of Judah, she did whatever she had to do,[37] God helping her, to make sure that it would be her egg that would hatch. From the beginning, Satan has been after the woman and her seed. His war has been against her, not against him.

Satan makes war against "hims" only to the degree that we become "hers" in relationship to Christ.

A father is a seed planter. The life is in the seed. A mother is a place where new life grows. God is the one who gives the growth or "increase."

In order to have a new race, there must first be a new father, a new kind of a father, in this case, a heavenly one. The heart of God is that everyone become a new race. This can only happen by His Fatherhood, which is to say, by His seed, even Christ. In the first instance, what we bring to the process is the egg. He makes us pregnant by Christ through an act of love, the cross.

We then become partakers of the Divine nature; once that happens, we are no longer the old race that we were, the race of the first man Adam. More than that, we are no longer male or female. In any given situation we might be either in spiritual function. At one point Paul was in labor pains, at another he was taking new believers to his breast for nurture, at another point he was planting Divine seeds.

You are no different than Paul in this regard. You can be a seed planter. You can be a life nurturer. In Christ, you have it all. All you need is the revelation and the faith to appropriate what is yours in eternity. You are pregnant with new life and are able to get others pregnant with new life.

---

[37] Genesis 38:6–26.

God certainly wants us to notice that, in the first instance, he has made us male and female; not to notice is inexcusable (Romans 1:20), but, armed with what we have noticed, he wants to take us to a place of intimacy that leaves what we have noticed in the shadows of who we used to be. If we just can't stay out of the shadows, that's okay, but whatever we do, let's not miss the light.

God does not want us to miss the graphics, but in the process, let's not miss the otherwise invisible reality about God, about which the graphics are only a shadow.

When Jesus went to the cross, it was an act of love with the potential of getting the whole world pregnant. We have been caught up in a very exciting—and fulfilling—process, if we only could understand it from God's point of view. Properly understood, life is an act of love.

I've got to run to Pilates. A couple of things—I mailed you Penny's book today....

Thank you so much. I have another tape I am sending to you. This one is by my older brother in the Lord, Nate Krupp.[38] Tony and Felicity know of him. The tape was made at a meeting in our living room back in Connecticut. Nate was speaking about "Church" that night. It also has an authentic manifestation of tongues in it.

...Also, I sent your overview to my dad and to my massage client—as I told you. Gave them your email address—hope you don't mind—in case they would like to correspond about your work.

Again, thank you, I will look forward to hearing from them should that seem good to them.

Time to go get a little more sleep now. The cats help me with my correspondence by getting me up around 4 in the morning to let one or the other of them out.

You are in my heart and prayers for a wonderful day today!
Jay

---

[38]For information on where and how to obtain this tape, go to www.notleftbehind.net.

NOT LEFT BEHIND

CHAPTER 15

OLD WOUNDS

Dear Jay,

Well, your prayers and thoughts are certainly working! I had a wonderful weekend, in particular yesterday. Let's start there, moving around as needed.

It's difficult untangling the events from the feelings—the internal experience—so you'll get both. Going to Tony & Felicity's for the baptisms was an experience all in itself. There were probably about 30 people there—families and friends of the two girls who were baptized. One of the girls was their son, Matt's, girlfriend—so it was a "Dale family" event as well. The girls were both probably early 20s—part of a group that Tony and Felicity work with. (They also work with a group of high school students—I got to meet a few of them as well). T & F's daughter, Becky—who just recently got back from some training event in Hawaii—helped with the baptisms (Matt's girlfriend, Kristen, is one of Becky's good friends). She was awesome. She prayed for the girls when they came out of the water. The prayers just flowed out of her—like your milk and honey. It was such a moving experience to watch this group of people interact with each other. The love that was present was so real. The commitment to one another was apparent. One of the girls talked about how she had always thought of herself as Christian, but that it wasn't until she met with this group (they've only been meeting for six months) that she really felt a personal connection with Jesus.

Jay, these people that God has brought into our lives—Tony and Felicity—and you—really do "glow in the dark." I've never encountered people like this. Jesus with skin on. The spirit just radiates thru you. When Tony addressed the group of people, he was so warm, unpretentious, inviting. He has a way of listening to people—both in this group and with our group at home—where, not only are you comfortable talking intimately, but then he's able to pull the rest of the people into the conversation without breaking the intimacy. It's as if one by one these people's lights get turned on, and before long the whole room is glowing. It's truly incredible to watch.

At our house, I felt different this week from last week—much more peaceful but still with that sense of anticipation (like you said). I'm aware of a huge shift in me—pregnant is a very good description. Radiant. And not at all nervous about the "structure" of the meeting—and I had absolutely no problem with discussing the Bible. I was very much aware that what was occurring there was very sacred—the spirit was very present. People talked about being drawn to be there: Abigail said, "I don't know what we're doing here, and I don't know why, but I have to come here week after week." Pat has said for the last two weeks that she doesn't know why she's coming, but she feels led—and as long as she feels people will accept her she will come. Barbara was "blessed to be here." Lenora didn't make it this week due to arthritis (weather changed)—but will probably come next week. Sandy and Bob—new this week—committed to bring the "meat" next week (main dish—I've been providing so far—I was thrilled for their commitment not so much for the meat, but to the group after just one meeting). There were 13 of us in all—I feel certain that everyone left feeling somewhat changed. Tony and Felicity even hung out for a while after everyone left, talking about how they sensed that everyone seemed glad to be there. This shift in me has certainly made me feel closer to everyone.

When we broke into groups for prayer, I got Felicity. That was such a blessing. I needed someone who was "on the same page" with me for this week. We crammed a lot into that little prayer—intimacy with Kurtis, guidance from God, understanding of Christ. Their "House2House" publication[1] *is picking up again, and her prayer needs included hearing from God what needed to be said thru that and other developing interests. I'm struck by the enormity of what they're being called to do. Talk about responsibility!*

I shared some in the beginning of the group, when we did the "God events," about how significant this week had been for me. I told them that I couldn't go into specifics—because it was still "undigested"—but that I felt I was having some understanding of the

---

[1]This publication is available on the Web at www.house2house.tv.

significance of the Cross, salvation, and the Body of Christ. That even in my limited understanding, it was obvious that there was so much more involved—and it was so much better—than anything I had ever imagined. That I had had such a limited view of Christ and limited understanding of what Christianity was. I was blown away at the love—not only of Jesus but of this body of people who were put in my life—who were laying their lives down for my spiritual growth. I was filled with love and a deep sense of wanting to do the same for others as my understanding grew. Paul pointed out, as you have, that even with my limited understanding, I can, and have, talked about what I'm capable of talking about. There were tears in people's eyes as I was talking. It was precious. And very obviously not the "old Lisa."

Once again I'm running out of time. This last email about the Fatherhood of God was very clear to me. I think, with some practice, I might even be able to talk about it with people. It's an incredible, extraordinary plan—the way God arranged to make His spiritual race. Thank you so much for committing your thoughts to paper in such a succinct manner.

*I poured over last week's emails over the weekend, and—as I said—I'm still digesting. But oh so agreeably! So much more is making sense, and I'm feeling so incredibly privileged to be a part of the "family." I'll have some time tonight to continue (I'm reading **The Message**, too—skipped ahead to read Galatians and Corinthians, as you suggested. Good stuff! It seems that Paul is one of your favorites. Can you tell me more about him?) and will focus on those more tomorrow.*

Loved your "mother to mother" conversation. Such a wonderful way to describe the experience that you're having nurturing me! You're such a wonderful mother—I hope your milk never dries up!

I've watched "The Power of Myth"—just recently it was on PBS. Would love to see it again—mesmerizing.

Question: What keeps some people from being "drawn in by God"? Is it that we just ignore Him?

Kurtis is loving having people come to the house; he is participating and his face glows when he talks. He seems in awe when the people leave. There's no way that he can deny that something wonderful is going on here. He's asking questions that so far I'm not feeling digested enough to answer. I believe that he would feel comfortable talking one-on-one with Tony. He's much better talking in person than by reading and writing. Felicity actually suggested that Tony and Kurtis could get together for lunch. I will follow thru with Tony to see if he would initiate that.

Am so looking forward to your tape! Exciting! I listened to your other tapes over and over all weekend while recording them. Will have them memorized soon.

I love you! And am feeling qualified to say "Yours in Christ,"

Lisa

Lisa wrote: *Well, your prayers and thoughts are certainly working! I had a wonderful weekend, in particular yesterday. Let's start there, moving around as needed.*

Dear Lisa,

Carleen and I are very encouraged to hear that your weekend went so well!!!

It's difficult untangling the events from the feelings—the internal experience—so you'll get both. Going to Tony & Felicity's for the baptisms was an experience all in itself. There were probably about 30 people there—families and friends of the two girls who were baptized. One of the girls was their son, Matt's, girlfriend—so it was a "Dale family" event as well. The girls were both probably early 20s—part of a group that Tony and Felicity work with. (They also work with a group of high school students—I got to meet a few of them as well). T & F's daughter, Becky—who just recently got back from some training event in Hawaii—helped with the baptisms (Matt's girlfriend, Kristen, is one of Becky's good friends.). She was awesome. She prayed for the girls when they came out of the water. The prayers just flowed out of her—like your milk and honey....

There are some who seem to have a special gift for prayer. They are capable of taking others to heaven with them.

...It was such a moving experience to watch this group of people interact with each other. The love that was present was so real. The commitment to one another was apparent. One of the girls talked about how she had always thought of herself as Christian, but that it wasn't until she met with this group (they've only been meeting for six months) that she really felt a personal connection with Jesus.

We are rejoicing with you!!!

Jay, these people that God has brought into our lives—Tony and Felicity—and you—really do "glow in the dark." I've never encoun-

tered people like this. Jesus with skin on. The spirit just radiates thru you....

Thank you. It's hard to tell from in here. I can certainly see Him in you!!

... When Tony addressed the group of people, he was so warm, unpretentious, inviting. He has a way of listening to people—both in this group and with our group at home—where, not only are you comfortable talking intimately, but then he's able to pull the rest of the people into the conversation without breaking the intimacy. It's as if one by one these people's lights get turned on and before long the whole room is glowing. It's truly incredible to watch.

This is a truly wonderful report!!

At our house, I felt different this week from last week—much more peaceful but with still that sense of anticipation (like you said). I'm aware of a huge shift in me—pregnant is a very good description. Radiant. And not at all nervous about the "structure" of the meeting—and I had absolutely no problem with discussing the Bible....

WOW!!

...I was very much aware that what was occurring there was very sacred—the spirit was very present. People talked about being drawn to be there: Abigail said, "I don't know what we're doing here, and I don't know why, but I have to come here week after week." Pat has said for the last two weeks that she doesn't know why she's coming, but she feels led—and as long as she feels people will accept her she will come. Barbara was "blessed to be here." Lenora didn't make it this week due to arthritis (weather changed)—but will probably come next week. Sandy and Bob—new this week—committed to bring the "meat" next week (main dish—I've been providing so far—I was thrilled for their commitment not so much for the meat, but to the group after just one meeting). There were 13 of us in all—I feel certain that everyone left feeling somewhat changed. Tony and Felicity even hung out for a while after everyone left talking about how they sensed that everyone seemed glad to be there. This shift in me has certainly made me feel closer to everyone.

We are so blessed to hear about this!! I'm reminded of what Paul wrote to the Corinthians. It is especially good in **The Message**: 2 Corinthians 2:12: In **The Message**, it begins with "An Open Door."

When we broke into groups for prayer, I got Felicity....

Doesn't get much better than that!

...That was such a blessing. I needed someone who was "on the same page" with me for this week. We crammed a lot into that little prayer—intimacy with Kurtis, guidance from God, understanding of Christ. Their "House2House" publication is picking up again,[1] and her prayer needs included hearing from God what needed to be said thru that and other developing interests. I'm struck by the enormity of what they're being called to do. Talk about responsibility!

As Carleen and I were straightening up around here in preparation for the Krupp's arrival Friday evening, I came across an old issue of "House2House," and a notebook of study materials compiled by Felicity. She's a treasure!

I shared some in the beginning of the group, when we did the "God events," about how significant this week had been for me. I told them that I couldn't go into specifics—because it was still "undigested"—but that I felt I was having some understanding of the significance of the Cross, salvation, and the Body of Christ. That even in my limited understanding, it was obvious that there was so much more involved—and it was so much better—than anything I had ever imagined. That I had had such a limited view of Christ and limited understanding of what Christianity was. I was blown away at the love—not only of Jesus, but of this body of people who were put in my life—who were laying their lives down for my spiritual growth. I was filled with love and a deep sense of wanting to do the same for others as my understanding grew. Paul pointed out, as you have, that even with my limited understanding, I can, and have, talked about what I'm capable of talking about. There were tears in people's eyes as I was talking. It was precious. And very obviously not the "old Lisa."

Again, I'm reminded of Paul: 1 Thessalonians 2:19–20 in **The Message**, the last two verses.

Once again I'm running out of time. This last email about the Fatherhood of God was very clear to me. I think, with some practice, I might even be able to talk about it with people. It's an incredible, extraordinary plan—the way God arranged to make His spiritual race. Thank you so much for committing your thoughts to paper in such a succinct manner.

I'm so glad that you could so easily receive it. In 2 Corinthians 5:17 Paul writes: "Therefore, if anyone is in Christ, he is a new creation; the old has gone, the new has come!" New International Version (only because, in this case, it works better for what I want to add to the Fatherhood of God.) Perhaps the best way to understand this verse is to put it this way. "Therefore, if anyone is in Christ, he is a new 'race'; the old has gone the new has come."[2]

I poured over last week's emails over the weekend, and—as I said—I'm still digesting. But oh so agreeably! So much more is making sense and I'm feeling so incredibly privileged to be a part of the "family." I'll have some time tonight to continue (I'm reading **The Message***, too—skipped ahead to read Galatians and Corinthians, as you suggested. Good stuff! It seems that Paul is one of your favorites. Can you tell me more about him?) and will focus on those more tomorrow.*

Where Paul is concerned, for now, perhaps it's enough to say that Paul is the one who got to say, "my gospel,"[3] This is to say that there is an unfolding revelation that is set before us in the New Testament, and Paul is the one that the Lord chose, as one born out of season, to end up with the ball.

Loved your "mother to mother" conversation. Such a wonderful way to describe the experience that you're having nurturing me! You're such a wonderful mother—I hope your milk never dries up!

Me too. There is a supernatural vitality that comes with being a nursing mother. It only becomes a problem when there is a refusal to let go of that season of nurture and progress to the next.

I've watched "The Power of Myth"—just recently it was on PBS. Would love to see it again—mesmerizing.

If you saw before you were revitalized, I'm guessing that you would be looking at it with very new eyes if you watched it again.

Question: What keeps some people from being "drawn in by God"? Is it that we just ignore Him?

Romans 9 strongly suggests that a big part of the reason lies with the sovereignty of God. **The Message** is really good in its translation of this chapter!!!

---

[2]Galatians 3:28-29. Warren Litzman was the first one I heard share this understanding.
[3]Romans 2:16, 16:25, 2 Corinthians 4:3, Galatians 1:6-12, 2 Timothy 2:8.

Kurtis is loving having people come to the house, he is participating and his face glows when he talks. He seems in awe when the people leave. There's no way that he can deny that something wonderful is going on here. He's asking questions that so far I'm not feeling digested enough to answer. I believe that he would feel comfortable talking one-on-one with Tony. He's much better talking in person than by reading and writing. Felicity actually suggested that Tony and Kurtis could get together for lunch. I will follow thru with Tony to see if he would initiate that.

We are tickled silly!!!

Am so looking forward to your tape! Exciting! ...

I had hoped to get it in the mail to you yesterday and then got ambushed, but it looks like I'll succeed today. On my way to Shepherds, I go right by a little post office. :-)

... I listened to your other tapes over and over all weekend while recording them. Will have them memorized soon.

I'm impressed. :-)

Here Jay discussed some exchanges he had had with several Deida list members. He concluded that discussion with the following material:

Lisa, I have had some further exchange with the Deida list, but it is not clear yet if they are ready to listen to someone looking at reality from a "Christian" perspective. This list has made it very clear to me, if there was any doubt, just how offended the world is with what we have called "Christianity" and "Church"

Yesterday I sent the following to a pastor friend of mine: (We were speaking of inordinate sexuality)

Les wrote:

...I have often wondered if this form of reproductive suicide is, in part, the result of the great liar and his minions seducing mankind into extinction.

Dear Les,

Thank you for your very thoughtful response to what I had sent. I had not meant to completely ignore the genetic causes of the problem. I think they are real, even if rare in comparison to the primary cause. I had meant only to address the primary cause, and I believe you have nailed it in what you have said here. At root there is a wounding or weakness or vulnerability or insecurity. That is where, and when "the great liar" and accuser attacks. Three words come back to mind in connection with the foundations of every life; "Source," "Destiny," and "Identity." At best, the wounding I am talking about makes sand of all three. This is the sand that "the great liar" tempts us to build on. Whatever other builders might do with the "head stone at the corner," these sand builders must surely reject that Stone at the very outset.[4]

LES: Much work has been done—even within the homosexual community—in trying to understand the overwhelming violent and suicidal concomitant corollaries with this "lifestyle." There is more at work here than apostasy and rebellion on the part of man.

JAY: Yes. It goes deeper than "apostasy and rebellion"; it goes to the wounding that lies beneath the rebellion, the wound of Cain, for instance.

LES: It also appears strange that some of these people - while cutting themselves off from joining in creation - nevertheless crave to be part of the creative process through surrogate mothers and sperm donors or even, as you paraphrased Paul, '...went looking for a sense of meaning and purpose in mere men or even birds, animals and reptiles.'

Some of them, at least, still deeply feel the pain of their 'cut off' state and try invalid substitutions that can never come close to Godly fulfillment.

JAY: Again, this well describes the attitude and offering of Cain.

LES: I am thankful for folks like Desert Stream Ministries and others who see this as a sign that some of them can be set aright through the gospel of Jesus Christ.

JAY: Of course, nothing in any of us is going to be "set aright" except by "the gospel of Jesus Christ," if only we could just figure out what that gospel is.

LES: It would be interesting to get your views of some proactive strategies for the church while we are still able to engage in public dialogue. For sure, the night is coming when no man works, but there is still some light to see by—even in the approaching dusk.

JAY: "Proactive strategies." That is an interesting way to put it. Over the weekend, I was thinking about "proactive strategies," but not by that name. I was thinking of them in terms of "the new commandment." What finally struck me was what the new commandment wasn't. For instance, it wasn't, "A new commandment I give unto you, that you should 'go to church.' " It wasn't even "...that you should 'go to house church.' " It was "... that you should 'love one another.' "

Seems like that should be a lot easier than "going to church," and yet, compared to going to church, it is hardly even on our radar. It only takes two or more people, but it does take two at a minimum, not to exclude God, without whom nothing is possible.

As I write this, I can hear in my spirit that which is written, "...He sets aside the first to establish the second."[5] What strikes me is that, somewhere in Church history, we seem to have thought that, if He could set aside the "sacrifices and offerings" that the law required, then why shouldn't we set aside the sacrifice and offering that He established. We seem to have set aside the new commandment in favor of "going to church."

---

[4]In 1 Peter 2:7, Jesus is described as "the stone that the builders rejected."
[5]Hebrews 10:9.

I take the time to mention this, because I believe that Jesus' new commandment is foundational to everything, especially to fixing things that otherwise seem unlovable.

It's not clear what the life expectancy of "a church" might be, whether it be the church in a town or the church in a house, but one thing is clear, and that is Jesus's love lasts forever.[6] If that's the case, and again, I believe it is, then loving one another as He loves us should also have a long life expectancy, longer than the life expectancy of any given "church." I am not using "church" here in the sense of the "church universal."

What I want to say is that we tend to take our eye off of loving one another in favor of preoccupation with establishing and maintaining buildings and institutions. The result is that, rather than the world seeing a people who love one another, the world has seen a people preoccupied with buildings and institutions, even preoccupied with "house groups." This preoccupation was not to be the sign of Jesus's credibility.[7]

If there is a human condition, which provides greater evidence of a paternal love deficit, then sexual disorientation or confusion, I don't know what it is. In short, homosexuality is a sign that the hearts of the fathers have not been turned to the children. (Last verse of the Old Testament.)

If that is the root cause of most of the problem, then the question becomes, is there anything that we, as believers, can do about it. I passionately believe that the answer is "YES!" and that what we can do about it is "Love one another." The root problem is a "storge deficit" "without natural affection."[8] Romans 12:10 mandates to us who believe the responsibility of getting rid of the deficit.

The problem is that, when there is a deficit of parental love, "storge," almost invariably there is a pressure to compensate with inordinate sexual love "eros." The over-compensation can take the form of heterosexual excess or homosexual orientation/excess. Fact is, people need love, and if they don't get it in the right place, they will "go looking for love in all the wrong places."

[Lisa, I don't know if you have noticed, but I'm leading us out behind the wood shed.]

In a recent exchange, a woman I know [Lisa, this is you] wrote:

"Also, please give my love to Carleen. I was thinking this week about how generous she is in allowing you to spend so much time with other people (me!). Many thanks."

I responded: "Carleen is amazing in this way. One of the greatest obstacles to intimacy that exists in Christian leaders is that their spouses will not allow them to lay down their lives for others. This is a very big problem. It ranks very close to not knowing who you are in relationship to others."

[Lisa, you see you are already helping me to be a better communicator with others. :-)]

I needed to share that up front, because I believe that the solution to the problem of inordinate sex lies with the love of the brethren, and I'm not talking about "lip service" and or "liturgical hugs."

---

[6]1 Corinthians 13:13.   [7]John 17:23,

[8]Romans 1:31, 2 Timothy 3:3.

One other essential is that "storge" is communicated by look, and touch, and tone. We are talking about a storge transfusion here. It has to do with the blood of Christ, again: "Don't leave home without it."

I know from experience that it is possible to shut down libido with a transfusion of storge.

I believe that this is the answer to the problem, not only for homosexuality/lesbianism, but also for inordinate heterosexuality.

Yours in Christ,
Jay

I love you! And am feeling qualified to say "Yours in Christ,"

Lisa

Yes, and more than qualified!!

You are a great writer. There is a vitality in your ability to communicate in writing that is a great gift. I am covetous!!

I have to get going. Shepherds day today, and things are heating up there too. By the time Nate and Joanne get done, we should have "lift off."

Yours in Christ,

Jay

On Tuesday, February 10, 2004, Lisa wrote again:

Hi Jay—

I had other stuff to talk to you about—actually made a list of questions from the correspondences from last week. But my spirit directs me to tell you something else. Hence the attachment. I'm saving it thinking that, like you, it looks like I'll need a body of information to draw from while corresponding with people. So I'm starting my computer files.

Pretty written out again. Hope your trip to Charlotte went well and would love to hear how your weekend went with your friend there.

Love you!
Lisa

Lisa's attachment:

Dear Jay,

I've got something that is really on my heart to talk with you about today. I've never talked with anyone about it, not even my therapist. Maybe it just never seemed relevant, or maybe it was just too painful. But now seems like the time because it really ties in with all we've been talking about lately.

Let me start by telling you that I talked with Kurtis last night about some of my understanding of what you've been writing lately. I started it by asking if he would feel comfortable talking with Tony about some of the things he was asking me. He wouldn't let me off the hook so easily. He wanted to hear from me. So I opened my mouth and did my best to let the spirit guide me. I think it was pretty good for my first attempt. Kurtis listened and at the end said that was enough for one session. Then he said something that really hit my heart. He asked would I still love him if he never got an understanding of all of this. I was quick to reassure him that I would. That what was most important to me was that he went about this process at his own pace, in his own way. That I didn't want him to feel pressured to think like I think or to be like I am. I could see he was relieved. The thought didn't come till later to reassure him that God loves him, too—way more than I ever could—no matter what. But what seemed most important to him at the time was reassurance of my continued love—no matter what.

I was thinking this morning about how other people have reacted when I told them about my emerging faith. I've heard this over and over again, "Will you still love me?" I remember feeling the same way earlier in our conversations with you, "Will you still love me, Jay, if I can't accept the Bible? If I never understand these concepts?" It's not a challenge but a sincere yearning of the heart. When we find someone who can love deeply—and express and transmit that love—it becomes paramount to hold onto that love.

When I look back over my "spiritual life," it's very apparent to me that the spirit has been with me from an early age. I remember the first opening of my heart. I was probably four, and my mom and dad had recently divorced. My mom must have been working, because she was not home when I came home in the afternoons. Sometimes a lady down the street, named Dorothy, whom I must have really liked, would watch me. Sometimes our black maid, also named Dorothy, would watch me. I remember one day I was so excited thinking I was going to get to be with "Dorothy down the street." When I found out it was Dorothy the maid, I was so disappointed. I struck out, saying to Dorothy, "I don't like you!" Dorothy said, "Why not?" I said (maybe because I had heard it somewhere), "Because you are black!"

She promptly said, "Well, I don't like you because you are white." I was instantly rebuked inside. I had deep sorrow about saying what I had said. It was so apparent to me—even at that young age—that what I had said had hurt this woman. It never bothered me what she said to me—I was just so sorry for hurting her—and told her so. I don't know if she was able to accept my apology—but I sure got a big-time understanding of how wrong it is to be hurtful to someone—by thought, word, or deed.

I had another occasion—I was probably about five—when I was at pre-school, Catholic school (that's as far as I got in the Catholic system—we stopped going to church about then). I got mad at a fellow student and kind of accidentally on purpose pushed her chair over. She started to bleed—actually a scab came off an old wound—and again I was instantly rebuked. I went to her, apologized, held her while she cried. The nun in attendance was speechless for a while, then started proclaiming something like how God's spirit was working thru me.

I've always been a champion for the underdog. I befriend the lost and lonely—the outcasts. I've had a number of people tell me—throughout the years—that I'm the most loving person they have ever known. Even my therapist, who worked with Kurtis and me for six years, and who himself is a very loving man (Christian—and guided me some—but had some "ethical" issues, I think, of mixing too much spiritual with psychological, unfortunately. Because of his "ethics," he doesn't interact with old clients, either, which made him unavailable for ongoing spiritual nurturance), said that Kurtis and I both had the purest and least mean-spirited hearts he had ever seen. I'm not sure why I'm telling you this, except to tell you that I think people have always responded to this spirit inside of me—sometimes so that my biggest fear of intimacy has been that they would somehow just suck the life right out of me. Sunday night Tony said, in response to Kurtis talking about how wonderful he thought Tony was and how anyone would want to do business with him, "There's not enough of me, Tony, to go around for everyone; but there's plenty of Jesus." Having the love of Jesus to guide people to is a huge relief to me—they can suck as hard as they want and there will be enough for everyone—including me. Yet when people see me, and the love in me, they still see ME—and are not always ready to accept that the love they feel is from God. What they want most in that moment is to feel the love—regardless of where it's coming from. To feel totally accepted and loved just where they are—by someone who is present, tangible. This is where I feel some of the people in our group are. They are coming because I've been feeding them and they want more—and God is drawing them. It's paramount that they feel the love. The words will eventually follow and at a time when it will hit their hearts. So it is a challenge right now to get the right balance—for me—in setting up this fellowship. But what I have to remember is that it is the love people see coming out of me that they are responding to, and how important it is to primarily focus on that.

Having said that, I'd like to tell you about my first "saving" experience. I was about 22—in a very desperate place in my life. I had been working full time—11 p.m. to 7 a.m. at a local mental health institution—and going to college full time getting a degree in speech pathology and audiology (never practiced—disliked school and clinical settings—but was determined to get a degree and too tired to change paths). The nature of this degree required lots of "clinical time," which took up most of the afternoon (classes in the morning). Hence, I wasn't getting much sleep. Three years of this really took a toll, and by the time I was off to finish the last stage—student teaching—I was starting to lose it. I moved home to my mom's house in San Antonio to do two semesters of student teaching in one semester so I could be done with it.

At the time, my mom was in a desperate place. My stepfather had just recently left her, and she had pretty much confined herself to her room. My little brother was about 10 at the time, and my sister was 7. They had the "run of the house": they got very little guidance and were starving for love and attention. I struggled with trying to "hold it all together." My dad was pretty much out of the picture at this time—I reconnected with him after getting married. In short, there was really no family capable of nurturing any of us.

I rediscovered an old friend from grade school at that time, who had recently married and had a baby. She and her husband were ardent Christians, Baptists. Both were born again—he was from a Catholic background and she was probably agnostic—but fairly new to their born-again lives. I'm not sure they were quite ready for me. They tried their best but were unable to give the long-term nurturance I needed at the time.

They introduced me to this concept of Jesus and salvation. Drew me a picture (literally) depicting how God wanted to reach us but he couldn't, so Jesus had to come as the middle man. I was drawn to their love like a magnet. Could not get enough of them. I would have done anything to receive the kind of love that they were demonstrating, so I willingly accepted Jesus.

I went to church at a big Baptist church in San Antonio for a few months. I sang in the choir and was filled with the spirit—overflowing—when watching people come up to the altar to accept Jesus. I cried a lot during this time—at the time it was so confusing. Here was this amazing feeling—spiritual filling—and around me my life was falling apart. I remember some "higher ups" from the church walking past me while I was sobbing on the grounds one Sunday—just looking at me like I was some alien. Nobody asked what was wrong or could they help. I don't remember anyone from the church trying to befriend me. I was really hurting and afraid to ask for help.

My mother pretty much disowned me during this period. I probably offended her with my religious enthusiasm and I'm sure she thought I was judging her. It was the first time in my life that I felt completely cut off from her, and—since she was my lifeline all my life—it hurt bad. Other friends shunned me too. Not openly, but they didn't want to have anything to do with this religion stuff, and I got the message that I was not to talk about this. And perhaps the worst, I was "dating" Kurtis at the time—we had started to get fairly serious—and he told me that, if I was going to get all weird with religion, he didn't think he could stay in relationship with me.

Kurtis by this time had become my lifeline. He was the only relationship (male) that had ever sought me out. He was living in Lawrence, Kansas (where we met our freshman year—then I moved back to Texas), and would come see me on holidays. He was very good-hearted and wanted to take care of me. I was starved for someone to take care of me. And pretty much emotionally and physically at the end of my rope. So I traded my new-found faith for the security of Kurtis. God, how it hurts to talk about this!

I remember I tried to continue reading the Bible for a while after that. But without Christ-filled people around me, I was unable to sustain the practice. It was probably about five years later when Dad introduced me to the Urantia book. There was some harmony there—I was quite fascinated with the Jesus part. And having the attention and guidance from my dad was so important at that point in my life.

So that is my Christian background. When you talk about "formula Christianity," I know from experience that it works. But without ongoing support and Christ love from at least one other person (and, I'm sure, maturity and a stable lifestyle helps), I don't think most people can sustain faith. With this experience, I'm reluctant to mess with anyone coming to Christ without full assurance that I'm willing and capable to go all the way with them. It's just too painful and guilt-producing to come part way.

And, perhaps you can see my reluctance in regards to talking with Kurtis about all of this. Granted, we've come a long way, and we're really two different people from that time. But there's a lot riding on this. I'm not turning my back on my faith again.

Thank you, Jay, for listening once again. You are such a blessing to me!

Lisa

On Wednesday, February 11, 2004, Jay responded:

Dear Lisa,

Well, here by attachment is my preliminary response to your "background" piece. I await your pleasure as to where to go next.

Love,

Jay

Jay's attachment:

Dear Jay,

I've got something that is really on my heart to talk with you about today. I've never talked with anyone about it, not even my therapist. Maybe it just never seemed relevant, or maybe it was just too painful. But now seems like the time because it really ties in with all we've been talking about lately.

Dear Lisa,

My seat belt is fastened, and I have my "buddy-breathing apparatus" at the ready.

Let me start by telling you that I talked with Kurtis last night about some of my understanding of what you've been writing lately. I started it by asking if he would feel comfortable talking with Tony about some of the things he was asking me. He wouldn't let me off the hook so easily. He wanted to hear from me. So I opened my mouth and did my best to let the spirit guide me. I think it was pretty good for my first attempt....

I'm glad to hear that you are not discouraged from your first attempt. This is one of the most difficult things in the world to do. The root problem as I have experienced it is that "the flesh warreth against the Spirit, and the Spirit against the flesh."[9] In short, the flesh connection can make spiritual communication very difficult. Paul puts it this way: "Wherefore henceforth know we no man after the flesh: yea, though we have known Christ after the flesh, yet now henceforth know we him no more."[10]

Once you know a person in the flesh it is more difficult to know that person in the Spirit. This is a problem that even the original 12 disciples/ apostles had. Paul had never known Christ "after the flesh."

...Kurtis listened, and at the end said that was enough for one session. Then he said something that really hit my heart. He asked would I still love him if he never got an understanding of all of this. I was quick to reassure him that I would. That what was most important to me was that he went about this process at his own pace, in his own way. That I didn't want him to feel pressured to think like I think or to be like I am. I could see he was relieved. The thought didn't come till later to reassure him that God loves him, too—way more than I ever could—no matter what. But what seemed most important to him at the time was reassurance of my continued love—no matter what.

You are doing GREAT!!

I was thinking this morning about how other people have reacted when I told them about my emerging faith. I've heard this over and over again, "Will you still love me?" I remember feeling the same way earlier in our conversations with you, "Will you still love me, Jay, if I can't accept the Bible? If I never understand these concepts?" It's not a challenge but a sincere yearning of the heart. When we find someone who can love deeply—and express and transmit that love—it becomes paramount to hold onto that love.

Jesus doesn't do "date rape," and neither should we. "He stands at the door and knocks."[11] He loves, without forcing His love on others. That's our job description.

When I look back over my "spiritual life," it's very apparent to me that the spirit has been with me from an early age....

I've always been a champion for the underdog....

Me too!!

---

[9]Galatians 5:17.   [10]2 Corinthians 5:16.

[11]Revelation 3:20.

...I befriend the lost and lonely—the outcasts. I've had a number of people tell me—throughout the years—that I'm the most loving person they have ever known. Even my therapist, who worked with Kurtis and me for six years, and who himself is a very loving man (Christian—and guided me some—but had some "ethical" issues, I think, of mixing too much spiritual with psychological, unfortunately. Because of his "ethics," he doesn't interact with old clients, either, which made him unavailable for ongoing spiritual nurturance),...

I like the way the Jesus does it better. Isaiah 9:6–7.

...said that Kurtis and I both had the purest and least mean-spirited hearts he had ever seen. I'm not sure why I'm telling you this,...

Perhaps to confirm the impression that I already had.

...except to tell you that I think people have always responded to this spirit inside of me—sometimes so that my biggest fear of intimacy has been that they would somehow just suck the life right out of me....

...But what I have to remember is that it is the love people see coming out of me that they are responding to, and how important it is to primarily focus on that.

Someone said, "People don't care how much you know until they know how much you care." That pretty well says it.

Having said that, I'd like to tell you about my first "saving" experience....

...I don't remember anyone from the church trying to befriend me. I was really hurting and afraid to ask for help.

Someone else said, "Church is like a cornucopia, you enter the wide end dazzled by all the fruit, then you get more and more restricted, and after a while, if you are blessed you get to escape through the little hole in the other end."[12]

My mother pretty much disowned me during this period. I probably offended her with my religious enthusiasm and I'm sure she thought I was judging her....

I did the same thing to my older brother and his wife. Hardly saw them again for 20 years. Their two children got saved, both marrying wonderful believers, and my brother and his wife finally

---

[12]Warren Litzman was the one I heard share this understanding

caved in and the relationship was restored. The attractiveness of new love in Christ works better on our friends than it does on our relatives.

...It was the first time in my life that I felt completely cut off from her, and—since she was my lifeline all my life—it hurt bad....

I can imagine.

...Other friends shunned me too. Not openly, but they didn't want to have anything to do with this religion stuff, and I got the message that I was not to talk about this. And perhaps the worst, I was "dating" Kurtis at the time—we had started to get fairly serious—and he told me that, if I was going to get all weird with religion, he didn't think he could stay in relationship with me.

Kurtis by this time had become my lifeline. He was the only relationship (male) that had ever sought me out. He was living in Lawrence, Kansas (where we met our freshman year—then I moved back to Texas), and would come see me on holidays. He was very good-hearted and wanted to take care of me. I was starved for someone to take care of me. And pretty much emotionally and physically at the end of my rope. So I traded my new-found faith for the security of Kurtis. God, how it hurts to talk about this!

Look at Song of Songs, Chapter 4, paying careful attention to verse 12 and beyond. "North wind" speaks of death. "South wind" speaks of resurrection. Your fragrance has been spread abroad once more.

I remember I tried to continue reading the Bible for a while after that. But without Christ-filled people around me, I was unable to sustain the practice....

If it could have worked in isolation, it would have worked in the Garden; the surroundings have never been better since. Now you have something more than they had in the Garden, but the encouragement of others is still very important.

... It was probably about five years later when Dad introduced me to the Urantia book. There was some harmony there—I was quite fascinated with the Jesus part. And having the attention and guidance from my dad was so important at that point in my life.

So that is my Christian background. When you talk about "formula Christianity," I know from experience that it works. But without ongoing support and Christ love from at least one other per-

son (and, I'm sure, maturity and a stable lifestyle helps), I don't think most people can sustain faith....

Without Koinonia (normally translated "fellowship," but much deeper in its original meaning), even the "mature" and the "stable" lose their luster.

...With this experience, I'm reluctant to mess with anyone coming to Christ without full assurance that I'm willing and capable to go all the way with them. It's just too painful and guilt-producing to come part way.

This is a very big subject! It is just here that we need revelation as to who we are, and whom the Lord has made us to others. Again, someone said, "If the devil can't defeat you any other way, he will overload you." To be overloaded is to be beyond the grace of God.[13]

When we first opened our home to what I call "the household dimension of our inheritance in Christ," over 30 years ago now, we didn't know what we were doing and had no where on earth to go to find out. We just had to learn the hard way. About 1980, I got knit together with a pastor from a town where I was working. It was about an hour and a half from our home. We were like Jonathan and David. This is the relationship that I touched on at the beginning of my "Getting Personal" chapter that I sent you fairly early on. Bob and I saw each other just about every day for years. He has since passed away from cancer. He was pastoral, and I was more prophetic. We made a good pair.

When he saw the numbers of people who were coming to our home on Wednesday nights, around 50, at the peak, and that many were coming in and out at all hours of the day and night the rest of the week, his pastoral heart for me prompted him to give me some advice. "Don't let people traffic through your life."

He wasn't saying don't let anyone into your life, but just to be careful who and how many we tried to care for. It was very good advice and given just after I got the revelation at the conference in Dallas, Texas, the one where I discovered who I was and that God had put me in a spiritual family. That was so that I could come to understand who I was to others.

I learned that people tend to bond to the one who does the most talking (if what they are saying makes sense). I had been doing too much of the talking. As a result too many people were led to have unrealistic expectations about my calling and ability to be

---

[13]Hebrews 12:15.

there for them. In that same time frame, I read somewhere that "*love* is spelled T-I-M-E, *time*." Clearly I didn't have enough of it. The Lord showed me I had exactly enough time for doing exactly His will. There were more people in my life than were God's will for me or them.

I learned what it meant, "...that which is written...." Well, I guess it's past time for me to send you the following:

Where the cost of following Jesus is concerned, most of us remember His response to a young man: "Teacher, I will follow you wherever you go." Jesus replied, "Foxes have holes and birds of the air have nests, but the Son of Man has no place to lay his head."[14]

Surely, having no place is a great cost, so great that most of us can dismiss it as not having relevance for our present circumstances. In seeming contrast to this verse, however, how many of us noticed that Jesus did have a home?

He "...went and lived in Capernaum."[15]

He "...went out and began to talk freely, spreading the news. As a result, Jesus could no longer enter a town openly but stayed outside in lonely places. Yet the people still came to him from everywhere."[16]

"A few days later, when Jesus again entered Capernaum, the people heard that he had come home. So many gathered that there was no room left, not even outside the door, and he preached the word to them. Some men came, bringing to him a paralytic, carried by four of them. Since they could not get him to Jesus because of the crowd, they made an opening in the roof above Jesus and, after digging through it, lowered the mat the paralyzed man was lying on. When Jesus saw their faith, he said to the paralytic, 'Son, your sins are forgiven.' "[17]

"They came to Capernaum. When he was in the house..."[18]

Whether or not Jesus or His family owned the house, rented the house, or were more or less extended houseguests, it is clear that there was a place called "home," and it apparently included a house.

In the Gospel of Luke, we find the story of the man lowered through the roof just following Jesus preaching in the synagogue at Nazareth:

"He went to Nazareth, where he had been brought up..." and read the following from Isaiah: "The Spirit of the Lord is on me, because he has anointed me to preach good news to the poor. He has sent me to proclaim freedom for the prisoners and recovery of sight for the blind, to release the oppressed, to proclaim the year of the Lord's favor."[19]

Having spoken of His anointed agenda in the town "where he had been brought up," He next went to the town, even to the house where He was then living. This is where the man was lowered through the roof.

I need to confess that I do not lose much sleep contrasting my own ministry to that of others, that of Mother Teresa, for instance. My

[14]Matthew 8:19-20; Luke 9:58 (NIV).   [15]Matthew 4:13 (NIV).
[16]Mark 1:45 (NIV).   [17]Mark 2:1–5 (NIV).
[18]Mark 9:33 (NIV).   [19]Luke 4:16–19 (NIV).

problems of conscience come from what I am doing or not doing in my own home.

Jesus's agenda was to "preach good news to the poor, proclaim freedom for the prisoners, bring recovery of sight for the blind, release the oppressed, and proclaim the year of the Lord's favor."

It is apparent from His lifestyle, together with that of the early Church, that Jesus did not intend to accomplish this agenda in an institutional context. It was not His heart to institutionalize people, but to meet them in their brokenness and transform their lives in a vital community of faith. He brought His work home with Him, one consequence of which was that the roof was torn off of the house where He was staying.

Institutional ministry by its very nature is limited liability ministry. The ministry of Jesus was unlimited liability. Where having a place is concerned, an unlimited liability mindset is one that does not claim even bird's nests or foxholes. It is capable of occupation without possession or grasping.

Our point for present purposes is that having a home does not disqualify us from following Jesus. The important thing is our attitude about the things we possess, even the place where we live. If our homes are not going to be off-limits to the agenda of Jesus, then we must face up to the cost. Jesus wants to accomplish His agenda from house to house. This means opening our homes, our families, and our lives, to poor, broken, and oppressed people, and broken people break things. In their desperation they and/or their friends have even been known to tear the roof off.

Are we ready for this? Are we ready for unlimited liability? Or would we prefer to go on touching lives at the relatively safe distance of our institutional programs, churches, and buildings? Perhaps a vital community of faith could both risk and hope to walk in the agenda of Jesus.

Having flirted with His agenda in the past, it is clear that isolated individuals and families are quickly overwhelmed by the enormity of the task and the world's response to even limited success. There are more broken people than occasional even semi-sold-out saints can handle. Making the effort, one quickly discovers why, in so many cases, those who take the Lord seriously, do so by appointment, some place else, and for earthly compensation.

Isn't it time for the nets, torn by our institutions, to be mended, and the limits of liability be removed from the Church? Isn't it time for "church" to cease being something that we do some place else?

—Jay Ferris—2/14/91

Lisa, I think you have the right understanding so you can make your own mistakes. You don't have to repeat mine. Love everyone, but keep your eyes open for those that the Lord has made yours. Otherwise you will very quickly be so drained that you will not be able to take care of those that the Lord has made your own. It sounds to me like there is a wonderful openness working in Kurtis. Keep your eye on him, and remember that, while a woman is wooed by love, a man is wooed by honor.

And, perhaps you can see my reluctance in regards to talking with Kurtis about all of this. Granted, we've come a long way, and we're really two different people from that time. But there's a lot riding on this. I'm not turning my back on my faith again.

Lisa, with your sensitivity, I am sure you will be able to notice those moments of spiritual fertility in Kurtis, and you will know whether to water or plant,[20] 1 Corinthians 3:6-9, and what to plant. The Lord will show you by His Spirit.

Thank you, Jay, for listening once again. You are such a blessing to me!

For you, I'm all ears. Well perhaps a little bit keyboard as well.

Yours in Christ,
Jay

On Wednesday, February 11, 2004, Lisa wrote:

Dear Jay,

I'm still a little shell-shocked from writing the "background" piece yesterday. It was really not much effort—it spewed out of me in a relatively short period of time—but the emotional component is taking some recovery time. Hence, assimilating your response is coming at a slower pace. So please bear with me.

In fact, perhaps today isn't the best time to try to respond to your response. Let it just soak in a bit. I can say that you are very encouraging and loving, as usual, and that I feel very safe talking with you. I hear your advice about not overloading myself and to watch for those who are our own. It makes total sense that Kurtis would be my first "own." Perhaps it's perfect that I start with him, because the stakes are so high that I will be extremely careful to proceed slowly and listen intently. It's clear that this will have to involve supernatural guidance, because I feel clueless. The only thing that I feel certain I can do is love him.

I will watch for which of the others seem to be "my own." I'm guessing that that will be a very limited number of people—so that

---

[20] 1 Corinthians 3:6-9 (NIV).

I have time for them. The other people that come for fellowship will perhaps find "their own" in each other? How does that work in your group? How many of them do you count as "your own"?

So far, I've listened to my internal voice about whom to invite to the meetings. I, personally, don't want the group to get too large. Both so there remains a feeling of intimacy, but also because of the fear of spreading too thin. It helps to think of letting the group evolve while sitting back and waiting for guidance about whom to do what with.

In the meanwhile—what is your experience about group size? What about when people start bringing people? Tony says I'll be amazed at how the group will start reproducing. He says to just keep inviting people. What does that do to intimacy? Is this something to talk about with the group?

I'm getting more excited about the possibilities. So far, it's been all of the unexpected twists and turns—the hand of the Lord—which as been the most enriching. I suppose that's part of the "abundance."

Okay. There's a lot going on here. Good stuff. Very exciting! Keep breathing....

Oh yeah—before I go—Tony emailed today wanting Kurtis's work number so he could call him for a one-on-one lunch! No prompting from me!! Now, that's a God thing.

Love you,
Lisa

On Thursday, February 12, 2004, Jay responded:

Lisa wrote: *I'm still a little shell-shocked from writing the "back-ground" piece yesterday. It was really not much effort—it spewed out of me in a relatively short period of time—but the emotional compo-nent is taking some recovery time. Hence, assimilating your response is coming at a slower pace. So please bear with me.*

Dear Lisa,

I'm reminded of the song, "Nice 'N' Easy."

In fact, perhaps today isn't the best time to try to respond to your response. Let it just soak in a bit....

Of course!!

...I can say that you are very encouraging and loving, as usual, and that I feel very safe talking with you....

I'm so glad, I want to be a safe place for you, and if I am succeeding, it must be the Lord.

...I hear your advice about not overloading myself and to watch for those who are our own....

It can seem like a remote possibility until it hits you, and that's when you need to remember that you may have taken on a greater load than Jesus has for you.

...It makes total sense that Kurtis would be my first "own." Perhaps it's perfect that I start with him, because the stakes are so high that I will be extremely careful to proceed slowly and listen intently. It's clear that this will have to involve supernatural guidance, because I feel clueless. The only thing that I feel certain I can do is love him.

That's a great thing to feel certain about!

I will watch for which of the others seem to be "my own." I'm guessing that that will be a very limited number of people—so that I have time for them. The other people that come for fellowship will perhaps find "their own" in each other? How does that work in your group? How many of them do you count as "your own"?

Paul wrote to the Corinthians: "Even though you have 10,000 guardians in Christ, you do not have many fathers…"[21] You may find that the Lord has made you a guardian to some, in which case, the thing to do is to help them find their home in Christ. That doesn't mean that you boot them out, it just means that you don't try to parent everyone who comes along, and you don't give people any false relational expectations. Sometimes you have to have a "rose ceremony."

In our little group there is a clear spiritual parental bond between Carleen and me, and the two girls. There is a very close bond with their flesh and blood parents, and a more tenuous bond with the rest. It's close enough to look a lot like the book of Acts, but there is a variation in closeness and intimacy among those in the group. By staying clear on the relational dimension, it provides the greater opportunity, as you have said, for them to find relationship with others in the group or outside of it. For some their place may be elsewhere, and the Lord is still preparing that place in the Spirit.

---

[21] 1 Corinthians 4:15.

So far, I've listened to my internal voice about whom to invite to the meetings. I, personally, don't want the group to get too large. Both so there remains a feeling of intimacy, but also because of the fear of spreading too thin. It helps to think of letting the group evolve while sitting back and waiting for guidance about whom to do what with.

It sounds to me like you are doing a very good job of allowing the peace of God to reign in your heart.

In the meanwhile—what is your experience about group size? What about when people start bringing people? Tony says I'll be amazed at how the group will start reproducing. He says to just keep inviting people. What does that do to intimacy? Is this something to talk about with the group?

The time will certainly come when it needs to be talked about, but to press the matter too soon is to risk becoming programmatic. There is such a thing as "spiritual adolescence." It is as difficult to live with in the faith as it is in the flesh. Knowing when and how to let go takes a great deal of spiritual sensitivity. Adolescence is a season of identity crises. Adolescents are no longer who they were and not yet what they are to become. If you give them too much space too soon, it can feel like rejection, and they are encouraged to rebel. If you hold them too close or too long, that can also cause rebellion or relational retardation. Somebody once said, "Timing is everything in life." I have found it to be true no matter which life we are talking about.

Of course the greatest intimacy is possible when there are only two. (Sometimes you have to give the kids a couple of bucks and tell them to go to the movies. Sometimes even spiritual parents have to lock themselves in the bathroom to get the privacy needed to discuss the challenges/problems of parenting.) The size you are now is a good size. It can also depend on the maturity of those in the group, and their maturity as a group. It can depend on whether it is what might be called a "closed group" or an "open group." Carleen and I always felt that we needed to be open, so that the Lord was free "to [add] to the Church daily them/those who were being saved."[22] Where there was a need for privacy among some or all of those in the group, we would just meet at another time or place.

I am glad that Tony used the "reproducing" word, and not the "dividing" word. Premature reproduction is cloning, it does not spring from life. As those in the group come of age, reproduction,

---

[22]Acts 2:47.

"leaving and cleaving," is the blessed outcome. It is not always easy to leave for the purpose of reproduction rather than because of alienation.

I'm getting more excited about the possibilities. So far, it's been all of the unexpected twists and turns—the hand of the Lord—which as been the most enriching. I suppose that's part of the "abundance."

It sure is!!!

Okay. There's a lot going on here. Good stuff. Very exciting! Keep breathing....

Lamaze!

Oh yeah—before I go—Tony emailed today wanting Kurtis's work number so he could call him for a one-on-one lunch! No prompting from me!! Now, that's a God thing.

That's wonderful, God bless Tony and Felicity!!

Yours in Christ,
Jay

CHAPTER 16

SPEAKING IN TONGUES

Eleven days elapsed between the e-mails of the last chapter and the ones that follow here. During this time, much happened: Nate and Joanne Krupp spent a wonderfully productive time with Jay and Carleen, and Lisa took a trip to San Antonio with her sister Traci and Penny Dale. The purpose of the trip was to visit Lisa's mother, but much else was accomplished, as will be seen below. Lisa and Jay, of course, remained in frequent contact through e-mails during this period; much of the content of those e-mails, however, deals with material that the two have decided belongs in a future volume.

On Monday, February 23, 2004, Lisa wrote:

Dear Jay,

It was wonderful to hear from you this morning. I'm so glad that you had such a memorable time over these last days. Thank you for sharing your thoughts and adventures with me. It must be difficult to separate from Nate and Joanne. I've often had the thought that all of our loved ones should be gathered in one place to live and share together. Like a big commune. It saddens me that we have to be separate from one another. It helps to think of us all as one body of Christ—that somehow the spirit moves between us so that we're never completely separate. Still, I like the closeness and intimacy of one on one. Can't seem to get enough of it these days.

I've thought recently about what it would be like to get to know you "in the flesh." There is something so powerful about knowing someone only from writing. It's like the difference between reading a

275

book and watching a movie. The book is always much more intimate and personal. There's much more communication at a soul level—it's an internal experience rather than an external experience. And then communicating with God is a whole other level of intimacy. Thru impression or word or vision knowing that it is from God and I get to participate with Him in this very real and intimate way. It's mind-boggling!

All this is to say, I suppose, that it's becoming clear to me that I probably will be meeting you—maybe not such a long time from now. I have visions of being there. When you talk about North Carolina and the surroundings, I feel a yearning to go there and to experience the area, the people, and, of course, you. It's a very pleasant thought, yet for the meantime I still treasure the unknowingness.

Meanwhile I'm enjoying getting to know the people in my life in a whole different way. The trip to San Antonio was extraordinary in many aspects. First, I asked Penny to tell me about how she became baptized in the Holy Spirit. She did, going into wonderful detail, giving names, dates, circumstances, passages of the Bible that she studied leading up to it. It blows me away how she had this experience so long ago (in the 50s), in China, on her own (she went to a friend's house to find out about the Holy Spirit in the Bible as directed by the Lord). She's quite a woman!

Traci was in the back seat listening. She listened a lot over the weekend, processing. She is contemplating a move to Michigan to date a man she's been in relationship with over the last year or so and determine whether there's a future for them. In the process she would be leaving her 10-year-old daughter with her ex-husband. As you can imagine, she is in turmoil. We talked at length over the weekend. I was moved to pray over her—that was an amazing experience. These words just came out of my mouth. All weekend, actually. We talked about God and faith and prayer and the Holy Spirit—all sorts of spiritual stuff. It was such a treat to talk with my sister on this level. No matter what she decides, we have a bond and an understanding and acceptance of each other that wasn't there before. I'm so glad we had this time before she leaves.

I talked with Mom about her spiritual beliefs, too, and about some of my emerging ones. She was very encouraging. I can see how God has been working in her life, too. It's hard to see a lot of what is going on for both her and Traci—the difficulties that they face and the methods they use to cope. But I have way more peace about knowing that God is working in their lives and that I don't need to be anxious for them. I'm finding that I'm becoming better at trusting *that He will involve me as needed and He will make clear to me what role to take. In the meanwhile I can just love them.*

The Sunday evening gathering was very interactive. We talked about the Holy Spirit and how part of the Christian experience was in inviting God to fill us with the Holy Spirit! I was amazed that Tony was being guided to take us into this area. Yet it was clear that the Holy Spirit was working within us. Felicity talked about her experience of accepting the Lord and how she was led to ask the Holy Spirit to fill her. It was such a blessing to have Felicity, in her quiet and believable way, share this with the group. Lots of spontaneous prayer—and Tony burst into song at one point (joined by others—I didn't know the song or I would have joined in). Barbara was there with her spiritual mom (who was a well-cooked trip!), and they were vibrating with the Spirit. Sandy was sitting next to me and she cried for most of the meeting.

Tony said at the end if there was anyone who wanted to pray with someone about anything that came up to be sure to get someone and do so (he and Felicity were offering to pray with people one on one). Sandy and Felicity and I prayed together. Felicity asked Sandy if she had ever asked Jesus to come into her heart. Sandy said that she had been raised Lutheran and always thought of herself as a Christian but didn't think she had ever really done that. So she did! Felicity also prayed for Sandy to be filled with the Holy Spirit! We talked at length about some of the feelings Sandy was having (what had been prompting her crying), and, with prayer and discussion, I think she was assured that God would be dealing with her emotions and behaviors as He worked with her from the inside out. It was precious!

I had them pray with me, too. I wanted to be certain that the Holy Spirit was in me and that any other dark spirits would be driven out. After praying and asking for that, Felicity asked if I would like to receive speaking in tongues as a spiritual gift. I said yes (I had been nervous about this—it's all so supernatural!—and what if nothing happened?), and she said to just start talking—praying—and that she would also talk in tongues. I can't believe it, Jay, but it actually happened. It was halting and felt awkward—but Felicity said that it was normal to be that way at first. To just practice and to email her about it! So I did (practice) this morning on the way to work. It was right there. No effort. Just flowed out of me. I can't tell you how wonderful I feel!

Felicity also had a vision of God holding me—as a baby—and His being so happy and so full of love for me—welcoming me and saying how glad He was that I was born.

So, I guess you could say that it wasn't your average weekend!

Kurtis praised Tony in his "facilitating" the meeting—I had no sense that he was put off by anything Tony said. I told him about my experience and he seemed cautiously open to hearing about it. God is definitely working with him, too. He told me this morning about how he had turned his life over to God during this very difficult job that he had about eight years ago selling light bulbs door to door. It was a turning point for him. His whole demeanor changed from that point on. I'm excited about him learning how having Jesus and the Holy Spirit in his life will make it even that much better! He's definitely moving in that direction.

You asked how his and Tony's visit went. Kurtis said it went very well. They talked about prayer—Kurtis wanted to know why we pray if God already knows what we need. Tony said it wasn't to help God, but to help us. (That reminded me of the line in the movie[1] when C.S. Lewis —Anthony Hopkins— made that same statement.) They seemed to have a good connection. Kurtis thinks they have many similarities as well.

Tony and Felicity are hosting a "Luke 10" meeting for six days at their home starting Wednesday, I think. It is why they won't be at the meeting on next Sunday. They said they would have invited us if we had not already made plans to be with Kurtis's dad. That would be awesome—being with a group of Christians night and day for six days! Will have to do it in the future. Our gathering will take place next week at Pat's house.

I'm looking thru your notes and am wondering what kind of clarification you need in regards to what I wrote, "Jay, it's obvious that God has chosen me to share in this way. He wants me to share my struggles so that I can be equally strong in my witness when He heals me."

My best attempt at this time is just to say that it appears that God puts things in my heart to say—whether writing about it to you or in sharing with my friends and/or group. It always seems to be about some area where He is working in my life. Oftentimes I don't have a full understanding about what is happening, and many times I have inner conflict as I'm coming to an understanding and acceptance of what I'm learning. Sharing this inner conflict, I think, is just as valuable to both believers and non-believers, as it is when I reveal the gifts that God has given me—the baptism in the Holy Spirit experience, the spirit of unworthiness lifting, the speaking in tongues. People get

---

[1]From the 1993 movie **Shadowlands.**

comfort in knowing that this is a process, that there are challenges along the way, and that it's okay to talk about them. In fact, the out-comes (or "healings," as I've perhaps loosely termed them) are much more believable and so much more apparently "God-given"—thus a witness to God—when the whole process is included. People don't want icons, they want to see how this applies to their lives. God has prepared me for this role in many unique ways. I don't know if this helps with clarification—let me know if you need something else.

The dream that you shared sounds very relevant in regards to all that you've been writing to me since day one[2]—bringing in the feminine – even as she is maturing—to bring light (or love) on the subject. I loved your thought of how the "new commandment" of the 21st century might be to "love one another as He loved us." I feel that as well. I'm so glad that that is what is in your heart!

Thanks so much for Joanne's book. It's fascinating! I would love to send her a note—could you send me an address—email or snail?

Guess I'd better go for now. Feel like I talked your ear off. All good stuff, though. Can't get enough of that, can we?

Love you,
Lisa

Lisa wrote: *It was wonderful to hear from you this morning. I'm so glad that you had such a memorable time over these last days. Thank you for sharing your thoughts and adventures with me. It must be difficult to separate from Nate and Joanne. I've often had the thought that all of our loved ones should be gathered in one place to live and share together. Like a big commune. It saddens me that we have to be separate from one another. It helps to think of us all as one body of Christ—that somehow the spirit moves between us so that we're never completely separate. Still, I like the closeness and intimacy of one on one. Can't seem to get enough of it these days.*

Dear Lisa,

Thank you for your wonderful gift of communication!! I'm a little jammed again this morning, what with having to leave soon for Shepherds, but I wanted to, at least, make a start in response to all you had written.

2Lisa is referring to a dream Jay shared with her concerning a gathering he had at-tended. We will be sharing that dream in a future volume.

I've thought recently about what it would be like to get to know you "in the flesh." There is something so powerful about knowing someone only from writing. It's like the difference between reading a book and watching a movie. The book is always much more intimate and personal. There's much more communication at a soul level—it's an internal experience rather than an external experience....

The nice thing about the internal part is that, internally, we are probably about the same age, and that's closer to 21 than either of us has seen for a while.

...And then communicating with God is a whole other level of intimacy. Thru impression or word or vision knowing that it is from God and I get to participate with Him in this very real and intimate way. It's mind-boggling!

It's the best!!

All this is to say, I suppose, that it's becoming clear to me that I probably will be meeting you—maybe not such a long time from now.....

I suppose!

...I have visions of being there. When you talk about North Carolina and the surroundings, I feel a yearning to go there and to experience the area, the people, and, of course, you. It's a very pleasant thought, yet for the meantime I still treasure the unknowingness.

What a gift for words you have!

Meanwhile I'm enjoying getting to know the people in my life in a whole different way. The trip to San Antonio was extraordinary in many aspects. First, I asked Penny to tell me about how she became baptized in the Holy Spirit. She did, going into wonderful detail, giving names, dates, circumstances, passages of the Bible that she studied leading up to it. It blows me away how she had this experience so long ago (in the 50s), in China, on her own (she went to a friend's house to find out about the Holy Spirit in the Bible as directed by the Lord). She's quite a woman!

That had to be a real treasure!!

Traci was in the back seat listening. She listened a lot over the weekend, processing. She is contemplating a move to Michigan to date a man she's been in relationship with over the last year or so and determine whether there's a future for them. In the process she would be leaving her 10-year-old daughter with her ex-husband. As you can imagine, she is in turmoil.

Ouch! Yes, I can imagine.

We talked at length over the weekend. I was moved to pray over her—that was an amazing experience. These words just came out of my mouth. All weekend, actually. We talked about God and faith and prayer and the Holy Spirit—all sorts of spiritual stuff. It was such a treat to talk with my sister on this level. No matter what she decides, we have a bond and an understanding and acceptance of each other that wasn't there before. I'm so glad we had this time before she leaves.

Wow!!

I talked with Mom about her spiritual beliefs, too, and about some of my emerging ones. She was very encouraging. I can see how God has been working in her life, too. It's hard to see a lot of what is going on for both her and Traci—the difficulties that they face and the methods they use to cope. But I have way more peace about knowing that God is working in their lives and that I don't need to be anxious for them. I'm finding that I'm becoming better at trusting that He will involve me as needed and He will make clear to me what role to take. In the meanwhile I can just love them.

"That's the deal!"[3] [:-)]
I rejoice with you both!!

The Sunday evening gathering was very interactive. We talked about the Holy Spirit and how part of the Christian experience was in inviting God to fill us with the Holy Spirit! I was amazed that Tony was being guided to venture us into this area. Yet it was clear that the Holy Spirit was working within us. Felicity talked about her experience of accepting the Lord and how she was led to ask the Holy Spirit to fill her. It was such a blessing to have Felicity, in her quiet and believable way, share this with the group. Lots of spontaneous prayer—and Tony burst into song at one point (joined by others—I didn't know the song or I would have joined in)....

Those two are such a treasure!!

...Barbara was there with her spiritual mom (who was a well-cooked trip!) ...

---

[3]Another line from the movie **Shadowlands**.

Love it.

...and they were vibrating with the Spirit. Sandy was sitting next to me and she cried for most of the meeting.

Tony said at the end if there was anyone who wanted to pray with someone about anything that came up to be sure to get someone and do so (he and Felicity were offering to pray with people one on one). Sandy and Felicity and I prayed together. Felicity asked Sandy if she had ever asked Jesus to come into her heart. Sandy said that she had been raised Lutheran and always thought of herself as a Christian but didn't think she had ever really done that. So she did! Felicity also prayed for Sandy to be filled with the Holy Spirit! We talked at length about some of the feelings Sandy was having (what had been prompting her crying), and, with prayer and discussion, I think she was assured that God would be dealing with her emotions and behaviors as He worked with her from the inside out. It was precious!

I had them pray with me, too. I wanted to be certain that the Holy Spirit was in me and that any other dark spirits would be driven out. After praying and asking for that, Felicity asked if I would like to receive speaking in tongues as a spiritual gift. I said yes (I had been nervous about this—it's all so supernatural!—and what if nothing happened?), and she said to just start talking—praying—and that she would also talk in tongues. I can't believe it, Jay, but it actually happened. It was halting and felt awkward—but Felicity said that it was normal to be that way at first. To just practice and to email her about it! So I did (practice) this morning on the way to work. It was right there. No effort. Just flowed out of me. I can't tell you how wonderful I feel!

Wow!!

Felicity also had a vision of God holding me—as a baby—and His being so happy and so full of love for me—welcoming me and saying how glad He was that I was born.

Yes, this is the storge that comes down from above that we need so badly to experience.

So, I guess you could say that it wasn't your average weekend!

Not normal lately, anyway. I think it was normal in the early Church right after Pentecost.

Kurtis praised Tony in his "facilitating" the meeting—I had no sense that he was put off by anything Tony said. I told him about my experience and he seemed cautiously open to hearing about it. God is definitely working with him, too. He told me this morning about how he had turned his life over to God during this very difficult job that he had about eight years ago selling light bulbs door to door. It was a turning point for him. His whole demeanor changed from that point on.

I'm excited about him learning how having Jesus and the Holy Spirit in his life will make it even that much better! He's definitely moving in that direction.

Words fail me to express my gratefulness to the Lord for all that He is doing there.

You asked how his and Tony's visit went. Kurtis said it went very well. They talked about prayer—Kurtis wanted to know why we pray if God already knows what we need. Tony said it wasn't to help God, but to help us. (That reminded me of the line in the movie when C.S. Lewis —Anthony Hopkins— made that same statement.) They seemed to have a good connection. Kurtis thinks they have many similarities as well.

Nice!!

Tony and Felicity are hosting a "Luke 10" meeting for six days at their home starting Wednesday, I think. It is why they won't be at the meeting on next Sunday. They said they would have invited us if we had not already made plans to be with Kurtis's Dad. That would be awesome—being with a group of Christians night and day for six days! Will have to do it in the future. Our gathering will take place next week at Pat's house.

I'm looking thru your notes and am wondering what kind of clarification you need in regards to what I wrote, "Jay, it's obvious that God has chosen me to share in this way. He wants me to share my struggles so that I can be equally strong in my witness when He heals me."

The clarification I was looking for was an understanding of whether the healing was already complete or whether there was more to come.

My best attempt at this time is just to say that it appears that God puts things in my heart to say—whether writing about it to you or in sharing with my friends and/or group. It always seems to be about some area that He is working in my life. Oftentimes I don't have a full understanding about what is happening, and many times I have inner conflict as I'm coming to an understanding and acceptance of what I'm learning. Sharing this inner conflict, I think, is just as valuable to both believers and non-believers, as it is when I reveal the gifts that God has given me—the baptism in the Holy Spirit experience, the spirit of unworthiness lifting, the speaking in tongues. People get comfort in knowing that this is a process, that there are challenges along the way, and that it's okay to talk about them. In fact, the outcomes (or "healings," as I've perhaps loosely termed them) are much more believable and so much more apparently "God-given"—thus a witness to God—when the whole process is included. People don't want icons, they want to see how this applies to their lives. God has prepared me for this role in many unique ways. I don't know if this helps with clarification—let me know if you need something else.

It is enough for now to say that you are gifted with a very attractive transparency!!

The vision that you shared sounds very relevant in regards to all that you've been writing to me since day one—bringing in the feminine – even as she is maturing—to bring light (or love) on the subject. I loved your thought of how the "new commandment" of the 21st century might be to "love one another as He loved us." I feel that as well. I'm so glad that that is what is in your heart!

Me too. An old sage advised me years ago "not to major in minors." Love is the principal thing!

Thanks so much for Joanne's book. It's fascinating! I would love to send her a note—could you send me an address—email or snail?

I will give you that address.

Guess I'd better go for now. Feel like I talked your ear off… .

That's what my ear's for!! [:-)]

… All good stuff, though. Can't get enough of that, can we?

Nope!

Have to run. Love you!
Jay

Epilogue

When our correspondence began, the subject line of our emails read "Three Points." The points were raised by Lisa in her email to the Deida list. Some time later, as I revisited that early correspondence, the three points seemed to be:

1. The desire for intimacy/sexual parable
2. The fear/garbage removal
3. Storge

What I realized was that there is a certain order here that is not unlike what has happened between us.

1. Quality conversion
2. Wounds/fear/healing
3. The closeness or "storge" between us that has been made possible by knowing who we are to each other.

Yes, that is how it looks to me, too. It looks like that will be the content of three books. Another way I look at it is "the Son, the Father and the Holy Spirit." It's incredible the way His Spirit has been revealed to me thru my relationship with you, Jay!!

As we got to know each other in this first portion of our correspondence, the meaning and depth of those points were explored, with a question here, a word there. Little by little a bridge of understanding developed, across which a greater weight of truth could pass.

I wonder if you have any idea what a WONDERFUL journey this has been for me! Certainly the most enlightening, exciting, and breathtaking journey I could ever imagine. Really, it's been unimaginable!

After the thought to share the correspondence with others had surfaced, our sharing continued without the hindrance of self-consciousness. We continued without any sense of where this was going or any conscious agenda. We simply continued to open to each other.

Looking back on what has already been shared here, and being aware of what remains to be shared in the future, it becomes clear that foundational truths were being set in place. (Hebrews 6:1-3)

Truths that can only be shared and fully realized in the context of relationship with another.

Having now arrived at Lisa's "baptism in the Spirit," the next season of our conversation opens an understanding of the Church. We talk about the offendedness that has been the result of what has been calling itself "church," as contrasted with the healing that is ours in what God calls "church," as revealed in the Bible.

On looking back, we discover that the answers Lisa was seeking for her own personhood and marriage were a kind of a parable of truth on another level, truth concerning Christ and His Church. Healing on these two levels mirror each other in ways that result in the wholeness of both.

I've been so blessed in all of my relationships, especially with my husband and with those the Lord is giving me.

In the next book, Lisa and I discover who we are to each other. On the foundation of that knowledge we are able to explore the depth of her "want" and wounding. By now we have had the opportunity to share that healing encounter with others. The result has been healing for them as well.

Even with years of therapy, I never knew that there could be healing so complete and everlasting!

As this first book prompted the inclusion of others in our correspondence, the next book provides the confirmation. It is our sincere hope that you will join us there!

Yes, as I told you, Jay, this first book is wonderful, but in regards to going to really deep places in Spiritual love and intimacy, my money is on the second and beyond! :-)

—Jay *& Lisa*

APPENDICES

APPENDIX A—
The Love Patent

> From Chapter 3, pg. 51; taken from an e-mail written by Jay to Lisa on Wednesday, December 31, 2003.
>
> Jay wrote the following based on insights he received in a patent office in Dusseldorf, Germany, in 1987—a "life-changing, paradigm-shift moment," in his words.

Perfect love casts out fear: [All Bible references are to the NIV.]

I John 4:16-18:
"And so we know and rely on the love God has for us. God is love. Whoever lives in love lives in God, and God in him. Love is made perfect in us so that we will have confidence on the day of judgment, because in this world we are like him. There is no fear in love. But perfect love drives out fear, because fear has to do with punishment. The man who fears is not made perfect in love."

This is a word spoken in faith, the faith founded on a rock, Jesus Christ, himself being the cornerstone. Faith, that lives and moves and has its being in God's love (Acts 17:28). By faith we are like Him in this world, God's love dwelling in us. By faith we know that we are accepted in the beloved (Ephesians 1:4-6). If this truly is the content of our faith, then we are without fear. God's perfect love which we have believed and received in the person of Jesus Christ has driven the fear of punishment out of us. If we continue to fear, then our faith is imperfect or has an improper object.

The only way we know what love is:

I John 3:16,4:10:
"This is how we know what love is: Jesus Christ laid down his life for us. And we ought to lay down our lives for our brothers. This is love: not that we loved God, but that He loved us and sent his Son as an atoning sacrifice for our sins."

We do not know what love is from our kind of love, but from God's love, and more specifically, from the love shown in the sacrifice of His Son for us. God's kind of love is the kind with which He loved us first.

Our kind of love, the state of the art before Christ:

John 15:13:
"Greater love has no one than this, that he lay down his life for his friends."

Beyond friendship:

God wants to take us beyond human friendship, where our ability to relate to and serve others is concerned:

Luke 14:12-14:
"Then Jesus said to his host, 'When you give a luncheon or dinner, do not invite your friends, your brothers or relatives, or your rich neighbors; if you do, they may invite you back and so you will be repaid. But when you give a banquet, invite the poor, the crippled, the lame, the blind, and you will be blessed. Although they cannot repay you, you will be repaid at the resurrection of the righteous."

Romans 12:20 (also Proverbs 25:21–22):
"On the contrary: 'If your enemy is hungry, feed him; if he is thirsty, give him something to drink. In doing this, you will heap burning coals on his head.'"

God's demonstration:

Romans 5:6-8:
"You see, at just the right time, when we were still powerless, Christ died for the ungodly. Very rarely will anyone die for a righteous man, though for a good man someone might possibly dare to die. But God demonstrates his own love for us in this: while we were still sinners, Christ died for us."

The word, here translated "powerless" is the same word that is translated "weaker" in I Peter, 3:7 "... the weaker partner..."

Romans 5:10:
"For if, when we were God's enemies, we were reconciled to him through the death of his Son, how much more, having been reconciled, shall we be saved through his life!

While we were still powerless, This is to say that "While we were still unable to stand under God, having nothing in us of value, while we were still ungodly, Christ died for us. The best kind of love found among men, that is our kind of love at its best, might possibly dare to die for a good man, but God's love is that much superior to ours, that Jesus Christ died for men while they were not good. His death demonstrated the superior, even the perfect love of God.

Our kind of love is vulnerable to failure in its object, to the inability to stand, in its object. The real source of our kind of love is the value of its object. Because imperfect love has its source in its object, it creates fear in its object:

I John 4:18:
"There is no fear in (perfect) love, God's kind of love. But perfect love drives out fear, because fear has to do with punishment, especially rejection. The man who fears is not made perfect in love."

Our kind of love is a response to the value of its object. "For a good man someone might possible dare to die." Our love has its source in the goodness of the one we love. If mistakes are made or the goodness goes away, our love is withdrawn. As a result, the object of our kind of love lives in the fear of failure and consequent rejection or "punishment." That was the problem before Christ.

Enemies in our minds:

Colossians 1:21:
"Once you were alienated from God and were enemies in your minds because of your evil behavior."

The fear of rejection due to failure, is the result of, and confirmed by, past experience with our kind of love. God abolished that relationship between behavior and love:

Hebrews 2:10-15:
"In bringing many sons to glory, it was fitting that God, for whom and through whom everything exists, should make the author of their salvation perfect through suffering. Both the one who makes men holy and those who are made holy are of the same family. So Jesus is not ashamed to call them brothers. He says, 'I will declare your name to my brothers; in the presence of the congregation I will sing your praises.' And again, 'I will put my trust in him.' And again he says, 'Here am I and the children God has given me.'

Since the children have flesh and blood, he too shared in their humanity so that by his death he might destroy him who holds the power of death—that is the devil—and free those who all their lives were held in slavery by their fear of death."

Ephesians 2:14,15, Colossians 2:14:
"For he himself is our peace, who has made the two one and has destroyed the barrier, the dividing wall of hostility, by abolishing in his flesh the law with its commandments and regulations. His purpose was to create in himself one new man out of the two, thus making peace."
"...[H]aving canceled the written code, with its regulations, that was against us and that stood opposed to us; he took it away, nailing it to the cross."

The barrier to relationship was the law which said in effect, if you will be good, I will love you. This is a kind of set of expectations which must be met as a basis for relationship. God abolished that basis for relating. He nailed it to the cross in order to make peace. God abolished it, not only for himself, but also for us, so that we can love, and go on loving even when those we love do not live up to our expectations. Since we no longer have to live in fear of failure or judgement for past failures, neither do those we love.

Perfect love has its source in God:

I John 4:7-17:
"Dear friends, let us love one another, for love comes from God. Everyone who loves has been born of God and knows God. Whoever does not love does not know god, because God is love. This is how God showed his love among us: He sent his one and only Son into the world that we might live through him. This is love: not that we loved God, but that he loved us and sent his Son as an atoning sacrifice for our sins. Dear friends, since God so loved us, we also ought to love one another. No one has ever seen God; but if we love each other, God lives in us and his love is made perfect in us. We know that we live in him and he in us, because he has given us of his Spirit. And we have seen and testify that the Father has sent his Son to be the savior of the world. If anyone acknowledges that Jesus is the Son of God, God lives in him and he in God. And so we know and rely on the love God has for us. God is love. Whoever lives in love lives in God, and God in him."

I John 4:19:
"We love because he first loved us."

Acts which are not done in faith, not having their source in the love and acceptance of God, are acts done for the purpose of recognition, approval or acceptance. God condemned this at Babel. [Genesis 11:4,8] Jesus Himself characterized those who approach God on that basis as "evildoers." [Matthew 7:22–23] At the cross, God abolished behavior as a prerequisite for love, and established love as a prerequisite for behavior.

Love is a fountain:

John 4:14,7:38,39, Galatians 3:2,5:22, Romans 5:5, I John 4:13:

"...but whoever drinks the water I give him will never thirst. Indeed, the water I give him will become in him a spring of water welling up to eternal life." "Whoever believes in me, as the Scripture has said, streams of living water will flow from within him.' By this he meant the Spirit whom those who believed in him were later to receive. Up to that time the Spirit had not been given, since Jesus had not yet been glorified." "...Did you receive the Spirit by observing the law, or by believing what you heard?" "...the fruit of the Spirit is love, joy, peace, patience, kindness, goodness, faithfulness..." "...God has poured out his love into our hearts by the Holy Spirit, whom he has given us." "We know we live in him and he in us, because he has given us of his Spirit."

In all of this, the baptism in the Holy Spirit [*Luke 3:16, Acts 1:5,8*] and ongoing filling with the Spirit [*Ephesians 5:18*} are essential.

The redemptive love of God has the power to change your life:

It is of first importance that we see the crucifixion of Christ as the expression of God's love, because that is the focus of our faith. The Gospel is the announcement of the fulfillment of the promise to Abraham, that we have relationship to God by faith, and that God's antidote for the effects of law, is the revealed love of God in Jesus Christ. The only cure for the effects of the knowledge of good and evil, the effects of the law is death.

God knew this from before time began, and provided a "...Lamb that was slain from the creation of the world. He that has an ear, let him hear. If anyone is to go into captivity, into captivity he will go. If anyone is to be killed with the sword, with the sword he will be killed. This calls for the patient endurance and faithfulness on the part of the saints." [*Revelation 13:8–10*] To create the tree of the knowledge of good and evil was to slay the lamb. From the beginning, the work of anti-christ was to replace the work of Christ, with the work of the law. The spirit of anti-christ is already in the world [*1 John 2:18*], and it is clear from the scripture that the work of anti-christ would intensify rather than diminish as the end approached. The work of anti-christ is not blatant evil, it is man-made goodness. [*1 Timothy 4:1*]

A continued or renewed preoccupation with the law as an external command, after the revelation of Jesus Christ is anti-christ. To fall away from the powers of the age to come, ours in Jesus Christ, is to "...Crucify the Son of God all over again and subject him to public disgrace." [*Hebrews 6:6*] The little anti-Christs or anti-Christians are little angels or messengers of light. They carry little rules and regulations, enough to spoil the vineyard. [*Song of Songs 2:15*] The final anti-Christ will carry the greatest light of all, the law. The law is the brightest object there is outside of Jesus Christ.

If what you know interferes with your ability to love, then you do not know as you ought. [*1 Corinthians 8:2*] The measure of how spiritual you are is seen in that which offends you. [*Proverbs 17:9, 19:11*] God's kind of love does not take offense. [*1 Corinthians 13:5*] You can nail it to a tree and it will keep on loving. "Yet I hold this against you: You have forsaken your first love. Remember the height from which you have fallen! Repent and do the things you did at first. If you do not repent, I will come to you and remove your lamp stand from its place,…He who has an ear, let him hear what the Spirit says to the churches. To him who overcomes, I will give the right to eat from the tree of life, which is in the paradise of God." [*Revelation 2:4, 5, 7*]

Christianity is the result of faith in the love of God that was willing to die for us while we were still bad. "The Gospel is the power of God for the salvation of everyone who believes:…" [*Romans 1:16*] The Gospel is the power of God for the transformation of your life. The Gospel is, God loves you regardless of your works. If, by the Grace of God, you can believe that, it will change your life. Only works resulting from faith are pleasing to God. All God wants from you is you, together with the transformation resulting from faith in His love. He does not want people going through a lot of "religious motions" in misguided effort to please him. This is anti-christ, and the Bible says it is based on the doctrine of demons. [*1 Timothy 4:1–3*]

A word about the resurrection:

"So it will be with the resurrection of the dead. The body that is sown is perishable, it is raised imperishable; it is sown in dishonor, it is raised in glory; it is sown in weakness, it is raised in power; it is sown a natural body, it is raised a spiritual body. If there is a natural body, there is also a spiritual body. So it is written: 'The first man Adam became a living being'; the last Adam, a life-giving spirit." [*1 Corinthians 15:42–45*]

The Scripture is certainly clear concerning the resurrection of the body, the second or final resurrection. [*Romans 8:22–25, 1 Corinthians 6: 12–29, 15:50–55, 2 Corinthians 4:14, Philippians 3:21, Colossians 3:4, 2 Thessalonians 4:13–18*] What is not so clear is the nature and timing of the first resurrection. It is important to have clear understanding about these things, for it is written: "…'I believed; therefore I have spoken.' With that same spirit of faith we also believe and therefore speak…" [*2 Corinthians 4:13–14*]

The first resurrection takes place every time believers arrive on the other side of suffering, as demonstrated by the fact that they are walking in newness of life. [*Matthew 3:8, Acts 26:20, James 1:18, 1 Peter 1:22, 2:3, 4:6, 1 John 2:28–5:21, 2 John 4–11, 3 John 11*] The first resurrection is in the Spirit. [*Matthew 3:11*] "And if the Spirit of him who raised Jesus from the dead is living in you, he who raised Christ from the dead will also give life to your mortal bodies through his Spirit, who lives in you." [*Romans 8:11*]

Christians are people who are no longer living in darkness, although they are surrounded by people who are. They are a people for whom the lamb is the light. [*Revelation 21:23*] They in turn are the light of the nations. [*Revelation 21:24*] Whomsoever will may join them. Both "the Spirit and the bride say 'come'…Whoever is thirsty, let him come; and whoever wishes, let him take the free gift of the water of life." [*Revelation 22:17*] Christians live on the resurrection side.

"And God raised us up with Christ and seated us with him in he heavenly realms in Christ Jesus, in order that in the coming ages he might show the incomparable riches of his grace, expressed in his kindness to us in Christ Jesus." [*Ephesians 2:6–7*]

Perfect love is never selfish, it knows that it has already inherited all things:

"…All things are yours, whether Paul or Apollos or Cephas or the world or life or death or present or the future - all are yours, and you are of Christ, and Christ is of God." [*1 Corinthians 3:21–23*]

Jesus knew that the Father had put all things under his power, and that he had come from God and was returning to God; so he got up from the meal, took off his outer clothing, and wrapped a towel around his waist. After that, he poured water into a basin and began to wash his disciples' feet drying them with the towel that was wrapped around him. [*John 13:3–5*]

If you know that you have already received all things, then there is nothing else to want, nothing else to be selfish about, not time, not money, not attention, or even kindness, perhaps only encouragement in the faith that makes it possible to do without all of these things, [*Hebrews 10:25*].

I Corinthians 13:5:
"Love is not rude, it is not self seeking, it is not easily angered, it keeps no record of wrongs."

Nothing, and no one can separate us from the love of God:

Romans 8:35-39:
"Who shall separate us from the love of Christ? Shall trouble or hardship or persecution or famine or nakedness or danger or sword? As it is written: 'For your sake we face death all day long; we are considered as sheep to be slaughtered.' No. In all of these things we are more than conquerors through him who loved us. For I am convinced that neither death nor life, neither the present nor the future, nor any powers, neither height nor depth, nor anything else in all creation, will be able to separate us from the love of God that is in Christ Jesus our Lord."

Our work is to believe all of the above, and encourage others in that belief.

—Jay Ferris, May 1987

TRUST AND OBEY

The implications of the Love Patent for horizontal trust:

Transparency

We need to look at still another aspect of our expectations, this time having to do with Authority and trust. It is written that "...Jesus would not entrust himself to them, for he knew all men. He did not need man's testimony about man, for he knew what was in a man." [*John 2:24–25*] Trust is an important word. We are a people who are heading for a transparency, perhaps best described in the Book of Revelation: "...before the throne there was what looked like a sea of glass, clear as crystal...." [*Revelation 4:6a*] In Chapter 17 the sea is interpreted to signify "...peoples, multitudes, nations and languages." [*Revelation 17:15b*]

The sea representing the nations, is heaving, it is tossed about. In Ephesians, Paul puts it this way: "Then you will no longer be infants, tossed back and forth by the waves, and blown here and there by every wind of teaching and by the cunning and craftiness of men in their deceitful scheming." [*Ephesians 4:14*] The sea before the throne, is like a sea of glass. It is no longer tossing. It represents those who have been saved out of the heaving sea, the redeemed. They are those who are no longer tossed about, and they are those who have become clear as crystal.

Wounded

Zechariah 13:6:

If someone asks him, "What are these wounds on your body?" he will answer, "The wounds I was given in the house of my friends."

Our present difficulty is with vulnerability in transparency. We have all had the experience of sharing our inner thoughts and feelings, only to experience betrayal and rejection as a result. In some sense, we see this in Matthew 7:6, "Do not give dogs what is sacred; do not throw your pearls to pigs. If you do, they may trample them under their feet, then turn and tear you to pieces." Having experienced this, we then become defensive and closed. By the time most Christians become leaders, they are very reluctant to share their innermost thoughts, struggles, and feelings. There is a crises of trust. The temptation, at that point, is to go looking for others who can be trusted, but the search is in vain. Better to trust God, and walk in faithfulness with those he has placed in our lives, in the relationships that God has established.

The problem with trust is that it presupposes expectations. Trust means that expectations will not be violated. If there are no expectations, than trust ceases to be an issue. Jesus knew what was in a man, as a result he had no good expectations, nothing that could serve as a basis for trust. As a result, He did not trust himself to any man.

DON'T TRUST MEN

Where does this leave us? According to the Scripture, there is good reason to believe that we cannot be trusted: Psalms 146:3 Do not put your trust in princes, in mortal men, who cannot save.

Jeremiah 9:4–5:
"Beware of your friends; do not trust your brothers. For every brother is a deceiver, and every friend a slanderer. Friend deceives friend, and no one speaks the truth. They have taught their tongues to lie; they weary themselves with sinning.

Jeremiah 9:6–8:
You live in the midst of deception; in their deceit they refuse to acknowledge me," declares the Lord. Therefore this is what the Lord Almighty says: "See, I will refine and test them, for what else can I do because of the sin of my people? Their tongue is a deadly arrow; it speaks with deceit. With his mouth each speaks cordially to his neighbor, but in his heart he sets a trap for him.

Jeremiah 9:9–12:
Should I not punish them for this?" declares the Lord. "Should I not avenge myself on such a nation as this?" I will weep and wail for the mountains and take up a lament concerning the desert pastures. They are desolate and untraveled, and the lowing of cattle is not heard. The birds of the air have fled and the animals are gone. "I will make Jerusalem a heap of ruins, a haunt of jackals; and I will lay waste the towns of Judah so no one can live there." What man is wise enough to understand this? Who has been instructed by the Lord and can explain it? Why has the land been ruined and laid waste like a desert that no one can cross?

Jeremiah 12:5–8:
"If you have raced with men on foot and they have worn you out, how can you compete with horses? If you stumble in safe country, how will you manage in the thickets by the Jordan? Your brothers, your own family--even they have betrayed you; they have raised a loud cry against you. Do not trust them, though they speak well of you. "I will forsake my house, abandon my inheritance; I will give the one I love into the hands of her enemies. My inheritance has become to me like a lion in the forest. She roars at me; therefore I hate her.

Micah 7:1–2:
What misery is mine! I am like one who gathers summer fruit at the gleaning of the vineyard; there is no cluster of grapes to eat, none of the early figs that I crave. The godly have been swept from the land; not one upright man remains. All men lie in wait to shed blood; each hunts his brother with a net.

Micah 7:3–4:
Both hands are skilled in doing evil; the ruler demands gifts, the judge accepts bribes, the powerful dictate what they desire—they all conspire

together. The best of them is like a brier, the most upright worse than a thorn hedge. The day of your watchmen has come, the day God visits you. Now is the time of their confusion.

Micah 7:5–7:

Do not trust a neighbor; put no confidence in a friend. Even with her who lies in your embrace be careful of your words. For a son dishonors his father, a daughter rises up against her mother, a daughter-in-law against her mother-in-law--a man's enemies are the members of his own household. But as for me, I watch in hope for the Lord, I wait for God my Savior; my God will hear me.

IN GOD WE TRUST

Micah 7:8–9:

Do not gloat over me, my enemy! Though I have fallen, I will rise. Though I sit in darkness, the Lord will be my light. Because I have sinned against him, I will bear the Lord's wrath, until he pleads my case and establishes my right. He will bring me out into the light; I will see his righteousness.

John 14:1:

"Do not let your hearts be troubled. Trust in God; trust also in me."

Acts 14:23:

Paul and Barnabas appointed elders for them in each church and, with prayer and fasting, committed them to the Lord, in whom they had put their trust.

Romans 15:13:

May the God of hope fill you with all joy and peace as you trust in him, so that you may overflow with hope by the power of the Holy Spirit.

Hebrews 2:13:

And again, "I will put my trust in him." And again he says, "Here am I, and the children God has given me."

It is apparent from the above, that putting our trust in people, mere "mortals," is not only a highly risky business, but would seem to be an act of disobedience, as well.

In a very real sense this is another area that boils down to government. "...The government is on His shoulder," all government. Jesus is in charge, and we must trust in him. When Peter said "not me Lord, I'll never betray you," Jesus put no stock in what he said. He did not trust him. Are we better than Peter? Jesus is in control, and He alone is trust-worthy.

There are many reasons why we cannot be trusted, not the least of which are to be found in the very roots of what it is to be mortal; "...frail, fee-ble desperate, incurable, sick, woeful." To make it personal, my problem is that if I am hurt badly enough, I become offended. Because of human frailty, humans are to be loved, not trusted. If we are able to trust God, and love each other, we have some hope that God, who is faithful, by His Spirit, will show us who we are to be open with. If we know each other in this way, "...after the Spirit, and not after the flesh..." then the Spirit will be in charge of the outcome. If, on the other hand, we know each other after the flesh, and put our trust in the flesh, "...arm of flesh will fail us." And we are bound to be defeated in every relationship.

By trusting God in everything, and in relationships in particular, we can and will look to Him for the relationships of our lives. God is the one who determines who we should walk with. Knowing this, that a given relationship is ours by the will of God, we will be able to be faithful in that relationship even when the relationship is painful. Again, our call is to trust God and love each other.

This is particularly true in relationships where there is a protective or authoritative dimension. As a husband, and father, for instance, I have a protective, enabling, and providing role for my wife and family. This is a role in which I often fail, in that sense, a role in which I can't be trusted.

To the degree that I have been trusted in this role by my wife and children, where they have had great expectations, my failures have led to great disappointments. Their trust, over time has had to be adjusted away from me and directed toward God. By making this adjustment, rather than being shaken in the face of my failures, they are able to provide encouragement and strength when I need it most.

The same is true for me in relationship to them. If I am counting on God for the things that come from them, I am able to minister strength and encouragement to them at the points of their weakness. I have used myself as an example, but it is clear that the same can be said of any relationship that includes a dimension of authority, pastors and their flocks, for instance.

Proverbs 21:22:
A wise man attacks the city of the mighty and pulls down the stronghold in which they trust.

II Corinthians 10:3-5:
For though we live in the world, we do not wage war as the world does. The weapons we fight with are not the weapons of the world. On the contrary, they have divine power to demolish strongholds. We demolish arguments and every pretension that sets itself up against the knowledge of God, and we take captive every thought to make it obedient to Christ.

"Grace and truth" and "the law of the Spirit of Life" "came by Jesus Christ." [*Romans 8:2, Ephesians 4:30*] Continued legalism, after the Grace of God has been revealed, is either a rejection of that Grace or an indication that it was never received, and is everywhere in Scripture, candidate for the unforgivable sin. [*Matthew 6:5, 12:31–32*] "But now that you know God-or rather are known by God-how is it that you are turning back to those weak and miserable principles? Do you wish to be enslaved by them all over again? You are observing special days and months and seasons and years! I fear for you, that somehow I have wasted my efforts on you." [*Galatians 4:9–11*]

Jesus's Kingdom is not of this world, [*John 18:36*] neither should we be of this world, [*2 Timothy 2:4, James 1:27, 4:4–10, 1 John 2:15–17*] but rather the Kingdom of God is "righteousness, peace and joy in the Holy Ghost." [*Romans 14:17*] It is true, however, that the Kingdom of God is not a matter of talk, but of power, [*1 Corinthians 4:20*] power to transform lives, and the power of transformed lives. Believers are, first of all, the fruit of the Gospel, fruit containing seed, for the generation of new life, but fruit, none the less. As such our lives should manifest; "...love, joy, peace, patience, kindness, goodness, faithfulness, gentleness and self-control." [*Galatians 5:22*] These things do not come from eating the law. They come from eating the Passover Lamb.

These qualities are not to be held aloof from the world, rather they are to be the salt of the earth. A people so imbued can change the world. Commandments cannot change people for the better, on the contrary, they only serve to reveal our wretchedness. Paul says the law is good if one uses it properly. [*1 Timothy 1:8*] Strictly speaking, the law is useless as a source of how to live, for it can only kill. Its proper use is to determine whether or not the life that is being lived, the walk being walked, the deeds being done, the words being spoken, the thoughts being thought, are in the Spirit.

Rules and regulations can only serve as an indicator of whether or not the fruit of the spirit is present in a person or a people. "All men will know that you are my disciples, if you love one another." [*John 13:35*]

APPENDIX B—
Scripture and Experience

From Chapter 3, pg. 53; taken from an e-mail written by Jay to Lisa on Friday, January 2, 2004.

Bill to Jay wrote concerning the various levels of difficulty in coming to make decisions about the objective meaning of the Scriptures. He contrasted our own personal experience with five levels of decision-making that stood between present translations and what had been originally spoken. He describes his concern as the conflict between "scripture and experience."

Bill wrote:

Ralph's long memo on experience and miracles evokes a few comments, but my observations may not correspond exactly to Ralph's own statements in his memo. Some of you, Ralph included, have at times wrongly assumed that my comment must be a direct attack on a memo you have written, even when it really dealt only with possible questionable inferences. Sometimes I could not tell for sure how strong an implication might be, but I wanted to deal with what looked like a likely inference.

For example, Ralph has set up a dichotomy between scripture and experience, and this can be understood as near enough to cogency, to get across what he wants to get across.

Nevertheless, it could represent a false dichotomy in our deciding what the most basic determiners of 'guidance' ought to be.

Could such a dichotomy, that is: seeing 'scripture' and 'experience' as alternatives, be accurately true? What follows will at the least suggest what some of my most serious questions about it would be.

If an individual studies, assimilates, or appropriates any portion of 'scripture', could not that be regarded as a subjective experience? Would this be a far-fetched technicality, the relevance of which would be remotely conceivable?

Suppose an adherent of shuldom and churchdom claims that 'the bible' says this or that. This process comes loaded with many factors that could be quite subjective. To understand these factors more clearly, it be best to move backwards in time from, say, an English version of Revelation back toward John's pen. (I do not say 'to', because I would not know how to get there.)

A speaker or writer quotes a supposedly 'objective' statement from 'the scriptures'.

The one who does the quoting must decide which words in his native language best express the statement. That's always a subjective choice. Usually it's a very subjective choice.

Will he say <<washed their robes>> or <<do His commandments>>? Which one "means what it says and says what it means"?

Elements of the subjectivity in choosing a translation may reflect positive reactions, as in the following fictional quotation:

"When Rotherham translated 'the habitable world' in Acts 17,31, I looked it up in 'Thayer'. He said, in effect, that that's what the Greek meant. I think he could look at the Greek text and understand it. Therefore I like Rotherham's." (Most probably think that Thayer wrote Thayer. Reading title pages has never been much in vogue.)

Note the subjectivity of 'thinking' instead of knowing. Note too the subjectivity in the jump from liking one instance of import to 'liking' the entire general version. Thousands in churchdom continually commit such illogic.

Elements of subjectivity may also reflect negative reactions, as in the following fictional quotation:

"A cult that teaches false doctrines distributes a version of its own. In 2nd John 07 that version has 'coming' instead of the 'is come' of the King James Version. I believe it's safer to stick to the King James Version."

Note the subjectivity of letting general dislike dictate one's decision on specific matters. Nonetheless, on a specific point, a largely rejected group may represent a more valid understanding than much larger, widely accepted groups. On the point at stake here, 'coming' would be closer than 'is come' to the concept of the epxomevov = erchomenon in the manuscripts. Note too that 'coming' could be understood as contrary to a major dogma of the group, if the Watchtower should be in mind.

At any rate, from a positive or negative approach such factors inject awful subjectivity into the average disciple's choosing a translation. They 'like' the ones they choose. And that's about it.

In choosing English text labeled 'bible', many may cite bible dictionaries or commentaries. And yet they do not have the skills required to evaluate the opinions of the authors or 'authorities' they cite. The managers of the printing companies who publish translations, dictionaries, commentaries, etc., do their best to represent the authors as celebrated scholars. They want to make money, but they themselves cannot evaluate what they publish.

Another ploy would be that someone who adopts an English representation as 'bible' may have done word studies in Young's or Strong's. In doing so they sometimes deceive themselves in the conclusions they reach. They often have no concept of any foreign syntax and that often affects import more than the definitions ascribed to detached words.

Those who want a word to have a peculiar sense in one context may often infer it from another, even when its usual signification includes other senses that would more likely have been in the mind of the author. For example, our 'scholar' may find the 'Lord's' occurs as kupiakh = cyriace in Revelation 01,10:

<<I was in the Spirit on the Lord's day and heard behind me a great voice, as of a trumpet ...>>

He may assume that that meant 'Sunday.' Then from this he may transplant this idea and so inject it into the form kupiakov = cyriacum or -on 'Lord's' in 1st Corinthians 11,20:

<<When ye come together therefore into one place, this is not to eat the Lord's supper.>>

Presto. We have supposedly proven that Sunday is the day to eat the Lord's Supper. For many that is 'scripture', which "says what it means and means what it says."

This memo has already become too long, and I have barely finished the first level. As we move down to the second and third levels, bear in mind that in making their subjective decisions, the doers try to do what they do as objectively as possible. Even our imagined objectivity must be subjectively determined. Think about the respective processes indicated. Perhaps this will dawn upon you too.

Perhaps someone will claim regarding this level one that the Holy Spirit has given you exact answers on some or all of the questions. That could terminate the discussion or divert it to other avenues.

The second level would deal with the subjective decisions of the one or more translators. Which of the many possible 'originals' should the translator translate? Which printed text will he try to represent? Will he stick to the Leningrad manuscript of the Hebrew? Will he incorporate decisions based on 'the LXX' or the partial copies from Qumran? Such decisions must be pronounced subjective, even when they have been made as objectively as possible.

As for 'Matthew through Revelation', will the translator of the Greek work from a single printed text like that of Tischendorf, Souter, Westcott and Hort, Tasker or Merck? Will he work from one of the even more eclectic UBS editions or a work of limited scope like 'NT of the Majority Text'?

In churchdom anybody who could get it printed could have his name on a new and different text of the 'Greek NT'. A certain and complete text of 'the original' only exists in the minds of the ignorant. If a translator chooses a printed edition, that will be his own subjective decision.

Or will a translator instead of the above make eclectic decisions and work from the differing manuscripts himself, himself determining in each instance which reading to translate? Every such decision will be subjective.

Perhaps someone will claim regarding this level two that the Holy Spirit has given you exact answers on some or all of the questions. That could terminate the discussion or divert it to other avenues.

The third level concerns how the translator 'at rock bottom' can find out what the words or their combinations meant to the linguistic pool that first heard or read them.

Those devoid of experience in these areas labor under several delusions. They may think that lexical observations, like those printed in so-called Thayer (really mostly Grimm and Wilke) or so-called Arndt and Gingrich (really mostly Bauer), must surely be correct. Few understand that those observations may prove mistaken, if they have misjudged import within specific citations or if they have failed to find and analyze relevant instances. No student of Greek scripture has ever done for Greek what Rashi did for Hebrew. The methods of Rashi who did what he did with a minimum of technical terminology remains head and shoulders above anything ever done for Greek on the churchdom side of linguistic investigation. Numbers 19,11, for example, would far more nearly determine the import of yuxh = psyche in Revelation 06,09 than any use of the word in a Hellenic metempsychotic source like Plato.

Failure to detect how syntax or positio in situ (placement within a verbal setting) should be related to questions of import also vitiate the 'results' of translators as well as multitudes of opinion-makers of shul and church. For example, take an alternative syntax for Romans 11,26:

<<And so all Israel shall be saved, as it is written: "There shall come out of Sion the Deliverer, and shall turn away ungodliness from Jacob.">>

One use made of this has been to disconnect what looks like an obvious syntactical relationship. The result has been to take <<all Israel shall be saved>> as if it did not have the 'as' clause attached. This turns it into a mere simple assertion. Then users of it often add their own conclusions about the possible conversion of Israel before the second coming, etc.

As over against this, note the syntax of the 'so' as modified by the 'as'. A saner understanding of it would probably be that all Israel that will be saved will be thus saved, namely, by the direct intervention of the Redeemer in human affairs, as described in the prophecy of Isaiah 59.

Whether this be wrong or right, it may help clarify the point that the most valid ultimate tools for understanding the text would not be grammars and lexicons, much less monographs and commentaries, but usage within or as close to the linguistic pool in question, as a final court of appeal.

I have detected spirits on this list who have no patience for such matters and may therefore be condemning themselves to be 'often in error, but never in doubt'.

Perhaps someone will claim regarding this level three that the Holy Spirit has given you exact answers on some or all of the questions. That could terminate the discussion or divert it to other avenues.

The fourth level had to be mentioned on the second level, above. Most of the composers of printed editions of 'texts of the original' have looked at as many manuscripts of the source documents as they could. In each instance of difference, most of them have tried picking their chosen reading as objectively as possible. On any band, or spectrum, from objectivity to subjectivity, each of these decisions hits a different mark. Who can critique each decision? If you do not know what has been done, you certainly cannot.

Let me emphasize that the situation of the Greek differs greatly from the Hebrew.

Theoretically, and maybe practically, the Hebrew ktiybh, the printed text, never changes. The sprinkling of the marginal qrey, however, heard in public readings of Hebrew, must be regarded as subjective decisions. These can be known to have changed.

The state of any printed Greek text of Matthew through Revelation, however, proves radically different. None of them follows church wide principles. Every such Greek text ever printed amounts to a set of subjective decisions by the individual or group that gave the text to the printer.

In such matters 'infidel scholars' and 'believing scholars' display about equal smartness and stupidity. Contrary to what most of infidel churchdom thinks, many assertions about 'the original' by John Shelby Spong deserve high marks for stupidity.

If we had any original copies handed down directly from, say, Moses or Paul, then 'scripture' as an objective fact would be a reality.

The situation, of course, proves markedly different from impressions left regarding the Islamic Quran or the Book of Mormon. In those scenarios the Most High has been featured as dropping one whopping bundle right off his table in heaven into the lap of a single go-between.

Perhaps someone will claim regarding this level four that the Holy Spirit has given you exact answers on some or all of the questions. That could terminate the discussion or divert it to other avenues.

Although many more levels may need to be added, a fifth level will be the last in this memo. It concerns the fictions to which those resort who assume a 'canon of scripture'. If you are Roman Catholic, that was decided for you by the Council of Trent and those who do not accept it have all been anathematized. If you are not Roman Catholic, your guess will have been as good as mine, if it is as well informed as mine. If not, I pity you. But we can both take comfort in the fact that our results probably affect the standings of only a few source documents. For a start look at the charts under the entry 'Canon' in the unabridged Dictionary of the Bible by William Smith. Take time to master the abbreviations, so that you can comprehend the real picture. Most of you have probably never realized the 'real picture'.

Perhaps someone will claim regarding this level five that the Holy Spirit has given you exact answers on some or all of the questions. That could terminate the discussion or divert it to other avenues.

What could one say? Several choices seem open. One could deny that He has. Another could claim a different revelation from the Holy Spirit, if it seemed so. Another may even claim that you have been deceived by a demon, if that seemed like a valid discernment. Why, trudging down that lane could end up pitted against each other like Jannes plus Jambres versus Moses, right? Or it could be more like Jannes versus Jambres.

shalom,

b

Jay responded: "Or it could be more like Jannes versus Jambres…"

APPENDIX C—
Getting New Life into a Woman

From Chapter 7, pg. 124; taken from an e-mail written by Jay to Lisa on Sunday, January 18, 2004.

Some time before the e-mails in this book were written, Jay asked for Bill's help in understanding how the first city of Jerusalem was captured. The revelation that Jay received was that this is part of the sexual parable. The city is a woman, and she is captured by the penetration of her stronghold. Here's how this exchange went.

Dear Bill,

I need some help!

As I understand it, the following passage is somewhat unclear in the original, particularly the translation, "up to the gutter"[1]:

Was the city or fortress captured by using a waterway, and, if so, was it water in or water out?

"And the king and his men went to Jerusalem unto the Jebusites, the inhabitants of the land: which spake unto David, saying, Except thou take away the blind and the lame, thou shalt not come in hither: thinking, David cannot come in hither. Nevertheless David took the strong hold of Zion: the same is the city of David. And David said on that day, Whosoever getteth up to the gutter, and smiteth the Jebusites, and the lame and the blind, that are hated of David's soul, he shall be chief and captain. Wherefore they said, The blind and the lame shall not come into the house. So David dwelt in the fort, and called it the city of David. And David built round about from Millo and inward."[2]

I think I just saw something very important where getting around paradigms is concerned, but it depends on a proper understanding of how David's men took Jebus/Jerusalem.

Thanks in advance for any insight you can give me!

Bill responded with:

probably does mean what jps tanakh has = water channel

yours & His & shalom

b .
_____

[1] 2 Samuel 5:8. [2] 2 Samuel 5:6–9.

Jay pressed him further:

Dear Bill,

Thanks! Can you tell me whether it's water in or water out of the fortress?

I'm trying to figure out how to take fortified cities,[3] and my sense is that the taking of the "stronghold of Zion" may be a real key.

The following is a smorgasbord of my present wrestling with the subject:

"We are heading for a city whose builder and maker is God, you know, the one with foundations. I would like to consider that goal for a little bit, particularly as it relates to how to best take a city. When the Israelites entered the promised land, there were cities that they had to take, even strongholds. All this happened to them as an example, and was written down for our instruction on whom the end of the age has come.[4]

Taking Paul, and through him, the Lord, seriously about this, I would like to consider the taking of a city, even Jerusalem. Here is the passage that came to mind in this connection, the opening salvo directed at my own paradigms, so to speak. "Nevertheless David took the stronghold of Zion: the same is the city of David. And David said on that day, Whosoever getteth up to the gutter, and smiteth the Jebusites, and the lame and the blind, that are hated of David's soul, he shall be chief and captain. Wherefore they said, The blind and the lame shall not come into the house. So David dwelt in the fort, and called it the city of David. And David built round about from Millo and inward."[5]

Keep in mind Proverbs 18:19: "A brother offended is harder to be won than a strong city: and their contentions are like the bars of a castle."

The city was occupied by the Jebusites. It was called, "Jebus," interesting name. According to Strongs: "from 947; trodden, i.e. threshing place;…" 947: "boos; a prime root; to trample (lit. or fig.): -loath, tread (down, under [foot]), be polluted."

They took "the strong hold of Zion:" Perhaps I should also cite: "For though we walk in the flesh, we do not war after the flesh: (For the weapons of our warfare are not carnal, but mighty through God to the pulling down of strong holds;) Casting down imaginations, and every high thing that exalteth itself against the knowledge of God, and bringing into captivity every thought to the obedience of Christ;"[6]

Now this sounds to me like a war that is going on in the hearts and minds of men. The war is against, "philosophical" strongholds or paradigms, together with their root causes, whether it be the devil, demons, the futility of Gentile thinking, wounds of the past, insecurities, you name it.

---

[3]Proverbs 18:19.
[5]2 Samuel 5:7–9.

[4]1 Corinthians 10.
[6]2 Corinthians 10:3–5.

Those things hold up inside the fortress on men's minds, interesting, they do, in fact, make us "lame, and blind." Arguments, like bars in the windows, only reinforce their position or stronghold. Even Jerusalem was/can be/is, occupied by thinking, thus polluted, or trodden down.

How does King David take the stronghold? Through the "gutter." The more I look into it, the more it seems to me that it is the water coming out of the stronghold. I'm guessing it was/is polluted by the occupants, the Jebusites.

My additional impression is that the water source may have been in the stronghold itself. It was probably clean at its source but became polluted as it passed through the stronghold. (I hope you're still with me, on at least two levels.) I feel like the Lord has taken me to John 7:37-39: "In the last day, that great day of the feast, Jesus stood and cried, saying, If any man thirst, let him come unto me, and drink. He that believeth on me, as the scripture hath said, out of his belly shall flow rivers of living water. (But this spake he of the Spirit, which they that believe on him should receive: for the Holy Ghost was not yet given; because that Jesus was not yet glorified.)"

Somewhere it is written, it is "not that which goeth into the mouth defileth a man; but that which cometh out of the mouth, this defileth a man."[7]

Another passage that comes to mind is: "But as it is written, Eye hath not seen, nor ear heard, neither have entered into the heart of man, the things which God hath prepared for them that love him. But God hath revealed them unto us by his Spirit: for the Spirit searcheth all things, yea, the deep things of God. For what man knoweth the things of a man, save the spirit of man which is in him? Even so the things of God knoweth no man, but the Spirit of God."[8]

About at this place in my meditation, Bill answered:

"about all i know so far about the 'gutter' would be that it seems to be a container like an aqueduct, which is usually assumed to be conduit to within, but i doubt that inheres in the word. whether in or out, the circumstance could be that it would be useful as an access hole for warriors to get in. why would it need to be 'taken', unless it was defended from without, if indeed it was an aqueduct?"

Jay responded:

Dear Bill,

Thanks for your continuing help with sorting this out.

There is also a passage in Isaiah, 22:9 that might have some bearing on our understanding of this. Yesterday I was speaking with a good friend

---

[7]Matthew 15:11.   [8]1 Corinthians 2:9–11.

who was certain that this is the way that the Medes took Babylon. He was also sure that it was in Daniel 5, but, alas, it is not there. I'm as sure as my aging brain can be that I read it somewhere else in the Scripture, concerning the taking of a city, and I thought it might have been Babylon. But, with all my searching, I have not yet been able to find it."

Bill continued:

"as for the 'Jerusalem above' of Galatians 04, it would be, obvious to me, not the church or a wicked city, but the new covenant."

I continued my response:

I think we are in agreement about that. But, in Revelation 3:20, Jesus seems to be knocking at the door of a "new covenant" church. Presumably this "church" had walls as well as a door. In any case, Jesus is on the outside, looking to get in, and whether He is in or out seems to require a decision on the part of the doorkeepers. It seems to me that a church where Jesus is on the outside of the door is a church, which is, at least, in deficit where the "mind of Christ" is concerned. I believe that our default mode is the "carnal mind."

What I am exploring is the possibility that there are attitudinal door-keepers in the mind of each of us. Those doorkeepers are not always so obvious or easy to reach. Some of them seem to be holed up in strongholds. Paul, for instance, provides us with some pretty good lists: Romans 1:29-31, Galatians 5:19-21, 2 Timothy 3:2-5. It is these strongholds, that I would like to get better at pulling down, whether in myself or in others. It looks to me like we have been given the very powerful weapons necessary for the successful execution of this war, but I would like to get better at identifying those weapons and knowing how to wield them.[9]

Bill continued:

"i would caution against our becoming too ready to dismiss individuals or groups as 'carnal minded'. now and then i have realized that it had been a carnal thought to picture the one or the other brother or sister as 'carnal'."

Jay responded:

It goes without saying that all must be found—and done—in the spirit. It's our/my carnal mindedness that gets in the way of making sense out of it all."

Bill:

"it also seems most likely to me that the new Jerusalem of Revelation 21–22 fits that much better than it does any church,"

---

[9] 2 Corinthians 10:4.

Jay:

At least, any church that I have yet seen being called "church."

Bill:

"no matter how many spots or wrinkles get removed."

Jay:

Well, that remains to be seen.

Job's characterization of what it took to get the wrinkles out of him, what it took to get him from where he had been in his understanding to where he wound up,[10] was, "That which I've feared the most has come upon me." Well, if I might be permitted to borrow that assessment and apply it to the "great tribulation,"[11] it seems to me that that should be fairly effective in removing the "spots and wrinkles" from just about any "church." We will yet be a city on a hill, the salt of the earth, the light of the world, but I don't think it's going to be a pretty sight to see what it's going to take to get us there. As Daniel says, "It will be rebuilt in troublous times."[12] If kings haven't shut their mouths already, I think they will by then.[13]

Bill:

"the church there would be the guests gathered to the wedding feast, not the bride who marries the lamb (for the first time?)."

Jay:

Paul says he has "espoused" us,[14] so, whatever it takes to consummate the marriage, even so, "Come, Lord Jesus."

Bill:

"afterthoughts:

i do not mean to suggest that the spiritual application you apparently aim at ought to be neglected. i want to settle in my mind first what the 'surface' narrative states, its import regarding the ancient physical situation."

Jay:

Thanks Bill, I understand, and I really appreciate your searching out what this meant in the first instance.

---

[10]Job 42:5.
[11]Matthew 24:21.
[12]Daniel 9:25.
[13]Isaiah 52:15.
[14]2 Corinthians 11:2.

APPENDIX D—
Burning Babylon

From Chapter 8, pg. 138; taken from an e-mail written by Jay to Lisa on Wednesday, January 21, 2004.

In this piece, Jay contrasts two economic systems, the familiar system of buying and selling in a marketplace, where the gospel has been focused up to the new covenant, the other a system that is based on love and requires no "trip to the marketplace" at all.

One of the ways of summarizing where the gospel takes us, as contrasted with where we have been, is a contrast between two economic systems. One system finds its expression in a market place, a place where people go to buy and sell. The rock bottom object of the market place is a re-distribution of the necessities of life.

There are many ways of determining or describing a market place; capitalism, communism, socialism, fascism, etc., even "black market." What I would like to present as the best-case market scenario is a "free market."

This phrase has been so misrepresented, and so often that, for present purposes, I'll try to define it.

A free market in its simplest essence is what happens when two people come together, each with something of value that the other wants. They make a voluntary exchange, each of their own free will, with no outside interference or coercion. The process is facilitated when they have a common understanding concerning a medium of exchange, money. Everything else being equal, the money itself is one of the commodities exchanged in the market place. Historically this has been silver or gold. Biblically, it is undefiled only when the silver or gold is measured by weight, and not by image. The silver or gold is corrupted when it is marked with an image, the work of man's hands.

Babylon on her best day might possibly attain to being a free market. A free market is still a place where merchants come to make deals. Theoretically, it is even possible that they might make honest deals, if only any of us were truly honest without Christ.

In Jesus's days in the flesh, it is said that, "He didn't trust himself to any man, because He knew what was in a man."[15]

---

[15]John 2:24.

We need to know the same thing, and own up to what is in us. It is our only hope of becoming the lovers Jesus died to make us.

What I saw was the "now" implications of the fact that, in the end, there will no more be the merchant in the house of the Lord of Hosts;[16] none; not dishonest; not honest; none; end of story. Jesus offers us an alternative to both Wal-Mart, and Wall Street.

The Biblical best-case scenario is a free market, which is to say, a market where the medium of exchange is silver and gold by weight. For present purposes, I don't need to go into the complexities, even the Biblical complexities of making images of silver and gold. The present revelation is closer to the core than that.

Peter's response, as stated, suggests a best case market place scenario, "… silver and gold have I none…" From Peter's response, we know it was a forgone conclusion in his mind that the beggar was looking for silver and/or gold. The only reason the beggar would have wanted silver and/or gold was so that he could go to the market place, and buy what he needed.

Peter didn't have the medium exchange of the market place. He had something else. In either case, the meeting of a human need was the object, but Peter had another way of meeting the need, one that did not require a trip to the market.

A market place is a place of merchants. The People that God chose as examples for us on whom the end of the age has come,[17] were a people, whose promised land was occupied by Canaanites. "Canaanite" means "merchant." They were told to take the land, wiping out the Canaanites/merchants in the process."[18]

In the end we are told, "Every pot in Jerusalem and Judah will be holy to the Lord Almighty, and all who come to sacrifice will take some of the pots and cook in them. And on that day there will no longer be a Canaanite in the house of the Lord Almighty."[19]

In other words, God's house is not to be a market place, not even under the best of circumstances. There are only two alternatives to a free market, a forced market or no market. A forced market is still a market. There are only two ways I know to deviate from a free market. One deviation always involves force or fraud. At root, it enters the market place with a gun. The other deviation involves the grace of God. At root it enters the market place with love. This is a deviation that you can read about in the early chapters of Acts.[20]

Unfortunately, it did not last long. The religious network marketers came on the scene early, got their hands in the cookie jar, (the "Jeru-

---

[16]Zechariah 14:21.
[18]Deuteronomy 7:1–10.
[20]Acts 2:41–47, 4:32–35.

[17]1 Corinthians 10:11.
[19]Zechariah 14:21.

salem pots"), and tore the body of Christ apart.[21] Paul cried over this problem, especially with the Church in Ephesus.[22]

In those early days of the Jerusalem Church, however, we got enough of a look at what God has in mind.[23] Enough so that we can have confidence that neither the mind of a merchant nor the mind of a politician have any place in the Kingdom or household of God. The evidence of God's intervention in human affairs is lovers, not regulators, and not peddlers. This to say, that even after the politicians have been removed, we still have a choice between an economy of merchants, and an economy of lovers.

Returning then to our simple example; two free people each having something that the other wants, the only alternative to a free exchange is either a gun or love. In the end those are our only alternatives.

Babylon is the mind of a merchant. "Let's make a deal." "What's in it for me?" When the man of sin, the last antichrist, comes on the scene, he burns Babylon. That is the end of the free market, if there ever was one. From then on, no one buys or sells without the "mark of the beast."[24] This is the mark of antichrist; even the mind of antichrist. When the antichrist puts an end to Babylon by burning her with fire, he sets up his alternative. He does this as a counterfeit Christ.

When the Real Christ returns, He also puts an end to the status quo by burning it with fire.[25] This is "the real thing." The other is a deception. Jesus said, "I have come to cast fire upon the earth; and how I wish it were already kindled. But I have a baptism to undergo, and how distressed I am until it is accomplished!"[26]

What I saw was two ways of thinking, the mind of a merchant, and the mind of Christ. The merchant mentality is burned up by, both Christ, and antichrist. Where externals are concerned, it looks like it's first burned up by antichrist, then by Christ. That's not really it. When Jesus went to the cross He went there as the last Adam.[27]

When the fire fell at Pentecost, that fire burned up the mind of a merchant. The result was that there was not a needy person among them.[28]

The market place was replaced by the love of Christ operating through the new citizenship of the Kingdom of God. The economy of merchants was replaced by the economy of love.

---

[21]2 Corinthians 2:17.

[23]Acts 2:41–47, 4:32–35.

[25]Revelation 20:9.

[27]1 Corinthians 15:45.

[22]Acts 20:29–31.

[24]Revelation 13:16–17.

[26]Luke 12:49–50.

[28]Acts 2:41–47, 4:32–35.

APPENDIX E—
The Mark of Cain

From Chapter 10, pg. 162; taken from an e-mail written by Jay to Lisa on Friday, January 23, 2004.

The material that follows is the result of thoughts Jay had after the terror attack on the Twin Towers on September 11, 2001. Aware of the religious, and even the genetic background of the terrorists, Jay was reminded of Ishmael and the terrible rejection he had suffered as an oldest child being sent away in favor of a younger brother. What Jay shared had to do with what happens to first children when the second or subsequent children come along. They are displaced from center stage before their source people. In the content of their heart, this results in "Abba" being replaced by "Uh Oh!" This is often our first wounding, and carries marks with it late into adult life. And very often into the heritage of the generations to come.

"For this is the message that ye heard from the beginning, that we should love one another. Not as Cain, who was of that wicked one, and slew his brother. And wherefore slew he him? Because his own works were evil, and his brother's righteous. Marvel not, my brethren, if the world hate you. We know that we have passed from death unto life, because we love the brethren. He that loveth not his brother abideth in death. Whosoever hateth his brother is a murderer: and ye know that no murderer hath eternal life abiding in him. Hereby perceive we the love of God, because he laid down his life for us: and we ought to lay down our lives for the brethren."[29]

To bring this a little closer to where we are now living in history, let's say that Cain was the first "terrorist." In answer to the why question, we are told, "Because his own works were evil." It is also written that Cain was "of that wicked one." In a sense then, we are given a choice between two role models, Cain and Abel. Since they both had the same father in the flesh, we are also given a choice between two spiritual fathers, "the wicked one," and God who is LOVE. The word, "poneros" here translated "wicked," traces its root through "ponos" to "penes" which, according to Strong's, has the meaning, "(to toil for daily substance); starving, i.e. indigent:-poor."

---

[29]1 John 3:11–16.

(Note: "The thief cometh not, but for to steal, and to kill, and to destroy: I am come that they might have life, and that they might have it more abundantly."[30] The One who said this, also said, "And the Father himself, which hath sent me, hath borne witness of me. Ye have neither heard his voice at any time, nor seen his shape. And ye have not his word abiding in you: for whom he hath sent, him ye believe not. Search the scriptures; for in them ye think ye have eternal life: and they are they which testify of me. And ye will not come to me, that ye might have life."[31] In other words, what we are reading about in Genesis, and on, is all about Jesus.)

Viewed in that light, I am reminded of what God said to Adam after the fall: "And unto Adam he said, Because thou hast hearkened unto the voice of thy wife, and hast eaten of the tree, of which I commanded thee, saying, Thou shalt not eat of it: cursed is the ground for thy sake; in sorrow shalt thou eat of it all the days of thy life; Thorns also and thistles shall it bring forth to thee; and thou shalt eat the herb of the field; In the sweat of thy face shalt thou eat bread, till thou return unto the ground; for out of it wast thou taken: for dust thou art, and unto dust shalt thou return."[32]

Notice the distinction that is made between Cain and Abel in their occupations: "And Adam knew Eve his wife; and she conceived, and bare Cain, and said, I have gotten a man from the LORD. And she again bare his brother Abel. And Abel was a keeper of sheep, but Cain was a tiller of the ground."[33]

At some point in time, they both brought offerings to the LORD: "And in process of time it came to pass, that Cain brought of the fruit of the ground an offering unto the LORD. And Abel, he also brought of the firstlings of his flock and of the fat thereof. And the LORD had respect unto Abel and to his offering: But unto Cain and to his offering he had not respect."[34]

Cain tried to offer human doing, "the work of his own hands" to God, but human doing had been cursed as a result of the fall. Where attitude in connection with "offering" is concerned, human doing is born of either pride or guilt, and results in either pride or guilt. Righteousness cannot come from the law, from outer things. A focus on outer things, our own doing, can only produce pride or guilt, it can never produce gratitude or love. Cain was under the curse, but Jesus, "being made a curse for us" is "The Lamb of God who takes away the sin of the world."

"For as many as are of the works of the law are under the curse: for it is written, Cursed is every one that continueth not in all things which are

---

[30]John 10:10.
[31]John 5:37–40.
[32]Genesis 3:17–19.
[33]Genesis 4:1–2, 3–7, 8–12, 13–16.
[34]Genesis 4:3–5a.

written in the book of the law to do them. But that no man is justified by the law in the sight of God, it is evident: for, The just shall live by faith. And the law is not of faith: but, The man that doeth them shall live in them. Christ hath redeemed us from the curse of the law, being made a curse for us: for it is written, Cursed is every one that hangeth on a tree."[35]

"And Cain was very wroth, and his countenance fell. And the LORD said unto Cain, Why art thou wroth? and why is thy countenance fallen? If thou doest well, shalt thou not be accepted? and if thou doest not well, sin lieth at the door. And unto thee shall be his desire, and thou shalt rule over him."[36]

"If thou doest well": "doest well" is apparently the translation of a single word, "yatab" which, again, according to Strong's has the sense of a good attitude: "…happy …accepted …cheerful …content …glad …merry …sweet…"

In that sense we could understand The Lord's word to Cain as being: "If thou hast the right attitude, shalt thou not be accepted? And if thou hast the wrong attitude, sin lieth at the door. And unto thee shall be his desire, and thou shalt rule over him."

The New Testament perspective on this is well expressed by James: "Blessed is the man that endureth temptation: for when he is tried, he shall receive the crown of life, which the Lord hath promised to them that love him.

Let no man say when he is tempted, I am tempted of God: for God cannot be tempted with evil, neither tempteth he any man: But every man is tempted, when he is drawn away of his own lust, and enticed. Then when lust hath conceived, it bringeth forth sin: and sin, when it is finished, bringeth forth death.

Do not err, my beloved brethren. Every good gift and every perfect gift is from above, and cometh down from the Father of lights, with whom is no variableness, neither shadow of turning. Of his own will begat he us with the word of truth, that we should be a kind of firstfruits of his creatures. Wherefore, my beloved brethren, let every man be swift to hear, slow to speak, slow to wrath: For the wrath of man worketh not the righteousness of God. Wherefore lay apart all filthiness and superfluity of naughtiness, and receive with meekness the engrafted word, which is able to save your souls.

But be ye doers of the word, and not hearers only, deceiving your own selves. For if any be a hearer of the word, and not a doer, he is like unto a man beholding his natural face in a glass: For he beholdeth himself, and goeth his way, and straightway forgetteth what manner of man he was. But whoso looketh into the perfect law of liberty, and continueth

---

[35]Galatians 3:10–13.   [36]Genesis 4:5b–7.

therein, he being not a forgetful hearer, but a doer of the work, this man shall be blessed in his deed."[37]

"...drawn away of his own lust..." The word here translated "lust" is a very strong word with very deep roots, perhaps the deepest of which is "thuo." Again, according to Strong's, the word has the sense of: "...rush (breath hard, blow smoke) i.e. (by implication.) to sacrifice (prop. by fire, but gen.); by extens. to immolate (slaughter for any purpose): kill, (do) sacrifice, slay."

In that light then, returning to Cain's problem: "If thou hast the right attitude, shalt thou not be accepted? and if thou hast the wrong attitude, sin lieth at the door. And your wrong attitude desires to have you, to carry you away to do its will, but you don't have to be mastered or fathered by a wrong attitude, you can take it captive, pull it down, you can master your bad attitude.... Get a grip!"

Would that it were so, but instead: "...Cain talked with Abel his brother: and it came to pass, when they were in the field, that Cain rose up against Abel his brother, and slew him."[38]

"And it came to pass," who knows how long that was, but outwardly, at least, it could have looked like everything was fine, that is, until they took a walk together. Our attitudes of heart can be well hidden until we go to do something with each other, then what is hidden in the heart comes to light.

"And the Lord said unto Cain, Where is Abel thy brother? And he said, I know not: Am I my brother's keeper?"

It is quite possible to have that attitude hidden in the heart long before we ever get around to physically murdering someone. It's an attitude of heart that wants that person not to exist would be very happy to never see or hear of that person again.

The Lord, however, will not allow that attitude to go unchecked. The Lord will continue to bring that person to remembrance: "What hast thou done? the voice of thy brother's blood crieth unto me from the ground. And now art thou cursed from the earth, which hath opened her mouth to receive thy brother's blood from thy hand; When thou tillest the ground, it shall not henceforth yield unto thee her strength; a fugitive and a vagabond shalt thou be in the earth." (The territory of terrorists certainly has this look about it.)

"And Cain said unto the Lord, My punishment is greater than I can bear. Behold, thou hast driven me out this day from the face of the earth; and from thy face shall I be hid; and I shall be a fugitive and a vagabond in the earth; and it shall come to pass, that every one that findeth me shall slay me."

---

[37]James 1:12–25.   [38]Genesis 4:8.

(Again, certainly descriptive of the post 9/11/01 situation.)

But wait:

"And the LORD said unto him, Therefore whosoever slayeth Cain, vengeance shall be taken on him sevenfold. And the LORD set a mark upon Cain, lest any finding him should kill him. And Cain went out from the presence of the LORD, and dwelt in the land of Nod, on the east of Eden. "

(Where does this fit in to our present situation? Could it be that there is a better alternative to killing Cain?)

"For we wrestle not against flesh and blood, but against principalities, against powers, against the rulers of the darkness of this world, against spiritual wickedness in high places."[39]

"For though we walk in the flesh, we do not war after the flesh: (For the weapons of our warfare are not carnal, but mighty through God to the pulling down of strong holds;) Casting down imaginations, and every high thing that exalteth itself against the knowledge of God, and bringing into captivity every thought to the obedience of Christ."[40]

Now Cain is not the last "only child" who had a problem with "... imaginations, ... high things that exalt themselves against the knowledge of God, ... thoughts."

There would be others, perhaps most notably, Ishmael. Paul draws upon Ishmael's situation in order to make a very strong point to the Galatians: "Now I say, That the heir, as long as he is a child, differeth nothing from a servant, though he be lord of all; But is under tutors and governors until the time appointed of the father.

Even so we, when we were children, were in bondage under the elements of the world: But when the fullness of the time was come, God sent forth his Son, made of a woman, made under the law, To redeem them that were under the law, that we might receive the adoption of sons. And because ye are sons, God hath sent forth the Spirit of his Son into your hearts, crying, Abba, Father.

Wherefore thou art no more a servant, but a son; and if a son, then an heir of God through Christ. Howbeit then, when ye knew not God, ye did service unto them which by nature are no gods. But now, after that ye have known God, or rather are known of God, how turn ye again to the weak and beggarly elements, whereunto ye desire again to be in bondage?

---

[39] Ephesians 6:12.

[40] 2 Corinthians 10:3–5 (By the time of this publication, Mel Gibson has provided a wonderful example of a spiritual weapon. **The Passion of the Christ** is probably the most effective weapon yet devised in the war on terrorism.)

Ye observe days, and months, and times, and years. I am afraid of you, lest I have bestowed upon you labour in vain.

Brethren, I beseech you, be as I am; for I am as ye are: ye have not injured me at all. Ye know how through infirmity of the flesh I preached the gospel unto you at the first. And my temptation which was in my flesh ye despised not, nor rejected; but received me as an angel of God, even as Christ Jesus.

Where is then the blessedness ye spake of? for I bear you record, that, if it had been possible, ye would have plucked out your own eyes, and have given them to me.

Am I therefore become your enemy, because I tell you the truth? They zealously affect you, but not well; yea, they would exclude you, that ye might affect them. But it is good to be zealously affected always in a good thing, and not only when I am present with you.

My little children, of whom I travail in birth again until Christ be formed in you, I desire to be present with you now, and to change my voice; for I stand in doubt of you. Tell me, ye that desire to be under the law, do ye not hear the law?

'For it is written, that Abraham had two sons, the one by a bondmaid, the other by a freewoman. But he who was of the bondwoman was born after the flesh; but he of the freewoman was by promise."[41]

In Abraham's case, the two sons had different mothers, one a slave and one free. But it is also possible to have two sons by the same woman, one born when she is a slave and one born when she is free. Take the case of Eve for instance. Cain was born first after Adam was ejected from the garden, and the ground was cursed for his sake. That rejection had to be a pretty big blow. Something like that hurts a lot and takes quite a while to get over. (There is plenty of evidence that we are not over it yet.)

But, wounds do heal with time, and in time, she had another son, Abel. It is quite possible that she had mastered the feelings of rejection by the time Abel came along. Keep in mind that Slavery is an attitude of heart, "Know ye not, that to whom ye yield yourselves servants to obey, his servants ye are to whom ye obey; whether of sin unto death, or of obedience unto righteousness?"[42]

"Servants" is really not a strong enough word, it is "slaves" and its root is "bind," to be bound. We are bound to obey our inner attitude of heart. "As a man thinks, so he is." Or, as the author of Hebrews puts it (my personal belief is that the author of Hebrews was probably Priscilla), "And truly, if they had been mindful of that country from whence they came out, they might have had opportunity to have returned."[43]

---

[41]Galatians 4:1–23.   [42]Romans 6:16.
[43]Hebrews 11:15.

Somewhere else it is written, "But sin, taking occasion (opportunity) by the commandment, wrought in me all manner of concupiscence. For without the law sin was dead. For I was alive without the law once: but when the commandment came, sin revived, and I died. And the commandment, which was ordained to life, I found to be unto death."[44]

In Luke it is written: "And when the devil had ended all the temptation, he departed from him for a season."[45]

The NIV has it "until a more opportune time." In the wilderness, the devil tempted Jesus in a time of deprivation. At the cross, the devil tempted Him at the point of rejection. "He was despised and rejected of men…"

Continuing now with our quotation from Paul's letter to the Galatians: "Which things are an allegory: for these are the two covenants; the one from the mount Sinai, which gendereth to bondage, which is Agar. For this Agar is mount Sinai in Arabia, and answereth to Jerusalem which now is, and is in bondage with her children."[46]

(Works of the flesh, even those according to the "Law" are born of bondage, they come from being married to a husband whose influence is death; for the letter kills, but the Spirit gives life, and from being born of a different father, "that wicked one," the "father of lies" the father of bad attitudes.)

"But Jerusalem which is above is free, which is the mother of us all. For it is written, Rejoice, thou barren that bearest not; break forth and cry, thou that travailest not: for the desolate hath many more children than she which hath an husband.

Now we, brethren, as Isaac was, are the children of promise. But as then he that was born after the flesh persecuted him that was born after the Spirit, even so it is now. Nevertheless what saith the scripture? Cast out the bondwoman and her son: for the son of the bondwoman shall not be heir with the son of the freewoman. So then, brethren, we are not children of the bondwoman, but of the free."[47]

There is a great vulnerability in being an only child. An only child is center stage where the focus of his source is concerned.

"And Adam knew his wife again; and she bare a son, and called his name Seth: For God, said she, hath appointed me another seed instead of Abel, whom Cain slew."[48]

When Eve gave birth to Cain she said: "And Adam knew Eve his wife; and she conceived, and bare Cain, and said, I have gotten a man from the Lord."[49]

---

[44] Romans 7:8–10.

[45] Luke 4:13.

[46] Galatians 4:24.

[47] Galatians 4:26–31.

[48] Genesis 4:25.

[49] Genesis 4:1.

God had said something to "that wicked one" which contained an implied promise to Eve: "And I will put enmity between thee and the woman, and between thy seed and her seed; it shall bruise thy head, and thou shalt bruise his heel."[50]

"Her seed" would bruise the head of "that wicked one" The way we are given the story, it is as though Cain was somehow passed over as the focus of the promised seed of the woman, and with the arrival of Seth, it is apparent that he is the replacement for Abel as that seed.

One is left to wonder how Cain might have felt about all of that, except that there are so many Biblical examples of older brothers who are jealous of younger brothers, and this seems to echo the experience of this present life as well.

God, the Father seems to have stood by, and gone along with all this rejection, whether the rejection of Cain or the rejection of Ishmael, the rejection of Esau, and finally the "forsaking" of His own Son, who was also the "first born of many brothers."

This is to say, there is no parental rejection with which Jesus is not familiar. He bore it all on the tree. He is the redeemer of older brothers, and rejected siblings.

"And Jesus answered and spake unto them again by parables, and said, The kingdom of heaven is like unto a certain king, which made a marriage for his son, And sent forth his servants to call them that were bidden to the wedding: and they would not come. Again, he sent forth other servants, saying, Tell them which are bidden, Behold, I have prepared my dinner: my oxen and my fatlings are killed, and all things are ready: come unto the marriage. But they made light of it, and went their ways, one to his farm, another to his merchandise: And the remnant took his servants, and entreated them spitefully, and slew them.

But when the king heard thereof, he was wroth: and he sent forth his armies, and destroyed those murderers, and burned up their city. Then saith he to his servants, The wedding is ready, but they which were bidden were not worthy. Go ye therefore into the highways, and as many as ye shall find, bid to the marriage. (Lisa, that's where I went to find you.)

So those servants went out into the highways, and gathered together all as many as they found, both bad and good: and the wedding was furnished with guests. And when the king came in to see the guests, he saw there a man which had not on a wedding garment: And he saith unto him, Friend, how camest thou in hither not having a wedding garment? And he was speechless. Then said the king to the servants, Bind him hand and foot, and take him away, and cast him into outer darkness;

---

[50]Genesis 3:15.

there shall be weeping and gnashing of teeth. For many are called, but few are chosen."[51]

"Lie not one to another, seeing that ye have put off the old man with his deeds; And have put on the new man, which is renewed in knowledge after the image of him that created him: Where there is neither Greek nor Jew, circumcision nor uncircumcision, Barbarian, Scythian, bond nor free: but Christ is all, and in all. Put on therefore, as the elect of God, holy and beloved, bowels of mercies, kindness, humbleness of mind, meekness, longsuffering; Forbearing one another, and forgiving one another, if any man have a quarrel against any: even as Christ forgave you, so also do ye. And above all these things put on charity, which is the bond of perfectness."[52]

"And when the thousand years are expired, Satan shall be loosed out of his prison, And shall go out to deceive the nations which are in the four quarters of the earth, Gog and Magog, to gather them together to battle: the number of whom is as the sand of the sea. And they went up on the breadth of the earth, and compassed the camp of the saints about, and the beloved city: and fire came down from God out of heaven, and devoured them."[53]

Yours in process,

Jay

---

[51]Matthew 22:1-9, 10-14.
[52]Colossians 3:9–14.
[53]Revelation 20:7–9.

APPENDIX F—
Inflation: The Ultimate Graven Image

From Chapter 11, pg. 179; taken from an e-mail written by Jay to Lisa on Saturday, January 28, 2004.

The following contains, as Jay puts it, "a testimony, summary, and taste from the **Inflation** book." The book was written about 25 years ago, but for the most part, it still reflects Jay's understanding.

AN OVERVIEW

Why do the heathen rage and the people imagine a vain thing? The kings of the earth set themselves, and the rulers take counsel together against the Lord, and against his anointed,.. (Psalms 2:1,2).

In the chaos of today's world there are many events, which find points of reference in the Word of God, and this is particularly true of money. Money is basic to the problems of the western world, and the Bible has much to say about it.

We have only to stop for a moment to realize how central money is to our problems as individuals, as families, as towns, states, nations, and the world.

What may not be so obvious is that God knew this would be a problem, if not the problem from the beginning. That being true, it seems only reasonable that the Bible, should have something to say on the subject, and, in fact, it has everything to say about it.

In studying the subject of money, I have gone through many stages of thought, and while, like the apostle Paul, "I count not myself to have apprehended" the entirety of the subject, I believe that I have glimpsed its breadth and found the ultimate conclusion to the matter.

But how did I come to the answer? It is difficult to say, but maybe it started with Walt Disney. I grew up on Scrooge McDuck comics. For those of you who never had the pleasure, or perhaps have forgotten, Scrooge McDuck is the rich uncle of Donald Duck. He gets involved in fantastic entrepreneurial ventures. He has a money bin which he swims in and through, and his fortune is constantly being threatened by his archenemies, the Beegle Boys.

Or perhaps it began with my exposure to the writings of Ayn Rand, which for me began in high school with her novel, **The Fountainhead**.

Wherever my search began, it was firmly established by the time I read her novel, **Atlas Shrugged**, while I was in the navy. That book opened my eyes to some of the finest statements on money that I have ever read.[54]

Having thus had my interest well established, I concluded my college career by studying economics, particularly economic systems. During that period of study I came across the book **Capitalism and Freedom** by Milton Friedman.[55] Reading it, I became convinced that controlled paper money was the best system. Thankfully, that stage lasted only about a year, my final year in college.

It ended when I was introduced to a book by Andrew Dixon White, **Fiat Money Inflation in France**.[56] This book was placed into my hands by a then new and now good, but passed on friend, Leonard Read of the Foundation for economic Education. Essentially, the book demonstrated to my satisfaction that controlled paper money, if not an impossible medium, is highly improbable while men are imperfect. Thus began my "gold bug" stage which had lasted ten years to the first writing of this book.

In April of 1972 my wife Carleen and I committed our lives to The Lord. No fanfare or fireworks, that I was aware of, we just didn't find enough answers anywhere else. All the writers, philosophers, heroes, and all the causes seemed to wind up in a dead end. Little did we know at the time, how dead. The commitment to Christ that began out of that void has been abundantly blessed.

In September of 1974 I was invited to address a business men's luncheon on the subject, "Inflation, Depression, and Survival." The talk was to be given at the end of November. It was God's timing. The week before the luncheon I was scheduled to attend a monetary conference in Washington D.C., sponsored by The Committee for Monetary Research and Education.

Because the conditions in the economy were changing rapidly at that point, and wishing to be up-to-date with my talk, I decided to prepare for the luncheon after attending the conference. The congregations of three churches prayed that I would get an insight there on which to base the talk the following week. It was more prayer than had ever been brought to bear on a single event in my life, so far as I am aware.

---

[54] Ayn Rand's The Foundtainhead is now available in a 50th Anniversary Edition, published by New American Library in 1996; Atlas Shrugged is similarly available in a 35th Anniversary Edition published by Signet Books in 1996.

[55] **Capitalism and Freedom**, by Milton Friedman, 2nd edition, published by The University of Chicago Press in 1982.

[56] **Fiat Money in France**, by Andrew Dixon White, published by The Foundation for Economic Education in 1959 (out of print).

The day of the conference arrived; the first workshop began; the first speaker opened his mouth to speak; and it occurred to me that inflation begins the moment government calls money something else. At the time I didn't begin to see the Biblical implications of the thought, but it was obvious that, if it were true, and if we wanted to stop inflation, then we shouldn't allow the government to call money something else. I could have gone home right then, and the conference would have been worthwhile, even though I hadn't yet begun to discover what would become of that insight.

The following week I spoke at the businessmen's luncheon and was well received. But even on the way to the talk many ideas and questions began to force themselves to my attention. I thought, in calling the money something else, man puts a mark on it. In Christ's time the mark was Caesar's head.

I thought about the passage in Matthew 22 where Jesus was asked if it was lawful to pay tribute. He Jesus looked at a coin with Caesar's head on it and said, "Render unto Caesar the things which are Caesar's and unto God the things that are God's."

I asked myself, What would Jesus have said if Caesar's head had not been on the money?

I had just finished reading the Bible through for the first time and decided that I would immediately have to go back and take another look at Scripture in the light of the new insight.

I didn't have to go very far before discovering, to my great delight, that the first thing God called good after creation was gold (Gen. 2:12). For a Christian "gold bug" this could hardly have been better news. It would be another twenty years before The Lord would reopen the passage to me in its greater and deeper meaning. But more about that a little later on.

About a year previously I had read the book, **The Day The Dollar Dies**, by Willard Cantelon.[57] This book had brought home to me the monetary importance of the "mark of the beast" (Rev. 13:16-18). As I was meditating on the "good gold" at the beginning of the Bible, a close friend reminded me of the "bad beast" at the end.

That did it.

The evolution of money, perhaps better wording would be "devolution" or "degeneration" of money, both through out world history and the history of nations, begins with gold and ends with fiat money - money that is money by law, rather than by substance or choice. All fiat money has this in common; it all has man's mark upon it, a mark, which I have since learned is a "graven image" (Deut. 4:16), the work of man's hands.

---

[57]**The Day the Dollar Dies**, Willard Cantelon, published by Logos International in 1973.

But the history of money isn't over yet. A brief period remains ahead. The international money of the Western world was gold. The money toward which the international financial community is now driving us is an international credit system, a universal credit system, if you will, where in place of gold we will have "Special Drawing Rights," "Computer Transactions," "A Number System," "No more paper work."

We haven't gotten there yet, but this is clearly the direction in which "the powers that be" are taking us.

If this is true, if the history of money is to be gold on the one end, and "the mark of the beast without which no man may buy or sell," on the other end, then it seemed reasonable to me that the history of money should be found in the Bible somewhere between Genesis and Revelation. On that assumption I took another look at the Scripture, a rather substantial look, in fact, by the first publication of this book, a seven year look, and discovered that, not only is the history of money there, it is all there.

But even beyond all this, just as the Scriptures gives us a perspective on human history, the unfolding of history opens the great truths of Scripture to us for application in our own day (Dan. 12:9). The events of today's world in the area of monetary affairs provide us with the most graphic confirmation of the truth of God's word since the time Christ walked the earth as a man. This continuing study, and these unending discoveries have been the most exciting and rewarding experience of my life.

Right now, today, there is a battle going on for control of the world. As a practical matter this battle comes down to man's doing versus God's doing. It's a control issue. Abraham left the city of man's doing and headed for the city of God's doing. What man does shakes, but the city of God's doing is a "city with foundations" (Heb. 11:10), a city which does not Shake, (Heb 12:26,27). In fact one way of looking at it is that God's purpose is to bring us to a place that doesn't shake. There is a sense in which God does not want us to shake economically, emotionally, mentally, psychologically, morally, spiritually or in any other way.

It is written that God has set eternity in the hearts of men" (Ecc 3:11). In Romans we are told that "the invisible things of God from the creation of the world are clearly seen, being understood by the things that are made, even His eternal power and Godhead; so that men are without excuse. Several years back a book was published called "Eternity in Their Hearts."[58] In it, the author explains that the world is full of "redemptive analogies." Redemptive analogies are facts of life from which we can

---

[58]**Eternity in Their Hearts**, rev. edition, by Don Richardson, published by Regal Books, in 1984.

come to understand God. Economics and money are two very powerful redemptive analogies.

The battle, which is going on is a matter of control, who is in charge, who governs in the affairs of men. The real issue is that of government. Who or what is it that determines how and what we think, say, and act? Or, even more basic than this is who or what determines how you relate to others. A, perhaps, "the" foundational confession of the Christian Faith is Jesus Christ is Lord. He is Lord of all. One of the most important and foundational areas of His lordship is in the area of relationships. Jesus Christ is Lord of relationship.

It is at this point that money, or more precisely a medium of exchange, comes in. The medium of exchange is the way that men relate to one another for the fulfillment of their needs and desires. If Satan through his agents, "the kings of this earth," can control your medium of exchange, then he can control you. This must be understood if we are to have any grasp of what inflation is all about.

Inflation is nothing more nor less than the monetary manifestation of a grab for power, power to run your life, and/or dispose of it.

Inflation, Biblically speaking, is corruptible riches in the process of corruption. It is by one kind of riches or another that we relate to each other. As your riches are corrupted, you become controlled. It is by your riches that you are controlled, "For where your treasure is, there will your heart be also" (Matt. 6:21).

In a sense this book is a study guide to the subject of money in the Bible. The major question of this study is: What is keeping you? The greater significance of the question will become apparent as the book unfolds.

Under that question are to be found the Biblical alternatives. They are, in the broadest sense, the keeping of God and the keeping of this world. The keeping of God includes all of His promises right up through and including the completed work of Jesus Christ. The keeping of this world includes all of the different kinds of idols that man looks to for his happiness and security.

Not to miss the broader significance of the "mark of the beast," its generic meaning: in principle it is, "the work of man's hands," man's doing, man handling, the mark of man. Clearly the Scripture says, don't be man handled, don't let man do a number on you. The message is summarized by symbol in the book of Revelation and elaborated in Paul's letter to the Galatians. The "mark of the beast" is the mark of man.

As the end of the age approaches, we are increasingly man handled in every area of life. Man is doing a number on us morally, governmentally, educationally, medically, relationally, mentally, emotionally, economically, and even religiously. It is a constant temptation to define evil in such way that it does not apply to ourselves. Religious people are particularly adept at this. That said, in the present study our focus will be on graven images and money.

In between our two alternatives is our response to the question. The source of our keeping is the object of our love. It is by nakedness that this love is expressed. If we look to God for our keeping, then it is God whom we will love and before God that we will stand naked. If we look to the world for our keeping, then it is the world that we will love and before the world that we will stand naked.

One of the things that distinguishes us as human is that we are decision makers. If we understand economics in its broadest sense, it deals with the selection, production, and distribution of man's values. The economist tries to figure out the answer to the question, "What's keeping you?" The Bible reveals the answer.

In one sense the alternatives are personified in Satan and Jesus. They are the bidders for your love and loyalty, you are the spoils. You are won or lost by purchase. You are either purchased by Christ who has paid the whole price and has redeemed you, requiring nothing of you but your confession of your inability to pay your own way, and your acknowledgement of His life as the full and sufficient price for your own; or you can "sell your soul for a nickel," "sell your birthright for a pottage of lentils" (Gen. 25:29-34) as did Esau, or in some other way put your trust in uncertain riches.

In fact, of all the things, which stand between you and your salvation, it is riches that make the decision most difficult.

"They spend their days in wealth, and in a moment go down to the grave. Therefore they say unto God, Depart from us; for we desire not the knowledge of thy ways. What is the almighty, that we should serve him? and what profit should we have, if we pray unto him? "(Job 21: 13-15).

"And again I say unto you, it is easier for a camel to go through the eye of a needle than for a rich man to enter into the kingdom of God." (Matt. 19:24)

It is your answer to the question, What's keeping you?, that determines whose spoils you are, and in the ultimate sense, whether you are a winner or a loser.

In summary, The Bible shows us three systems - one that leads to death, one that men couldn't (or wouldn't) live with, and one that leads to life. These three systems are injustice, justice, and grace. Expressed another way, they are unmerited penalty, the merit system, and unmerited favor.

Each of these systems has a people. The people of injustice are the Gentiles, the people of justice are the Jews, and the people of grace are the Christians. These are the three basic people types of which the Bible speaks. Christians were formerly either Jews or Gentiles, (Gal 3:28). Each of these systems and peoples has a medium of exchange. Injustice is Satan's system, the world system. Its medium of exchange is the graven image, fiat money, money that is money by force, not by substance.

Justice is the system of God, and in this regard, it is either God's justice or it isn't justice. "Except the Lord build the house, they labour in vain that build it" (Ps. 127:1). The medium of exchange of this system is gold and silver, and the Bible tells us that, of the two, gold has the more stable value.

But man wouldn't live by this system. Instead, he combined the gold of God's justice with the graven image of Satan's injustice. Thus inflation was released, and the gold was corrupted. That began the continuum of monetary corruption, which we are still caught up in today. Gold has substance. A graven image has none. It is by the elimination of anything of substance and the placing of the graven image on you that inflation achieves its ultimate purpose, your enslavement.

Anticipating the unwillingness, even the inability of men to keep God's justice, God provided the third and final system, grace - The Love of Christ. The medium of exchange of this system is the love of Jesus, our incorruptible riches. Whether or not men ever had any other options for their long term keeping, they haven't any longer. It is in the love of Christ that our only true keeping lies.

We hope to make the reality of Christ's love as a medium of exchange clear as the book develops. For the present, however, it may help to grasp this idea if we consider the love of a father for his child and the way it replaces the child's need of money. The father's love is sensitive to the desires, and especially the needs of the child and impels him to meet those needs and proper desires as well. The love of the father is all the medium of exchange the child ever needs (Matt. 7:11). This is also true for the Bride of Christ - the love of Christ is all the medium of exchange the Bride will ever need; for He is sensitive, faithful and true.

Each of these mediums of exchange has a mindset, a way of thinking, which goes along with it. The graven image mindset is that of getting. One has the medium of exchange in order to get. Needs are met by getting. In its ultimate form - the mark of the beast - giving is all but un-thinkable.

The mind set of gold, or justice, is a "break even" mindset. "You don't cheat me; I won't cheat you." An eye for an eye." It has the advantage of desiring no more that what is yours, as opposed to wanting something for nothing inherent in the graven image system.

The mindset of grace is the mind of Christ. It is a giving attitude of mind. It is a other centeredness as distinct from a self-centeredness. The medium of exchange, which is the love of Christ meets needs by giving -

giving without keeping track of or thought of return. Whatever options may be open to Christians prior to the end of the millennium, beyond this, lies only love. Because the love of Christ is the ultimate money, the Love of money, worldly money, is a denial of Christ, a rejection of God and His provision; hence "the love of money is the root of all evil" (I Tim. 6:10).

At the present time, whatever question there may be from a Judeo-Christian point of view as to the use of gold as money, and the use of love as money, the graven image is not an option that is open to us either under the law or under Grace.

When we abandon gold as the medium of exchange, the question becomes not what, but who. Where money is concerned, gold is the ultimate "what." Graven images get their value by force - the force of the state, the force of Satan acting through his agents, the kings of this earth (Psalms 2:2,3, Rev. 16:14,17:2,18 18:3,9, 19:19). Hate lies at the root of that force. The love of Christ has value because it is the love of Christ. When we abandon gold, we must choose between Christ or Satan, love or hate, giving or getting, life or death.

There are a number of facets to the monetary implications of the Bible, among them nakedness. Nakedness is woven as a continuous theme from beginning to end. This theme begins in the Garden of Eden before the fall of man with the beauty of nakedness and continues through the shame of nakedness after the fall. It is brought out in various ways, times, and places throughout the Old Testament and leading to the righteousness of Christ, given as a covering for our nakedness. This contrasts to the ultimate shame of the nakedness inherent in the mark of the beast, there, in the economic sense, man is stripped completely naked before the central authority of this world, to whom his every economic transaction is revealed.

Even now you are being stripped naked in the same sense, if not yet to this ultimate degree, as the central authorities of this nation reduce you to a computer entry and the Internal Revenue Service gains greater and greater access to your financial dealings, particularly where banks and banking transactions are concerned. To the degree that we rely on the provision of the central authorities, those authorities have a hook in us and strip us naked. This has always been so.

So this book is written to Christians and gold bugs on behalf of the Bible, and asking the question, What's keeping you? Whom do you love? To whom are you exposing your nakedness? God or mammon? The King of kings or the authorities of this world? The reality of Jesus Christ or the image of the beast.?

The present task is to retarget the book from "Christians and gold bugs" to Jews, Catholics, otherwise unbelieving participants in the world of high finance, and monetary policy. The further I get into the rewrite,

APPENDIX G—
Adoption and Birth

From Chapter 13, pg. 212; taken from an e-mail written by Jay to Lisa on Thursday February 5, 2004.

Some time before these e-mails were written, Jay had exchanged a number of emails with his friend Bill, discussing the difference between adoption and birth, as it relates to the application of these two ways of relating to the spiritual truth of relationship in Christ. Bill is a Messianic Jew, a convert to Christ from Judaism. As Jay puts it, Bill, whose given name is William S. Thurman, is "the deepest well on the web I know where Greek and Hebrew are concerned. As it happens, he does not live far from me, and we get together quite often." Jay continued, in his e-mail to Lisa, saying, "For the most part, Bill is way over my head, so if you feel like you are drowning for a minute or two in reading the following, we'll just 'buddy breathe' for a bit, and then we'll resurface shortly."

Dear Bill,

Even in my ignorance to follow after you closely, you are such a delight and blessing to my spirit. For me the timing of this latest is, once again Divine. The other subject which was in my hopper, when I sent the last concerning the "codification of the highest truth," was "adoption vs. the new birth." As a parallel to your exploration here, I should say that the only difference would appear to be the word order of our subject titles. As I am presently looking at it, Adoption has to do with "authority," and the new birth with power or as you put it further down in your own exploration, "e" and "d."

With that introduction I would like to note the following in what you have written and then include what I have put on paper, so to speak, thus far.

William S. Thurman wrote:

Power and Authority

...The mere position did not confer the authority needed. The position conferred responsibility. After that, acquiring the authority depended on how the man discharged his responsibility. The better the handling of the responsibility, the more extensive the authority acquired...

... You might put duvamic = dynamis as 'power' and e3oucia = exusia as 'authority' out of your mind for a minute and decide what the citations' settings show about the two respective words, denoted by d. and e., so that d. = duvamic = dynamis and e. = e3oucia = exusia..."

My response to Bill:
In 1987-88, I was in Germany, working for a machine building firm. I wasn't there very long before I realized that my ability to perform was hampered by a lack of authority. Actually, I found that I was lacking both language and authority. Then I went to my employer, the founder and C.E.O. of the company, and pointed out that I had not been introduced to his staff, as one having authority, and therefore was unable to perform my expected function, He responded by saying, "Just fight for the authority."

Responsibility without authority is a lose/lose situation. I responded by saying that I do not believe that authority is something that can be taken, it must be given. The principle is the difference between Satan and Christ. "All authority in heaven and earth has been given to me..." "I give you authority to..." I told him that I would not accept one gram more responsibility than I was given the authority to carry out - "... one comes whose right it is to rule..."

With the "position" comes the authority to perform its duties, the "e" to perform its duties. The "e" without the "d" makes us nothing but unprofitable servants, what's lacking is the "d," so the servants are told to go nowhere, and do nothing, until they receive the "d," the "d" that, in our case, can only come down, "from on high." No matter where we are where responsibility is concerned, authority and power must go hand in hand, if we are to prove faithful even in the small things.

Adoption vs. New Birth, ("e" vs. "d")

I have been thinking quite a bit in recent months about the "new birth." There are many verses of Scripture that were part of the meditation, but perhaps the following two passages are a good place to begin:

"But as many as received him, to them gave he power ("e") to become the sons of God, even to them that believe on his name: Which were born, not of blood, nor of the will of the flesh, nor of the will of man, but of God." John 1:12,13

(Lisa, I call this, "the birth control passage." If you read it closely, you will see very clearly that the difference between our first birth, and our second birth is, whose idea it was. God is generally given credit for our first birth, but not according to this passage. He only takes credit for our second birth. It's all about control.)

And: "But when the fullness of the time was come, God sent forth his Son, made of a woman, made under the law, To redeem them that were under the law, that we might receive the adoption of sons. And because ye are sons, God hath sent forth the Spirit of his Son into your hearts, crying, Abba, Father." Galatians 4:4-6

Here is where this is going:

The debate of the past century where the "Baptism of the Holy Spirit,"

(Lisa, we need to talk about this. Let me know when you are ready to have that talk.), is concerned centered on something which was sometimes referred to as a "second blessing." The Evangelicals, generally said, "No such thing, we got it all in the original package of salvation." The Pentecostals said, "No, being baptized into Christ was not all there is, there was also the Baptism of the Holy Spirit, with the confirming sign of 'speaking in tongues."

In general, the Pentecostals acknowledged the salvation of the Evangelicals, but argued that they had not yet received the power of The Holy Spirit.

Without reopening this whole debate, which by now has almost become mute, I would like to focus on two distinct aspects of our "salvation."

"Jesus said, "No man can come to me, except the Father which hath sent me draw him: and I will raise him up at the last day." John 6:44

A clear implication of what Jesus said is that, before the new birth, there is a "drawing." This drawing process can take time, short in some, and long in others. Our reliance on "confessional" or, "repeat after me regeneration," can, and I believe does, cause a presumption of new birth where the new birth has not yet taken place. The person may well be being "drawn," even to the point of receiving their "adoption as sons," but they are not yet there as a matter of saving faith, in the sense of, "... how much more, having been reconciled, shall we be saved through His life!" Romans 5:10

In the first two passages cited above, there is a chronological distinction made between, "receiving Him" in the one passage, "adoption" in the other, and being empowered to be a child of God, in the first, receiving the "Spirit whereby we cry 'Abba" in the other passage. This to say that there is a difference between being adopted and having the same nature, the same DNA. Where being included in the family of God is concerned, adoption is a necessary, and legal precondition for receiving the very nature of God. (Lisa, adoption has to do with the legal disposal of our garbage. We are not allowed in the house with our garbage.)

Adoption is a legal matter; a new birth is a matter of impregnation. We had been "under the law." Under the law, it would have been illegal for God, The Father to adopt us, so Jesus took care of the legal obstacle to our adoption, so that God the Father could legally adopt us. That was a necessary precondition to our adoption. That having been taken care of, and we having availed ourselves of that provision by faith in Jesus Christ, His blood, and His righteousness, we were adopted.

The fact is we were the wrong species to be part of God's household, and adoption did not change our species. In my case, it was as though God had adopted a chimpanzee. God was looking at me through the blood of His son, so it was ok for me to be there, but for my part, I was still a chimpanzee.

Now some chimpanzees are quite good at doing imitations, even imitations of Christ, but Christianity was not to be built on imitations, but the reality of Christ.

Having adopted me, however, and because I was a consenting recipient to my legal adoption, God then poured out His Spirit into my heart, so that I was able to cry out in Spirit and in truth, by a brand new nature, "Abba." Everything to that point was the drawing of the Father to receive the Son, but at that moment I became born again by an incorruptible Seed.

Now, if sometime prior to that moment of Divine conception, the process is aborted by some kind of manhandled confession, after which I am told that I have just been "born again," then I am "still born" or born dead.

Here's another passage, which supports this perception:

"For if, when we were enemies, we were reconciled to God by the death of his Son, much more, being reconciled, we shall be saved by his life." Romans 5:10

First reconciliation by the blood of Christ then salvation by His Life.

Adding premature baptism to this deception only compounds the problem. What I am suggesting is that, as a result, we have a "Christian culture" born out of a subnormal or, in a sense, aborted response to the gospel. I say aborted, because before the new life has truly been formed, the birthing process is terminated, and the "would be" child of God is born dead. Actually it is more fundamental than that, the confessional salvation doctrine, as it has been practiced, acts as a kind of birth control technique which blocks conception.

Please don't misunderstand me, I would be very reluctant to make that judgment in any particular case, but the track record or witness of "nominal Christianity" is not looking too good.

Let me also quickly add, that while the Kingdom of God may not come by appearances, there is a substance to the relational integrity of the genuine which ought to have taken place in time for the "... world to know."

What I am saying is that, "adoption," and the "new birth," are not the same thing, they are two separate aspects of being included in God's house.

Please allow me to say this once again; there is a legal aspect to adoption. You can't just go around picking up any child you want. It has to be legal. In God, our Father's case, until the sacrifice of Jesus, it would have been illegal to adopt any of us, for all have sinned and come short of the right to live in The Father's house. So, we were reconciled to God by the death of His Son. That got us in the door or through the curtain, by the blood of Jesus, by adoption, having gotten rid of the legal obstacles to our being included, and because we were now qualified by the blood of Christ for adoption, and, in fact, adopted by our faith in Christ, and His sacrifice for us, God was then able to send the very Spirit of His Son into our hearts, without which there is no supernatural heart's cry of "Abba, Father." That heart's cry only happens at the moment of the new birth, when we actually become partakers of the divine nature, when we are actually born from above by the incorruptible seed of Christ. Everything short of that is only the drawing of the Father, but not yet the new birth. The "drawing" precedes the impregnation.

The seed necessary for that impregnation was not available until the day of Pentecost. Until Jesus died, there was only one seed. It was the seed of Eve, and God watched over it all through human history making sure that it never died until it died in Jesus. The seed was always passed along prior to the death of its carrier. It finally gave birth to Jesus, and in Him it died. (Interesting, it was the seed of Eve, but without the intervention of a man, it gave birth to the last Adam.)

Jesus said, "Verily, verily, I say unto you, Except a corn of wheat fall into the ground and die, it abideth alone: but if it die, it bringeth forth much fruit." It takes more than, just planting a seed to multiply it. It has to cycle through death, and come up out of the ground as fruit, because only in the fruit is the seed multiplied.

"And God said, Let the earth bring forth grass, the herb yielding seed, and the fruit tree yielding fruit after his kind, whose seed is in itself, upon the earth: and it was so. And the earth brought forth grass, and herb yielding seed after his kind, and the tree yielding fruit, whose seed was in itself, after his kind: and God saw hat it was good."

Only in the resurrection did the fruit come into existence. Jesus' resurrection was the first fruit of death.

"But now is Christ risen from the dead, and become the first fruits of them that slept. For since by man came death, by man came also the resurrection of the dead. For as in Adam all die, even so in Christ shall all be made alive. But every man in his own order: Christ the first fruits; afterward they that are Christ's at his coming."

But, before the seed in that fruit could be made available to others, it had to be presented to the Father. Only then could God deliver on His promise. Only then did the "promise of the Father" become available. That promise was poured out on flesh on the day of Pentecost. It was poured out on those He had adopted by faith, their faith, given by Him, and because they had been adopted, God sent the spirit of His Son into their hearts whereby they cried out "Abba."

This to say, before the baptism of the Holy Spirit, there might have been legal adoption, but there was no new birth. If this understanding is correct, the implications for "the church" in our own day are far reaching.

As I understand it, human cloning does not require the seed of a Father. Is it possible that a "Christianity" that stops short of the baptism of the Holy Spirit, is after all, just religious cloning without any authentic new birth?

"But as many as received him, to them gave he power to become the sons of God, even to them that believe on his name: Which were born, not of blood, nor of the will of the flesh, nor of the will of man, but of God."

"But ye shall receive power, after that the Holy Ghost is come upon you: and ye shall be witnesses unto me both in Jerusalem, and in all Judaea, and in Samaria, and unto the uttermost part of the earth."

Were they His before Pentecost? Yes they were: "I have manifested thy name unto the men which thou gavest me out of the world: thine they were, and thou gavest them me; and they have kept thy word."

They were His, but they did not yet possess His life. Only death and resurrection could accomplish that.

For the first time in human history, a Seed which was both human and divine and which had already passed through death and resurrection was made available for the propagation of a whole new race, one that was born of a Seed that would never have to die again."

About the Authors

In his hometown of Greenwich, Connecticut, Jay was running for congress in 1972, when the Lord began to pull him over to the curb. In late 1973 or early 1974, he and his wife Carleen opened their home, their family—by now including four grown children—and their lives to what they had just begun to see was "the household dimension" of their inheritance in Christ. That happened on Wednesday nights. Since then, as they have experienced relationship with many "churches," they have continued to gather with others in homes, mostly their own.

In the process of making the transition from his old set of values to his new ones, Jay spent seven years researching God's position on money. In 1982, **Inflation The Ultimate Graven Image** was published by New Leaf Press.

That assignment done, his heart since then has been in discovering what it is that God calls Church. By now, it has become clear to him that God's purpose is to bring people to a place that doesn't shake. Or, as he has come to understand it in the past year or so, "The Glory of the former house" is the glory of the fellowship in the Godhead before the world began—"The Glory of the latter house" is the glory of the fellowship in the Godhead, including us, after the world comes to an end. Jesus died for the difference. It's all about That!

Jay is now in his mid sixties, living in the mountains of North Carolina, and for the past eight years has enjoyed fellowship with "The Shepherd's of Charlotte," a spiritual gate into that city for over 30 years.

Lisa has been described as the "quintessential party girl." These days, the truth behind that description rings with the understanding that engaging people in the most loving, connected, and joyful way is her heart. Perhaps Lisa can best be understood as a seeker: for a better life, for a better understanding, for a better way of loving and being with one another. Being in Christ and in the Love that He pours into her has been the ultimate experience in her life. Sharing it with others is a close second.

Lisa lives with her husband in Austin, Texas, and meets with a group of believers in their home. She has a heart to share the life that Christ makes available with those seeking a better life and with those whom the Lord draws close to her.

For more information, go to the *Not Left Behind* website at:

www.notleftbehind.net

The authors are available for speaking engagements and personal appearances. For more information contact the publisher at:

ADVANTAGE BOOKS™
PO Box 160847
Altamonte Springs, FL 32716

To order additional copies of this book or to see a complete list of all **ADVANTAGE BOOKS™** visit our online bookstore at:

www.advantagebookstore.com

or call our toll free order number at: 1-888-383-3110

Advantage BOOKS

Longwood, Florida, USA

"we bring dreams to life"™
www.advbooks.com